AF412670

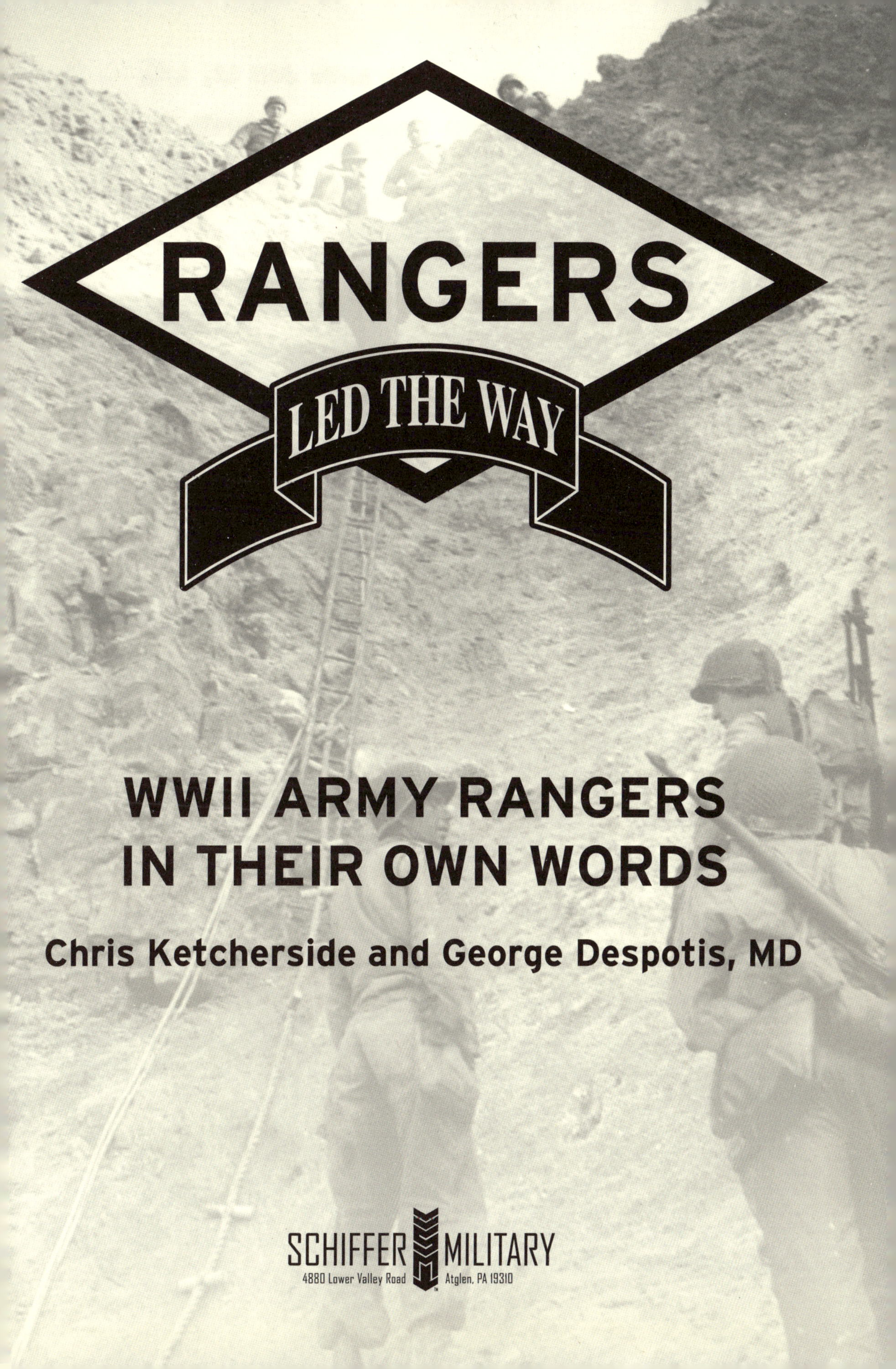

RANGERS

LED THE WAY

WWII ARMY RANGERS IN THEIR OWN WORDS

Chris Ketcherside and George Despotis, MD

Designed by Justin Watkinson
Type set in Interstate/Minion Pro
Cover artwork, *Cliff Hanger*, courtesy of the artist, James Dietz

ISBN: 978-0-7643-6036-7
Printed in China

Published by Schiffer Publishing, Ltd.
4880 Lower Valley Road
Atglen, PA 19310
Phone: (610) 593-1777; Fax: (610) 593-2002
E-mail: Info@schifferbooks.com
Web: www.schifferbooks.com

For our complete selection of fine books on this and related subjects, please visit
our website at www.schifferbooks.com. You may also write for a free catalog.

Schiffer Publishing's titles are available at special discounts for bulk purchases
for sales promotions or premiums. Special editions, including personalized covers,
corporate imprints, and excerpts, can be created in large quantities for special
needs. For more information, contact the publisher.

We are always looking for people to write books on new and related subjects.
If you have an idea for a book, please contact us at proposals@schifferbooks.com.

The included photographs were taken by the authors obtained from the interviewed
Rangers, or are part of the collections at the National Archives or Army Historical
Education Center. Maps are by R. H. Britton, with additions by J. C. Ketcherside. We
express our appreciation to John Brueck for providing the pictures of the Ranger
headstones from the Normandy American Cemetery at Colleville-sur-Mer, France,
where 9,388 US soldiers are interred, and to Gwenaël Jacob (Normandy Coordinator
Best Defense Foundation) for providing aerial pictures of Pointe du Hoc as well as
the picture of the Ranger Memorial plaque that lists the Rangers that gave their lives
on D-day at either Omaha or Pointe du Hoc contained within one of the batteries.
Many of the interviews were completed with the help of Matt Lary, and we would
like to express our appreciation to Matt for his support of this project.

George and I would like to thank Col. (Ret.) Robert Black and his lovely wife, Carolyn, for their help and their gracious hospitality. Also, much gratitude to both Dave Lavely and Gen. (Ret.) John C. Raaen, who provided invaluable help and detail with their revisions. However, any mistakes noted are the authors' own. We would also like to express our appreciation to Steve Stroot and the 2nd Ranger Battalion of the St. Louis (reenactor) organization for their support and critical assistance with the interview process and multiple other aspects of this project. We would like to also express our appreciation to Don Korte and his colleagues for their technical support (transcription of the videotaped interviews).

We would like to express our appreciation to the Voges, Schlichter, and Messel families for their support of this project and their fathers' service during World War II: Sgt. Schlichter (Scott Air Force Base, Army Air Force) and SSgt. Forrest Messel (B-17 tail gunner, 99th Bomb Group, 15th Army Air Force), and PFC Bob Gion (US Infantry, Pacific Theatre of Operations).

For both of us this has been a labor of love. But, of course, we owe a large debt of gratitude to our families, my wife, Kara, and George's wife, Vonna, and their two daughters, Alyssa and Lea, who have supported our passion for this endeavor because they understood its importance.

Most importantly, we would like to thank all the Rangers interviewed in this book, the Rangers who have previously or are currently serving to protect our country, and, most importantly, those Rangers who gave the ultimate sacrifice for our freedom.

CONTENTS

Introduction 6

General Notes 8

Part I: 1st, 3rd, and 4th Battalions

CHAPTER 1 **The WWII Rangers Battalions Are Born!** 11

CHAPTER 2 **First Blood** 13

CHAPTER 3 **Operation Torch** 15

CHAPTER 4 **The Rangers Invade Europe** 18

CHAPTER 5 **Up the Italian Boot** 21

CHAPTER 6 **The Interviews** 25
    TSgt. Wayne Rouona 25
    Sgt. Carl Lehmann 32
    Sgt. James McVay 40
    SFC William C. Fauber 49
    1Sgt. Lawrence Gilbert 61
    PFC George Sabine 73
    Maj. Bing Evans 79

Part I Photo Section 98

Part II: 2nd and 5th Battalions

CHAPTER 7 **Rangers in Western Europe** 130

CHAPTER 8 **Day of Days** 131

CHAPTER 9 **Assault on the Port of Brest** 138

CHAPTER 10 **Hill 400** 139

CHAPTER 11 **The Irsch-Zerf Raid**. **141**

CHAPTER 12 **The Interviews**. **144**

    PFC Raymond Tollefson. 144

    Sgt. Warren Burmaster 151

    SSgt. Dan Farley 162

    PFC David Owen 170

    Cpl. Francis Coughlin 177

    PFC Lewis Haight 183

    1Lt. Frank Kennard 190

    2Lt. Leonard Lomell 197

    PFC Richard Lemnitzer 205

    Maj. Gen. John C. Raaen 214

    SSgt. William E. Boyd 233

    Sgt. Alvin Rustebakke 241

    Lt. Col. George Kerchner 249

    SSgt. Bill Hoffman. 274

    1Lt. Charles Ryan. 283

CHAPTER 13 **Diary of Capt. Walter E. Block**. **295**

Part II Photo Section **306**

Endnotes **332**

Bibliography **333**

Ranger Hall of Famers **334**

INTRODUCTION

Churchill faced a seemingly impossible strategic situation in the dark days of 1940. He had for years stated that war with Hitler's Germany was inevitable, and as prime minister it was now his to fight. And fight he would, although in the summer of 1940, the situation seemed grim. The British army had been driven off the Continent, and as heroic as the miracle of Dunkirk was, it was still a defeat. The skies over Britain darkened almost daily with swarms of Luftwaffe aircraft, and while British pilots fought heroically, the war of attrition was going slowly and surely against them. At sea, Admiral Karl Dönitz's U-boat fleet was wreaking havoc on Britain's merchant fleets, eventually cutting imports, which threatened Britain's ability to subsist, not to mention what was required to wage a global conflict. Having already lost in France, British ground forces were unceremoniously ejected from Greece and Crete by the Wehrmacht and were suffering reversals in North Africa.

Despite all this, Churchill was sure the war would be won, if for no other reason than it *had* to be won. He knew that as long as Britain could hold out, time was on their side. Thus he was able to inspire and motivate the population to resist. However, Churchill knew that prolonged deprivations, shortages at home, defeats abroad, and the bombing of the Blitz could crush British morale. Their cause was just, but with so many brothers, sons, fathers, and husbands being killed and wounded in one defeat after another, the home front being no safer, it seemed, than the battlefront, and worries about being able to simply feed children or even keep them safe, the situation could eventually cause the toughest will to break. Britain needed some hope that victory was possible.

Churchill's ideas of military strategy were as romantic as they were pragmatic, though often too much of the former. Looking for some way to strike back, he supported the idea of creating special forces to employ unorthodox tactics that would keep the enemy off balance and provide victories, however small, for the people. These forces came to be called "Commandos."

The name originates from conflicts Britain fought from 1899 to 1902 in South Africa, which came to be called the Boer War. Churchill himself had fought in these conflicts. The Boers organized themselves into units called kommandoes.[1] This translated from their Dutch German language as "command." Each "command" was led by a local village leader or man of local respect, and the command was usually named after him. These commands operated as a military unit, and, lacking the numbers or heavy weapons of the British army, they used asymmetric tactics. These consisted of combinations of hit-and-run attacks, ambushes, and raids. They remained highly mobile on horseback, and while they could disappear easily into the countryside, which they knew very well, they had no base on which they were dependent and vulnerable. And they were excellent shots at long distances. They fought few conventional battles but instead relied on guerrilla warfare to defeat the British. Their expertise at this, and the British misunderstanding of the word, caused them to call such tactics "commando" warfare. When the British decided to conduct special warfare on the Germans, it would be done by Commandos.

In one of the first raids against a radar station in Bruneval, France, Commandos destroyed the station and captured key components of the German radar system for British scientists to study. This was trumpeted as a great success. A later raid on the port of Saint-Nazaire was successful in shutting down the docks but was far more costly in lives. Two of the casualties were British officers who refused to answer any questions from their German captors, not even about the timed explosive that would kill them as well as their enemy. Such courage was exactly the sort of thing Churchill needed to bolster British morale, and served as an example of what highly trained and skilled warriors could accomplish.

On December 7, 1941, the United States entered the war with the Japanese attack on the naval base at Pearl Harbor, Hawaii. President Roosevelt found himself in a similar situation as that of Churchill; he needed to boost morale in the face of defeat. In addition to the catastrophic attack at Pearl Harbor, the United States suffered defeats on Wake Island and the Philippines. By early 1942, U-boats attacked almost with impunity off the East Coast, sometimes sinking ships within sight of beachgoers at Virginia Beach and Cape Hatteras. Meanwhile, the United States seemed almost powerless to strike back at her foes. Against Japan, he authorized the tactically minimal but strategically crucial Doolittle Raid against Tokyo in April 1942. Against the Germans, Roosevelt found himself also looking to use special forces, for the same romantic and pragmatic reasons. The authorization to develop special forces for the United States was soon forthcoming and would lead to the formation of the Ranger Battalions.

GENERAL NOTES

The following section should help the reader with some understanding of the interviews. It provides some definitions and explanations of common terms used. Many of these are second nature to the Rangers, so that they often do not describe or define them, and rather than bury the reader in footnotes (although some of those are used), this section should be used as a reference for unfamiliar terms and acronyms/initialisms.

First, a brief synopsis of rank. A complete breakdown of ranks is not required, only that they were broken into three broad categories; enlisted, sergeants and higher noncommissioned officers (NCOs), and officers, which were second lieutenants and higher.

A brief description of units. A soldier's most basic unit is his squad, which is a group of between ten and twelve soldiers. This was primarily the entire social world of the World War II infantry soldier. Usually, it was led by a sergeant. Keeping in mind, the numbers between what was authorized and what existed on a day-to-day basis varied widely because of losses and replacements. Three squads composed a platoon, between thirty and forty soldiers, at this level led by an officer, a lieutenant, although in practice the platoon was often led by a sergeant or other NCO. Two platoons combined to form a company, which had between 100 and 120 soldiers, although Ranger companies were substantially smaller, between sixty and seventy. Six companies formed a Ranger battalion numbering around five hundred. The Rangers operated only at the battalion level but often were attached to higher units. For the most part, this will suffice for the purpose of this book, since the Ranger battalions were attached at the division level. Ranger battalions were substantially smaller than normal infantry battalions, which numbered approximately eight hundred. The larger units that the Rangers were attached to never seemed to grasp the difference. This led to the Rangers being assigned tasks that would normally be borne by much-larger regular-line units.

Which brings up the subject of attachment. As you read this book, you will see that the Ranger battalions were attached to one division and then another. This is because the Ranger battalions were independent battalions; they had no parent unit structure. That is, they weren't permanently part of a regiment or division and so on. So, they would be attached to divisions who may have employed them tactically but were in any case responsible for the Rangers administratively. This included ensuring they were fed, received mail, and were resupplied. The lack of a parent structure gave the Ranger battalions a great deal of tactical flexibility but made these administrative chores a challenge. This is why Ranger commanding officers such as Darby and Rudder had to spend so much time personally canvasing replacement depots for replacements.[2] Additionally, the issue of what division they were attached to is important for research purposes; gaps in operational records of Ranger battalions can sometimes be filled by researching the records of divisions they were attached to.

The administrative tasks for military units of battalion strength and higher were considerable, so staff sections were specifically created in order to accomplish them. These sections are known, at the battalion level, as the "S" sections and are often referred to by the Rangers:

S1 Administration; responsible for pay, mail, daily records of where soldiers were and their status, etc.

S2 Intelligence; responsible for developing information on the enemy

S3 Operations; responsible for planning

S4 Supply and logistics

S6 Communications

At the division level, the *S* is replaced by *G*, for G1, G2, etc., but their functions are the same.

This is not to be confused with D-day date designations, such as D+1, D+2. These are dates used for planning purposes. D-day was June 6, 1944, although the term "D-day" was used for all amphibious invasions. But for the example here, D+1 would be June 7, D+2 would be June 8, and so on. Essentially the "+" indicated the number of days after the invasion day.

It is also important, for several reasons, to understand the hierarchy of awards. While most are familiar with the Medal of Honor, this is not only the nation's highest award, but one that is only awarded in very extreme cases. There are a number of awards under this, in the following order from lowest to highest: Bronze Star, Silver Star, Legion of Merit, and the Distinguished Service Citation.

A quick note on medical evacuation procedures may prove helpful for readers. A number of Rangers were wounded, and by the nature of being wounded they will have little recollection of their evacuation. The United States had arguably the best evacuation system of the war. Upon being wounded, a soldier could count on either himself or his buddy administering his allotment of morphine, which minimized pain and thus limited shock and panic. Also, sulfa powder would be applied to prevent infection. Usually within a few minutes at the most, the unit medic would be there and would conduct any procedures necessary to maintain life until transportation to the battalion aid station was ready. Usually this was via jeep after the wounded soldier had been brought off the lines by medics or his buddies. This was the most difficult and dangerous part of the ordeal and usually took the longest. If the soldier survived this, he almost always survived his wound. The battalion aid station had a surgeon who could conduct surgery and whatever else was needed to ensure the soldier's survival until he reached a field hospital. Here, he was treated fully. From the field hospital the soldier either recovered and was returned to combat or was sent home for long-term rehabilitation.

The Rangers in these interviews will also refer to certain enemy devices with frequency. One of these will be a pillbox, which is simply a small-sized bunker made of reinforced concrete and containing a machine gun. Often, more than one pillbox would be encountered, and they would be positioned to protect each other. Another device referred to is the "88," which is short for the German 88 mm high velocity anti-aircraft cannon which was converted to an anti-tank and anti-personnel weapon. This was a particularly effective German weapon and was highly respected by GIs. Last, in the sections regarding Normandy, you will read about hedgerows. These were high, thick growths of dirt and trees found in the Normandy region of France. The phenomenon resulted from generations of French farmers throwing dirt and rocks out of their farm fields, creating, over time, rows that were often 10 to 20 feet high and almost as thick. They were impenetrable by anything but tanks equipped with special devices, and formed perfect defensive positions for the Germans. They lined roads and fields all over the Normandy area. Often, Rangers and other US soldiers would be fighting Germans who were as close by as the opposite side of a hedgerow.

Finally, some discussion of routine patrolling is warranted. The Rangers will discuss patrolling as very routine because they did a lot of it. It was generally a very exhausting and dangerous but necessary task. Patrolling was the only effective method for gathering intelligence on enemy activities and possibly capturing enemy soldiers. Also, patrolling was necessary in order to prevent the enemy from collecting information on friendly units.

Interestingly, the Rangers would be among the first and usually only US soldiers to employ certain techniques and procedures learned from the British Commandos. They usually patrolled wearing only a GI stocking cap instead of the larger and more distinctive helmet. They also blackened their faces with camouflage makeup: soot, burnt cork, or other materials at hand.

Usually conducted in squad strength, but sometimes with as few as three men, a patrol would leave friendly lines and venture into the no-man's land between friendly and enemy forces. With few exceptions, this was done at night. The object was to gather information about enemy activities by observing them without being seen. This was difficult, of course, because the enemy was looking for patrols or anything else in no-man's land. And, of course, the enemy would have patrols out as well. Simply moving around at night without getting hurt or lost was a challenge; added to this was the presence of a deadly enemy. Finally, once the patrol was completed, there was the challenge of reentering friendly lines without being shot by friend forces. All of this took a great deal of training, experience, coordination, and planning. Rangers, due to their extra training, were superb at patrolling, and so their interviews make it seem very routine. It was only routine due to its frequency, but it was not ever easy or safe.

Other acronyms or terms encountered should be explained in context or in footnotes.

1ST, 3RD, AND 4TH BATTALIONS
PART I

CHAPTER 1

THE WWII RANGER BATTALIONS ARE BORN!

FIRST BATTALION FORMATION AND TRAINING

Gen. George Marshall issued the orders for a formation of US Special Forces. Ostensibly, the group formed for the purpose of training a cadre of soldiers in special tactics who would then return to their units to train others.

The soldiers came from the units forming in Britain for the eventual cross-channel invasion. Specifically, they primarily came from the 34th Infantry and 1st Armored Divisions of V Corps. They were officially formed on June 19, 1942, and Capt. William Darby was assigned command. He subsequently interviewed all those who volunteered for the unit, asking them questions ranging from attitudes toward their leadership to whether or not they had been Boy Scouts. His intent was to ensure that the unit would be full of the type of soldier with the proper physical fitness, aptitude, and attitude.

Unofficially, at first, they were known as "Rangers." Who first suggested this as a name and how it was adopted is not entirely clear. Several members claimed credit for it and several stories exist, all as creditable as the next. What is known is that all agreed that US forces would not use the term "commando," since that would always belong to the British as a title of honor. In any case, the exploits of Roger's Rangers were well known as a unit formed during the French and Indian War from British colonial militia. They fought using the same asymmetric tactics and techniques that the Native Americans were using with great success against the British. These tactics included many things that modern special forces would recognize, such as long-range patrolling, ambush, raids, and even the use of camouflage and stealth. To this day, Ranger candidates must memorize Roger Robert's standing orders. Roger's Rangers were greatly successful, and their efforts were immortalized in a book popular during the 1930s and 1940s called *Northwest Passage*.

The Rangers conducted their training at the Commando School at Achnacarry, Scotland. Their instructors were combat-experienced British Commandos. This training also served as a weeding-out process. The training consisted of intense physical exercises, including log drills, swimming, and calisthenics. Additionally, there were obstacle courses, speed marches, cliff climbing, fording, river and stream crossings, amphibious exercises, map reading, first aid, patrolling, hand-to-hand combative training, live-fire training, and explosives. There was a special emphasis on operating at night. Here the Rangers learned, among other techniques, to blacken their faces with paint or burnt cork when operating a night, and to tape down pieces of equipment to minimize noise. These techniques became standard operating procedures for the Rangers.

The Rangers trained on all manner of weapons that were then in the US inventory. What made the Rangers exceptional is that every Ranger became an expert on every weapon, instead of focusing on specialties with a brief familiarization for others. In this way, any Ranger could operate any weapons system and could take over a job from a wounded or killed Ranger. Rangers were proficient with all weapons the US could provide them, as well as a few others, such as brass-knuckle trench knives and the Fairbairn-Sykes knife.

Initially, the principal weapon they used in training was the 1903 Springfield, a .30-caliber bolt-action weapon used by the US Army in the World War I. Since World War II had caught the United States largely unprepared, this weapon was the predominant weapon initially in use. Also used was the Government Model .45-caliber semiautomatic pistol. This weapon had also been used in World War I and was considered a powerful and reliable sidearm. Other weapons included the standard US-issue hand grenade, as well as the similar British models. They also received training on the Thompson .45 submachine gun, a weapon primarily known for its use by gangsters in the 1930s. This would remain a standard weapon for the Rangers due to its heavy firepower, reliability, and ease of use. For heavier fire support, the Rangers also had the M1919A4 light machine gun, and the .30-caliber crew-served weapon. However, since these were heavy to carry and required two men to operate, they would remain at the battalion headquarters level, to be used as needed. They were considered too heavy for the light, fast-moving commando force. Instead, for fire support, some Rangers would be issued the Browning Automatic Rifle, or BAR. This was also a .30-caliber machine gun, with a twenty-round magazine. The magazine limited its rate of fire, but it could be carried and operated by a single Ranger.

Prior to deploying to their first mission in North Africa, the '03 Springfields would be replaced with the M1 Garand. The M1 was a .30-caliber semiautomatic rifle with an eight-round magazine. This larger-than-usual magazine size, along with the M1's hitting power, reliability, accuracy, and ease of use, made it arguably the best infantry rifle of World War II. It would prove especially lethal in the hands of Rangers. Also used was the M1 Carbine, a .30-caliber rifle that had less range and hitting power than the Garand but was smaller and lighter. Usually it was issued to officers and specialist troops, but the Rangers for the most part abandoned it in favor of the Garand.

For additional indirect-fire support, the Rangers were issued the 60 mm mortar. While this was also a heavy crew-served weapon, it could be carried by Rangers and would be useful, since they would often operate out of the range of other artillery assets. These were also consolidated at the headquarters level as needed. For antiarmor capability, the Rangers trained with the 2.36-inch antitank rocket launcher, commonly known as the "bazooka."

A last weapon that must be mentioned is the satchel charge. This was an explosive device that was contained in a canvas bag, similar to a messenger bag, but contained various amounts of explosive. It was activated by pulling a fuse and could be used in any number of ways but was usually employed by Rangers to demolish bunkers. The fuse was pulled, and the charge would be thrown into the bunker through the firing slit or some other opening. The explosion was usually enough to kill or incapacitate anyone inside.

The Rangers also trained with various German weapons in order to be able to operate those as well if required.

This period of training also served as a "shakedown" period for the battalion. Darby, quickly promoted to major, had no intention of training men and disbanding them to rejoin their units. His men shared this attitude. In fact, Darby stamped his ethos into the battalion to the extent that they would be known as "Darby's Rangers" for the rest of the war. So in addition to individual training, Darby was selecting company commanders, building his staff, and seeking larger and more-permanent allocations of equipment.

Training continued, and with it the weeding out of those unsuited. The "dark mile" at Achnacarry was a portion of every speed march and was lined with epitaphs on fake tombstones showing reasons that Commandos had died, such as "Forgot to maintain his weapon" and so on. The dark mile was the reason for many dropouts.

Unfortunately, dropping out was not the only way the battalion lost members. Believing in the maxim of sweating in training to prevent bleeding in combat, the Rangers did not sacrifice realism for safety, and a few Rangers were killed during training—some by mines and some by drowning, as well as other causes. Others were wounded in live-fire exercises.

The Rangers impressed their Commando trainers with their enthusiasm and hard work. The only thing they still lacked was combat experience.

CHAPTER 2

FIRST BLOOD

While the Rangers were training, the British were planning an operation that required the use of the British Commandos. It was decided that some of the Rangers in training would be selected to participate. This gave the United States a boost in morale by seeing forces being committed against Germany, and provided Rangers with the invaluable experience of combat.

This was Operation Jubilee, a large-scale raid on the French coast at a port called Dieppe. There were several objectives for the raid. First, the raid was to test the feasibility of capturing a port by amphibious assault. Second, it was to test various amphibious tactics, techniques, and equipment in anticipation of the cross-channel attack being planned by Britain and the United States. Additionally, the Royal Air Force (RAF) wanted to fight an offensive local action against the Luftwaffe. There were strategic reasons as well. Churchill wanted to keep up British morale with an offensive action, and it was hoped that this would keep the Germans off balance and force them to retain forces in defense of France that might otherwise be sent to reinforce the Eastern Front. Stalin, who was fighting the bulk of the German army, had been clamoring for the Americans and British to open a second front in Europe, and in part Operation Jubilee was launched to appease the Soviet dictator.

The raid was scheduled for August 19, 1942. Fifty Rangers were selected to take part. These Rangers would be among some significant "firsts." Some of them would be the first Rangers to see combat, among the first Americans to set foot in occupied Europe, among the first to inflict casualties on the German army, and some of the first Americans casualties suffered fighting the German army.

The operation had three parts. The main part was a landing on the beach at the port, to be conducted by the 2nd Infantry Division of the Canadian Army along with the Royal Marines, a Canadian tank regiment, and the Scottish Fusiliers. Concurrently, No. 3 and No. 4 Commando Troop would land to the east and west, respectively, in order to destroy large guns that could wreak havoc on the beachhead. In total, over six thousand men would be involved.

Naval gunfire support was limited, since the Royal Navy could not risk capital ships in the narrow confines of the English Channel under a powerful Luftwaffe threat, and heavy bombers would not be used for fear of excessive civilian casualties. Instead, the raid depended heavily on surprise.

Rangers were assigned to forces in each part of the operation and would have varying roles. The Rangers assigned to the Commando troops were well received, integrated into the plan, and matched with a Commando as part of the Commando "Jack and John" system of pairing men for combat. These Rangers had the advantage of being sent over to the Commandos on August 1, giving them time to prepare. The Commandos were aware of Ranger training and capabilities from their colleagues at Achnacarry.

The Rangers assigned to the Canadian forces were not as fortunate. They were not transferred over until August 17, a mere two days before the raid, and were treated as observers at best and interlopers at worst. In defense of the Canadians, from their point of view they were being burdened with inexperienced strangers on the eve of a major operation. The Rangers were basically told which ship to board, where to go, and so on but were not integrated into the plan or paired with any other soldiers.

For the operation, thirty-six Rangers embarked with No. 3 Commando, headed for the eastern guns, four embarked with No. 4 Commando, headed for the guns on the western end of the beachhead, while six Rangers went in with the Canadians.

Unfortunately, the Dieppe Raid was to be an unmitigated disaster. Lacking the support of a heavy air or naval bombardment, the surprise the raid depended on was lost in the predawn hours when the assault ships encountered a German convoy. Several Rangers with No. 3 Commando were wounded in this engagement. The battle itself was a draw; the German gunboats were escorting tankers and wanted to carry on their mission as much as the British ships did theirs, but the crucial element of surprise had been lost.

Nonetheless, No. 3 Commando landed at their designated beach, Yellow Beach II, and moved to attack the German guns. The Germans had six 150 mm guns at Berneval that the Commandos targeted. While they were not able to destroy the well-defended guns, they maintained a heavy volume of fire that prevented the guns from hampering the main raiding force.

Another group from No. 3 Commando was not as fortunate. They landed at Yellow Beach I, but all of their wire-cutting gear was lost when the landing craft it was loaded on was destroyed. Thus they were delayed in penetrating the heavily barb-wired gully to attack German positions. During this delay, the Germans were able to surround them, and they were driven back to the beach. Lacking any landing craft able to extricate them, they were captured.

Meanwhile, No. 4 Commando landed smoothly at their designated beaches, Orange I and II, on the western flank. Quickly moving inland, they brought small arms and mortar fire to bear on the 150 mm guns that were their objective. One of the mortar rounds hit the enemy's ammunition cache and blew one of the guns to pieces. Other portions of No. 4 were able to reach and destroy the guns with demolitions. Their mission complete and under increasing pressure from German reinforcements, No. 4 conducted a withdrawal to the beach and was extricated. This success was the exception on this day.

While the Commandos prevented German heavy guns from firing on the Canadian landing beaches at Dieppe, the Canadians and accompanying Rangers still met with disaster. In short, this was the biggest loss of men and material in the raid. The Germans had fortified the town, and German forces reacted quickly and were able to pin down and destroy most of the invading forces almost at the water's edge. The bulk of the Canadian forces were killed or captured, including several Rangers.

Dieppe was a heavy price to pay for the key lessons learned and later applied at Normandy. Among them was that assaulting a port was too difficult; it is too easy for the enemy to fortify. Heavy fire support is critical; air and naval dominance must be present to assist the landings. If it is not safe for aircraft and ships, it is not safe to land troops. In the actual event, the RAF was barely able to hold its own against the Luftwaffe at Dieppe and was not able to provide any support, while suffering heavy losses. Painfully learned by No. 3 Commando was to load critical gear across several landing craft, so that the loss of one craft does not result in the loss of all of one kind of critical gear, such as wire cutters.

At Dieppe, the Rangers were "blooded," killing their share of Germans but also suffering their own killed, wounded, and captured. While Dieppe was not an American operation, the Rangers had contributed, proved themselves, and paid in blood. Perhaps most importantly they learned many key lessons about amphibious assaults.

OPERATION TORCH

Debate raged between the US and British members of the Combined Chiefs of Staff (CCS). Formed even before the US entry to the war, this body of men was composed of the top military leaders of each country, charged with directing and combining strategy. Both sides had agreed on a "Germany First" strategy. Despite the moral outrage caused by Pearl Harbor, Germany posed the greater military threat, and so Allied forces would focus on its defeat first. The argument was over how to defeat Germany.

The United States argued for a cross-channel invasion as soon as possible, if not in 1943 then in 1944, at the latest. Destroying Germany's armed forces and occupying Berlin was the only sure way to defeat the Third Reich. The British wanted to first attack German forces peripherally, such as in the Mediterranean theater, to whittle down German forces while building Allied strength. They pushed for immediate operations in North Africa, and then perhaps Italy or the Balkans before the cross-channel attack. The US leaders, on the other hand, saw any peripheral operations as delays and distractions from building up and attacking Europe directly.

The argument was settled mainly by the availability of landing craft. There would not be enough landing craft to consider an attack on the European mainland for one to two years. In the meantime, despite the risk of siphoning off forces, it was agreed by the CCS to invade North Africa. The British were already fighting the Germans and Italians there, and it would serve a strategic purpose of destroying Axis forces. Additionally, it would serve the political and moral purpose of getting US forces into the war against Axis ground forces. Thus was born Operation Torch, the invasion of western North Africa by US and British forces. The Rangers would play a key role in this major amphibious operation. And the enemy they would fight first was the French.

The US forces would be landing at several points on the west coast of North Africa. The principal objective was the port of Oran. The command general of this operation, Gen. Fredendall, planned to seize the port by a pincer movement, with landings on both sides. The Rangers would land at Arzew, on the east side of Oran.

As at Dieppe, Arzew had gun batteries in high positions overlooking the port that could inflict heavy casualties on landing forces. The Rangers' mission was to destroy these positions; in the north, Superieur, which had four 105 mm guns, and a smaller fort on a point of land in the harbor itself called Ford de La Pointe, which had three 75 mm guns.

The main landings could not take place until these positions were destroyed. Given the distance between these forts and the concern that an attack on one would alert the other, Lt. Col. Darby and his XO, Maj. Dammer, decided to split the battalion and attack both positions simultaneously.[3] Darby would lead Companies C, D, and F against Superieur, which was on high ground, while Dammer would lead Companies A and B against the harbor fort.

In the predawn hour of 0100 on November 8, the Rangers embarked on landing craft for the assault. Maj. Dammer's force landed after some difficulty, but at no point did it seem the French were awake or alert, expecting an attack.

Company B established a blocking position, then Company A infiltrated and assaulted the fort, in part by speaking French to the few sentries who were out. With few shots fired and only one casualty, a French soldier killed, Maj. Dammer signaled success by 0215.

Starting thirty minutes after Dammer, Darby's force embarked on their mission with only one small issue: one of the assault craft was mishandled and its cargo of equipment was lost. This would become important later. Despite the confusion of the spilled boat and the effort of recovering Rangers out of the ocean, the Rangers still landed by 0130. After scaling the cliffs, they were in position and began their attack on Superieur. However, while cutting through the barbed wire surrounding the fort, the French opened fire. The Rangers used supporting mortar fire to suppress the French forces, and by 0400 the fort was taken.

The plan called for Darby to signal his success by firing a prearranged code of colored flares, flares that had been loaded in the boat that spilled, and were now at the bottom of the ocean. Because of this, the landings were delayed, but ultimately successful. And another hard lesson about amphibious landings had been taught.

The Torch landings were successful across western North Africa. Once the political machinations and complexities of Vichy France had been sorted out, most French forces quickly ceased resistance. The same could not be said of German and Italian forces in North Africa.

Immediately after the invasion, the Ranger battalion was attached to the 1st Infantry Division (the "Big Red One"), and C Company was committed to a pitched battle to capture the village of St. Cloud from French forces still resisting. The Ranger company cut the village off from reinforcement or escape, and the 1st Battalion of the 18th Infantry Regiment captured the village.

Meanwhile, E Company attacked with the 1st Battalion of the 16th Infantry Regimen and cleared the road to La Machta. With the remaining French forces surrendering or switching to the Allied side, the Rangers received reinforcements and integrated them with training, incorporating the lessons learned from combat operations.

As the Allies pushed east into Tunisia, the winter weather forced a stalemate along the lines. During this "static" defense, the Rangers were involved in raids and aggressive patrolling, the precise type of operations they had been raised and trained for. Also, they were finally facing an Axis enemy, the Italians.

The raid on Sened Station is an example of the type of operations they conducted. On February 10, 1943, A, E, and F Companies moved out on a 12-mile night march to get into attack position. They spent the next day lying in wait and conducting reconnaissance of the Italian positions. That night, they attacked and drove the Italians out of their positions, then moved back to US lines before sunrise. The Italians at Sened Station were the 10th Bersaglieri Regiment, distinctive for the black feather they wore on their helmets. They were also distinctive for their qualities of being skilled marksman and of high physical condition. While not the equivalent of Rangers or other special forces, the Bersaglieri were elite troops that had been bested by the Rangers.

Not long after this, however, the German military struck back in an attempt to neutralize US forces in Africa. On February 14, 1943, the Germans launched an attack that came to be known as the Battle of Kasserine Pass. Along with other US forces, the Rangers were forced to retreat and take up defensive positions. However, they kept up their aggressive patrolling, seeking to keep their enemy off balance and insecure even in "static" defense.

Soon after this battle, Gen. George S. Patton was placed in charge of US forces in North Africa and immediately planned offensive operations. The Rangers were ordered to conduct reconnaissance to determine enemy strength in El Guettar. Finding El Guettar empty of German forces, the Rangers located enemy forces in the mountain pass of Djebal El Ank. In this position was a formidable force, the Italian Centauro Division, an armored division of long acclaim, highly experienced in desert warfare from operations over the last two years.

The 1st Infantry Division would attack the pass, with the Rangers supporting the northern flank, next to the 26th Infantry Regiment. On March 20, the Rangers set off, moving 6 miles over terrain considered impassable by the Italians, to get into attack position. Then the Rangers attacked, with the accompaniment of a bugle and Indian war cries. They decisively defeated the Italians in this area, taking over two hundred prisoners and clearing the way for the 26th. Chaplain Father Albert Basil's fluent Italian-language skills were as important as the surprise and fury of the attack in inducing the Italians to surrender.

The Rangers then attempted to assist in exploiting this success. Over the next few days they advanced, suffering under German dive-bomber attacks and counterattacks by the German 10th Panzer Division.

On March 24–26, the Rangers defended Djebel Berda, protecting the flank of the 18th Infantry Regiment. Here the Rangers held on for almost three days with no support against elite German paratroopers.

After repulsing German counterattacks, the Rangers regrouped. The Africa campaign was over for them, as it soon would be for the Germans and Italians. On April 19, two more Ranger battalions were authorized, the 3rd and 4th. Darby immediately recruited men to fill these units from replacement depots in theater, each man passing muster by him and his experienced NCOs. The men of 1st Battalion were then spread throughout the 3rd and 4th to even out these new units with combat-experienced Rangers. They began immediate training in order to be prepared for whatever campaign was next.

For their time in Africa, Patton himself would remark that the Rangers were "the best damned combat soldiers in Africa."

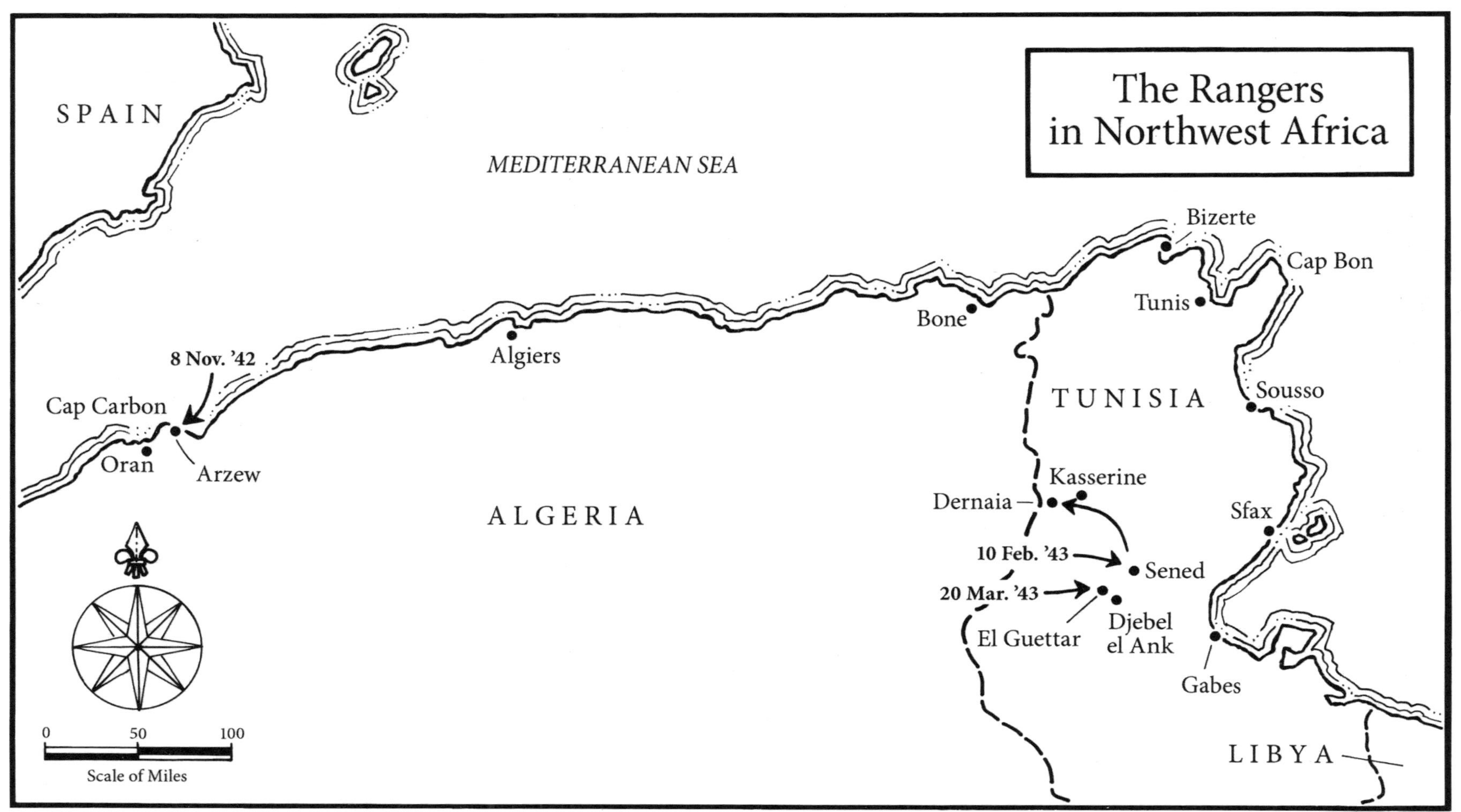

The Rangers
in Northwest Africa
SPAIN
MEDITERRANEAN SEA
Bizerte
Cap Bon
Bone
Tunis
Algiers
8 Nov. '42
Cap Carbon
Oran
Arzew
TUNISIA
Sousso
Sfax
ALGERIA
Dernaia
Kasserine
10 Feb. '43
Sened
20 Mar. '43
El Guettar
Djebel el Ank
Gabes
LIBYA
0
50
100
Scale of Miles

THE RANGERS INVADE EUROPE

That next campaign would be the invasion of Sicily, code-named Operation Husky. The Allied High Command determined that capturing Sicily would ensure the safety of Allied shipping in the Mediterranean and perhaps cause Italy to surrender. In any case, at the conclusion of the North African campaign there were hundreds of ships and hundreds of thousands of soldiers with no other mission at hand. Logistics precluded moving them to England, so invading Sicily would keep them busy at the task of killing Germans, and Darby's three battalions would play a key role.

The invasion took place on the night of July 9, 1943. Airborne forces landed that night, with follow-on landing forces early in the morning on the tenth. The Ranger battalions were in the initial landing forces, attached to the 1st Infantry Division. The 1st and 4th battalions would be in the first waves, designated as Force X. Their objective was the town of Gela. The 3rd Battalion would land at Licata, with the 3rd Infantry Division (the Rock of the Marne) about 20 miles to the west.

The port of Gela was divided by a long pier, and the battalions landed on either side of it—1st Battalion on the west and 4th Battalion on the east. Debarking from the transports USS *Dickman* and HMS *Albert* and *Charles*, the Rangers encountered problems again with amphibious operations. One landing craft containing seventeen men of Company E capsized, drowning all Rangers aboard. The others hit the beachhead at 0300 on July 10. After fighting through the maze of wire and land mines on the beach, the Rangers were immediately engaged in difficult urban combat in Gela, fighting house to house. While there was some fire support from destroyers, the mortars belonging to the Rangers were not available because key radio equipment had been lost at sea during the landing. The Italians had machine guns and an 8 cm gun, but by 0800 the Rangers had cleared Gela and set up defensive positions on the outskirts inland. They captured the gun intact, which would prove useful very soon.

Meanwhile, 3rd Ranger Battalion encountered far-fewer problems. They aggressively cleared the beach and the high ground beyond of Italian defenders, clearing the way for the 15th Regiment of the 3rd Division. By 1500 on the tenth, they were put in the division reserve guarding the port of Licata, which, contrary to the usual, was a very dangerous place due to German aircraft attacks.

As the day wore on at Gela, the Italians counterattacked. This attack was composed of both infantry and artillery from the Italian Livono Division. The Italian infantry was driven off by naval gunfire, but a number of tanks made it into Gela, where they were destroyed by the Rangers using captured artillery, satchel charges, hand grenades, and bazookas. However, the fight for Gela was not over. It would be within these first forty-eight hours that the Axis forces of both Italy and Germany would make their best bid to destroy the American beachhead.

The Italians struck again early on the eleventh. The attacks were uncoordinated though. First, the Rangers fought off another Italian infantry assault, and then separately from another direction, their tanks attacked. But skilled employment of artillery and naval gunfire by the Rangers destroyed or drove off this attack. The Axis bid had failed. Gela and the beachhead were firmly in US hands.

Before the battalions were reunited, the 1st and 4th were tasked a few days later with another challenge. This was the capture of the Italian fortress town of Butera, which sits on top of a high-rising, dominant feature several thousand feet over the surrounding area. Garrisoned by Italian troops, it was a difficult objective to take. Using artillery and naval gunfire to suppress it by day, the Rangers made their way up the single road to Butera the night of the fourteenth. After overrunning initial Italian positions, Rangers who spoke Italian convinced the garrison to surrender. Thus the fortress town was captured quickly, with few losses.

The 3rd Battalion was also busy. Having moved out of reserve, they moved north as well, taking the town of Montaperto on the sixteenth by a furious and efficient flanking maneuver, destroying enemy artillery batteries there. Interestingly, en route to Montaperto the Rangers encountered Italian forces at Agrigento, who fled in a panic at their approach. Perhaps they knew the Rangers were coming.

Moving ahead of other US forces, 3rd Battalion next captured the town of Porto Empedocle on the same day. Their reward was being accidentally shelled by US naval gunfire, friendly fire being an unfortunate but not uncommon occurrence in World War II. That night, 3rd Battalion fought off an attack by fifteen Italian tanks. Then on the seventeenth they were ordered back into reserve at Montaperto.

Over the next few weeks of the short campaign, the Rangers were employed seizing key terrain, such as crossroads and high ground, for follow-on forces. In this they were used much like other infantry battalions, but with more-challenging objectives.

Following this, the Rangers were used principally as security forces and for guarding prisoners until the conclusion of the campaign, when finally all three battalions were reunited. They took in replacements and resumed training, which included more training at night. The Rangers had learned that fighting at night offered distinct advantages they could use that the enemy did not have. This would prepare them well for the next campaign, wherever that would be. However, unlikely to go with them would be Rosebud, Lt. Col. Darby's personal mule, who, according to him, attempted to bite him in the rear to avoid being ridden.

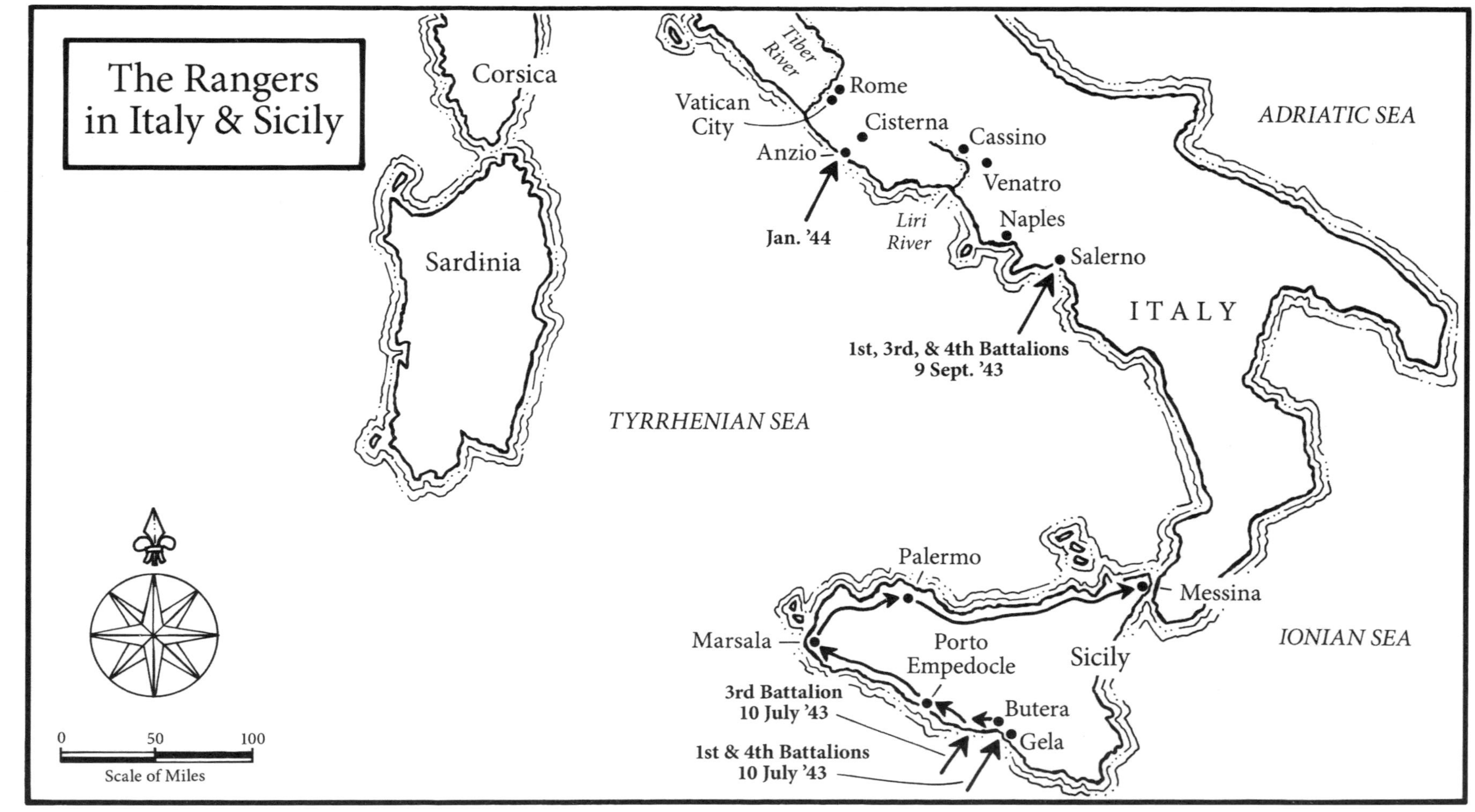

The Rangers
in Italy & Sicily
Corsica
Sardinia
Tiber River
Rome
Vatican City
Cisterna
Cassino
Anzio
Venatro
Liri River
Naples
Jan. '44
Salerno
ITALY
ADRIATIC SEA
1st, 3rd, & 4th Battalions
9 Sept. '43
TYRRHENIAN SEA
Palermo
Messina
Marsala
Porto Empedocle
Sicily
IONIAN SEA
3rd Battalion
10 July '43
Butera
Gela
1st & 4th Battalions
10 July '43
0
50
100
Scale of Miles

CHAPTER 5

UP THE ITALIAN BOOT

War often writes its own geography. Military forces can find themselves fighting in places that have no inherent value, or places that they did not plan to fight in but to which circumstances, the actions of the enemy, or the numerous other factors in war compel them to go. In short, war often has a momentum of its own that causes it to go to unexpected and unintended battlefields. One such example is the campaign in Italy.

As before, the debate raged among the senior commanders of Britain and the US British commanders, who were mostly echoing Churchill, arguing that invading Italy was the next inescapably logical step. It followed the momentum of success in Sicily, it would knock Italy out of the war (it was already teetering), and it would tie down German forces on a second front, and, as Churchill put it, a campaign in Italy would allow a drive into the "soft underbelly" of Europe.

The US commanders were suspicious of British motives, believing them to base strategy in part on protecting their postwar empire. They saw no real military *need* to invade Italy, and, they noted, with its narrow width and numerous mountains, it presented anything but a soft underbelly. But, again, the principal issue was whether it would delay the cross-channel attack planned for summer of 1944. Since it would not, the Allies decided to invade.

The campaign began with an invasion by British and Canadian forces on September 3, 1943, at the bottom of Italy's "boot." On September 8, Italy formerly capitulated. However, the Germans had been prepared for this and quickly seized Italian weapons and captured any Italian soldiers who might have been inclined to switch sides. By the end of the day on the 8th, the Germans in fact controlled Italy.

On September 9, US forces invaded Salerno. The 1st, 3rd, and 4th Ranger Battalions landed with British X Corps at Maiori. The landings were very smooth. Brought in on a British Landing Ship Infantry (LSI), one Ranger remarked that the British crew were so cooperative and supported the Rangers so well, "It was as though they were wearing Ranger patches."

They moved 6 miles inland and were able to seize the high ground overlooking the road to Naples. The Germans had fought only to cover their withdrawal up the Italian peninsula. This action would be typical of the fighting in Italy, fighting for high ground, and a German retreat to the next high defensible position.

By September 11, the Rangers were moving inland, along with the 504th Parachute Infantry Regiment, against the Hermann Göring (HG) Parachute Panzer Division. Following this, the 1st and 3rd Ranger Battalions were pulled off the line, while the 4th continued to operate. While able to seize Sala, the Rangers suffered steady losses through attrition. Meanwhile, the Germans were pulling back farther north to positions that promised to be far more formidable.

The Germans prepared a series of defensive lines across the Italian peninsula. These consisted of fortified positions on high points that were mutually supporting. Each of these lines was named; the first was the Volturno Line. The 4th Ranger Battalion was attached to US 5th Army for the assault on this line.

On November 3, the 4th Battalion infiltrated the Volturno Line and penetrated 12 miles in. On the fifth, they attacked a key position at Hill 689 but were repulsed by overwhelming German firepower. The Rangers were operating without fire support or with other units. Additionally, the very cold and wet Italian winter had set in; the Rangers fought the weather as much as they did the Germans. Within a few days they were forced to withdraw because the Volturno Line held against other US attacks.

On November 8, the 1st Battalion was back on the line, and the next day the 4th was on the line. The Rangers here were not being used as intended, but as regular infantry battalions, and suffered the commensurate rates of attrition. For the Rangers, though, the attrition was of highly trained soldiers who could not be quickly replaced. On the twelfth, the battalions fought off a major German counterattack but for the remainder of the year suffered from constant combat and the weather.

Meanwhile, the 3rd Ranger Battalion was attached to the 36th Infantry Division, and on December 8 the battalion captured Hill 950, and subsequently San Pietro. With this feather in their cap, the Ranger battalions were taken off the line in late December, and redesignated as the 6615th Ranger Force (Provisional).

By January 1944, the Germans were emplaced in their next defensive line, the Gustav. Here, the 5th Army developed a plan to circumvent the German line, in effect an "end run" around the Gustav line by landing in their rear. This was an amphibious assault at Anzio code-named Operation Shingle, conducted in sync with offensives against the Gustav Line from the south. As always, the Rangers would play a major role.

The Ranger force, consisting of the 1st, 3rd, and 4th Battalions, would land in the center of the US beaches, with 1st Infantry Division on the left and the 3rd on the right. They would seize port facilities, destroy enemy batteries, and clear the beach area, while linking up with the units on their right and left. The landing was on January 22 and achieved complete surprise. The Rangers were able to complete all objectives by 0900.

However, two actions led to a lost opportunity. The commanding general of the invasion forces, Gen. Lucas, decided to consolidate his forces before driving inland. Even though there were no significant enemy forces in contact, he wanted to wait until all of his forces were ashore before driving inland toward Rome. Meanwhile, the Germans, while surprised, reacted with their customary speed and quickly surrounded the beachhead with armored forces. They soon had over 40,000 troops, including a parachute corps and elements of several panzer divisions in the high ground surrounding the beachhead.

The result was stalemate. By January 26, the Rangers were already preparing defensive positions. Several furious German counterattacks failed. The Germans could not push the US forces back into the sea, but the US forces could not break out of their perimeter. On the twenty-ninth, the Rangers were relieved.

The 6615th was attached to the 3rd Infantry Division for an attack planned for January 29, to break out of the Anzio perimeter. The 3rd was facing a familiar foe, the HG Division, which was defending in depth. This means that instead of all their forces holding a single line, they were arrayed in echelon, so that after breaking through or overwhelming the closest enemy units, additional enemy forces were close at hand. Closest to the US forces were outposts that would not hold against a strong attack but were meant to detect an attack and warn the rest of the German forces. The next-closest defenders the US would encounter were strongpoints that would hold out to break up an attack and destroy its momentum. Then, finally, would be the main line, which would slow the attack enough to enable counterattack by reserve forces. This type of defense economizes troops and allows for a flexible defense, but it also allows opportunities for infiltration. This is exactly the sort of weakness the Rangers were trained to exploit.

The objective was the village of Cisterna. The village was 4 miles behind German lines and controlled movement along Highway 7, otherwise known as the Appian Way, the road to Rome. While British and US forces conducted an attack to break out the Anzio beachhead, the Rangers would infiltrate to seize and hold Cisterna, preventing German reinforcement and allowing 3rd Infantry Division forces to move on Rome.

Unfortunately, the deployment of German forces and tight time restrictions would limit the amount of reconnaissance the Rangers could do, and the nature of the mission would limit their fire support. Also, no armor was available. What the Rangers did not know was that the location of the Germans main line was wrong on their maps; it was 6 miles closer to the US line than they thought. Additionally, the Germans occupied the positions with higher numbers than anticipated by the Rangers. Coupled with the fact that Cisterna was composed of stone buildings, surrounded by featureless flat plains devoid of concealment or cover, would make this one of the toughest missions the Rangers had ever had. The attack was set for January 30 at 0200. The 1st and 3rd battalions would infiltrate directly toward Cisterna to capture it. The 4th Battalion would move on their left.

The afternoon of the thirtieth the Rangers spent in preparation. Many were unshaven, given their hectic pace of action, being described by a paratrooper who saw them that they "looked like cutthroats." Extraneous gear was stowed and the Rangers put extra grenades in their pockets and bandoliers around their necks. Mail arrived, but with no time to read it, it was held in the rear. Rangers never took personal mail into combat, to avoid giving any type of intelligence to the enemy. Before moving out, Darby asked a young Ranger who was shaking if he was nervous; the Ranger replied, "No sir, I'm just shaking with patriotism."

The Rangers crossed the line of departure that night as planned.[4] Since there was no cover, they used small ditches that crossed the area to mask their movement. Nonetheless, by 0300 they were detected, and the veteran German forces reacted with a fierce volume of fire. The lack of fire support, armor, or cover forced the Rangers to dig in, and by daylight they were on the defensive in the open. The 4th Battalion had also been stopped by the unexpected number of Germans. As they later learned, the 1st and 3rd Battalions had infiltrated into a German camp and had been largely stopped short of Cisterna by the ensuing firefight. The fighting was so intense that one Ranger described how the wood stock of his rifle was smoking from having been fired so much. Supporting forces from 3rd Infantry Division were stopped by mines and accurate fire from the Germans' dreaded 88 mm guns.

As is their standard operating procedure, the Germans counterattacked with artillery support and armor. With no support of their own, surrounded, outnumbered, and outgunned by German armor and artillery, the 1st and 3rd Battalions largely disintegrated. By the end of the battle, Darby himself had been moved to tears by the destruction of his unit.

The 4th Battalion, with help from elements of the 3rd Infantry Division, was able to open and hold a road to Cisterna, but this was done at great cost to the battalion.

Cisterna largely destroyed the 6615th. Of 767 men from the 1st and 3rd Battalions, only eight returned. The 4th Battalion suffered over 50 percent casualties. After the battle, a mortar round hit the command post, killing an additional six Rangers.

Who is to blame for Cisterna? Possibly no one, but definitely not the Rangers. Intelligence had been faulty as to what Germans faced them, the terrain was not conducive to infiltrating, and, above all else, the mission was not one for a Ranger force trained in special missions. What was needed here were several battalions with heavier fire support. This was the case months later when Cisterna was captured by the 3rd Division.

After Cisterna, the 4th Battalion moved into the reserve, but in Anzio the reserve endured constant small-unit actions in the surrounded beachhead. The losses to the battalion had been significant, so on March 25 the battalion was disbanded. Rangers were transferred to other infantry units, some to the 1st Special Service Force, serving in Anzio, and others returned to the States to help train the newly forming Ranger battalions.

Perhaps the most significant accomplishment of the Rangers was that in their short time in combat, the 1st, 3rd, and 4th Battalions had validated the need and value of a Ranger force.

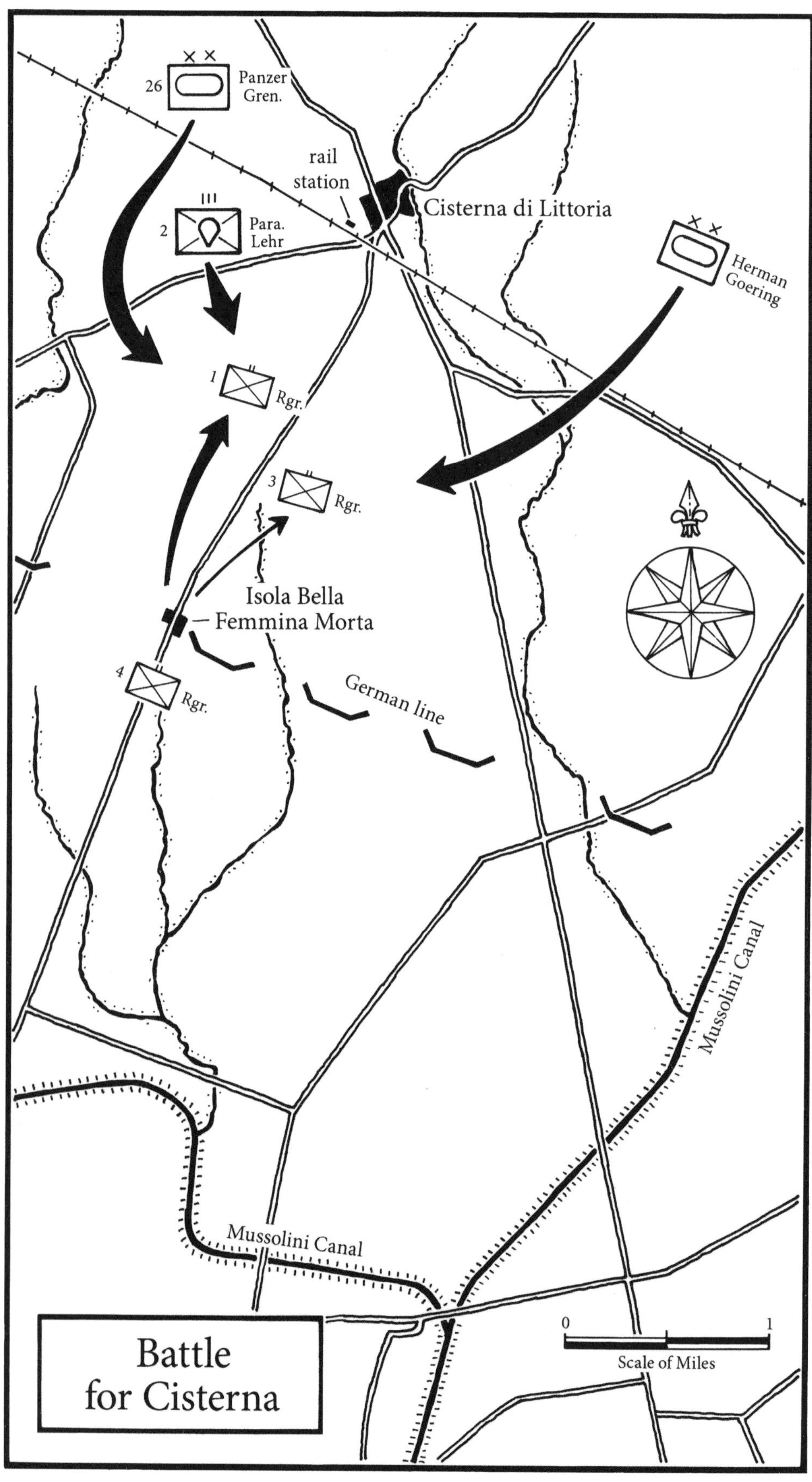

26
Panzer Gren.
Para. Lehr
2
rail station
Cisterna di Littoria
Herman Goering
1 Rgr.
3 Rgr.
Isola Bella
Femmina Morta
4 Rgr.
German line
Mussolini Canal
Mussolini Canal
0
1
Scale of Miles
Battle for Cisterna

CHAPTER 6

THE INTERVIEWS

Ranger Rouona

TSGT. WAYNE ROUONA

This is Mr. Wayne Rouona, and he served in the 1st and 3rd Ranger Battalions in World War II. So, right before Pearl Harbor, what were your aspirations? What were you thinking about before the war broke out?

I had been farming with my dad at that particular time. I had to sign up for the draft in September of 1940. And I stayed with that until I was drafted on April 22, 1941. I got sent by rail car to Fort Snelling, near Minneapolis. And we were given physicals and a bunch of shots, which affected me. What part of that shot affected me, I don't know, but anyway I had 106 temperature and I was put into bed. I thought, "Well, maybe this will keep me out of going anywhere." But they gave me some antidote that knocked out the temperature, so I had to go south with everybody else. We went to Camp Claiborne, Louisiana, where the 34th National Guard Division was, and we were put into the National Guard Division. I was placed into I Company to help fill up the company. When we got there, the National Guard guys were quite resentful to have somebody else come in there, and they had to take care of us and try to get us trained. In fact, I'd been there for a while, and they had some shacks along the road where they sold beer and they had some dances, and some women there. So I went down there, and the first sergeant came down there. He was one of the guys who was resentful of us being in his organization. And after we were there for a little bit, we had to get back at a certain time. The clerk of I Company was one of my neighbors out from Park, and he pulled me aside and he says, "Don't get too close to the first sergeant, because after he's had a few drinks, he gets pretty ornery." I said, "Okay." So I tried to avoid him. And finally the first sergeant . . . we happened to run into each other. He says, "What are you doing here?," so I told him, I says, "I just came down to see what was going on down here and see what the people are doing and then go back." "Well, look at your shoes. They should have been polished and your pants are not in good shape as far as convention was concerned." And I said, "Hell, this is what they gave me from the stocks of the Army, and if this is what they gave me, I'm satisfied. I'll wear them as they are." "Oh, yeah." So we had to go back to camp headquarters . . . I Company headquarters . . . so we took the taxi and went over there, and I rode with these guys and they resented the fact that they had to take me along in the cab to go to the I Company. The reason I'm stressing [this] is because we got into a problem a little later.

Do you remember volunteering for the Rangers?

Yes. We'd been there about a week in this new place, and the first sergeant got up in front of us, and he said that there's a new outfit going to be established, and it's going to be considered a crack outfit like the British Commandos, and that they needed volunteers to step forward.

And what made you step forward?

I stepped forward because of the poor training I had in the 34th Division, 'cause I had been reading about how well trained the Germans were, and I figured I wouldn't be able to compete with them if I stayed in the 34th. They asked those of us who wanted to volunteer to step forward, and there were eight of us who did.

Do you think that the Ranger training you had made you a better soldier?

It helped keep me alive. The full tactics of Ranger training was carried out by the British Commandos, and it was enough to overcome the poor training we had in the 34th Division, and that's what bothered me. With the poor training we had in the 34th Division, I figured, good God, we would get over there and it was proven after they got to Africa. I guess they lost one of their regiments because of the poor training. Well, anyway, we trained right in the northern part of Ireland. We were told not to go into the south, because if we got there we might be put under arrest. So we just stayed away from there. But anyway, on the way over, a German submarine was caught trying to attack us, and the battleships that were with us opened up with depth charges. Well, one of them went off too close to our ship and damaged our hull. So we had to limp into Scotland while the rest of the convoy went on ahead. But we got into Scotland, and they took us in smaller boats and got us to Northern Ireland, where they put us in the barracks. We went into training there for a while, and then we moved closer to the border of main Ireland, and we were there about a week.

Moving on to your first battle, you were at first in the 1st Battalion, so your first battle encounter was Arzew, North Africa, right?

North Africa. That's right.

Do you remember, when you were on the ship before the invasion, what you were thinking about? Were you scared, were you apprehensive?

No, I wasn't; neither one. I was just wondering if it would turn out the way we wanted it to. Two companies—A and B, and I was in B—were to make the invasion into the harbor of Arzew, which was a good depth for ships. And four other Ranger companies (there were six in a battalion) went in the backside of naval guns that were posted up there in the mountains. They were going to open up on any enemy that came in there, but they knocked out the controllers of the guns up above. But when we came in, there was wire netting in front of us, and we were told that it was up. So they asked for volunteers to go in there to take care of it, and I volunteered. But finally, word came to us that the barbed-wire chains protecting the beach were open, so we went in and hit the docks. The landing craft I was in happened to hit another ship, and immediately a French officer popped up on the deck of the ship that our boat had hit, and, in French, he wanted to know who we were and what we wanted to do and how come we were hitting them. Well, it so happens we had Capt. Meade, who could speak French, so he let the guy know that "Oh no, we were just a fishing outfit coming in." So we docked there so he could see. So the Frenchman said, "*Oui, oui.*" Anyway, he left.

I see. On that invasion, did you have a lot of fire or artillery on the beach?

No. It was a pretty quiet invasion. A Company was to take the fort, and there was kind of a peninsula right there. At the end of the peninsula, the French port loaded with French troops, so we fought the French for three days. But we entered, and B Company formed an arc protecting A Company from being attacked. And the only damage done was one of our guys got killed by a shot, and the guard at the gate of the fort on the peninsula got shot and killed. But one of our guys went on his own into town and found the barracks, where about thirty to forty French troops were in, and he was loaded with a submachine gun and a rifle. He had them both cocked, and he walked in and told the commander there that we were here to take over the country and the French troops. We want them to march back up to the fort. So he led them out and he said, "The first one who wants to get shot, try it. I'll take care of it." So he came back with a group of these French soldiers, and they went into the barracks at the fort. Right below us was an oil refinery, lit up with lights. We were in a cemetery, and we could see this guard walking back and forth. So our lieutenant went down there to capture this guy, but the guy ignored him. He kept walking back and forth. The lieutenant didn't know what to do; whether he should just kill him or what. So he came back, and about this time it got daylight, and there was a rock abutment all the way in about 300 feet from the shore out into the water of the harbor. And on the end of this here rock abutment, they had built a machine gun nest from some brush and soil that they had brought in there. We didn't pay any attention to it. We figured it was all right. So I'm leaning against the concrete wall of the cemetery, and two of the other guys were with me when the French opened up with their machine gun. And I'd be on the right side of the group, clipped the concrete off of that wall in my face, and as soon as that happened, I hit the ground so hard that I lost my breath for a while. But we didn't care to be shooting at the French, because we were told not to be too harsh on them because they should be our friends after a while. Which turned out to be the case.

So the firefight at Arzew wasn't that intense?
No, it wasn't. No.

So let's move on to the next invasion you were involved with, which was Licata, Italy, right?
Yes, that one was a little more intense. We had to take out quite a fortress right on the beach. There was a rock that they had plowed into for protection.

What time of day did you invade Licata?
At the nighttime. Yes.

Was there a lot of artillery fire on the beach?
No. They gave us machine gun fire on both sides, but they couldn't see us or anything. They had a barbed-wire entanglement along the beach on both sides. And the machine guns were firing on water side, between the Mediterranean Sea and the barbed-wire entanglement. I had to get the rest of the guys off of our boats, and the reason we had a little problem on that [was] because the Mediterranean was a little rocky from the storm we had the day before. So it washed enough rock to block out the intensity of the artillery that was tied up to these barbed-wire entanglements.

I see. So did you guys take out the machine guns at that point?
Well, we got through one side of the barbed wire, cut that up. The guy who dashed out came from the rear side of the machine gun nest. It took a while. We took two prisoners, but most of the rest were killed.

And that's how you advanced up the beachhead then?
Then we advanced forward on the beach to allow the 1st Division to come in without any problems, which they did.

So you basically secured the beachhead and then the 1st Division came in?
Yes, yes. And then we went up and we got to the hill up there. I was on the mortar at that particular time, except I had a new lieutenant with me, and he said, "I want to watch what you do because I want to learn to see what's going on."

And were you a sergeant at that time?
I was a sergeant, yes. I was a three-stripe sergeant.

Now did you employ your mortars right there on the beachhead toward the enemy, or did you wait until you went inland?
Waited until we got inland and we got up on the wall, and the 1st Division went through us, and about that time we started to get artillery fire to the left and right of us, and I was waiting for our commander and the assistant to tell us what to do. Seeing they didn't do anything, I ordered the guys to follow me and do as I do. We were under a tree, and I figured, well, they shot over here and shot over here, so the next fire was going to be right in the center. So I got the rest of the guys with me, and we dashed off a little ways from that tree when I heard the artillery coming in. We got pretty close and down we went, and a shell hit that tree and knocked it

out. And the captain was back about 20 feet from the tree that got blown up. He was talking to the lieutenant and he had his back braced off of this rock wall that was there, and they both got jolted pretty hard. That's when the lieutenant said he got bad enough, so he left the outfit.

So you were in charge of an assault team of maybe seven or ten guys? And your lieutenant was in charge of your platoon?
Yes. Yes, he was supposed to be in charge.

It sounds like you were leading your men?
Who else was going to do it, because he hadn't been in combat yet.

When you got to the top, you secured the beachhead. Were there a lot of firefights beyond that?
No, they backed away from us, but then the other Ranger battalions—there was only two Ranger battalions that came where we were—went into Gela, and they had a rough go there.

You didn't go there?
No. But we swung along the north shore of Sicily and advanced. We were supposed to clean out the beach all the way until they wanted to turn north to Palermo, which is the capital of Sicily. The 3rd Ranger Battalion, which I was in, moved forward and we got way ahead of the infantry. We cleaned out all of the enemy armor that was ahead of us.

But it wasn't too intense?
No, not at all, until we got to Port Empedocle, which was a beautiful beach; landing ships and things like that in the Sicilian area.

But that was more fortified?
It was fortified. But they were fortified to the Mediterranean, and we came in from the back and they didn't know what to do. So we captured them.

How many soldiers did you capture there?
I think it was about five hundred.

Five hundred. Was that your platoon, or was that your company?
Just our company, C Company. First we had to get on top of another mountain in front of us and take out the headquarters of the Italian division that was in front of us. So we got behind them, and we got up there and our captain ordered me to come up there with the mortars to open up where they were bivouacking up there.

So your company of probably eighty guys captured five hundred guys?
No, the rest of the guys went the other way. See, we had to go up on the hill over here, and the rest of the guys went this way. We went up in the mountains, and they didn't have to follow the mountain. They went down below. So we took over the garrison of the divisional command post, and how many there was I don't know.

The German forces?
No, Italian forces. And the Germans were down below protecting the beach.

I see. So when you compare the landing at Licata and Arzew to Salerno, was Salerno worse?
Salerno. Oh yes. That was much more heavily fortified.

Can you describe that invasion? What time of day did you go in on Salerno?
It was night when we came in. Something like one or two in the morning.

And so there was heavy fire on that beachhead and a lot of artillery?

No. No fighting until we got partly up the hill that was right in back of this town. I forget the name of the town. We went up the road to the top of the hill, but we had to stop because the Germans had it fortified, and we killed them off.

How many were up there?

Of Germans? It wasn't too big of a force because it was a small town on the way up.

How about the fighting of Valterra in Naples?

We went over to Valterra to help destroy some of the armament they had there, and it was by a river. I forget the name of the river.

That was in the mountains? Was there heavy firefight there?

Not for us, 'cause we took care of ours in a hurry and pulled back and let the regular infantry go forward. And then we swung around the backside and was going to go around the rear. We had to go through Naples.

And so with Anzio, it was the same kind of situation? On the beachhead, you had no problems entering Anzio?

No, they had a little firepower at Anzio. There was some strength. We took out some pillboxes and a tank or two. I don't remember how many tanks. And we had the British with us. I think they had some Australian troops as well, and we took the beach and controlled it for over two weeks. Our general had never been in combat before and was ready to retire. So he wanted the chance to tell people that he was in combat before he retired. So he was going by the book and had us make the arc around the two cities that were along the beach. I forget their names right now.

I see. Well, let's go to Cisterna. What about you never being deployed for Cisterna?

Yes. After we had been there for a while, they ordered us to move into Cisterna and take it over. That was in the middle of the night.

You were traveling along a little ravine?

It was quite a ditch. Yes, because Mussolini wanted that to be for cropping, and it must have been wet before that, because they dried it out and the ditch was pretty deep.

But you were moving along the ditch upward?

That's right. Up. And we got to a point . . .

And that was sometime around 3:00 or 4:00 in the morning?

We got part of the way and then we ran into problems after that. We had been there since about five or six in the morning. The 1st Ranger Battalion was ahead of us. The 3rd and the 4th were over here on the left side about half a mile from us, and they were going to protect us from the flank.

Your left flank, right?

Our left flank, yeah. And we got to a bridge or a culvert on the road. It was still dark, and a German command car drove by us and busted our group. The 1st Ranger Battalion was way ahead of us, and the German car split us in half. They figured something was wrong. It was getting daylight, so they turned around and came back and parked the command car on top of a culvert that was about 4 feet deep. We opened fire, and it was one of these jeeps that had the motor in the back, not the front.[5] So we killed all the officers in it and the driver, because they had the driver come out to pretend he was working with the machine gun. Well, that didn't work, because we shot them all. And the motor kept running. That was really part of it. The motor on this here command car kept running. By this time we were getting into Cisterna, just about over there. Two German divisions had moved in, so we had the 1st Ranger Battalion hit them first, and they knocked out six tanks and I knocked out one in the 3rd Division from our side.

How did you knock out that tank?
I had the guys with me in my platoon, down in the culvert. And here comes a tank on top, and he couldn't deflect his artillery piece down low enough to get us below there. So I had a new guy who had a rifle grenade. I told him to get that rifle grenade in there. Then if the tank came by here, shoot it in the bogey wheels to stop it, and then we could kill off the guys inside. Well, he didn't pull the pin on the grenade. So it hit the bogey wheel and that was it. It bounced off. So I said, "Now what the hell did you do?" He said, "Well, I guess I didn't pull the pin." So I dashed up the bank of the ditch and dropped a grenade inside of the tank, and it blew up. These guys started coming out, and they killed them as they came out. That was in the morning, and we fought until . . . well, I did and another guy. Most of our guys quit, 'cause we were surrounded.

Did a lot of your guys raise their hands and surrender while you were still fighting?
Yes, that's right. Behind us.

How many guys around you surrendered versus how many of you were fighting?
Well, first of all there were artillery guns behind us. They turned the artillery guns our way and threw up a shell, and our commander from the 3rd Ranger Battalion got killed right away. There was quite a group around him as they crossed that road that had a culvert underneath, and they got killed. I suppose there were twenty or thirty guys.

How many of you were in your proximal area?
I had about fifteen.

Fifteen. And of all the guys in your area, how many surrendered?
Oh, well, in the 1st Ranger Battalion, there were about three hundred guys there, and the 4th Battalion over here on our flank. Well, in all, thirteen guys got back and half of the rest got killed and the other half taken prisoner. I was captured.

At the time, though, when you kept fighting, you said some people surrendered and you kept fighting. At what stage did you decide you were going to be captured?
I figured that I was going to be captured when I saw this circle around us on the back. There was no way we could even get anywhere, but I figured, "What the hell, we'll kill as many as we can. Okay, if they kill me, I saved somebody from getting shot."

So how much longer did you fight?
Until about three in the afternoon.

And how many guys did you lose?
Another guy and myself would fire and shoot a German, and they'd shoot one of our men. They held the men right by them, and they might have killed more than one. I know they killed one. So me and the other guy, we'd shoot and kill another German and they'd kill some of our guys.

So how many did you lose out of the fourteen guys that were with you? How many of them were killed?
I don't really know. They went somewhere else, because we left the ditch for a while and went to a building about 300 to 400 feet from where we were, and the Germans opened up on us. The lieutenant with us got shot right through the breast, and we thought that was the end of it. Somebody said, "Get the medics and help him out," and one of our guys said, "To hell with him. He's shot and killed anyways." And, by God, he made it. But anyway I gave up when our first sergeant came from down below and he says, "They're killing our men. Quit firing." At first I decided, "To hell with him." But then I thought, "Why should I keep on killing them guys when they're killing ours." So I stomped my M1 into the mud that I was in. And I finally looked up, and here's a German 10 feet from me with a machine gun. He was ready to pull the trigger on me, and I looked at him and I said, "Shoot, you son of a bitch." And instead of me, there's two guys over here that had dug themselves a foxhole, and he turned around and shot them instead.

Is that right? Did you shoot him then?

No, hell, I had dropped my gun before that and stomped it in the mud. I didn't know there was going to be somebody next to me. No, I didn't want to do that. They would have shot me in a big hurry if I'd done that.

So they shot the other two and then you just raised your hands?

I raised my hands before that, and they had their hands up in the air and he shot them. And he had his machine gun pointed right at me and was ready to pull the trigger. But he looked at me and then he turned over there and shot the other two.

Isn't that amazing?

It is. Why he would do something like that, I don't know. So that's when I got captured. Well, they brought us out, and a lot of the guys were wounded and couldn't walk. So I got a blanket and got one of the guys on there, and we were going to start carrying him to the first-aid station. I heard there was a first-aid station down the lane where our doctor was. Then a German officer who spoke good English came up and said, "You leave that man there, or else we'll shoot you too." So he shot him. So we started moving forward with the German. He got ahead of us, so we got about a hundred feet from him, and I got another blanket and I got another guy on this blanket. He was bleeding out of the mouth and nose. He was in bad condition, but I put him on the blanket and we carried him over to the first-aid station. Then the Germans took us back a ways. Our troops were firing at us with their artillery, and the Germans on this side were firing at us. So we were in between. Well, anyway, they took about twenty of us from there, and they said if one is missing, the rest will get shot. So the sensible thing to do was to stand there and wait. They had one truck, and they used that to take us to a business establishment. What it was, I don't know. They took us there, and I was one of the last twenty that got over there, and it was midnight. The Germans had fed the first group that was there. And of course I missed out on that until I got there, and I was so damned tired by that time and hungry that I fell asleep while the other guys had something to eat. I said, "What the hell is wrong with you guys. Why didn't you wake me up so I could eat?" Well, anyway, we were in this building, and they separated the officers from the noncommissioned officers. So I went over to the officers, and here's one of our officers had told the Germans that if somebody is waving an orange flag or someone's got some orange powder, that's our troops being told that we're in trouble. And he told this German officer that. So I told the lieutenant of ours, "Why the hell don't you shut his mouth up?" But he didn't.

So where did you go from there?

We went by railroad car to northern Italy, by the Arno River. Before that we were down in Naples, and they took films of us for reporting to the public. "Well, here's the Rangers. And we whipped the hell out of them."

Did they walk you through Rome though?

Oh yeah. They walked us in Rome, and there's a crowd on both sides. And we were guarded by the SS troops. The guy in front of me was a fascist Italian officer on the side, and he had arm signals, whatever they were, and told them that we were a bunch of asses. And this Palumbo, who was in front of me, understood Italian and what he meant. So he grabbed his helmet and he was going to hit him over the head, and I grabbed him by the neck and I pulled him back in there. I said, "You get in there. That's just what they're waiting for so they can open up with machine gun fire." So they kept marching us out of town, and they used all that film that they got for propaganda purposes.

What were the Italian people doing? Were they cheering you on?

Some of them. They were crying even because we were in such a bad situation. A few of them. Not too many. 'Cause they had given up already.

Now were you marching as a formation march?

They were formation-marching us out of there from Naples up into the country. In a column.

In a column. And you just had your wool shirt and wool pants and that's it?

That's right. And they got us to a prison camp just a little ways out of town. There was a barbed-wire entanglement. I suppose it was about an acre or so. And they took each one of us in the column, and one at a time they had us go through some officers and stripped everything we had. Well, I took and folded the 250 lira and put it in my mouth. And then right behind me . . . they'd take the Jewish kids or soldiers and put them on the side. And right behind me were two buddies. One was a Jew and one was a Catholic. So they were crying 'cause they realized that they were going to take this Jew and put him on the side. So I asked the other kid, "What religion are you?" He said, "I'm a Catholic." I said, "Do you have your rosary?" He said, "Yes I do." I told him to give that to the Jew. And I told the Jew, "Put that around your neck. Be sure that it can be seen." So they let him go right through.

Is that right?

Yeah. But they had the other Jews over here on the side, and we were put in this camp and we got a little bit to eat there. There was a horse that could hardly walk that come down the hill, and they butchered him and put in for soup. So we had him for soup.

So then they transported you up through North Italy and Austria?

Yeah, that's right. They took us to Dachau, and we were there for a week, and then they started moving us up north.

Carl Lehmann

SGT. CARL LEHMANN

I would like to begin by asking you where you were and what your plans were before America became involved in the Second World War. Did you have any career goals?

Yeah, I was in college, going into prelaw.

Okay, where were you and what were you doing when you heard that the Japanese had bombed Pearl Harbor?

I was already in the Army. I had been drafted and I was playing poker in Fort Bragg. I didn't know where Pearl Harbor was.

How were you recruited into the Rangers?

They sent me to the 176th Field Artillery at Fort Dix, and I went overseas with the 34th Division.

How did you get into the Rangers though?

They called for volunteers for an American commando, and I volunteered.

What was your motivation for getting out of your old unit and wanting to get into the Rangers?

I couldn't stand the first sergeant.

Did you receive specialized Ranger training?

Yeah, I went to Achnacarry Castle, Scotland. Achnacarry was where the commandos were trained. We were in Kerrick Fergus, Ireland, and Col. Darby and several officers interviewed some 2,500 infantry and others for the Rangers, and in Kerrick Fergus they trimmed us down to seven hundred, and the seven hundred went to Achnacarry to be trained by the commando fellas there. That took a month, and then we continued training in the Scottish Highlands and eventually went down to Dundee and then Glasgow, Paisley, and on the ship to North Africa.

How did your Ranger training compare to your basic training?
There is no comparison. Every day that you trained in the commandos, you were surprised at what the young human body could take. Marching, climbing, whatever.

When and where were you first deployed in combat?
We made the landing at Arzew, Africa.

Do you recall what was going through your mind as you were approaching the shore and about to embark on this engagement?
No, I had arranged with some of the British sailors to get their rum ration, and I had several shots of rum before I went in, and I was very brave with the rum in me. And for that reason I never took another drop before I went into action.

Could you describe the landing?
Well, there was a boom across the harbor, but they had neglected to close the boom, so we went right into the harbor and got off on the dock.

Were you fired on when you landed on the dock, or approached?
No, it was a complete surprise. There was a little firing after that.

Could you describe your first battlefield engagement?
Well, our first assignment was to form a perimeter around the cemetery which was on the outskirts of the town. I was taken under fire, straddled by a machine gun burst, and I dropped down behind a tombstone. I was straddled again, so I knew I was on the wrong side of the tombstone. And what I remember about that is, on the tombstone was a photograph of a French soldier who had been killed in Verdun and sent home to be buried.

What was your role in the squad?
I was a scout.

What was your impression of your noncoms and your officers? Were they capable men?
Well, the first sergeant was a capable man. My squad sergeant was a capable man. The platoon lieutenant wasn't worth a damn, and he got bounced out of the outfit after that action. But otherwise they were a pretty good bunch.

What was your next engagement or landing?
We trained a bit around Arzew for a while, and then we were flown to Tunisia and Gafsa to take part in the proceedings there. Well, that was about the time of Kasserine Pass, and our troops there took a licking. We were around Gafsa and had to withdraw, and my company, B Company of the 1st, was the rear guard. We were the last ones out of the position, and our instructions were to make our way back to Tebessa on our own. I was hiking down the road with another Ranger when we came upon a column of trucks that were filled with French goons, and they invited us on. We started to get on the trucks, and as we did, our lieutenant by the name of Dunnegan leaped on the tailgate. Then I saw two flashes and I didn't know what it was, but I was out of the truck and on the road when these two fragmentation grenades went off and made a mess out of the goons. The lieutenant was saved by a bunch of French francs that were in his hip pocket. He got one surret in his ass, and the rest of it went out. That's according to what he told me many years later anyway. I don't know what happened to him after that.

The next major landings were at Sicily? Did you participate in the invasion of Sicily?
Yes. Licata. At that time we had formed the 3rd and 4th Ranger Battalions and the reconstituted 1st, and I was in the 3rd Battalion. Capt. Kitchens was our new commander, and I had been trained to be a sergeant in the 60 mm mortar squad, so that's what I led into the beach—the mortar squad. My assignment was to take the first half of a Bangalore torpedo and blow the wire on the beach.[6] However, the storm the night before had

covered up the wire, so we just walked over it. My assignment was this place that Capt. Kitchens told me was a bunker, because he could see it through a spectroscope that would help your depth perception. Photographs that you look through; they're probably before your time. But anyway, it is supposed to aid your depth perception. However, I'm cockeyed anyway, and it didn't do a thing for my depth perception. So I said it didn't look like a bunker to me; it looks like a farmhouse. But he said no, and he pointed out the fields of fire and so on. He said, "It's a bunker, and you're to attack it." So I went in, bashed in a window, and pulled the pin on a grenade. But I was halted by cries of "mamma mia" in feminine voices. So I had to find a well to throw this grenade in, which I did. So I guess it was a farmhouse after all. We went on to Montaperto, Puerto Empedocle, Sciacca, Marsala, and so on, and then we were sent back to Corleone to rest. We rested for about two days, and General Truscott called for the 3rd Battalion to be on his right flank going towards Messina. So that's what we did. We went up and down these mountains on the right flank until we got to Messina.

What were your actions at Messina?
Well, not much. They were gone by the time we got there. We did a few things like making sure these houses were cleared of anybody.

You mentioned that you started off in the 1st Ranger Battalion and later transferred to the 3rd? Did a lot of the soldiers in the 1st go with you? Were you still with some familiar men?
Yeah. The A Company and B Company formed the 3rd Battalion. C Company and D Company formed the 4th Battalion, and the other two companies remained the reconstituted 1st Battalion. There's five hundred men in each battalion roughly.

I want to ask you about one of the next major landings at Maiori, Italy. What are your recollections of that assault?
The 4th Battalion went in first. Our landing was uncontested and we went 12 kilometers, almost all uphill to Chiunzi Pass. There were mountains on each side, and for the next fourteen days we defended that. We started off with 1,500 men, and before it ended, Darby was commanding a force usually commanded by a general. I mean there was a whole bunch of people there who gradually came to fill the gaps and so on. He was commanding at least a two-regiment-sized outfit up there.

Was there any particular engagement or firefight in that battle that stands out in your mind?
Yeah. About the third day the mortars were consolidated. They were given to somebody else, and I was a leftover sergeant, so I went with Kitchens. I was more or less the supply sergeant, and on the second day, I don't know what happened to the platoon leader, but he came to me and he says take the platoon and go up this path until you come to a house in the saddle between two mountains. D Company is up there, and they want some support. And he described the path. He said you will come to the end of the treeline, and you will see this white house in the saddle. So sure enough, I did, and there were people walking around this white house. And I yelled, "Is that D Company?," and they yelled something back that was unintelligible. I kept walking and yelling and they were yelling back to me and so forth, and then they said something that I understood, which was the word "Americana." I was carrying a tommy gun at the time, and I sprayed a burst with the tommy gun and ran like hell until I got back to my group. And I didn't hear a shot from them until I hit the trees. That was about the most exciting thing that happened for a while. But they tried to come at us all the time. The amazing thing . . . this is the most important thing about this part. When the 1st and 4th Battalions were at Gela, Patton came in behind them, and he was at the headquarters, and the 1st and 4th Battalions and the rest of the troops there were getting shoved back by Hermann Göring tanks, and Patton says, "Christ, can't somebody do something about those tanks?" And there was a junior lieutenant there, and he said, "I can do something, sir." He was from the cruiser *Boise*, and they directed fire on those tanks. So between our cannons that had landed and the *Boise*, and some of the destroyers there, they creamed these tanks. That was the first time they had ever engaged moving targets on land, and they made a believer out of Darby, and out of Patton as well. And from then on, Darby had naval observers to go with him. When we went into Maiori, the main thing was to wipe out this road and get any targets on this road. The *Rodney*, I think, was there, and another ship that they called the *Monitor*. It didn't have much armor on it, but it had big guns. It was a British ship, and they directed these guns

on targets that were down there. Also, we had a fellow whose name was Willie Fox. When he was a kid, he jumped on his mother's couch and he ran a darning needle up his trigger finger and the trigger finger became longer and fatter than any other finger, and he was always pointing at somebody, so we called him "the Finger." His commanding officer tried to send him back, but Darby decided to hang on to him, and he won the Distinguished Service Cross. He got that there because, on his own, he made a reconnaissance down there and came back with an Italian officer. This was the day that the Italians gave up, you know, September the ninth, and he brought back a young Italian officer with a briefcase full of maps and targets. Darby immediately sent the guy to the artillery control center, which was in the harbor under the control of the Navy. They creamed many of these targets, and as a result of this, he got the DSC. Willie Fox's commanding officer had him down for desertion but changed his mind and put him in for a Silver Star. The 5th Army sent it back and said, make it a DSC. There you are.

I would like to ask you next about one of the landings at Anzio. What are your recollections as you approached the beach and assaulted that area?
Well, I remember the British had this weapon, I forget what they called it, but it was filled with mortars, a mortar-type thing. And they bombed the beach with a big volley just before we went in, so when we went in there, it was no contest. We advanced some, and we fought some small arms for the next five or six days. Then they called us out to go over to make this incursion into Cisterna, which was several miles behind the lines, and we went up the Pontano Ditch. What we didn't know, and what Carlo D'Este (who I think had it right) said, was that Kesselring had sent in two divisions, or the best part of two divisions, at this time in preparation for a counterattack.[7] As a result of this we were engulfed by these two divisions. And we were in a line too. We couldn't very well fight out of a line, but we did it. We fought until afternoon, but eventually they marched unarmed prisoners towards us, and we couldn't shoot through them because they were our guys. We tried to run back, but the troops on either side just made that impossible, and so they captured us.

Did you get an order to give up from the commanding officer?
No. It was impossible. Nobody gave any orders or anything like that.

It was obvious that you were encircled, and there was no chance to fight your way out of that?
Right, yeah. It was automatic weapons all around.

Do you think that the Germans were dug in and waiting for you at that area where they captured you?
No, no. One historian copies from another, saying that we were ambushed. We were not ambushed, and I can tell you this on my own because the guy shouting orders to his gun didn't hear us. Because we went on the ditch and it was loud and then it faded out, and we could still hear him giving orders. And suddenly when the firing started, I went out of that ditch, and here were Krauts rolling out of their blankets. They didn't even have tents or holes or anything. They were just rolling out of their blankets, and we were shooting them going through. This was the most intense of any battle I was ever in. I ran up a hedgerow and stopped to load my rifle. I was out of ammunition by the time I got there, and there was a crest up here. We were in the shadows, and a half-track of some kind rolled up first with a 20 mm gun in the back, and we drove it off. Then we could see these guys' helmets, and we were just shooting at these helmets for several minutes. Now you may have never heard this before, but it happened to me. An M1 went automatic, 'cause it got so hot. There were like two shots left in it, and it popped this way in my hand. It had done it once before on an exercise where I had fired it until it got hot, and then it popped sideways in my hand. You couldn't hold it, you know. Four shots went off.

Were the German forces fairly brutal to you after you were captured? Did they shoot anybody right there?
No, but here's one for you. They lined us up and they searched us. Before I was searched, I had time to bury a Luger that I had, a German entrenching tool that I had, and my fighting knife. We were in a plowed field, so it was easy to bury them. But what I forgot was, Do you remember the Nazi eagle that was on the right breast of German soldiers? I had been in a sleeping area, and I went around stripping these scalps off, and I had them in my pocket. And this one guy who searched me stood me against the wall and begged the *Feldwebel* to shoot

me because of this horrible thing. And the *Feldwebel* kept saying "*Nein*," and I kept blessing his mother for giving birth to him. But anyway, when we left I saluted the *Feldwebel*, and he smiled and said, "You have a German name, Carl." That was about it.

So from there I'm sure you were herded up and brought to holding areas and went through northern Italy?
They lined us up in front of the Coliseum and took motion pictures of us. Not only us, but a whole bunch of prisoners that they had taken. Then they marched us past the Coliseum so they could show these pictures to the German people, I guess.

Were there Italian people lining the streets when you were walking?
Yeah.

Do you think they were sympathetic to you?
Yeah, I think they were.

So they weren't throwing anything at you?
No, I've heard this before, but I didn't experience any of that. I mean they weren't cheering or anything like that. You could see that they were sympathetic.

Then they transported you by train north?
Yeah.

And did you stop at certain locations before you actually got to your Stalag?
Yeah, we went to Stalag Moosburg, Stalag IV I believe. And we were there for a little while, and then they sent us to Stalag IIB.

At Stalag IIB were you assigned to the actual premises or were you taken off to the farm?
We went to the farm.

Was that an elective thing where they said did you want to go to the farm, or they just told you?
No, no. They just told you.

And so the majority of the people I believe were taken to the farms rather than the actual Stalag, right?
No, no. We were all in the Stalag, and you were taken out of the Stalag. I was taken with one other guy to this farm, and there were already twenty-one other GIs there and we made it twenty-three. We stayed in a compound at the farm. There were twenty-three of us who stayed in this little house. One of our guys was the cook, and he cooked for us.

How was life there? Did you get reasonable food?
We got Red Cross parcels occasionally. We were supposed to get them every week, but about once a month would be about right. But on the farm you got all the potatoes you could have to eat. And bread. They made the bread. Actually, the oven for the whole town there was in our barracks, so we got plenty of bread.

Would you ever get meat, fish, or cheese?
No.

Fruit?
No. It was basically soup, bread, potatoes, maybe some other vegetables once in a while?

So it was a fairly light meal for somebody that was working in the fields all day?
I don't recall being hungry there. Not at all. Don't recall being hungry. Of course one thing that helped me is that I volunteered for the cow barn and I milked cows. And when you milk cows, you can drink some milk, and that was one thing that helped me, I guess.

So how many soldiers were assigned your twenty-three or twenty-four guys?
Two.

I see. Did they treat you reasonably?
One of them had a very bad attitude. He had been banged up on the Russian front, and the other one was about sixty years old. But that was it.

Were there just privates or noncoms there? No officers, right?
We were only privates or noncoms.

When you were a prisoner of war, did you maintain your military status?
It all depended, I think, on where you were. I mean, our cook was named MacMahan, and he was a first sergeant and he was the boss, you know, but a friendly boss. I mean he was a friend.

So you still respected the rank that you had in the military?
Oh yeah.

Did they let you read any books, or did you have a radio hidden or have any information coming in?
No, not on the farm. But I escaped from the farm, and I was out about three weeks.

Do you think that being in captivity affected different people in different ways?
I guess so. There were twenty-three people on this commando,[8] and only two of us escaped. The escape was my idea. I had to talk this other guy into it, but I talked him into it because he told me that he had some experience with boats. Our plan was to go to Stolpmunde, which was 80 miles away, and somehow get into a halibut boat, which was manned by two men. From there we would go to Sweden, which was another 80 miles away. But it didn't work. We got caught.

Can you tell us how that evolved? How did you make the escape? What was your plan and everything?
Well, our plan was to go to Stolpmunde by foot. It was about 80 miles and it took us about two weeks. When we got to Stolpmunde, we cased the boats and so forth, and then there was a storm; the same storm that came on June 6. So we decided that we were going to try to get into this beach house. We stayed in that and we slept on a mattress; for the first time in years, we slept on a mattress. But it was 5 miles away from Stolpmunde and the storm came up, so we decided to try another house. Well, it happened to be a house that was housing a bunch of Luftwaffe, and they caught us.

Now, when you actually made that escape, how did you get away from the compound?
Somebody had a key to a back door, and they were holding it for somebody who wanted to escape. We wanted to escape, so we opened the damn door and it had barbed wire around it. But we cut our way through it with a pair of clippers, and we were gone.

So the guys that you came into that compound with had a key, but no one was interested in escaping. Why was that?
I don't know. They were fed pretty well. And it was much-better treatment than in the Stalag.

So you were not in civilian clothes when you escaped?
No, I'm not sure what I had on. I know when I was captured I had winter stuff on, like I think the armored fellows had.

But it was a uniform?
Yeah, and the reason I know is that they took pictures of us as we were going pass the Coliseum, and I was in this strange type of uniform, you know, like the tankers wore.

What did they do after they brought you back? Did they put you in solitary?
No, no. I was interviewed, and the guy wanted to know what happened and so on, but no, they didn't do anything.

You said you escaped a second time. Can you describe that?
Well, they sent me out on a town commando. I remember we were digging along the streets, and I remember uncovering a bunch of black marble with Jewish writing on it, where they had crushed these Jewish stores. They had buried this stuff to get rid of it, I guess. But that was one thing that stuck in my mind.

So there were no guards with you when you were sent out?
Oh yeah, they had guards with us.

How did you get away from them?
Well, I escaped from where they had us bunked. I went through a transom. I only weighed 140 pounds, I think, but I went through the transom. It was very well planned, I thought. I got a brand-new US uniform through the Red Cross. And I got some red dye somehow and dyed it red all the time I was a prisoner. I took all the buttons off, had a beret, and I was the best-looking Frenchman there. So I strolled into this railroad station where I had been told by the other prisoners that I'd probably be able to get a ticket. But no sooner than I opened my mouth, I could see that they were on to me, so I took off running. I ran back into the woods and decided to try to go to Stolpmunde again. I tried for about two days, and they say they found me on the side of the road with malaria.

When they brought you back that time, did they do anything to you that time, the second time?
No.

No solitary?
Oh yeah. Yeah, that was it. They sentenced us to a month. It was two weeks in solitary, and bread and water in solitary. But before we went in there, we had to go to this camp that was full of Frenchmen, who were on a questionable status. One of them was born going through Germany. Another had a German grandmother, and these were all questionable people. We stayed with these Frenchmen for a while, and then we were put into solitary confinement. After that, they put us back into the camp.

How was it in solitary?
There were two to the cell, but our buddies brought us the water, and they also brought us some food along with the water.

Otherwise, the German soldiers wouldn't have given you anything?
No, they would give us bread and water.

That's it?
Yeah, Joe Phillips was his name. He had the detail to bring water to these prisoners, and he knew me, since he was one of the Rangers. So he would bring me bully beef and spam and so forth.

So how did you go to the bathroom?

I forget. I think they had a pot. A can, a pot.

So at least you had another person in there you could talk to. Otherwise, you'd be by yourself?

Well, at first I had the guy that I escaped with, and I didn't get along with him anyway. Then I got an attack of malaria and went to the hospital. When I got out, I had to come back to complete my two weeks. That was the first time. The second time, the guy sentenced me to two weeks, and I had a surprised look and he said, "Why are you surprised?" I said, "Well, you told me if I did it again, it would be a month." He said, "Forget it." So I just did two weeks that time.

Did they take good care of you in the hospital for a while when you were sick?

I don't remember much about it. I know I was out of it for several days.

How about the third time when you escaped? How did you escape that time?

Well, we had evacuated the camp, and they marched us several hundred miles towards our lines rather than the Russian lines. You know, the Russians were coming in at Pomerania and Hammerstein. Visualize a column of maybe a thousand men, four abreast marching up the road. This is what we did for several hundred miles. Then imagine that they changed their mind and they're coming back. I said, "I am not taking one step back." And four other guys said, "What are you going to do?" I said when the curl comes here, we take ten steps and then fall flat, and hope it walks away from us. And that is the one time I led, and it worked.

How long had you been marching? For days or weeks?

Months. We started in January, and this was about March. We made the British lines on the day that Roosevelt died, April 14th or 12th.

You basically were behind the lines, but you were staying hidden so the Germans wouldn't see you until you got to the British lines. Of course the British took care of you then, when you got through their lines?

Yeah. They fed us and sent us back to Brussels. We stayed there for three or four days, and they sent us to Paris and then we went to a camp they had. And after that, they put us on a boat and sent us home.

Do you feel that your activity affected you psychologically after the war in any way?

I don't think so.

If you were to look at all your leaders in your military service, what characteristics would you say made effective leaders?

I don't know. There were just some people you trusted, some you didn't. Darby was great. I mean, everybody knew that he was a good officer. I don't know how they knew it or how I knew it, but I did. This fellow I mentioned earlier was a nothing, and I knew it, and the guy that was in charge of the camp at Achnacarry told Darby that this guy is not an officer and they ought to get rid of him, and he did. Boom, out. And the sixty men in the company agreed with that decision.

What do you think the saddest moment was during your military experience?

When they marched us past the Coliseum. That was the worst day of my life.

Is there any tribute that you would pay to anybody that you served with in terms of somebody that you admired or anyone that paid the ultimate price for our freedom?

Darby. Several guys, but I can't remember all the names. You interviewed one of them. We were in the same squad in the 1st Ranger Battalion. Rouona, Wayne Rouona. We were in the same squad. I was a scout and he was a BAR man. He was in the same Stalag. The only difference was he wasn't out in the farm. He was in the main complex.

Did you get the impression that in your situation, there were people that still had to maintain their military rank and leadership?

Yes. When I was sent back to the camp after my first escape, I told them I was going to escape again. And there was something about an escape committee that was there, so I went to them, and they said you don't speak German and blah, blah, blah. And I said, "Have you ever aided anybody to escape?" And they said no. So I said, "Well I escaped, and I want whatever help you can give me." So that's when I got the uniform and the dye and some instruction as to how to get a railroad ticket, which was all messed up and didn't work. But anyway, that's how it was. And then when I went back into the camp, there was sort of a self-government. I mean, we had something to say about what it was, and you elected the camp leader. And Rouona decided he didn't like the way it was run and he was going to run, and I was going to be his deputy. But the ones in power told us that we couldn't run against them, because they were in touch with the Secret Service using a radio they had. They had instructions as to what to do when the troops came in to liberate them, as to put something on the roof, and some other stuff.

So what lessons do you think you learned from your military service?

I don't know. When I got out of there, I went to law school and became a lawyer. I didn't have a damn thing to do with the Rangers. Well, I learned how to survive. That's for damn sure.

What attributes would you say would make a good Ranger?

You have to be tough. You have to be quick. That's one thing I attribute my survival to, is that I had these lightning instincts. I seemed to know what to do when I was scared to death, but I knew what to do.

What pearls of wisdom would you give to future generations?

Well, this probably has nothing to do with what you want to hear. Every time you see a war picture, you see people running doubled up. This was the first thing we were taught in Achnacarry. You run straight up like you were in a 100-yard dash. If you hear the crack of a rifle, you don't fall flat on the ground, because then you make a stationary target. What you do is you run as fast as you can, and you dive into a hole as soon as you can. And the first thing you do when you hear that crack of a rifle go past, you shoot back cause he's going to duck.

SGT. JAMES MCVAY

Sir, if you could just perhaps give me some background. Before Pearl Harbor, were there any aspirations you had as a teenager, what you wanted to do in life, or what you wanted to pursue?

Yes, I had intended to go to law school. I had an uncle who was a judge, and he encouraged me all the way down the line, so that's what I had geared my high school education on. But before I got out of high school, he was killed in an automobile accident. The brothers and Jesuits at the boys' school I was going to told us that we were going to be in the Army shortly after we got out of high school,

Ranger McVay

and that we would be fighting against Hitler. So I just figured, "Well,when I get out of high school, I'm just going to enjoy life for a year or so, and I intend to be in the military." I got a little job in a steel mill, but I got mad at some of the bosses, so about 3:00 in the morning when I was working, I decided to go down to the post office and sign up for the military when it opened later that morning. So I volunteered. It took three days before I would leave, so I could sell my car and pay my bills. Went down there on the bus and took off, and I wasn't home after that for three years. That was in 1942.

I see. Can you describe where you were and how you heard about Pearl Harbor and what your impressions were?
Yep. I was washing my car that Sunday afternoon, had a date with my girl for Sunday night. I had the car radio on and heard it then. I got the car washed and went home and told my dad. He was sitting reading. I said, "Did you hear the news?" And he said, "Yeah. I'll tell you, this is just the beginning." And that was it.

I think you both knew what it meant to the world. I understand that your initial division was the 1st Armored Division?
I was sent over as part of the replacements for the 1st Armored. Never got to the 1st Armored though. About two days after I landed over there in the replacement depot in Oran, there were guys coming back from the hospital who had been with the 1st Armored, and some of them had an arm in a sling or little bits of bandages on. I said, "Where are you guys going?" They said, "We're going back to our outfit." "What's your outfit?" "1st Armored." "How come you're going back like this?" "Hey, they want us back. We're going back." About that time, we heard this little Piper Cub flying around over the replacement depot. Pretty soon an announcement came over the PA system. "There's some colonel out here that wants to talk to anybody that wants to sign up and volunteer for a thing called Rangers." Well, I'll go down and talk to them. I went down. He's in a small tent, and he's telling us, "Well, you know, we got this outfit, the Rangers, and if you join up with this you're going to get the best of everything. You're going to get the best training. You're going to get the best clothes, the best food, and on top of that you're only going to be out on a raid maybe two or three days, four days maybe at the most. Then you come back, you rest, do a little more training, and you may not go out for another three or four weeks or a month, but it's going to be real easy." Right! I said, "That's for me." So that's how we got conned. But anyhow, I was glad that I did. Really glad.

So at that point, you were transferred where? Did you get some specialized Ranger training?
Yeah. About a day later, there were about five of us in all. After they interviewed us and decided who was going to be accepted, they just gave us all our records and said, "Now you guys are supposed to go from here to there. It's up to you as to how you get there." There was a little forty-and-eight train that left Oran. I don't know how far across Africa it went, but they said, "You're going to go to a place called Nemours." So we went down and got on this train, and it was loaded with Arabs and anybody you could think of, hanging on. Well, we were able to buy a little compartment on the train with the little bit of money we had. So we had our own little thing on the train. But these guys were sitting on the roofs because they were like a penny for a ride or something like that. For us, maybe it cost us ten cents. Anyhow, the train would go so far and then stop at these little cantinas like along the railroad. You'd go in. The only thing you could get mostly was fig bars, and since they had told us not to drink the water, we drank wine. Well, we had a real ball on that train. But the train was so loaded that when it would go up a grade, they'd say, "Well, everybody's got to get off, walk with the train until the train gets up on top, and then you get back on the train again." So it was probably a day or two to get over there on that train, and it was out in nowhere, just sand and rock on a cliff above the ocean.

Is that where you did your Ranger training?
Yeah, that's where we trained. They had ropes that went down the sides of the cliff. Of course, you did the speed marches on the sand so that you could strengthen your legs up. And then you'd take your shoes off, up and down the sand, and you'd go swimming. Then you'd go back up them ropes. In the evenings, a lot of times it would be so hot we'd even go down the ropes ourselves, just so we could go swimming in the Mediterranean. But it was a good one. I think there was about a hundred we started with, and we ended up with about thirty that was left at the end of training.

So do you think that Ranger training really exceeded what you got in basic training?

Oh, absolutely. Absolutely. There was no comparison. I think one of the things to me at least was that it made me more determined. You get to the point and say, "Well, I'm not going quit."

Okay. I guess at that point you were transferred to the 1st Ranger Battalion?

That was the 1st I was in at the time. Then they decided that they were going to create the 3rd and 4th. So that's when they moved some of us over into a place called Zeralda, and they formed the 3rd and the 4th there. And then they had other new recruits who were coming in, and they would put them in with us. Of course we had the old guys there also. That was around the time they were getting prepared for the landing in Sicily.

So your first real battle was the landing at Gela?

Right.

Do you remember what you were thinking about at the time? Were you nervous?

Apprehensive maybe. Yeah, we were on the boat probably for three or four or maybe five days. And they'd float around out there. We had these layouts of the town (Gela), and we were paired up, two guys together all the time. So then they briefed each two-man team. They'd bring us in and say, "Okay, now this is your objective. By daylight in the morning, you've got to be at this house or at this point. It may be three or four blocks inland from the beach, and this is how you're going to get there. You're going to go in this street and down that street, and you're supposed to wind up at this house at daylight." And then they'd have us tell them back exactly what we were supposed to do. So the guys knew pretty well where they were headed for as soon as they got there. And then the Britty was a converted British ship, and those British guys treated us like kings. Of course we ate good too. Tea, breakfast, 10:00, 2:00, 6:00 or whatever, tea, tea, baked bread, home-baked bread, orange marmalade (which I still like), and porridge in the morning. And they gave us one heck of a big dinner that night. It was steak, mashed potatoes, all the goodies. But a big storm hit there about 2:00 or 3:00 in the afternoon. Man, we thought that ship was going to sink. It was bad. Well, we ate supper about 6:00, something like that, and a lot of guys had gotten real sick. A lot of guys didn't even eat. So about 7:00, I thought, "Well, I'm going down to the latrine and maybe shave, wash up, and get cleaned up a little bit and look pretty presentable when I hit that beach." I was doing real good with holding my supper down until I got down to that latrine and I opened that door. About that thick on the floor, and the stench from everything. And then that hit me and that was it. That's all she wrote. But the storm calmed down around 8:00 or 9:00, something like that, and I got squared away. I'd go up and stand on the deck, and it was of course dark. A lot of the guys were still pretty sick when we got on the boats, but they had the boats on the deck, so we just got into the boats and they had davits that'd swing us out and drop us down. Some of the guys were still pretty sick yet, but generally it was pretty calm. I really just didn't have too much trouble. Everybody was just trying to feel better. "Let's hit that land and get on there and get some solid ground under us." That's about it.

What time did you get into the LCAs?

It was about 12:00 or 12:30, something like that, 'cause we hit the beach around 2:00.

And was there any fire on the beach when you hit it?

Well, everything was going real nice that night. Now these little boats that the British had were smaller than the Americans'. They explained it to us. They had a couple of Packard engines in them, with underwater exhaust so you couldn't hear them running. The only thing you could hear maybe in them was a cable to steer. Once in a while you hear that cable bang on it. Everything else was real nice and quiet. They were edging us in and telling us, "Okay, we're getting close. It won't be long." We must have been maybe 3 to 400 feet offshore. Some guy on the shore flicked a spotlight on and starting scanning out there. He picked up all of the boats. Man, it looked like the Fourth of July all up and down that beach. Everything opened up. So these guys of course still had to get in there and drop us off. Well, we got in there, and as soon as the boat scraped bottom on the sand, they dropped the ramp and started to put it in reverse. I was about the seventh or eighth guy off on my side of the boat. We had these Mae West vests. You'd squeeze them and there was compressed gas inside to blow them up. They told us to loosen up our stuff in case you had to inflate them. They went over your head, and you couldn't get up. Well, when I jumped off I must have been in about 8 feet of water, and I went right straight down. Aw, man. And I thought, "I'm going to keep my rifle and see how long I can go." So I started walking underwater. Finally I could feel that thing raising, and about that time I got above water. In the meantime, the guy in front of me, when he got off there, he tripped and fell in and went in headfirst, and as I was going by I happened to feel him. He was upside down. I grabbed hold of him and pulled him with me, and I got his head above the water and everything was lit up. So I got up on top of a sandbar. So now I've got to cross that sandbar. There was another stretch of water, but it was only about 4 or 5 feet deep, something like that. So I waded through that. We went through there, and when we hit that beach there was barbed wire. And man, it was like Fourth of July. Of course I remembered my training: "Lay on your back and go under the barbed wire." Which we did, and it kept everybody hard. Get off the beach. Get off the beach. That was thing you did. Get off the beach.

So when you got off the beach, was the fire as bad on the top? Did you climb up the bluff?
Well, there was a little seawall, just maybe a couple feet high. We got into town, first street. My buddy and I knew pretty much where we were. So we got to the place on the map where they said there was probably a little kind of a steep hill or cliff area, where we were going to have to go up to get up on the next level of streets. We had a rope and a grappling hook, and we got down there to where this supposedly hill or cliff was. Well, there was only one way to go, so we had to go up that way. Only it wasn't a cliff or a hill. And the street up on topside was where the civilians would back the wagons up and drop the donkey and horse manure. It was a dump. So we climbed up that stupid thing, and it stunk to high heaven. We finally got back up on the level where we were supposed to be, and got to the house, and it was just about breaking daylight when we went in. A family was living there. I felt sorry for them. They had a couple of little kids, and a husband and wife, and they were scared to death. So we told them to behave themselves and there wouldn't be any problems. It was a two-story, and my buddy and I decided to get up on the second floor. It had like a ladder to get up on this second floor. So we got up there, and the father was really accommodating. He said, "Do you want some vino?" We said, "Yeah." So he brought a big pitcher of red wine and a couple of glasses, and he came up there. There was a table up there, and he put it out there. He poured two glasses of wine, and I told my buddy, "Wait a minute." I told the guy, "You drink that first glass first." So he did. That's where they ran the tanks up the street. We all carried three half-pound blocks of TNT with us, and two or three different kinds of grenades—concussion, frags, and another British grenade. It was a plastic flash bang, really. It was just a regular old plastic, and it was round and it had a cap on it. You unscrewed the cap. There was a piece of cloth that went around, and there was a little lead weight on that cloth. When you threw it, it would supposedly unwind, and when it hit, it would drop a pit or a little BB or something down inside and hit the cap and explode.[9] About all it did was make a lot of noise. Anyhow, we had wired these half-pound blocks of TNT on a couple of concussion grenades. So then about 9:00 or 10:00 in the morning, that's when they ran the tanks down the street. Well, we were sitting right there, looking down at them. There wasn't a hell of a lot we could do, but we threw a couple of grenades with the TNT on them. We finally got one underneath one of the tanks and just blew it up off the ground about 4 or 5 inches, and that was about it. I don't know if it was Darby, but somebody got hold of a 75 mm cannon down the street and knocked one of the tanks out. Well, then a guy across the street came out of the house. He had a Bangalore, and it had blocked the rest of the tanks. So we were trying to get this guy out of the next tank, and we knew he wouldn't surrender. So this guy ran across the street and threw a Bangalore torpedo under the tank. Well, it really blew that track up. Of course, the top opened up and these guys came out with their hands up. Well, then one of the other tanks started backing up and going down the street. Well, then one of the guys threw a sticky grenade or something on the other one and blew the track off of that one. I think we caught three tanks on that one. It was very exciting.

So you were going into a house with two guys? You didn't have large teams then?
Right. It was just two guys each. You knew what you had to do. You had your objectives, and that was it.

And you were supposed to secure whatever house you were designated at?
That's it, yeah.

But it sounds like you had to stand off a counterattack, something like that?

Oh yeah, absolutely.

How long did the fighting last, and how intense? Was it intense for quite a while?

Well, the guys got into some pretty good scraps there in town, in the main square and when the tanks came; that was about the extent there until the next day. They moved us over into what they called the Mussolini Canal, which was a border of that town outside, and the Jerries[10] were forming up for a huge attack across the field. They were gonna have a big tank and infantry attack, and here again, we were on the other side of the barbed wire. They told us, "You guys don't come through the barbed wire. You stay here until . . . that's it." So of course the guys got some more grenades, and we lined the grenades up on top of the ditch and had extra ammo. We were watching the guys out there across the field, and they were starting to move. Here it comes. To go back a little bit, they gave us gas masks, but they were not the regular masks. They were just a little container of something, a canvas thing, which was to be used only for a short period. It had a can on the front of it and it went over your face. Well, since we thought there would be no gas attacks, everybody threw them away and kept the cloth and filled them with cigarettes. Well, of course, when this big attack was starting, the word came down—gas attack. Ha! No gas masks! But it turned out some of the shelling had hit an ammunition dump, and there were some gas shells that got hit and went off. That was it.

Well, how about Butera, Sicily?

That was a good one.

Was there a heavy firefight there?

Not that much. We ran a few machine guns down the road going up there. If I could go back to Gela. I always claim I should get a medal for shooting down a Jerry Stuka. They sent my buddy and me to a wee little brick or stone building out in this field. Well, this is after the supposed attack, which didn't come off. So they sent us out way up on the end of this field, where there were a couple of rows of Italian cypress. Then it kind of went over into a harbor down in there. It was a nice sunny day. We were on the other side of a house there, and we just took our shirts off to get a little suntan. Our M1s were leaning up against the building there. Planes were circling around overhead. If you ever heard a Stuka, you know what it is. They got this distinctive sound. But anyhow, this guy was passing around up there, and finally up over the trees down there, this guy made a hop over a tree. He must have been about 40 feet off the ground. And when he came down that field, his wings were lit up. Everything was lit up, and he just went by and made a big loop. In the meantime, we got up and grabbed our rifles. He went right back around again, but he had seen us there, so he was going to make another pass.

He went straight through the first time?

Well, yeah, but next time around we were waiting for him. So he kind of whooped up over there, and he came down through there, and I was standing right at the edge of the building. I watched that guy and thought, "Well, I'm not going to try to get him. I'm going to try to get that engine." So as he went by, I was pumping it into that engine, and I could see the pilot grinning at me. He kept going until he got down there just about to the other row of trees, and he made a big loop. Pretty soon, he went up and you could start seeing smoke coming out of there. Well in the meantime, the ack-ack had opened up on him. Now whether they got him or whether I got him, I don't know, but I always say I got a Stuka.

You had an M1 carbine at the time?

A regular M1. It wasn't a carbine. It was a Garand.

Was that standard issue for you guys at that time?

Yeah, oh yeah. We were pretty much the envy of the other infantry people 'cause they still had the old R3s.

The Springfield? Not too many carbines out there?

Well, I never liked the carbine. I never used it.

Okay, let's go back to Butera.

We were going down this road. The engineers were taking us over towards Butera. Now they had these big girders on these big, big, huge trucks. We were kind of behind these girders on the truck, going down this road. In the meantime, another bunch of guys had started up to Butera, so as we were going down the road, two machine guns opened up on us. Bullets were ricocheting off all the girders, so they stopped the truck. We got off the trucks, and there was a little orchard on both sides of the road. So we pretty well cleaned everything out of there, and we got back on the trucks and continued on up. Well, in the meantime as we were heading up the top of the hill, we saw a white flag go up. Out of Butera, right on the outskirts of town. So we got off the truck, and there was what must have been a regiment maybe, of mostly Italians. They were coming down and they were all surrendering. They had their knapsacks with them, and this one guy came over as he went by. He asked me in English, "Hey, you got a cigarette, Mac?" I gave him a couple of cigarettes, and he had this huge bag, which he couldn't even carry. He was dragging it. He said, "You know, my only problem is getting that to where I'm going." Anyhow, I went up there and there were some Germans holed out up there, 'cause they had controlled the town pretty well. So there were a couple of buildings that a buddy and I had. We got a couple of guys out of there. So then we went over towards a spaghetti factory. We went to that spaghetti factory to see if it was clean, and the people running it were the ones who owned it. There were no Germans there. So a woman there said, "I'm gonna make you a spaghetti dinner. You come in and sit down." So we sat down and they brought this liquor out. I never knew what it was, but it was good. Little shot glasses and hotter than blue blazes. About two or three of them, and man oh man. They cooked up these big, huge plates of spaghetti. My buddy and I sat and ate the spaghetti and had more drinks, until we couldn't even move. So they put us to bed. Seriously. So we must have slept for maybe three or four hours. Then we went out, and everything was fine with the world.

Probably the best sleep you'd had in a while?

Yeah, it was good. But Maiori, that was a good one. Nice, nice, quiet. Went in there. Not a whimper. Just about 2:00 or 2:30 maybe, something like that. They gave me and my buddy a flashlight, and it had two lenses. One was a red one, one was a blue lens, and we were supposed to go up this kind of a cliff and get up as high as we could. When we got up there, we were supposed to blink the flashlight. If there were no problems, we were to use the green lens. But if there were problems, we were to use the red lens. Well, we were blinking R with the green lens. So everything was good. About 4:00 or 4:30 in the morning, I heard somebody shifting around. There were little steps that went up, made out of cut stones. So I went out and saw something climbing up. I took my tommy gun and had about half the pressure already on the trigger. Always had bad dreams about this. It was a little old lady. She was about ninety-nine years old, with an old black dress on. I almost shot her. I asked her, "What are you doing?" I asked her in Italian, which I could speak a little bit. Turns out she had a place carved in the hillside, and they had a little stall there for a donkey. And she was going to go up and feed the donkey or give it water or something. Later that day we started up the coast road. I was first scout. We got maybe a couple of miles up the road, and the rest of the company was back of my buddy and me. So I heard this high-speed car coming. I told my buddy, "I'm going to stand out there with my tommy gun, and you get over on the side there against the bank, and if things happen, you shoot right into it." Well, here comes this little old car whipping around the curve wide open. I stand there with that tommy gun right in the middle of the road, and boy, they slammed the brakes on and skidded. I went over and told the driver to get out of the car. Well, he got out. In the back seat, there was an officer. I think he was probably a captain or a major or something. Anyhow, the driver got out and I told him to stand over there, and I told this guy in the car to get out. I told the driver, "You tell that guy to get out of the car." He said, "What's your rank? What are you?'" Oh, first he said, "Oh, you Anglais?" I said, "No, Americano." He said, "Americano." He was surprised. The driver said, "He won't surrender to anybody except an officer." And I said, "Of course. Can I say something? You tell that son of a bitch if he doesn't get out of that car, I'm going to shoot him right where he is," and I just rammed that tommy gun right in his face. Of course, the guy told him. So he got out of the car. He stood there, and he had riding boots and spurs on. I guess he was maybe going horseback riding or something.

This Italian?

He was a German, 'cause later on they found some more of them. Anyhow, I took his gun. He had a P.38. I got that one. So I told the driver, "You take those frigging spurs off of him. I want them." They were real beautiful and engraved silver spurs. He said, "Oh, no." I said, "Tell the son of a bitch if he doesn't give me them, I will shoot him right now." The driver got down there and took them off and gave me my spurs. So I told him, "Leave the car here." So about that time, the rest of the company was moving up, and Capt. Neil came around and said, "What are we going to do with the prisoners? We got no facility for them." I said, "That's not up to me." So he said, "Well go ahead and keep on going. We'll work it out." So we went up the road there, and I ran into a little old lady coming down with a donkey cart, just breaking daylight. She says, "You know, up in the building, *Sadeskies*," which is "Germans." "Big gun, big gun." So I told the captain about it. He said, "Well, it looks like there's a machine gun nest up in there." So we looked around. Well, this building was stone, and one side was carved right in the ocean, in the water, and it was about maybe four or five stories. Like maybe an apartment or something. And I asked her, "Well, where are they?" And she said, "I don't know, I don't know." So I said, "Well, we better get up above the road here and go up around. We'll go up around and drop back down sideways, and then we'll go around and see." So on the outside they had a stairway which went up, and then it would break on hallways going down each floor. Then there were doors off of that hallway down. So my buddy and I went down there. We were able to stay right against the building. I went up the first stairway and hit the first hallway. Well, in the meantime a door opened, and this woman came out. "Anglaise?" "No, Americano." "Oh, you're Americano." "Yeah." "I'm English. Yeah, I've lived here for twenty-five years." She says, "Come in, come in. I'll give you a little vino." I said, "I'll tell you what. We're looking to see if there are any Germans up here." She says, "Oh yeah, on the fourth floor." So I told her, "Okay, when we get done we'll be back down to talk to you." The stairway went up on the outside of the building, like this, and up to each floor. So we got up just before the fourth floor. A window was open, and you could see the snout of a gun sticking out. So I told my buddy, "Now, I'm going up and go in. Get your grenade. If you hear anything going on, if you hear a shot or anything, don't worry. Bail that grenade in the window, 'cause I'm gone." So I stood in front of that door, and I'm going to tell you, that was the hardest thing I ever did in my life. I stood there, lit up a cigarette, and I told you this monkey business of kicking doors in: don't do it. They had this latch on the door. Well, we'll try it nice and easy. I just raised that latch and I pushed the door open real easy, and there were six guys in there eating breakfast. One guy was just coming out of one of the bedrooms. He was just pulling his suspenders up, like this. I said, "That's it." None of them were armed, but they had stacks of rifles and that machine gun sticking out the window. "Come on, out, out, out, down." So we sent them down the stairway, and Capt. Neil was coming up around with the company and he said, "What do you have up there?" I said "I got seven of them." He said, "What the hell are we going to do with seven more prisoners? We have no place to put them." He said, "What do they have up there?" I said, "They have cases of grenades and ammo and rifles." He said, "Well, I'll tell you what. You guys stay there; break all that down, get rid of it, break that machine gun down, and get rid of it. Then you can catch up with us down the road there." So we took all the rifles, and on the other side was a room across the hall there. It backed up straight down to the water. So we went over there, and we just took the rifles and hit them over the windowsills and threw them out in the ocean. Then we stripped the machine gun and threw all the parts out. So we went back down, and I knocked on this door where this British gal was. Well, we went in there. She had this huge bottle of wine about this big, with that woven basket around; you know, halfway around it. We were standing over there. "You want some wine?" "Yeah." Took that basket over. So we told her, "Do you want a little cup of coffee, 'cause we had that powdered coffee?" And she said the coffee was unknown almost. So she made some hot water. So we had some coffee and wine, and we broke out a little bit of rations and we had a breakfast with her. Of course he and I stayed there, and we didn't leave there till it must have been 11:00 in the morning, and couldn't hardly find our rear end with both hands. Staggered out of there and staggered up the road. About that time, we heard some shooting, and when we got up to this little town, the company had got up there already. So we went in there and there were these guys laying [*sic*] out on this parklike area. Hell, they were half drunk. They got into a little shooting scrape up there, and there was a canteen, and they got in there and got some brandy and wine and they were all half crocked. Ha, ha. That's the way it went.

So how about the pretty heavy firefight in the Chiunzi Pass?
Oh, that was a good one. Yeah. Boy that was every day and night. Some guys got killed there. That was probably six or seven days up there.

And that was continuous fighting, pretty much?
Every day and night, at night too. It was pretty touchy. One morning I had to take the patrol out, and I was going around on a hill out there, and, like I said, instinct plays a big part. I got out there, had one of these walkie-talkies,[11] and I told the captain on the phone, I said, "I know they're here. I can smell them." He said, "You better not go any further. Just come on back and we'll run continuous patrols out." So I came back. They sent my buddy out then, and he was gone for maybe forty-five minutes or so. Heard the damnedest firefight. Nobody came back. So he sent other guys out to check. Couldn't find anything. Later, at a convention in Santa Barbara, the phone rang in my room and the guy said, "You McVay?" "Yeah." "4th Battalion?" "Yep." And he told me his name, Reynolds. And I said, "I thought you were dead." And he said, "Well, not quite. I just picked your name up in the roster here. Come on down and have a drink." So I went down. What had happened was an ambush, which I already knew. I knew it. And I had told him. I said, "Olsen, there's a problem out there. Keep your eyes peeled." Finally he says, "You were right. Boy, they had it set up for us." What happened was, they shot him, and there was kind of a bank there. He said, "I fell over the bank and fell down into some brush." And he said, "They got us all." There were five guys in the patrol, and they took him and they had shot him in his leg. He told me later they sent him back to a German hospital, but they didn't do anything with his leg right away. Well, it got infected, and over a period of time they finally did take care of it. At that time when I talked to him at the convention, his leg had shrunk about 2½ to 3 inches, and he had a terrible limp. But they had sent him to a prison camp and eventually took care of him, but it was too late to keep it going good. And then there was a ridge that went around, and you could look straight down into a valley which led into Naples. You could see everything going on. There were vineyards down there. You'd see the Jerries running everywhere. They had no problem down there, but they'd run patrols up. On this ridge, there was like a little peak out there. Well, my buddy and I had set up our little fort right there, and we could watch down there. We could see these eight guys coming up this pathway. We let them get so far and then we opened up. Well, the way it worked, there were two guys to a hole all up along these ridges. It was so far spaced between the guys that if somebody heard firing one place, then the guys in a few of the holes would come and reinforce you. So we'd get shooting down in there. Of course, these other guys would come running down there. Usually the platoon would come down and set their mortars up right away and drop some in there. There was like a saddle in there, and we were right up on the one tip there. Well, in this saddle was a little springhouse, with running water there, but it would take about ten or fifteen minutes to get enough water to fill a canteen. We didn't have any water, so every day we'd send two guys down there to fill up a string of canteens. There was a little stone wall that went around this springhouse. Well, the Jerries were using it too to get water, but we didn't know that. Well, two guys were down there getting the canteens filled up, and the Jerries were coming up there to get some water too. But we saw them coming there. Some of them got over the wall on the other side and we had a pretty good firefight then, but our two guys were in the springhouse and couldn't get out with Jerries all around there. But finally we got rid of them, and they brought the canteens back full of water.

Would you say Cisterna was probably your biggest firefight?
That was the biggest loss. Yes. That was really, really a bad one.

Obviously you were not going with the 1st and the 3rd up to Cisterna. You were on the flank, right?
We were there to back them and make an attack on the side. It was on the left side, and we were going up and we walked right into it too. They were sitting there waiting. And a couple of days later, we got into where the machine guns were. These guys were really pros at this stuff.

They were dug in?
They had holes, and then they had like railroad ties over the holes and dirt over it. They had just a little slot about like that for the gun, so the gun couldn't elevate much. Everything was pretty much level there, and that's

what they were doing. They couldn't get it up too high, so they were cutting the guys' legs out, you see. Just like a sickle going across there. Then as they would drop a lot of them, a lot of them were getting hit in the head. They'd go down and guys were still shooting, and they just hit them right in the head.

They were dug in and they were well defended?
Oh, man, and they had farmhouses and haystacks around. There were snipers in haystacks, and there were farmhouses, and little old barns around.

So did you know that the 1st and 3rd had been encircled?
They told us that they were fighting, and we had to get to them. Man, we made runs across the field.

But no one knew there were two divisions there?
No, no. It wasn't supposed to be that much. It was just supposed to have been a snap, you know. Get in there and get it done and get out.

What time of day did you actually start to run into them and start firefights?
It was before daylight. First time we ran into it was probably about 3:00 or 4:00 in the morning.

How could you see anybody? It was so dark?
You couldn't. But they knew you were there.

They heard something and they opened fire?
Yeah, and those tracers were going everywhere. Then they told us to hold up and pull back a little bit. We got a ditch away and then daylight. That's when they came back and said, "Okay, we gotta get through 'cause those guys are in bad shape." No matter what it takes. We made runs across that field, whew, every time.

How far were you between your position and the 1st and 3rd?
We might have been a mile away, maybe not even that much.

You got as close as a mile, but you couldn't get any farther?
Couldn't get any closer, because they just had it ringed.

Were they off on a ridge, on high ground?
No, no. It was all pretty much flat. Everything was pretty much flat.

Flat. They were all entrenched?
Yeah. You couldn't make a move.

So that was probably the worst firefight you were in?
Well, that, and Butera was a pretty bad one too. That was really close stuff up there. You were yelling at each other and throwing grenades at each other. Some of them were getting into hand-to-hand [combat] up there and fighting. Run out of, beating each other with rifles.

After that Cisterna battle?
Well, I went to the hospital.

You were injured there?
No, I wasn't. I got double pneumonia about the first part of March, and there wasn't anybody left. I mean, we'd go on patrols every night catching prisoners and stuff like that. The idea was to go on patrol, and if you didn't get prisoners, try to get in a firefight, and that way we could spot where the automatic weapons were. And it always had to be at night, so we could pick up on the automatics. I did that for about ten days, every night.

So what lessons would you say you learned from your military experience?
Determination. You don't quit, you do whatever. I used to stand on a deck before we made the landing in Maiori and Anzio, and I'd look and think, "What in the hell am I doing here?" And you could get out any time you wanted. Because if you didn't want in there, they'd let you go.

Is there something you would impart for future generations, any pearls of wisdom that you would give to future generations?
Well, I guess just learn whatever you're going to do as a trade, learn it well. Listen to who's going to teach you, and keep a good attitude about it and don't ever say quit. That's it.

Ranger Fauber in Naples

SFC WILLIAM C. FAUBER

I'd like to start off and ask you, before the US entered World War II with Pearl Harbor, what were your aspirations? What were you planning on doing before the war started?
I wanted to be in the military, because I was in military school when Pearl Harbor hit. I just loved the military. I always did. That's the reason I went to VPI[12] after I finished Fishburne Military School. They had a Cadet Corps up there (the whole thing was Cadet Corps), and I wanted to be in that, so I went up there. I registered as an engineer and that was my aspiration, to be an engineer in the service.

When did you enter the military then?
I entered the military actually in December of 1943.

Okay. So a year after Pearl Harbor had happened.
Yes. I was at Fishburne when Pearl Harbor struck. Then after that, I went to VPI.

Do you recall that Sunday, where you heard about Pearl Harbor?
Absolutely. We had gone to the Presbyterian church, which was right around the corner from the military school, and on our way back, we were getting ready to be dismissed for lunch. Then the colonel came out and told us about Pearl Harbor. We didn't know up until that time.

Did you think the world was going to change after Pearl Harbor?
Absolutely. I wanted to do something about it right then and there, because I felt it was a cowardly attack and I thought I could do something, but I wasn't sure what.

So what was your first assignment in the military? What division were you assigned to?
My first military assignment was at CMTC (Citizens' Military Training Camp) at Fort Meade, Maryland. I stayed up there for four weeks training, and after that I came back and finished high school, and then I went to Fishburne Military School.

And where did you complete your basic training?
Fort McClellan, Alabama. I was trained at the Intelligence School in Fort McClellan.

And was that the time you enlisted in the Ranger battalion as well?

Yes, actually. I came in from field maneuvers, and we saw it on our day room bulletin board. And my friend and I decided to apply. So we went down to see the first sergeant and signed up for the Rangers.

So you actually signed up, or were they looking for Ranger volunteers?

They were looking for recruits.

And they explained that it was a Special Forces kind of operation?

Well, I was gung ho at that time anyway, so I figured yeah. I was a football hero, a baseball hero, so I figured, heck, I can handle that.

So I believe you entered the European theater in Casablanca in the fall of 1943?

Yes.

Did you go through more-specialized training with the Rangers?

Yes. Some, not much. They didn't have time. My first assignment was at Venafro in the mountains there. And that's where I got a lot of my training. Right there, during that first week I was in combat.

I know a lot of other Rangers actually had quite extensive Ranger training. It doesn't sound like you had that extensive training?

No, I had a little bit more than the rest of them. I asked for it. We had a couple of captains there that would take you out and do all kinds of Ranger training with you. The physical training mostly.

It was more physical than anything else? How about cliff climbing? Demolition?

That's it, cliff climbing and demolition. And as an intelligence student, I had learned all about munitions and silhouettes and whatnot, so I knew most of that anyway.

Did you think that the extra training you had provided you with good insights when you got into the battlefield?

Yeah, I knew what I was doing then. I really did. Capt. Sundstrom and Capt. Sams were great teachers.

Did you think that the Ranger trainers who were the most stern had the biggest impact on you?

Absolutely. Absolutely.

So your first brush with battlefield conditions was at the Volturno River. Is that right?

Volturno, yeah. There was a river valley there. Naples was on one side of the valley and the Venafro Mountains were on the other side. They picked us up in Africa and took us by ship to Naples. They took us off the ship in Naples and put us in a repo depot for future assignment. Then they came to the repo depot and picked us up because we had volunteered for the Rangers. They took us up to Venafro, and we got there around 10:00 or 11:00 at night. They didn't have anything much to eat, but they did find something for us because it wasn't our fault we weren't there earlier.

Now was that early in 1944, or was that the winter months of 1943?

That was in 1943. Because my first Christmas was overseas with the Rangers.

All right, and so when you actually went into battle, it was in the Venafro Mountains, right?

Right. They stationed us on a long line and they told me, "You're a scout. You're trained in intelligence. We want you on the listening post." So they put me on the listening post that night. I was only supposed to stay four hours, but I went ahead and stayed all night. When I came back off of line, they said, "We heard some shooting last night." And I said, "Yes sir, you sure did. That little bush isn't going to bother anybody anymore."

So you suspected there were enemy soldiers down there?
Yeah, they were right below us. And so I suspected one was coming my way, and it was moving, so I kind of demolished that bush. So that was my first brush.

And what was your next major engagement?
Well, I guess the next major one was when Sgt. Hunt told me to go on patrol. I said, "Who do you want me to take with me, Sergeant?" And he said, "You pick." So I said, "I'll take you for one, and I'll take Bill Dallas." So we went on patrol that morning, and it was a foggy, rainy, misty morning because it had rained thirty-eight straight days when we were up on that mountain. There was a great big rock formation where the Germans had a whole view of the valley, and they could pick us off one at a time. So we had to get them out of there. That was what our mission was, to get them. But we got right next to the rock, and one of the Germans threw a grenade, and it just stopped short of Sgt. Hunt and blew the side of his face off. And so I didn't know what to do. I picked him up and carried him back to the line, and then the medics took over from there. Then I went back on patrol, and Dallas had picked one up in the leg. So I carried him back to the front line there, and then the medics took over that. And then I went back on patrol and finally got two Germans. But there were three of us out there still.

So you took the two injured Rangers back? You carried them back 100 yards or something?
Yes, 50 to 75 yards.

From there, you went back and attacked the small group of Germans?
Yeah. They weren't going anywhere. They were dug in, so to speak.

I see. Now were you awarded anything for that?
No sir. I was supposed to be, but I guess my papers never went through, and then we were captured and that ended the whole thing.

I think you deserve credit for that, and I think that if the powers that be knew about that action, they would give you something.
Perhaps we can still look into that. I checked today, and both Sgt. Hunt and Scotty Monroe, who was the first sergeant at the time, told me that I would be awarded for it, but no paperwork was ever pushed through.

So how much more time did you spend in those mountains after that?
We were up there for thirty-eight straight days on top of the mountain, and the sun came out one day and we thought, "Hot dog, we're getting a break." So everybody took their clothes off, laid them on rocks, and down it came.

When you left that assignment, then you went back where to prepare for Anzio.
We went back to Pozzuoli, which is near Naples on the beach. We had a bivouac up there, and we stayed there and got more training. They about ran the legs off of us.

So were you there a month, two weeks, how long?
We were there probably two weeks.

And that prepared you for the Anzio invasion?
Yeah. 'Cause we had one practice invasion. They took us out to sea and we came in.

So do you remember what you were thinking about when you were onboard ship, ready to invade Anzio?
I'm sorry, I was sleeping. People don't believe me when I tell them that, but I was sleeping. Then they got us up and said, "Fauber, Sergeant wants to see you." So I went on up and he said, "We're getting ready to go in." I said, "All right, so let's go."

So did you climb off the side of the ship and get into the landing craft, or what did you hit the beachhead with?
They had the landing craft high, and we just climbed into the landing craft.

You climbed in and they lowered the craft?
They lowered us in the LCAs.

How was the water? Was it pretty choppy that night?
It was pretty choppy the whole night. It wasn't real bad. They weren't very high waves, but you knew you were on water.

What time of the day was that when you landed in the water? When you got in the LCAs?
I guess it was probably somewhere between 1:00 and 3:00.

So you got in the LCA[13] and then you probably took an hour to ride in the LCA before you hit the beachhead?
No, it didn't take us that long. I would say less than thirty minutes.

Once the ramp went down, can you paint the picture of what it was like getting off on that beachhead?
Sure. I didn't know what to do. I was a little scared. Apprehensive, I'd say, more than scared, 'cause I knew that kind of stuff was going to happen anyway. So I just took my time, tried to stay calm, tried to calm everybody else down, and then we got in and went into shore. He got real close to beach with that craft, and so I barely got my feet wet. I went on first because I was the first scout, and they sent me on in to see what we needed. I said, "Give me the Bangalore torpedoes." And so we put twelve of them together and blew the barbed wire, and then everybody came.

Now, did you have much fire on the beach when you landed?
There was very light fire from them. Boy, we were tearing up heck though. There were some vehicles coming down the hill, and we were tearing those up like crazy. So we never did have too much resistance.

So there wasn't an artillery barrage or anything?
Not then. That all started later.

So the Anzio beachhead was uneventful for the most part, from your perspective?
Yes, from my perspective.

When did you become first scout?
As soon as we came off the hill from Venafro.

So after you took off the beachhead in Anzio, you just kept moving inland?
Yes. We kept moving inland and I kept scouting out ahead of everybody. I had my buddy with me, and we probably scouted out 5 miles, and there was nothing, really. We saw a little enemy movement, but nothing to be worried about.

So just you and your buddy went up as far as you could? Now, if you were up 5 miles, how far back was the main line?
The main line was back on the beach. They had found a place to cook their meal, and that's when we went out.

Did you have a vehicle?
No, we walked.

Before Cisterna, was there any major action that occurred from your Anzio beachhead to Cisterna? Was there any other firefight you were involved with?

Yeah. When we got captured. The day we got captured, we had a fight with the Germans, and that's when they surrounded us.

That was in Cisterna?

That's right.

Before Cisterna, how many days after you arriving on the Anzio beachhead was Cisterna? Was it just a few days?

Yes, just a few days.

So everybody combed out from the beachhead, secured inland, and basically waited until you were ready for deployment to Cisterna. What was your mission at Cisterna? Did they explain that to you?

Our mission at Cisterna was to block the highway there because that was the German supply route between Rome and Monte Cassino. We were to cut off the supply route to all the German forces south of there. And it didn't work.

My understanding is that the 1st and 3rd were supposed to go up the ravine, and the 4th was on the flank. Is that right?

Yes sir.

Obviously, you did not have intelligence to say that there was a huge German buildup on either side? Now, were you the lead scout on the 1st when they went up?

Yes. I got by the first two guards with no problem at all. And they told me I should have shot them, but I didn't. So I went up and came back, and I told the major (now this is my idea about what happened) that the Mussolini Canal was right there, and we went up the canal. There were three bridges crossing that canal. We were supposed to cross at the second bridge, and that would have dropped us down below the German buildup. We didn't know it was there anyway, but that's where we were supposed to go. But the second bridge had been blown out. So we actually crossed the third one, and that's how we ended up right in the middle of the German buildup. That's my thinking of it.

Now, since you were a forward scout, were you with a couple of guys or did you have a main body of soldiers?

The main body.

You were at the tip of the main body. Everybody was moving forward and going up that little ravine?

That's right.

From where you started on that campaign at Cisterna, how far in did you move?

Towards Cisterna? We probably went 4 or 5 miles.

And you really weren't taking any fire then?

No. Now, that all happened later when the whole group got through. That's when the Germans came out and started firing. I was above it.

So what time of day was that when you actually made contact with the German forces?

It was at night. Early in the morning, like 4:00 a.m. And we got by part of them, and then they all came in, and we scattered as much as we could to get to places to shoot. You know, strategic places. So I ended up on the side of a hill, under a grape arbor in a vineyard. Some of them were down in the ditch. There was a little ravine and a drainage ditch coming up through there below us, and that's where the Germans were coming from.

At 4:00 a.m, it was very dark, right? So they couldn't see you. You couldn't see them? Did anybody light any flares or anything?
No. They had fires. They were cooking or something.

So when you were going up that ravine, you really never knew that you were surrounded by a division on either side?
I never knew, no. No one else did either, I don't think, because they had built that up, and it was a secret movement on their part.

Okay, so you got to the end of the line there, and then all of a sudden you started getting some fire directed at you? And then basically you stopped in your tracks and laid some fire back into them? Can you describe what happened?
Well, I was laying [*sic*] on the side of the hill, under the grape arbor. The grape vines were all above us, and we saw the German tanks coming up. I wasn't very far from the channel there where the water was, so I saw the tanks coming and they had men following them. So we shot, but the troops that were with the tanks ducked back, and I saw one of my men had a sticky grenade. So I grabbed the sticky grenade from him and I went on the blind side of the tank, got in the ditch under the tank, and stuck it on the bed. Of course, I was out of the way by the time it went off. My buddy who was right with me also had a sticky grenade and he laid [*sic*] down in the ditch, but he couldn't get it on there. So he ran around the side and put it on the track. So we blew up those two tanks, and that helped us a little bit. It eased the situation for a few minutes. But then one of the tanks came up with maybe fifteen or twenty Rangers in front of it and gave us orders to surrender, or they were going to shoot them down. So that's when the orders came from headquarters for us to surrender.

Do you know who gave that order?
I think it was Morton.

It wasn't Col. Darby?
No, it wasn't Darby. Darby was with the 4th, and of course the 1st and 3rd were the ones that really caught the brunt of it.

So basically you received an order?
We received an order. It came over the radio to us. They wanted to know where our help was supposed to be. The 66th Division was supposed to come in and help us out, but they never showed up. And there was another division that was supposed to also come in there and help us, and they couldn't get there either. So we were on our own.

You mentioned that you and Cpl. Horton had knocked out a couple of tanks. Could you describe those sticky grenades? What were they like, and how they operated?
They call them jamming grenades. Jamo. It was like a ball, and it had a wire mesh over it. And inside that wire mesh was a film, and inside that film was sticky. I don't know what it was, but it was some sort of sticky solution. When you pounded it against something, it broke that mesh, and broke that skin, and let the sticky come out that held it wherever it was.

And at the same time, you're triggering a fuse?
Yes.

And what was the delay on that?
It was probably five seconds or fifteen seconds. Something like that.

So when you smashed it, you had to stick it and that's it? Unless you're at the tank and you just stick it immediately, right?
Well, you're going with it.

So you and your corporal took out the two tanks. There was also a sniper?
There were two snipers up in the tree, and they kept sniping all the men. We were laying [*sic*] on the bank, on our backs mostly, and they were up in the tree across the way from us, maybe 75 yards. And they were doing some damage to us. Not real heavy damage, but they were damaging us. I had my Thompson submachine gun, but I couldn't do anything with that, that far away. So I saw one of the kids down there with an '03 sniper rifle. It had a scope on it, and I said, "Let me have that thing." He wasn't using it. He didn't know what to do. So he handed it up there to me, and I pulled it up two out of three.

At least you eliminated them so they wouldn't do more damage?
That's right. We didn't have any more sniper fire after we got those two.

So how much later after that did you order the combat surrender?
Well, we hit the tanks and then we got the snipers, and then the tank came up the road with the Rangers in front of it and threatened to kill those men if we didn't give up. And they're the ones who told us to surrender. But we didn't listen to them. We absolutely did not listen to them. Then all of sudden we found out by radio that we were to give up. That they had orders from headquarters to give up.

I see. So they must have realized that you were surrounded?
Oh, they did. They absolutely did, and there was no help available to help us. We had been fighting them for maybe six or seven hours, and we didn't have any ammo left. I had two .45 cartridges left. That's all I had.

So that was about 5:00 a.m., your surrender?
No, it was after that. About 9:00 or something, but I'm not sure of the time.

So had the Germans set up a defensive position around that area so they were well entrenched, or did they just merge on you after they realized you were there? Were they prepared for you?
I think they felt that we were going to build up and come north, and they were going to stop us from coming north. They didn't want us to take Rome. So they had pulled in these troops.

So did they have established machine gun nests on either side of you?
Yes. They were waiting for us. Or rather, they had the buildup there. Now, whether they were actually waiting on us or not, I don't know.

And you came right up into it?
Yes.

And you had mentioned, I think, it was a lieutenant colonel that was killed in action there?
I wish I could think of his name. I can't think of his name. He was my CO at that time.

Well, can you then describe what happened to you after you were captured?
When we got captured, we had given up all our arms. We all field stripped our arms and threw the pieces all over the place. And then I had this idea about booby-trapping my pack. They told us to take everything off, all of our packs and everything. So that's when I came up with the idea of putting a grenade in there and strapping it down tight. I think I learned that somewhere or saw somebody do that or something in a movie. I can't remember where I got the idea, but I passed it on and everybody passed it on, and everybody had a grenade, put it in their pack, and tied it down and pulled the pin. So everybody field stripped their weapons, threw this, that, and the other away, or if they didn't throw it, they buried it. So the Germans didn't get any weapons from

us. Then they marched us all down in front of that tank and marched us around the curve and down into a big gully. So we were all down in there, and they were standing on the edge guarding us. So we were there for maybe forty-five minutes to an hour, and that's when I heard the packs blowing up. We got a lot of satisfaction out of that. Then they pulled us all out of the ditch, took us to this monastery, and put us upstairs. I think it was on the third floor of the monastery. So we stayed up there for about three or four days, and they would feed us what they had. They didn't have anything to feed us anyway, except for the food that we had in our packs, which they had taken from us. And that was also where they interviewed us. I was questioned by a captain in the German army who had gone to school at Northwestern. So he spoke better English than I did, and I don't know why they even questioned us, because they had all of our papers. They had all of the knowledge they needed on me. They told me where my mother and father were, where my brother-in-law was. I didn't even know my brother-in-law was overseas, but they told me where he was. We stayed there for a while, and then they took us down, put us on trucks, and took us to Rome. When we got into Rome, they took us off the trucks and put us in a vacant streetcar barn. There were no streetcars in there, so we had a roof over our head anyway. And that was the first time I'd ever seen any dehydrated cabbage. They had a piece of dehydrated cabbage, about the size of a cigar box. And they put that in a great big tub, and there was enough to feed every man there. And it wasn't bad either. But for the most part, they treated us very well. I mean, it wasn't a bruising thing at all. Then one morning they made us put our hands over our heads, and we walked from that car barn all the way through Rome for propaganda purposes. And for the most part, we got a lot of Vs for victory all the way through there by the people. They were cheering us on, you know. Not because we were captured, but because of who we were. They were ready for liberation.

That had to make you feel good.
Yes, it did, and we'd smile and talk to them. They'd say, "It's not over yet. It's not over yet." In broken English. And then they took us by truck up to Florence and put us in an old German army camp up there. We stayed there for about three days, and then they put us on the train and took us up through the Brenner Pass to Stalag VII-A. That was right near Munich, and that was where everybody went from Italy if they were captured. They went to VII-A first, since that was sort of a staging area, and then they'd send you out to the different camps.

So for the 1st and 3rd Battalions, you were probably a total of eight hundred men. How many do you think were prisoners?
There weren't as many casualties as people think until later on, when they started the barrage. I would say there were three hundred of us, something like that.

Three hundred in the 1st Battalion? Perhaps the same in the 3rd? So they marched about six hundred of you through Rome then?
Yeah. Everybody who got captured. Of course some of them got away without being captured.

And how long were you in Stalag VII-A?
I was there for about three days. Then they moved us to Stalag II-B. But when we were at VII-A, there was a Baptist minister there. And our understanding was that he had flown over and jumped out so he would be at that stalag as support for the troops. His name was Fox. They captured him, and since they knew he was a man of God, they didn't bother him. And he's the one who told us that if you wanted to be sent out of II-B, to tell them you were a farmer, and they would send you out working on a farm. That had advantages, since you were out in the air working, and you were clean and you got a little bit more food for working. It was just a little bit more freedom than being cooped up in a prison camp.

So if you were a farmer, you were let out in the day to farm, and then you would be brought back at night?
No. We were far enough that they built a building for us out there.

And they had a perimeter of guards basically?
No. It had two doors, and they opened up into a barbed-wire area. The barbed wire was maybe 7 feet tall, but for the most part we had to stay in the barracks when we came down.

I see. So you offered to do that?
Yes. There were seventeen of us on the farm. We had three or four Rangers. I knew two of them real well. Shorty Horton, the one who blew up the tank, was there, and so was Frankie Null, who had been my buddy all the way through.

And the other ones, were they Army Air Force?
No, they were from the 82nd Airborne, the 29th Division, and the 3rd Division. I think we had one 45th Division.

I see. So what time of year was it when you were transferred to II-B?
Well, we got captured the thirtieth of January, so it must have been early February of 1944.

And my understanding is that you actually escaped three times as well? Could you describe those escapes?
Sure. The first time we were in the field, we had a guard who was sort of stupid, I thought. So another sergeant and I decided we were going to take off. I said, "I don't know where we'll get, but we'll take off." So we were out in the field working at that time. I wasn't in the cow barn yet, and we left. We went over to the woods to take a leak. At least that's what the guard thought. So we went over there and just kept going. We didn't stop at the woods. We just kept going right on through the woods, and we got up the road maybe a mile or two. But they saw us walking on the road with no papers. Everybody had to carry papers over there, but we didn't have any, so they took us right back.

That was at nighttime, right?
No, that was during the day. The second time, we left right at darkness, when we were walking back down to our barracks. The guard didn't see us take off.

And he didn't count?
Well, he did when he got down there, but it was a little ways from the barn where we were working, to get back to our barracks.

A couple of kilometers?
No, not even that far. But he wasn't paying attention to us. He figured we'd do what we were supposed to do, I guess. Anyway, we took off and were gone for a day and a night. We were in this place getting something to eat, and one of the boys came in and asked us for our papers. We didn't have any, so right back we went. The third time we did pretty good. We got all the way to Berlin. We just walked down to the train station, bought tickets, got on the train, and went to Berlin. Took two steps off the train, turned right around, took two steps back on the train, and back to the camp.

They were waiting for you? I see. How did they know you were on the train?
They really didn't know we were on the train. It was just that they were asking everybody for their papers, and we didn't have any.

So explain to me how you got your ticket. I know that you had some German background in terms of the language, so you could communicate. How did you get the money for the tickets?
Well, they paid us. They paid us so many marks a week. They had to. The Geneva Convention said we had to be paid. And so we got paid, but it wasn't much. We had nothing to do with it, and we used to gamble all the time with it. That's about the only thing we could do. We could buy a keg of beer with it. Other than that, you had nothing to spend it on. So I had a lot of money and so did my buddy, and we just went down there and handed the guy a few marks and told him where we wanted to go. I could speak enough German to say, "Berlin," you know.

So basically, they didn't detect you had an accent?

No, no.

So once you were on that train, did you think you were free and clear at that point?

No. We were looking for them to pick us up at every station we stopped in. "Well, this is it, Frankie." "No, this is not the one, Bill. It's the next one after this."

Did you ever have the idea to jump off the back of the train and then you wouldn't have to go into the station to be caught?

We didn't want to do that. That would be too hard on us. We had a little sense, but not much.

So your third attempt was in March?

That was in March.

They didn't make you wear any special prisoner uniforms or anything?

No, no. We had regular US Army uniforms.

Well, how did they not detect you? When you escaped, what did you wear?

Well, the German had every color [of] uniform you could ever think of. And they didn't know one from another. The French were running around with their uniforms on, and they were the same color as ours.

So you had wool like this, and they didn't detect you?

No, they didn't say anything. They thought maybe we had the right to go. They didn't know who we were.

I'm wondering if they gave you the tickets and then they called Berlin and said, "Three guys who look suspicious are coming. You'd better be there at the station"?

No, that wasn't the case. When we got off the train, there were two gestapos checking papers, and I guess we looked suspicious, or maybe it was just a routine check. I don't know what it was, but anyway we took two steps and went back on the train.

So the bottom line is that had you changed your clothes and went in civilians' clothes, they would have shot you as spies?

Absolutely. That's what they said. I don't know whether they would have or not.

But if you were in your uniform . . . ?

Then you're just a prisoner of war.

So that's what saved you, in a sense?

That's right.

So from that point on, there were no more escape attempts?

No.

So I guess that brings us from March 1944, I guess, to the end of the war, which is the end of April 1945. Were you still in Stalag II-B at that time? The whole time?

Once we left Stalag II-B for the farm, we never went back unless we were sick. But I got yellow jaundice, so they moved me back to Stalag II-B and took care of me there. Then they shipped me back out to the farm.

So even though you made three escape attempts, they still let you work on the farm?

They figured we weren't going anywhere. And then a good guard came to watch us, and he was such a nice guy. Eric was his name, and he was Austrian and had been conscripted by the German army. But he had skipped the German army and gone into the French Foreign Legion, so he wouldn't be in the German army. Then Hitler decided he was going to pull all the Germans out of the French Foreign Legion and use them in his troops. So that's when Eric came along. They had sent him back to the Russian front, and he was wounded. So once he was wounded and couldn't do combat anymore, they sent him out as a guard. We were lucky enough to get him. He had been in the United States three times. He was a valet for a coal magnate in Germany, and he went with him everywhere he went. He could tell you the railroad stations on the southern route to California and also on the northern route to California. Couldn't speak English, but he knew those names. And he would do anything for us that he could, you know, within reason. He used to bring maps over, and he had a little radio he brought over, and we'd listen to the BBC and the AEF.

What was his last name? Eric what?
Hermann. His address is in that book in there.

So your three escape attempts were in the spring of 1945, right?
Well, one of them was right around Christmas of 1944, and the other two were in the spring of 1945.

Do you remember being liberated? Who liberated you?
The 102nd Calvary Recon. They were on recon and came up one road, and I was in charge of the prisoners in this group. We had heard small-arms fire two days prior, so we knew something was going on somewhere. So I went to the captain of the guard and I said, "You know, it ain't going to be long." He said, "You're right. It's not going to be long, and we'll surrender to you any time you want." But I said, "No, I want you to stay right where you are, because you're guarding us. You're protecting us." And that's what the guards were for—to protect us, not to harm us or anything. 'Cause they were just as good to us as they could possibly be. If somebody fell or hurt themselves, they'd see that he rode the supply wagon until he could get along by himself. So when that recon went by, I told him, "I'll go out there and bring them back down here, and that's when you surrender, not until." He said, "Okay." So that's what I did. I brought the tank back down there, and that was April 13 at 1:00 in the afternoon.

Is that right? So you went out there and brought the tank down?
I rode back down with them.

And they basically surrendered then?
Well, they surrendered their guns to me. They wouldn't surrender them to anybody else but me, 'cause I'd been with them the whole time.

Okay. So there were seventeen or twenty of you there who had been in the barracks?
No, this was the group that they had brought together, and there must have been 350 of us. The Germans moved us from where we were in East Prussia, and they were moving us west because the Russians were making their west plunge at that time.

So when did you start marching?
We started sometime in January.

So you left the II-B area in January. You must have marched quite a few miles then?
Seven hundred and fifty. We marched from where we were to Hanover, Germany.

And how many guards were there for three hundred of you?
There must have been twenty maybe. We didn't give anybody any trouble. What could we do?

I guess you could have overpowered them, but what would have been the point?
It would have been nothing. So we just strolled along with them, you know. They didn't harm us or abuse us or anything, so why not.

What were they feeding you along that march?

Well, they had a supply wagon, and they'd get stuff from local places and bring it in to us.

And you had adequate clothes. You weren't cold at night?

We froze at night. My feet got frostbitten. I've got neuropathy from it. I had neuropathy on all my limbs and extremities.

So they gave you some coats and that when you were marching?

No, we had all that. Each one of us had a shelter half and a blanket, and that's all we had.

And did you pitch tents when you were sleeping at night?

No, we covered. I had a poncho and I used that quite a bit. I'd lay that on the ground and sleep on that.

That was quite an ordeal to march all those miles.

Yes, it was. And we never had any problems because the German guards who were with us wouldn't let anybody do anything.

Okay. So where did you go after you were liberated?

We went to a little town called Dannenberg and Gen. Fox came up to see us and lined us up. He got up on the porch of a house and said, "Now, you guys have been sleeping out on hard ground, snow, sleet, rain. When I come back here tonight at 9:00, I want to see every one of you in a house in a warm bed." And so we said, "Yes sir." And he said, "If I come back and find anybody not in a house, you're going to be court-martialed, because I'm giving you a direct order." He said, "Take this town. This is yours."

That was a good night in Dannenberg?

Aw, man, you bet. And then he told us, "Up this road here about 2 or 3 kilometers, there's a ration depot." He said, "We'll send a truck up, and you'll go with them and load it up with rations and bring it on back down here to Dannenberg, and you'll feed off of that." So we said, "Yeah, we can do that. That's no problem there." The next morning when I woke up, I heard all this noise outside. Loud clatter and horns blowing. I went out to see what was going on, and what happened was, a group of guys had found the German motor pool, and every one of the fools had gotten a vehicle. So they were driving up and down the street. Just back and forth. Shorty Horton and I decided we'd do it too. The only thing left was a motorcycle, so I said, "Shorty, can you drive a motorcycle?" He said, "Yeah." So I said, "Okay, let's try it." So we got on the motorcycle and we're just flying down the road having a great big time, and all of a sudden the road dead-ended into another road. I knew we couldn't make the curve, so I said, "Shorty, hit the brakes." He said, "We don't have any brakes." So we hit that bank and both of us went flip, flop. Then we got back on it and came on back, and we remembered we didn't have any brakes when we got back, so we started dragging our feet. But that was fun. That was the best part of the whole thing.

So what were the greatest lessons you learned from your military experience?

Have faith in your fellow man. I'm not trying to be philosophical or anything, but I just think that's it. You've got to have confidence in your buddies, and they'll eventually develop confidence in you. Another thing. I learned how to live, and live right. I learned right from wrong a whole lot more than I would have outside, because you're ordered to do this and you have to have discipline. Discipline I guess is what I'm looking for all the way around.

Is there anything you would leave for future generations? Any pearls of wisdom for future generations?

I guess my few words on that would be "Stick to it. Go after it. Get there."

Ranger Gilbert

1SGT. LAWRENCE GILBERT

I understand that before America became involved in the Second World War, you were working with the Civilian Conservation Corps. Did you have any career plans or career goals?

No, at that time we just weren't thinking ahead. I tried to join the Army in 1937 or 1938, but they wouldn't take me because I wore glasses. And in those days, if you had a scar on your face or too many fillings or wore glasses, they wouldn't take you. If you couldn't read or write, they didn't care. They could have had a lot of guys who couldn't read or write, but if you had a scar on your face or you were just plain ugly-looking, they wouldn't take you because it didn't fit the image. I wore glasses, so I couldn't get in. But when the draft started, then if you walked through the door you were in.

Do you remember where you were and what you were doing on December 7, 1941, when the Japanese attacked Pearl Harbor?

I was in jail. We got in the CCC camp all right, and I was getting along good. So this guy convinced me to go honky-tonking down in New Jersey. So he came down and we meet the neighborhood. Here's Mike. Here's Joe. So we were out tomcatting around at some place they wanted to go, some honky-tonk. Well, here come the police cars. These are neighborhood guys though. I'm the badass from out of town, so the police blamed everything on me. So I spent the weekend in jail before I got a hearing. They could have checked my record in New Hampshire, and that made me the bad boy. So I finally got probation out of it. That's another thing. When I got back to New Hampshire, even when I got drafted I couldn't get in until I got relieved from probation. There were a lot of guys at that time who were on parole or probation before they got in the military. So here's the chance to behave yourself and straighten things out, see, so from there on in it was uphill.

So you were in jail when you heard about Pearl Harbor?

Yeah, that Sunday I was in jail.

When they told you, did you realize that you would be fighting?

Yeah, I knew. Been following what the British were doing and the bad luck they were having. So I almost went to Canada and tried to join the Canadian army that way, but Dad talked me out of it. I wished I had at that time, you know.

So what was your date of entry into the service?

I think it was in November of 1942.

Where did you complete your basic training?

Camp Funston, up by Fort Riley, Kansas. I went out there and went through the processing center, and they filled up the regiments. The outfit had been 2nd Cavalry, which consisted of four regiments, which made two brigades. They kept one brigade, and the other one became the 9th and 10th Black Troopers Cavalry. And at that time, one squadron of the 1st Battalion was armor. It had light tanks and half-tracks and scout cars, and the rest of them were horse. But the horse troops had the big horse carriers and semitrailers to transport equipment so they didn't wear the horses out. They didn't use the horses, and actually they called themselves cavalry, but the way they fought they were mounted infantry 'cause they never fought from a horse. They took their sabers away a long time ago. They came running, from the 2nd Cavalry to the 9th Armored Division. So we went out there, and they kept all the younger horse jockeys, but they shipped the older guys off somewhere. I don't know where the hell they went. They let them go 'cause they wouldn't adapt to armor. So we had more semi-infantry basic [training] for when we had to go to the rifle ranges. But we didn't have any real infantry training, just the rifle training. And the top seventeen high scores with the rifles became the tank gunners. There were seventeen tanks in the company, and they figured that if you were good with a rifle, then you could learn how to shoot the cannon good. You know, with the telescope sight. Well, I was one of the real top high scorers, so I became a lieutenant. I had a lieutenant for a tank commander, and we had real intensive training out there, realistic training at Fort Riley. They used to take us out in the middle of a field to get used to artillery fire. And you lay [sic] down, and they brought it in real close to you on three sides, with live ammo coming in over your head. Maybe 100 yards ahead of you and on either side of you. So you got used to the sound of it. And night training. We spent a whole week night training. We'd have reveille at 6:00 at night, eat breakfast, and by 8:00 you're in the motor pool and out in the hills. In Kansas in the middle of February, it's like walking around in the closet. We had the cross-country training, gunnery, and we had to rendezvous with our kitchen truck to eat the noon meal at midnight. And middle of the afternoon, you learned to go with your service truck to service the vehicle. Then you're back eating what would be the supper meal at 6:00 in the morning. We did that for a whole month. We ended up with some real good night drivers out there. It was realistic.

It sounds like you were settling in to serve with the Armor. How did you end up in the Rangers?
Well, they asked for two volunteers from each company. That made fifty from each armored regiment and twenty-five from the recon battalion for immediate shipment to North Africa to make up replacements for the 1st and 2nd Armored Division. Okay. I always say my claim to fame was I threw a pitcher of beer in the first sergeant's face and lived to tell about it. 'Cause after a month of night training, we had a beer bust in the mess hall after supper. Well, at 2:00 in the morning, the party was getting out of hand. The rowdies were taking over. And so the charge of quarters tried to shut us up, and we weren't paying any attention to him, so he called the first sergeant.[14] Well, I got tired of pouring beer, so I'm drinking out of a big pitcher. I'm drinking all that because I'm getting tired of pouring beer. So the guy behind me got a pitcher of beer, and he started pouring beer in my hip pocket. So I make believe I don't feel my hind end getting wet. So I'm carrying on a conversation when all of a sudden I roll around and let go of my pitcher of beer just as the first sergeant came through the door. Got him right in the face, and I didn't dare laugh.

Why weren't you sent straight to the stockade?
Well, that was the end of the party. The next day I'm on KP, and they give the grease trap. You know what the grease trap is? In the mess hall the water will go through that, and the grease will stay there, and you gotta clean that out. All the grease from the cooking, and it stinks like hell. Well, we left that keg of beer in the kitchen supply room, and when the mess sergeant left, three of us had a couple of beers, and I felt pretty good after that. So when I volunteered to leave, the charge of quarters came to the door and said, "Gilbert, get over to the dispensary." This was on a Sunday. I went over there and they gave me a physical, set up dental appointments, and everything like that. So by Thursday, we're on the train heading east, and we went to Camp Shenango, Pennsylvania, for a while. Just a short ways from Youngstown, across the border. When Hampton Roads was filled and Camp Shanks was filled, they'd hold people there until one of those camps shipped out. So we spent a week or two in Camp Shenango. They named it for the lake up there. And we went down to Camp Patrick Henry, which was down in Norfolk, for embarkation to head overseas. Well, that's when the Army lost us for about a week. There was one barracks full of us, and they couldn't find a boat to get us on. So they took us back to camp at 2:00 in the morning. The driver parked the truck and he said, "Take that barracks right there." So we had one guy who was a PFC, so he was automatically in command. We went in and made up our bunks and went to bed. In the morning, nobody came to bother us, so we got up and wandered over to the mess hall. They told us to get in four lines, and that was it. So this continued. We ate our meals, went back to our barracks, went to shower and got cleaned up, swept the place out, and we were doing this for about a week. We'd go eat chow and go to the recreational hall. Finally, a guy came through the door and started calling shipping numbers. He said, "What the hell is your shipping number?" Somebody told him, and he said, "Hell, they left a week or

two ago." We said, "We know it. They left us behind." So they put us on the next boat, in the middle of the night at West Point. It used to be a luxury liner, the SS *America*, and the only thing they left plush was the officer's mess on the fantail, which was the semicircle thing on the back of the boat. They left that plush and also the foyer where the elevators were, 'cause the elevators were for officers only. And some of the guys were down below the waterline. Well, we got on first, on the promenade deck, which came in off the open deck, 'cause they closed in the promenade deck where the storage used to be, and put bunks in there, six high. It was like slave quarters. Four days from Hampton Roads to Casablanca. The boat ran without a convoy. She had four 5-inch guns, two on the stern and two up front, with antiaircraft guns up on the stack. In the daytime, she was doing 17 knots on the zigzag. At night, she'd run straight at about 20 knots. The whole boat would be vibrating, right to the firewall. So we didn't have an escort till we got off at Casablanca, and then the destroyers came up to guide us through the minefields and then we got some air cover. We got into Casablanca Harbor and unloaded and went to the replacement center there. We only spent a couple of days there, and they put us on the train and ran up over the Atlas Mountains to Oran. There was a big replacement center there. I mean, it covered acres and acres and acres, and their idea of keeping us busy was close-order drill. Armored people, that's dismounted drill, manual arms, and all that. I never had too much manual arms. We'd just do a little bit of manual arms while we were cleaning our Springfield rifles. And after a while, we got tired of doing this all the time. So when they came by asking for recruits for the Rangers, I thought, why not? They almost didn't take me then, because I wore glasses. But my weapons qualification was good. I'd fired .50-calibers, then the .30s, and qualified good with them.

That was why you decided really to try to be a Ranger, because you didn't want to stay in the replacement depot anymore?

No walking up and down, doing the half miles. They were doing square bashes, the British called it. You're just out there drilling for no good reason. The one thing that's not going to help you win the war is "spit and polish." So I think there were about a hundred of us who volunteered. The 1st, 3rd, and 4th Battalions had already been formed, but in training they lost a lot of people, so they needed replacements for the people who quit or got hurt. So they gave us a hurry-up three weeks there from 6:00 in the morning to 2:00 in the morning. I had had night training in Kansas, so I was pretty suited for that. At the end, when they decided to process out to the battalions, lined us up in formation and just counted off half of us. They said, "Okay, 1st Battalion." The rest of them went across the road to the 4th Battalion. That's how I got in the 1st Battalion; I was in the right part of the formation. If I had been farther down, I would have been in the 4th Battalion. My first squad leader was there, and he became the first sergeant later on. Shortly after I got assigned, we started real serious amphibious training down in the Algiers harbor, for going into Sicily. One of our guys, for some reason or another, had a British training grenade. It was one of those that was like an M80 going off. It would jar your teeth loose, but there were no fragments from it. It was like a little Bakelite can about that big around, and it had a dynamite cap in it. You'd put the fuse in and light the fuse. Well, to make this thing safe, you undid the bottom and let the dynamite cap drop out, and put it back in upside down so the fuse ended up on top. And when you wanted to throw it, you'd take the top off, and there was a little piece of ribbon wrapped around the pin with a little weight on it. So you'd go like this and throw it, and when you'd throw it, the thing would unravel and the pin would fall out, and the minute it hit something, it would explode. So he was throwing them at people, and it might get them hard to hearing a little bit, but it wouldn't really hurt anybody. So he had those in his pack along with other stuff, and he threw his pack into the boat. It was about a 6-foot drop from the stone pier there into the boat, and the pack exploded and killed one guy and loused up two or three, 'cause he had other stuff that went off in his pack also. He had stuff he wasn't supposed to have. So that boat became a bad-luck boat. After the amphibious training, we pulled out to go to Sicily. They put my platoon right down in what used to be the recreational for the Coast Guard men. I'm right here, and there's a soda fountain right across from where my bunk was. The PX with cigarettes, cigars, and candy was right between the two bulkhead doors. And in there was a soda fountain with ice cream. Well, we went to general quarters the night we got on the boat, and all they had on was the red battery lanterns. So out came the wire cutters. You've seen those security cages with ⅛-inch wire, I guess, with a steel rim around it. Well, we just cut the wire and didn't bother with the lock. We opened it up and we had one 5-gallon can. The captain came down and said, "Well, where'd you get that?" "Well, the crew gave it to us when they went to general quarters." So we loaded up on cigarettes and cigars and everything else. I'm in the cage getting another can of ice cream. I was just pulling the can up and out. That was when they used to have old steel cans, metal cans with a paper lid on it. I was just pulling that thing up when the loudspeaker says, "First-boat teams, man your boats; first-boat teams, man your boats." So we went from there all the way to the boat deck and got into our boat and were lowered away. Well, the water was rougher than hell. There had been a hell of a storm, and we didn't think we were going to get off that night because the waves were rough. But they figured they got enough to launch us. So we were being lowered down. We were in the boat and the guy starts the engine up, and we're being lowered down and a big wave come up and picked our boat right up, and them shackles are designed so that when the weight goes off, they open up. When the boat goes down and hits the water, the thing will automatically open up. Well, when your boat's going down and you lift the boat up and slack them off, it could open up. Well, whoever was at the controls up there, up on top there, he threw it out of gear, I guess, because we went down with one hell of a bang. Then we pulled away and went around the boat to organize, and one of the boats on the other side was hanging by one shackle.

Were the men still inside?

No, all of them fell out. So we finally got the wave formed up, and we head for the beach. This is Gela, Sicily. The airplanes and the bombers had gone in. The paratroopers had gone in, and the wheat fields behind the town were all afire. So the town was backlit red, glowing, and you could see all the houses on the bluffs above where we were going to land, the beach, and they had about a 50-foot bluff from the beach up to the town. Well, they told me later that the plan was for us to land on both sides of the town and go on around the other side. But all the bad fortifications were out there, so Col. Darby recalled some of the submarines and looked it over. Fishing boats were coming in off that beach. So they used to pick the minefields up in the morning and put them back down at night after boats come in. Well, that storm came in and buried those mines, so over at the 4th Battalion some went off, but none of them went off in our area 'cause they were buried too deep. The waves were throwing sand up on the beach. Well, they had pillboxes and barbed wire all the way up the bluff. But they had to have these exits, so they go up like this, and there'd be a pillbox, and they'd turn like this, and, well, I think it was one here and one at the top and you were in town. Well, Darby convinced them that that's the way we're going to go. We're going to go straight in. And once we got off the beach and into town, we're behind all the other fortifications. Everything is pointing out way behind them. We always said, if Darby had had anything to do with D-day, they never would have landed in daylight. They would have gone in like we did, at 4:00 in the morning. Like I said, nobody ever took our picture, because when we landed it was like 3:30 or 4:00 in the morning.

It was still dark out?

It was still dark out, so they really couldn't see you to shoot very well. They might have known we were there, but they couldn't really see us. Well, like I said, we made the landing. I was the last man in the boat, and the guy had that thing in reverse before the ramp went down. So the ramp went down, and he was already backing her off the beach. Well, the guys up front hardly got wet. I go in and I'm in water up to here. The kid in front of me was small. He was out of sight. I had to pick him up and take about four steps before he could get his feet on the bottom. I think one of the Higgins[15] boats carrying E Company had a problem when they were going in. I never did get the straight of how it happened, but the ramp went down when they were going full speed ahead. So they lost the biggest part of the platoon that was in that boat because they couldn't get their gear off in time. Now, somebody said a 20 mm shell hit the cable or the safety latch. Or for some reason or other the thing wasn't latched right or the cable wasn't right, and the thing fell open when they bounced. Most of the stories say that a 20 mm shell hit the thing and cut the cable and the ramp dropped. They got picked up by the boats that came in from behind us just to pick up anybody that fell off. So we got to the edge of town pretty quick. That's where we started digging in. And come daylight, they start counterattacking. German tanks were coming down across the valley. The only artillery we had was the 4.2s, and the Navy was firing those at the Germans. We fired some 60s, but that just annoyed them. So once we cleared the beach, we were in behind all the fortifications. They were around like that, and we came in the easy way. And then from there, we went to a pass across the valley on the mountain road up to Butera. Well, we had to clear a path for us, and we got there in the middle of the night. They were firing at us, so we were firing mortars at them to keep their attention while the rest of the company went down the base of the hill, found a path, and knocked out the pillbox. It was the last one on top of the hill, and they all started surrendering. A combat engineer outfit was supposed to attack the pass about a mile across the other side of the pass. They never showed up because they got lost in the dark somewhere. I guess they just said, "To hell with it." We were getting all kinds of prisoners, and all of a sudden there was a white flag way over there, and they never had a shot fired at them. We had enough Italian prisoners; they could have licked us barehanded, if they had a mind to. But their heart wasn't in that war.

They were surrendering from the other side of the valley?
Nobody ever shot at them. The only ones that got shot up were on this side. And they didn't take much convincing. We knocked out the first pillbox. One guy said he walked in the back door with a tommy gun, and the guy inside was pretty surprised. The last one up on the hill. And then another company came out, and we spent half a day reconnaissance, and then we attacked Butera and took it right in the middle of the night. And then 2nd Armored came up and went right through us, and the next morning, daylight, they came up the hill where an Italian convoy had been strafed. We're going by this. Truck after truck and everybody's sitting in the back just like this. Dead Italians. P-38s had strafed that convoy and shot it up bad. They never got out of the trucks. We were walking by the truck and looking in the back, and there's a whole truckful of guys sitting there like they were on parade. All fallen over and everything like that. When we came back down, all of those trucks were gone. After the 2nd Armored went through the town. I know we were up there a couple of days, but when we came back down, all the trucks were gone and all the boys were gone and everything else. Somebody cleaned the mess up. They had some good trucks and they had some good Fiat diesel trucks, but I don't know how they ever got around the curves with the big trailers they had on back. They had a complete four-wheeled trailer, and the roads were like this. We had a hard job getting around with just a truck with no trailer on it. After Butera, we went back down and went up to Caltanissetta 'cause the Rangers didn't have any more operations going on, 'cause everything was moving pretty good. So we went up to Caltanissetta and we MP'd the town and ran the PW stockade. And while we were waiting for a train to take us up to Caltanissetta, we were sleeping on the station platform. So you're on the platform, and the rail goes right by, you know, on the station platform. Well, some engineer up in Caltanissetta thought Mussolini was still good. He turned loose about ten boxcars down the main line; a one-line railroad. These boxcars came down off the mountain there with no brakes on, and Licata was the end of the line. They gotta hit something there, 'cause it's the end of the road. Well, we were on the station platform, and them boxcars go by like this here. And they got down to the end of the track and finally crashed down there. I saw a little ball of fire like this, and the captain of transportation said, "Get that fire out." And the whole damn yard was on fire, 'cause there were gondola cars full of 5-gallon cans of gasoline. When they burned, the jerry cans would explode, and those cans would go clean out of sight. I mean it would come back down all laid open. They were coming down all over the place, and there was all kinds of ammunition going off. And the only thing that we had to fight it with was a little 1½-inch hose. Handy-billys, they called them, from the Navy. But they went down with the jeeps and pulled the boxcars away from the center of the fire. And then finally the train took us up to Caltanissetta.

Were there any casualties from this?
No, there was nobody on the train and nobody in the yard there when it went off. It just burned up a lot of gasoline and ammunition and other stuff. Then we went to Caltanissetta, and we were in the PW stockade and MP'd the town, and then the British went over to the town of Etna. The Canadians were shooting the town up at night there. So we went over there and put a kibosh on that. We had orders that if anybody was shooting, we could shoot them back. Then the 3rd Division was attacked up at Palermo. They were going to organize a mule pack train to support them in the mountains. The 3rd Ranger Battalion went in the mountains behind where Patton was going to land when they had that amphibious landing. Okay, we did that. We took to the hills and got on the high ground behind the beach. They'd make a landing, cut off; where's the Rangers? On our own artillery most of the time. Then they'd jump again. Well, one place we had to move up to, the road went through a tunnel. They'd turn like this right into another tunnel, and Germans blew out everything in between the two tunnels. We could barely walk through them, leading the mules in the dark. The engineers had to get down

there, but they didn't have anyplace to even put the Bailey bridge on. And there was no way to turn around at the other end, so they had to back through all the way the tunnel, do the job, and drive out to dump the load. So the headquarters' job was repairing that road. The German engineers were pretty good, but our engineers were better. That bridge no more than hit the ground than we got a Bailey across the hole. The last time we went out with the mules, we were overlooking Messina. I didn't go on that one because I was loading a 75-pound howitzer on the mules, and me and another guy were lugging a piece up the trail. It was pretty heavy, and I walked by the mule and the other guy said, "Watch out—she kicks." Well, when he said "kicks," I was already kicked. The mule hit me right in the hand, and it was all black and blue. I couldn't make a fist. So I stayed back and got into the rear end of the baggage. After Messina, we went to Corleone. I saw pictures of it later, and it didn't look anything like when I was there. It was a real country town back then. Now it's condominiums and all kinds of good-looking stuff. We did quite a bit of night training and refurbishing. We didn't lose too many people in Sicily. When we made the landing in Gela, 8:30 in the morning, and the captain was counting noses 'cause he knew one guy got killed on the beach. So we had two sergeants missing. Well, here they come around the corner, drunk. "Morning, Captain." The guy was from Texas or Oklahoma or somewhere. "Morning, Captain. Morning, Captain." We had a sand table of the town, and everything was marked. So they knew where this wine joint was, and when they cleaned out the bunkers going up the hill, the minute they got into town they broke the door open and proceeded to get drunk. A couple of regular Army drunks.

The next major action for your battalion was on the mainland at Maiori? What are your recollections of this engagement?

Okay, the 4th Battalion secured the beach 'cause the beach was small. The town was terraced steep right along the coast. That was the Sorrento peninsula, and it was beautiful terraced country. They landed and we came right in on their heels, I think five minutes behind the 4th Battalion. We landed in LCIs that time. We went by Capri off to the left, close by where we landed, and the minute we landed we took off up the road towards Chiunzi Pass. But before we hit the Chiunzi Pass, we went up in the mountains to a big peak. That gave us the high ground, and we could see everything that moved in the valley. The road down there came down from Naples, so we could interdict that road with artillery fire and Navy gunfire. So they had to detour way over around Mount Vesuvius. So that's when they attacked us on the hill, trying to move us off the high ground, but they never did. We didn't lose too many people there. Up on the mountain there at the same time when the Germans wanted to make a move, they just pounded the hell out of us, for fifteen to twenty minutes. Keep your heads down while they made a move. Usually they were withdrawing. So me and Tucker and a guy by the name of Filey were going to an outpost. Well, when they started blasting our area, I was in a hole about this deep, and that ground there was all ashes from when Mount Vesuvius blew up. The grass grows and the trees grow, but the ground is porous as hell. I get around and go off over there. The smoke would come right through the ground. So finally we couldn't get down in the hole any deeper because of the smoke was getting deep in the bottom of the hole. We had rounds bursting all around us, and we couldn't get any lower in the hole because of the smoke. So, when it finally quit and I get down with my squad leader, he was just sitting there like this. He had lost a piece of his shirttail, but no wound. He just got picked bodily right out of the hole and went down the hill to the hole with the lieutenant. About a few minutes later, they both got blown right out of the hole down over the bank. Not a scratch on them, just shook up.

The concussion lifted them right out?

Lifted them right out of the hole. That's where we ambushed some paratroopers with 60 mm mortars. We were firing a hundred-round concentration every time we fired. Twenty rounds across, five mortars. That would give you a hundred rounds in the air. They'd give us a little change in elevation, and you'd come back with another hundred rounds. And that's another thing. I've had guys with mathematics in ballistics explain to me why I could get fifteen rounds into the air before the first one lit, and when you have them all ready but they start coming down, and they go one, two, three, four, five, six, and all of a sudden they go "brrr." They all catch up with each other. It doesn't seem logical. They'd just come, and one, two, three, four, up to fifteen, one behind the other, but they'll start coming down one, two, three, four, five, six, and then all of a sudden there's a whole six or seven going off at once. We used to like to do that, get fifteen up in the air before the first one lit.

That has to be terrifying to be on the receiving end of that.

Yeah. They ambushed the German paratroopers that were coming up the mountain. The trees were just saplings really; there were no big trees. Every time they moved a tree, you'd see the leaves a different shade of green, and you could see a "snake" all the way down the mountain where these guys were climbing. I didn't see it, but I talked to the guys with the 4.2 observer, and they said they could see the whole line like a different shade of green all the way down the mountain as they pulled themselves up on the trees. So I told the guys at the Ranger camp there, never hang on to a tree when you're climbing a mountain, 'cause you'd give yourself away. Well, they asked Darby if he wanted to shoot at them. He said, "No, we'll suck them in." So that was when they pulled us off the mountain and went up and to the battery. We got up the Chiunzi Pass at night and couldn't find anybody to talk to, so we went to bed on the side of the road. About daylight we went down a little swale there. There were five or six mortars lined up, and they had a whole jeep trailer load of 60 mm mortar ammunition, so we broke it out and got it ready. I was the number one ammo bearer, so my job was to throw the safety off and pull the increments off and hand it to the assistant gunner to drop in. So I fired a couple of hundred rounds, and by the time I got done, I had a blister on my thumb from throwing that safety off. It didn't hurt until I stopped. When the shooting started, we could hear the Germans' pistols and machine guns going off less than 200 yards in front of us. And BARs and our tommy guns and M1s answered them back, and we started firing. Most of the rounds were tree bursts, so they didn't get to the ground. They went off in these saplings. Once you fired the mortar, the bore-safe pin pops; that thing is so sensitive it won't hardly go through a leaf. You know bore safe. There's a pin. Okay, when it's fired that breaks, but it will stay in until you leave the tube, and it finally pops up. And that really arms your fuse. All artillery rounds have that bore-safe capability. So the thing is not armed until it leaves the tube and the pin pops out. Well, anyway, these rounds came down on the trees, so it pretty well shot up that paratrooper company real bad. They didn't bother to come back, and finally the Germans started pulling out, so we let them get off the hill. We were with the British, XV Corps, on the extreme left flank of the whole beachhead. There was a tunnel along the coast to go to Sorrento and Castellammare, and we had to guard the tunnel, and then you go down the Sorrento Drive down to Sorrento. It was right along the coast with the ocean. There were all kinds of restaurants built right on a little peninsula. They put this British armored brigade in behind us, and they broke loose and went down into the valley, towards Naples. The whole armored brigade. So we just followed them on foot. We got down in Castellammare, and then we walked from there to Naples. Obviously, we had been sitting on our asses long enough, and we had to get back in shape with speed marching. So we threw the mortar on a truck and carried light packs, and we really got good exercise going to Naples. We stayed there a little while, and then we went back down to a school that had been for the Fascist kids there. All the sinks were low to the floor, for the kids. Then we went into training and picked up a few recruits, and then we went up to Venafro, and that's where we really lost the battalion. We went up the hill with seventy men, and by the time we got down, there were only about eighteen guys still active, between pneumonia, hepatitis, wounds, and getting killed. So when we got more recruits to go to Anzio, we weren't a viable outfit because we'd lost too many people, and we didn't have time to assimilate the new recruits.

Was your unit strong enough to land at Anzio then?

It was numberwise, but when some of the guys came back from the hospital, they weren't physically or mentally capable. They wanted to send them home, but the guys were noted for going AWOL from the hospital to try to come back to the Rangers. Anyway, we had enough people, but they weren't trained. When we left Africa, we had three battalions in top shape, but the wear and tear, just from July of 1943 to January of 1944, with no real time off, took its toll. They had a habit of misusing lead outfits like that. Besides, when you're attached to somebody, they think they can take care of their boys and let you do the heavy lifting. At the time, I didn't give it a thought. Later on, after reading the books and histories, I now know we were no longer a viable unit after Venafro. The 1st and 3rd and 4th Battalions all lost a tremendous amount of men.

So the battalions were already very weakened before they were committed to this heavy engagement?

Yeah, they were, and malaria had set in. A whole bunch of us contracted malaria at Corleone and up at Venafro. At Salerno and Chiunzi Pass, I came down with malaria. I had my first attack. It only lasted overnight.

You have a story about the goats?

Yeah. I'm a country boy, and one time I was up on the mountain and my canteen was empty. There was a whole bunch of goats up there, and I thought, "There's gotta be water up here somewhere." They couldn't have any goats on this mountain unless there's water. So I kept watching them, and one of them went up the hill there. I said, "He's spraddled, so he must be drinking." When they want to drink they spread their legs. But the guys said no. I said, "I know damn well that he spread his legs and put his head down. That's what they called spraddled." So I went up there, and there was a place where the rock was soft and they chiseled out a basin in the rock years ago.

So had the goats indeed found water to drink?

Yeah. The rock up on the hill was volcano rock, and who knows when they did it, but it was almost like a bathtub. There must have been 200 gallons in that thing from rainwater. And so, we were back there making coffee, washing up. Everybody else said, "Where the hell's the water?" So we said, "There's plenty of water around if you look for it." We finally broke down and told them where we got it from.

What were the circumstances of your capture?

Okay. When they finally decided to expand the beachhead, like we all say, "we were a day late and a dollar short." We war-gamed that we should have gone to Cisterna and the British up to Aprilia on the first day. Well, whether we could hold or not, but there was nobody there. The scout cars of the British went halfway to Rome. Never found anybody, see. But the corps commander was too cautious. When they finally decided to expand the beachhead, the plan of attack was for the 4th Battalion to clear the road for the armor to come up to Cisterna. The 1st and 3rd Battalions were supposed to cut cross-country, get into Cisterna, and set up roadblocks. So we took off about midnight. They scouted out the area and took out a German outpost. We were walking across the Pantano ditch, part of the Mussolini Canal drainage system. We were in that for cover, and it was a little bit down the bank. We went by German artillery batteries firing. In the movie when we crossed the road, they showed us crossing over in front of tanks. But they were actually trucks. It was a truck convoy, moving their people up for an attack they were going to make in the morning. We had been told there was going to be a regular German infantry regiment there, which was bad enough, but actually we attacked right around the assembly area. There were two divisions—the Hermann Göring Armored Division and the 15th Panzer Division. So we crossed over the road right about when it was what they call "nautical twilight." You could see movement, but you couldn't really identify what you saw. It wasn't light enough yet. I was in the last squadron in the company, and we took off up the road on a dead run and got to a bridge that went over the canal, and a German scout car came up. An officer got out and then he jumped back in, whipped that thing around, and went back the other way 'cause he didn't have a radio. So we were going up the road on a dead run. It was starting to get daylight. Well, we decided we were too out in the open, so they turned in this farm trail, but that was up by the German bivouac area. Everybody says, "You guys were ambushed." I say, "Four guys on guard duty is an ambush?" Everybody else was asleep, right in their holes. Some never got out of the holes. These guys just walked up. The guard sees the guys coming up, but he couldn't tell who was coming. He didn't challenge them until they came right on top of him. By then, it was too late.

At that point, it could be friend or foe?

Yeah. Well, that far back from the line, they didn't expect anything. Well, we were there, and that's when the fan got hit. The first fifteen or twenty minutes we thought we were winning, but after that they tried to overrun us with tanks that had been parked in town, and we took out twenty-one of them. My first sergeant was on top of one tank with a hand grenade in his hand. He was going to throw it into the turret, but they put a bazooka round on the other side and blew him off the tank, and he went cartwheeling through the air. He had that cast-iron grenade with the pin pulled. And Sgt. Gabriel, he mounted a tank and opened up the hatch. He said, "You ought to seen the look on the guy's face. He didn't have the hatch locked, and I hit him in the face with a fragmentation grenade and slammed the lid down. The only thing was, I needed to get clearing time. When the thing went off, the lid flew up and hit me in the teeth." That was the first time we were issued white phosphorous grenades. Like I said, when you get close enough to touch a tank, it can't hit you. They would throw a white phosphorus grenade up on the back deck, and when it went off, the intake fan would suck all that white phosphorus smoke right in and set everything on fire. The hatches would fly open just like the guys are waiting for their cue to come out. So after that, they never came back at us. Another time I took out one of the German self-propelled guns. One of them started up and came up the hill we were on. I looked at it and I said, "There's no machine guns on it. Cover me; I'll get that sucker when he goes by." I was standing by a house, and he drove by, trying to get out of the way. Well, I had two hand grenades. I missed him with the first one 'cause I didn't get close enough. So I ran after him and finally put the second grenade through the hole in the back there. For the gun recoil, or to throw the empties out. The brass out or something. So anyway, that grenade went off, poof. A little smoke like nothing happened. But pretty soon the whole thing was on fire. And it went through the camouflage line, and there was a tank truck in there with a lot of fuel on it. One of those old-fashioned round tanks, like they used in the old days to deliver kerosene. Well, there was about 500 gallons in a 700-gallon tank. A small tank truck. So he went down the hill and the thing was burning like hell, and he made a left turn, and the whole thing blew up. Well, this tank truck was on fire. I wasn't paying any attention to it. So I was using a German rifle, a K.98, which was a good bolt-action gun, standing by a gate post, which was a little cover for offhand shooting. I wasn't paying attention to the gasoline tank, which was on fire about 100 or 200 feet behind me. When it finally blew up, I was standing up and did exactly like they do in the movies. My helmet flew off and the rifle went in the air, and the ground in front of me went out. Dropped off like this. I went right straight out for about 20 feet before I landed, and it was hot. I thought for sure I was on fire, so when I hit the ground I started rolling around like they tell you to do when you're on fire. So finally I decided I wasn't on fire. Well, I got back up there, and the guys said, "What were you rolling around for?" And they were all laughing at me, so I said, "I thought I was on fire." Well, I was almost. My helmet and rifle were in the burning fuel, and I came to within about 2 or 3 feet of a post that I was standing by. Finally, the 3rd Battalion people got caught in the open up there, and the Germans rolled them up pretty quickly. They didn't have any cover, and the battalion commander got killed right off the bat, and things went to hell in a hurry. So they threatened to shoot our guys if we didn't quit. Well, we didn't believe it, but they did. This guy out in front of a bunch of prisoners dumped a whole magazine of his machine pistol into a crowd of prisoners. Then I think he was the deadest German there ever was, 'cause about fifteen of our guys shot him.

So he shot American prisoners?
Oh yeah. We had a bunch of prisoners there. He was standing about 6 feet away from them, and he dumped the whole thirty rounds out of that machine pistol into them. We were on the hill and watched the whole thing. And then everybody shot at that one guy. But we ended up surrendering, and we broke up our weapons into pieces. I had the .45, so when I went down the hill to a road, I went by that vehicle I'd set on fire. Had my .45 all apart, and I threw it up into the burning wreck. So I never got to use that pistol. The magazines and everything else. Then they loaded us on trucks and moved us out of the area. And to show how insensitive they were, they were using the cemetery for a supply dump. Had the aboveground tombs opened up and piled ammunition in there.

In the mausoleums?
Yeah. They opened up the mausoleums at the front of the gate and loaded them up with ammunition, rations, and water. And those big cathedrals had big doorways where they took the religious statues in and out. The Germans would open those doors and back a tank right in the cathedral, all the way down to the altar. 'Course all the pews and everything. So they could get in out of the rain and do service work on the tank. I had to convince our guys that every church steeple we saw out there probably had Germans inside with a big set of binoculars and a radio or telephone, so we should hit that steeple and drive them out of it. So when they were moving us out and we went by the cemetery, we saw all this stuff in there. They took us to Rome and paraded us by the Coliseum for propaganda pictures. They made a German newsreel film there, and they had German paratroopers guarding us. We went right by the Coliseum. Vatican City's right across the street there and showing us off. Took us up just north of Rome somewhere, had a little camp there, and finally they loaded some boxcars to go up to Germany. We got on the boxcar and they had the window barb-wired shut. But we managed to pull all of the barbed-wire staples, and that made a pretty good hole. Somebody reached out and undid the barbed-wire staples on the outside, and then we started escaping. Jumping from a moving train in the middle of the night was a stupid thing to do, but the guys were getting ready to do it.

This was on your car that you were on?
Yeah. Well, five of them got out before the guard on top started shooting. They had a guard on top of each car. I guess he was half asleep when the first guy went out, and something woke him up. So he started shooting, and the minute that happened, the train stopped. So five of the guys got away. Then the door opened and they yanked five guys out and shut the door. We were listening, but there was nothing, no sounds. They came back and got five more. Nobody wanted to be the first one. So finally somebody said, "What did you do with the other guys?" One of the Germans said in fairly decent English, "We're putting them in other cars." Well, they did, and they crowded us in another car. We were setting down there, but if you moved your foot you couldn't get it back where it was in the first place 'cause somebody else was there. And some of the guys had dysentery, but all we had was a bucket over there to go in. We'd take a leak in a can, which would get passed over and dumped out the window. So we were in the boxcar for about a week. There was no water. You could take the frost off the inside for drinking water. We got to Moosburg VII-A, Germany. Like I said, I had a heavy-duty moustache, and I hadn't shaved. This was January, and it was going on March by the time we got to Moosburg. So I had a real heavy beard, but I had to shave it off when I got in the prison camp. They wouldn't let you have a beard or a mustache, because if you had a beard you could just shave it off, and then you wouldn't look like your picture.

The one on your prisoner identification card?
Yeah. They had an identification file. All we had were the dog tags with the prison number on it. 22715 was my number.

So where did you end up as a POW?
In Stalag II-B Hammerstein. That's way up in Pomerania, almost up to the Baltic. You got the long days where the sun didn't go down until about 8:00 or 9:00 at night, and then you'd get daylight again about 3:30 or 4:00, 'cause you're that far north.

How long did you spend at the prison camp?
I was only at the main camp a short time. Then they sent us out to a farm, but we didn't like the job so we escaped. I spent four days out in the woods, and the fourth night out we came to a railroad train right in front of us. It had bales of straw on it, and the center one had two bales where someone had stretched a canvas over it to make a tent. So we crawled in. Said, "What the hell, we'll go for a ride and get out of the rain." So the train took off and we were moving pretty good. Every once in a while they'd pull into a siding and let another train go by, going the other way. Sometimes it would be the siding over here, and I could look through the grommet and see what the hell was going on. Well, about 4:00 in the afternoon, the train came to a complete stop and started backing up. So I'm looking through the grommet and all of a sudden I started laughing, so the guys said, "What's so funny back there?" I said, "This train just backed into a German army garrison." We went through the gate, and the German guardhouse looks like an outhouse with no door on it. The guard was standing there with a rifle, and a uniform on. Well, the only one who was perturbed about it was the sergeant of the guard, 'cause we got by his guard. The poor guard didn't have anything to do about it. He couldn't see us underneath that canvas. They took us up to the head shed, and there was a bunch of old World War I retreads there, colonels and majors, running training camp. They weren't on active duty, just training. So we're talking to them through an interpreter. Then they started to take us outside, and we get out on the sidewalk when one of these officers came running up and told us to go back inside. We go upstairs on the third floor. Man, I went into an office there. It looked like a movie set. This was the general's office. Big maps on the wall and pictures of all the old-time German generals and Hitler and Göring. They had that one with Bismarck and all the other ones. I think that's what he really wanted, but he had to have the other ones to be politically correct. So I said to the guys, "This is the head honcho. We'll give him the works when he comes through the door." Well, he comes through the door. We snapped into attention. We popped our heels and gave him a salute. So we're talking to him through an interpreter, and he said, "How did you get here? Where did you come from?" So I could see a map that showed where the town was, relative to the farm, 'cause the farm had been 15 or 20 miles from that town. So I pointed to that map on the wall and said, "The farm was somewhere around this place."

He looked at it and said, "How did you get here?" I said, "Well we were walking until last night. Last night we got on the train that brought us here." 'Cause he's thinking it's a big joke and it's funny. We thought it was too. So finally he stood up to leave, and that snapped them back to attention. We saluted and he left the room. They escorted us down to the guardhouse, and there was a lieutenant down there who spoke good English. He said, "Who the hell are you guys? The general called up and said turn the hot water on. There are some soldiers coming down." And a GI's a GI. I don't care what army they're in. I looked in the cell. On the wall, it said, "Sleeping, time twenty-eight days." The guy got twenty-eight days in the guardhouse for sleeping. So we had a shower and then got cleaned up. They had a stove in there, so we heated it up and made coffee. Asked the guard if he wanted a cup of coffee, and he said, "Sure." So two or three days later, the guards show up from II-B to escort us back to camp. Then they got their Gestapo guy, who wanted to know where our map and compass were. We didn't have any map and compass. "Who helped you?" "Nobody helped us." They looked at us and couldn't figure it out. That's another thing. You could easily recognize the plainclothes Gestapo, since they all wore the same type of hat, the same shirt, the same leather overcoat. They might as well have had a uniform on, the way they were dressed. It was all alike. The same style [of] hat, the same style [of] shirts and jackets and everything. Well, they asked us about maps and who helped us. Then the cooler. Bread and water down there. They had so many guys waiting there, they couldn't keep you in there for twenty days. They'd only keep you there for ten days, 'cause they had so many people go in. So then they sent us to a punishment camp, so called. It was one of the best camps, 'cause it was just a little building right down the middle of a dead-end street right in the town. And we're making rammed-earth houses in the Jewish cemetery. All they did was take the tombstones and level the ground off and start making footings out of the tombstones that were there, and pulled a slab and make a rammed-earth house on top of the footings.

They made a what on top of the footings?
Rammed earth. You made a form and you packed dirt in there. It was a clay-type dirt. You packed it real tight with sticks in it to stiffen it up, and once you stuccoed the outside and the inside and got enough overhang to keep the weather from beating against the wall, you had a nice wall, about 2 feet thick. It was well insulated, so it was cool in the summer and warm in the winter with very little extra heating. We were working with civilian contractors. So the guy had one of those big levels like you use when you're doing the chimney. He had a 6-foot level and he kept putting that on, to make sure the thing was plumb. So we kicked that thing into the form, and he didn't know where it was 'cause we were working too energetic. There's a couple wheelbarrows of dirt on it, and everybody's pounding away like hell. You know he didn't dare tear that goddamn form up and get his level back. But a GI's a GI. We were digging the trench and they got the German army on fatigue detail from the garrison in town. They were digging towards us, and we were digging this way. Well, we swung the pick this way, where when you bring the pick down you don't hardly move the ground. So down there was about 100 feet apart. Prisoners walking this way and the German soldiers on fatigue detail. So they quit for chow. The Hitler Youth camp was in town there, so the Hitler Youth camp kids come out, and when the German sergeant came back, he started kicking their asses all over it. They said the little bastards did more work in an hour than we did all afternoon. And then we had one kid that spoke good German, all the dialects. You get the kids singing, "Potato soup, potato soup all week. Potato soup, one time meat." We were doing the same thing as the Germans, but they thought it was funny, see. And even the guard thought it was funny. Except one Sunday, this guard's reporting in. The only day off we had was Sunday, so we were washing our clothes and we were sitting out there and looking up. Here he comes down the street. If you ever read *The Headless Horseman*, by Ichabod Crane (*The Legend of Sleepy Hollow* by Washington Irving), and this was it. The guy was about 6 foot 6, all knobby knees, and couldn't walk and chew gum at the same time. All I could think of was Ichabod Crane. And he was a real nasty. The first time he heard these kids singing potato soup, he got out there and was yelling and screaming, trying to kick them upside the head. That was the worst thing he could do, 'cause every time he walked up the street behind the bushes, all you could hear was potato soup, potato soup. And we had four houses all built—no roof on them—nice and square. It rained for three days, and I mean real bad. You could sit there and watch the edge go from square, start slipping, sliding off. So by the end of the third day, all four of those houses were right back down to just a pile of mud on the slab. And they made the tile out of cement, so it didn't have any strength in it. We found out you could take one of those tiles they made to put on

the roof, and all you had to do was hold it in your hand and go like this and you could break a corner off. They found out they didn't want us on that detail anymore. They put the girls to work on that. And this one guard, they called him Tony, but I don't know what his name was. He was a recuperating wounded. He had the junkiest rifle I'd ever seen in my life. I don't think I'd ever dare fire the damn thing. He had three rounds in it, another three rounds in his belt. So all he had was six rounds for that thing. And he'd lean the rifle against the wall, and he'd get lollygagging around the girls. He'd go over there lollygagging with the girls, and he'd get 40, 50, 100 feet away from his rifle. So we'd see somebody coming up the road looking important, and we'd grab his rifle and run it over to him 'cause we didn't want to lose him. So this kid that spoke the German; I don't know where he got it, but he started it. He says to Tony, "That don't mean *Heil, Hitler* no more. That's how deep the snow was in Russia last year." He told somebody, and I guess it was like getting on the internet. That thing went cross-country like a wildfire. So here come the Gestapo. They traced it back, I guess, somehow, that it started in our area, and they questioned us about it. So we had to make believe we never heard it before.

How long were you in this punishment camp?

I think they kept me about two or three months, I guess it was. But it really wasn't a punishment camp. They called it that, but we had a good barracks. The only thing was, we didn't have bathing facilities. 'Course we were washing up at the faucet out there. Had an outhouse. But we argued we didn't have bathing facilities. We were in a spa town. There was a lake down there. So they agreed that twice a week, we'd go down to the pier. You went in between the piers. The guard said that the only way he could tell us apart from the German troops who were also in the water was when we swam.

You had a different style of swimming?

Oh yeah. The Germans were just splashing around in there, but we were doing the breaststroke and the side stroke, and they're just in there splashing around. And then we'd take that little bar of soap that came in our Red Cross parcel, just like you get in a motel here, and we'd wash up with that, and the guards would look at us with the goddamn foamy soap. They ain't seen that since God knows when. And when we got done, we'd throw the sucker way out in the middle of the lake and watch the guy almost drown trying to get that soap. So the town had a swim team at the high school. And the kid who spoke German was going on the springboard and the platform diving, and he could do all the fancy dives. He was real good. So he was fooling around, and the German *Feldwebel*, the recreation sergeant there, I'd say a World War I man, a big old senior *Feldwebel*, senior sergeant. He spoke to the guy because the kid answered him in German, good German. He said, "How good are you?" The kid said, "Well, if you get the people away from the diving board, I could show them what I could do." So he blew his whistle and got them out of the pool. So everybody got out, and they watched him. He did the jackknife and everybody applauded him. Then he got up on the 30-meter platform and did the platform dives 'cause he was pretty good at it. I can't remember his name though.

Could you describe the liberation of your camp?

First they pulled everybody who was on these farm details into town. The Russians were coming, so they put us in a little bunkhouse we had there in town. They brought everybody in, and then we marched out. I marched from Poland to Bremen, clear across northern Germany. We were in good shape physically. We had Red Cross parcels, and the only thing we were missing was good waterproof, insulated footwear. We just had standard shoes like these here. I mean the old 6-inch boondockers they used to issue. That's all we had. But they moved us out in the middle of a howling blizzard with 2 feet of snow in the middle of the road. And they kept pushing us until we got over the Oder River at Stettin. Once we crossed the river, they slowed down to 10 or 15 miles a day. It all depended on the march unit ahead of us. If they were too close, they'd hold us back a day and let them get farther ahead. They didn't want too many people going through the same area at the same time. Then the last camp we were in was run by the German navy. Right over in Bremerhaven, a navy area. That was the last camp we were in before the British liberated us. Once they liberated the camp, they had the British version of the CID[16] or the CIC come up there and check you and make sure you're who you say you are. Check the rosters they got from the American army and who to look for. Then they took us down to the airport in Bremen. Boy, that was a beat-up place. We had to fly at night, so we went from there to Brussels, and the next night we went down to Camp Lucky Strike down near Le Havre. That was an exit port for about everybody in the area. So eventually we got processed and got on a boat. It went to Southampton, England, and we were on the last convoy that left to come back, because some German submarines hadn't come in and surrendered, so there were still German submarines out there. So we got halfway across before everything was accounted for, and then they told everybody to proceed at your own best speed. Well, our boat had a bent rudder post and a bent rudder blade. Anytime you tried to get above 6 knots, the boat would shake, and the crew was a bunch of seamen out of Boston. To run the boat to keep it in a straight line, you had to have the wheel hard over one way or the other, to straighten that bent rudder post out. If you centered the wheel, you had a bend on your rudder post. So to compensate that by yanking it one way or the other. So we were twenty-one days from Southampton, England, to New York. The slow boat to China.

A long journey?
A long journey. Cold. In May out there in the North Atlantic. Man, it was cold out there. The sky was just as blue. No clouds. It was pretty, but when you got on deck there, man we were cold.

So what were the greatest lessons you learned from your military experience?
Well, it's hard to say. One thing is, I never learned anything I could take home with me. Like I told my great-grandson going to Norwich University. He's going to be a second lieutenant, and I told him, "While you're up there going to college, get a degree in something you can take home with you." I said, "There ain't much market for machine guns. If you're good enough, get into controlled demolition, taking the big buildings down." Well, that's pretty good, but that's quite a science in itself. But there's very few people that do that. I told him to get a criminal justice or business administrator degree, or something that when he gets out of the Army he can take it with him. I went to work digging holes, setting poles, because I didn't have a trade when I went in the Army. I was working in a shoe shop, and it wasn't anything you could make a real living at. But the electrical-line work, I'd do pretty good. But working for the government, there were a lot more benefits than it sounded like. I had twenty-six days of vacation time. That don't count weekends and all the holidays. So like I said, during my military career I never learned anything I could take home with me to make a living at. But now you have all kinds of programs and computers and technical stuff, and you can get the education.

PFC GEORGE SABINE

What were your interests or career plans prior to enlisting or being drafted in World War II?
I enlisted. I was going to school at the University of Connecticut before I went into the service. I wanted to be a veterinarian, but I never made it.

Where were you when you heard about Pearl Harbor?
I was skating in New Haven Arena. It was with a couple of my friends and my cousins, and we used to go every Sunday afternoon. We'd go skate around on the rink. I was about eighteen.

What were your thoughts after you heard about Pearl Harbor?
I think it was anger. We were still all kind of thinking about the military one way or the other. It was a sobering thought.

Where did you complete your basic training?
I was in the Enlisted Reserve Corps. I signed up for the duration of the war plus ten years. I did my basic training at Camp Croft, South Carolina. I enlisted September 1, 1942. And the reason I did was so I could get into the Enlisted Reserve Corps and continue going to school at the University of Connecticut. I figured if I stayed out of the draft, I could stay a couple of semesters at the University of Connecticut. I wasn't ever assigned to a division.

How were you recruited for the Rangers?

I was in North Africa, and we were going through the replacement depots. I was with a friend of mine that I had gone through basic training with, and they came around looking for volunteers. So both of us volunteered. They took me and they didn't take him.

What did you know about the Rangers at the time?

Absolutely nothing.

You just thought it sounded interesting?

Well, let me digress just a minute. I got hurt playing football at the University of Connecticut. I tore up my knee, so I stopped going to school, quite frankly, and the Army called me up because I had signed up. And I didn't want to get into a regular infantry outfit. I had ROTC training at the University of Connecticut. We had to wear uniforms once a week, I guess, and we had formations and all. So I wasn't really enthused about going into an infantry outfit. I thought maybe I would go into the paratroopers, but then I thought, jeez, not with my knee. I'm still having problems with it. So I thought I'd never make it because when I jumped, it would go out of joint or something. So I didn't know what to do. I put in for Officer Candidates Service School [OCS] when I was up at Camp Croft and went through noncom school. But out of the class of thirty that we had, there was one man who made it, and he was an older guy. He was a sheriff of Dade County in Florida, and I think there was a lot of political rim-rams going on. So they shipped me overseas as an infantry replacement. We landed in Casablanca, and I was only there about a day and then we were shipped out. We started up the line to go to the 9th Division. They had gotten their butts wiped at Kasserine Pass, and they were getting replacements. So that's where we ended up, with the 9th Division.

And that's where you were recruited then for the Rangers? When you were there?

Yeah.

What additional training did you receive as a Ranger?

We did a lot of physical training, you know, physical work. And I had a company commander who was kind of picking people that he needed for certain jobs. So I got a lot of training from him and the first sergeant of the company, in scouting and patrolling. So I did a lot of training on that. We did a lot of weapons work too. It wasn't that long that I was training.

How did this additional training as a Ranger affect your performance on the battlefield?

Well, it's difficult to explain. We were kind of getting inoculated with the spirit that we were better. We were different than anybody else. That's what made us good.

Did your military training provide you with a reasonable perspective on what to expect with respect to battlefield conditions?

No. Well, the Army is not the most efficient organization in the country. And you had a lot of ninety-day wonders.[17] Also a lot of the officers were from National Guard outfits, and that's probably the worst. It's political. They became an officer because they knew somebody. And the government doesn't do a good job of training.

What do mean by ninety-day wonders?

Those were people who went to OCS. A classic example. I was only in Casablanca a short time. I had never slept out on the ground overnight in the Army until I got to Casablanca. That's the kind of training I had. But we were there in the replacement camp, and we had this fireball second lieutenant, and he said, "I'm going to show you how to take a shower without any problems, without any water." We said, "Okay, fine." So he took us out and marched the daylights out of us. It was in North Africa at the end of July, so it was hot. And when we came back into the camp, we were soaking wet. And then he said, "Take a towel and towel yourself off. This is the way to take a shower without any water." And I thought to myself, "If I had a chance with you, you're going to bite the dirt." You know, that was just stupidity.

Would you say that the officers that used the most-stern approaches, did that approach pay off on the battlefield?
I never had any trouble. There were only sixty-three men in a company of Rangers at full capacity, and we were never full. And the officers we had were really good, all of them. When the company is set up, you had the company commander, and he had two lieutenants under him. And each lieutenant had a platoon or section. So you didn't have too many officers. There weren't that many officers around. I had put in for OCS, but I never got in.

When were you first deployed to combat conditions?
When we went into Italy the first week in September of 1943. We went in below Naples. The name of the town was Maiori. It was on the left flank of the invasion of Italy.

Describe your first battlefield engagement.
Well, we were holding the ridgeline. In fact, we got Presidential Unit Citations for doing that. We were holding the line on the one side of the invasion, and we were up on these ridges. That was the first time I saw combat.

Was your first battlefield engagement similar to what you expected, on the basis of your training?
My first engagement was the Hun, with the Germans. I had been out on a patrol, and when I came back I was pooped. I had been out all night. So I was laying [*sic*] down, and the rest of the guys were spread out. That was the first time that I heard artillery fire, but I remember we never had the Germans come up close, so I woke up. I don't know if he woke me up or what, but I woke up and there was a big German standing at my feet. That's the first time I saw combat.

Were you shocked, scared?
You bet your life. Anybody that said they weren't is lying.

How did your noncom and commissioned officers handle the activities of you battalion?
We had good officers. That's the first time I got shot at. We were set up just like the British Commandos. We had sections, and there were twelve men to a section. We had a sergeant who was at the head of us and a corporal at the tail end. The corporal was a nice guy and he got killed right there. The first American I saw get killed was there.

Did you immediately respect your noncoms and your commissioned officers or did that process take some time?
They were good soldiers. If they told me to go, I'd go. I never had any problems.

How would you describe the best attributes that would make a noncom or a commissioned officer an effective leader, on the basis o your experiences?
It's just like a whole bunch of puppies. You've got a bunch of puppies and you got one leader in the bunch. It's the same way in anything. Playing football or when you were in business, the leader always came out. You didn't have to worry about it. They garnered respect from you.

What aspects of being a Ranger made you a more effective soldier?
I think we were proud. There were small things. You couldn't wear a Ranger patch or be promoted until you'd been in combat. You started at the bottom and you were made a PFC, but you couldn't do that until you were shot at. It was kind of their own rules.

You had to earn it, it sounds like.
Yeah, yeah.

Okay. What other major battles were you involved with?
Well, we lost a lot of people there at the start in Italy, and when we were going to Cassino. That's where the three battalions really took a lot of casualties up there, on the approaches to Cassino. We never got to Cassino,

but the approaches to it. The 4th Battalion was on the line the longest up there. Of the battalions, I think the 3rd was probably the luckiest, 'cause we didn't stay on the line too long. They'd take us in. We'd do whatever we had to do and then get pulled back after three or four days. The 4th Battalion stayed for a long time. I think it was over a month and a half that they were on the line. You didn't have a lot of people, and there wasn't a lot of support behind us. We were a small outfit, and the most people we had was sixty-three guys, and that included the first sergeant and everybody else. It wasn't like a regular infantry company.

What was the most intense battle or firefight that you participated in?
I got hurt the seventh of December 1943, and I think that was the hardest I saw. It was up on the approaches to Cassino.

Was this your biggest, greatest moment of fear; at that point when you got hurt?
I don't know. You know, you were afraid all the time. We didn't have much choice.

Were there any other isolated firefights or experiences that you would want to discuss?
No. After I was wounded, I went to the hospital. They stayed on the line there for about a week, I guess, and then they were pulled back and were sent into training for the invasion at Anzio. I was in the hospital. I came back to the company the day that they were captured at Anzio.

How were you wounded?
I got hit in the left side. I don't know what it was. I know it was a grenade that hit me first. But I don't know whether I set off a land mine before the grenade hit me. My sergeant, who was my section leader, and I were pinned down and there was an explosion, and I said, "Look, we got to get out of here." So I scooted back as far as I could and got into cover so I wouldn't get blown away.

What was your feelings or thoughts when you discovered you were wounded?
Staying alive.

Yeah, survival. Okay, do you remember where you were on Christmas Eve or Christmas day of 1944?
I was in the hospital in 1943. In 1944, we were in southern France. I was in the 1st Special Service Force. They put us in that when the Rangers were wiped out at Anzio. We were in Nice, 'cause we had been pulled off the line. We had been on the line for a month and a half or two months. It was Christmas Eve, and we had a big fight with another company, as a matter of fact. And a real good friend of mine was from Texas, and he could fight like a terrorist. He got in a fight with another guy from another company. I don't know why, but they were turning over cars in the center of Nice and setting them on fire. So we were going to be the good guys and stop it. So this big guy hit my friend in the nose and my friend went down. We had parkas. We had good equipment with us for Special Services. And I had my knife in the front pocket of my parka, and I was going to get it out and try to rescue my friend. Well, there was a big guy in back of me and one in front of me, and they got me between them and I couldn't get my hand out of the pocket. So by the time I got my knife out, my friend was down and we got out of there. I remember that very well. We had a good time.

That was an interesting way to celebrate the Christmas holiday?
The Christmas before that I was in an evacuation hospital, and we got pretty well geared up. We used the medical alcohol. We'd take it and cut it in half with water, and then we mixed that with grapefruit juice or whatever we had to make a drink. Christmas Eve the ward boy had some booze, and we got into that and got him all steamed up. The nurse that was in charge of the ward, she was going to shoot us all. She was playing footsies with this ward boy, I guess, but he wasn't in any shape to take her out.

No, I wouldn't think so.
So that's my story.

Your Christmas story. What was the saddest moment or moments during your time in the military service?
I guess that would be when they broke up the Special Forces and sent the Canadians back to Canada, and we were put into another outfit. I had been with them for almost a year, and we got real friendly. We knew the guys, and I think that was one of the saddest times.

How would you describe your most important contribution to a given battle or in the aid of a wounded comrade?
Well, after I got wounded, I could still walk. My arm was all banged up, but I had one good arm and I helped take out my platoon leader. His name was Parrish, 2Lt. Parrish. He hadn't been a lieutenant very long. He had been a first sergeant and then he made lieutenant. I don't know what he got hit with, but he got hit real bad, so I helped carry him out quite a ways. We didn't have a stretcher or anything, so we used a raincoat and two rifles to carry him. He died later on, and it was a good thing he did because he was all chopped up. He was in bad shape.

I'm sorry to hear that. Were there any individuals fallen or otherwise that you would like to pay tribute or would like to describe their impact on you or your company during a given combat engagement?
I probably had more close friends in Special Forces that I did in the Rangers. Some of them were Canadian and some were American guys. But I was probably closer to a lot of people in the Special Forces than I was in the Rangers.

What were the greatest lessons that you learned from your military experience?
Be patient. I think that we all grew up very quickly. I don't care what you were in, if you were in a bad situation you grew up.

You were never a POW, were you?
No.

What emotions do you feel when you look back on your past military experiences?
Well, you know, you lost a lot of good friends that you had, but on the other hand, you made a lot of friends. I think it made me a better citizen, and I think it made us a better generation. Let's put it that way.

Because of those war experiences?
Yeah. Well, you had to have a lot of faith in other people, and a lot of pride in yourself and the unit you were in. I think that was one of the things that we carried with the Special Forces and the Rangers. You were something special, and really it was all in your own mind. I mean, we wouldn't salute anybody but our own officers. You know, it was just little things like that.

Can you describe a fellow soldier's struggle for combat or a great combat achievement that was never officially recognized?
No, I can't. I helped a guy get a Silver Star. Most of it was being in the right place at the right time, so somebody saw what was happening. That's all. You know, I think a lot of the whole procedures of giving out medals and all this helped to hop up people after the war.

Who were the commanding officers or NCOs that made a lasting impression on you?
My company commander in the Rangers. His name was Evans, Bing Evans, and he lives up in Illinois now. He was a good guy. He was a nice guy. I didn't have any fault with him.

So you felt that he provided you with leadership?
Well, you know, you had a job to do. You had your own little group, your own squad that you'd had. You knew the guys, and they depended upon you and you depended upon them. That was what kept the units together.

Do you have any pearls of wisdom or comments or anything that you'd like to provide for future generations on the basis of what you learned as a Ranger?

I think that one of the things we've lost is pride in our country. You know, every time I see the flag it just brings up a knot in my throat. That's the way we were brought up. When I was a kid growing up, I was lucky my father always provided. He was a good man. He was more like a brother to me than a father. And my mother was the same. She was very, very good. I had a good upbringing. Maybe it wasn't right, but it was good. But little things come back to me, like we would never walk on the grass at school. We walked on the path, and nobody ever told us not to walk on the grass. You just didn't do that. The janitor of the one of the schools I went to was very, very good with me and all the kids. So even when I grew up, I called him Mister. It's just a feeling that you have. My father never once laid a hand on me, never. But if he told me to walk through that wall ahead of me, I'd have walked through the wall. The Army didn't have to teach me discipline. My father did.

What did you do after the war, then?

Well, I went to school for a while. I bummed around. I went to the University of Connecticut. I went up to Norwich. I went out to Penn State. I came back to Connecticut. I never did get a degree. I had enough time to get a degree, I guess, but I never did. Finally I quit school. I got married and then I went to work.

Is there anything else you want to add about your experiences as a Ranger?

No. I was proud of my time in the Rangers. They were a good outfit, and I was brokenhearted when they got wiped out. I had just come out of the hospital. I think it was the twenty-fourth of January that they got wiped out at Anzio. I came back to the outfit to the base camp the day of the night that they got wiped out. So I missed it by a day. And I went over the hill from the hospital. I never got checked out; I just left 'cause I was sick and tired of fiddling around with the medics. So I walked away and went back to the camp. I knew where it was. I thumbed a ride on a truck and got back to the camp.

And then?

Then they didn't know what to do with the ones of us that were left. It was an awful time. It was after Christmas, but we were still getting a lot of Christmas packages, and they'd give you little jobs to do around the camp. One time I was working and taking care of the mail, and there were other people there and we were opening up Christmas packages of the guys that we knew who were captured. Because we heard the Germans broadcast it on the radio with their name, rank, and serial number. And we were supposed to take out the valuables so they could be sent back to whoever sent them. But the goodies, the candy and the cookies that people sent, we kept that and gave it away, you know. There was more damn candy than we knew what to do with.

But it was sad to know that?

It was sad. Well, the thing of it was that every night at 7:00, the Germans would come on the radio, and they had this gal that gave the commentary. She spoke good English, and she'd give the name, the battalion that he was in, his name, rank, and serial number. And these were guys you'd been with for quite a while. All of a sudden you knew they were captured. It was sad. I talked to Bing Evans afterwards at one of the reunions that we had. And he said he was standing in the middle of the road, and he didn't know what happened. He said the next thing he woke up and he was captured. He got hit with something. He wasn't sure what it was. You know, you'd get hit with something, and you never knew if it was a hand grenade or what the hell it was. It came out of the darkness and it would knock you down. So he spent his time in the camp and came back. One incident and then I'll let you go. We got pinned down before Cassino. We were on kind of a big raid, and we got pinned down all day long. We lost a lot of guys. A lot of guys had been knocked off. But the Rangers never would leave anybody behind. Anybody got knocked down, they got picked up and brought back. It was a good morale builder. But anyway, they sent guys in to get us, and I don't know how the hell they got them in because we were pinned down. Every time we moved, they'd throw shells at us. They brought in a jeep with a trailer on it to take out some of our guys that got killed. And then they took the guys who were still able to get around. They were getting out, and there had to be 25 feet between guys going up this road. And we started up the road, and I heard this clunk, clunk, clunk. I said, "Those are chains." And I had made up my mind that

I wasn't going to get captured. If they came to grab me, I was going to fight. It was this little mountain road, and there was this big embankment on the right hand side, and I thought, "Well, if they come up the road and try to get me, I will go over the side here. Maybe I can get away." Come to find out it was just a jeep which had tire chains on all four wheels because there was a lot of mud up there. And the chains were loose, and every time they go over dead center, they'd go clink. That's what I was hearing. I didn't know about it until afterwards when I was talking to guys. But anyway, I can still remember that clink, clink, and I'd made up my mind that I'm not going to be captured. I don't know why. Some spirit, but that was it.

MAJ. BING EVANS

I understand you grew up in Aberdeen, South Dakota.

That's right. 406 South Seventh Street for the most part. That was my grandparents' home, although I grew up wild.

Ranger Evans

What do you mean by that?

It was a very small house, and it was on the wrong side of the tracks. My grandfather was keeping my uncle, my mother's brother, and he had five children all in this little bit of a house. In addition to my aunt, who was eight years older than I was, and my sister. So there [was] just no room for me. There just wasn't any room in the house, not even on the stairway.

I guess you had a good time in childhood and everything?

Well, I don't know. I never thought about it being a good time. I was hungry a lot with the Depression and everything. I was selling papers on the street. I had the corner with the Sherman Hotel, which was the best corner. The only reason I could keep it was because anybody who wanted it had to whip me to get it, and I couldn't afford to lose.

Do you remember specifically where you were and what you were doing when you heard about Pearl Harbor?

Yeah. I was at Camp Claiborne, Louisiana. We'd gone down there for a year of training. They took me out of college in my junior year, 'cause I was in the National Guard for spending money. I got a dollar a drill. So every thirteen weeks I got thirteen dollars. That was my spending money in college. I know it doesn't sound like much, but actually at that time it wasn't bad. So that's why I was in the Guard, and we were federally inducted on February 10 of 1941. I was with the 109th Engineers at the time, and we went down to Camp Claiborne. We were supposed to be through in a year, and of course you know that war was declared in December of that same year. So being the 109th Engineers of the 34th Division, I was in the advance party sent overseas, and as far as I know we were the first Americans overseas in World War II. We built some of the camps in North Ireland.

Now, when you disembarked probably from the East Coast, what were your thoughts when you were on that boat?

Well, my thoughts weren't about combat or anything like that, because my girl was on the way to marry me. When I got to Fort Dix, she knew I was about to go overseas, and she had just come from Camp Claiborne to marry me. She saw me for a half an hour on the station platform, and then we were shipped out. When she found out I was at Fort Dix, she borrowed her dad's car. Her dad was a farmer and had a gas ration, so she borrowed the car and started for Fort Dix, New Jersey, but she was in an automobile accident near Rockford, Illinois. So that's where she was, and they wouldn't let me go to her. There were two other women with her and their husbands got to go, because Bob Coffey was the battalion commander. He was my athletic director in college. I guess you'd call me a big-shot subsidized athlete in college. So he and Ray Schultz got to go to their wives, who were in the accident. But they wouldn't let me go. So I tossed the ring in the ocean in the middle of the night, along with the marriage license. I watched it flutter into the water. They seemed to be bad luck; I thought, well, I guess it was just meant to be. I didn't know what was going to happen. I was hoping she'd be there when I came back, but later as I became a company commander and was having to read all the correspondence that was sent back, I found out there were an awful lot of Dear John letters. But she waited three years and seven months.

So how did you hear about the Rangers, and what prompted you to join the Rangers?

Well I was in North Ireland when I heard about the Rangers, but they weren't Rangers then. They wanted some volunteers for the British Commandos, and I was tired of building camps, so I volunteered along with about three or four or five thousand others who were tired of what they were doing. So that group wound up being narrowed down to the original five hundred. Our first training as commandos was at Carrickfergus in Ireland, and it was there that we really became commandos. And then they moved us to Scotland in the Ben Nevis area, to the Cameron Clan Estates near Achnacarry.

So who interviewed you to be a Ranger?

I don't know. I would suspect it would either be Herman Dammer or Roy Murray, or both. Maj. Darby was interviewing at the time, but I don't recall him actually interviewing me.

So then you underwent more-extensive training with the Rangers?

Oh yes, on the Cameron Clan Estate. That's where we actually went through the very difficult part of the commando training. That was a commando-training base, and the British were bound and determined to weed us out and to prove that we couldn't do it. And they were pretty successful. As I say, out of the several thousand we started with, they wound up with five hundred of us. And then they tried everything they could to weed us out even from that. But I think we broke every record they ever had. They got five hundred pretty good men out of that first bunch. We had physical training like speed marches, as well as more-specialized training like cliff climbing, rappeling, and amphibious landings. Also obstacle courses and river crossings. They've got pictures of a lot of that stuff.

Do you believe that the drill work and the techniques taught during your Ranger training, and the discipline that was instilled, played an important role in your success on the battlefield?

I think the success on the battlefield came because of the weeding out of "weaker characters." I suspect we were pretty good physical specimens. I was 6 foot 3, 225 pounds, skinny as a rail. In those days you didn't have the weight programs like you do now. And so I was a pretty good-sized 225-pound football player, and I think my athletic background paid off, as well as the additional training.

Do you think your military training prior to battle provided you with a reasonable perspective of what to anticipate on the battlefield? Or do you think that training is good, but the experience you get on the battlefield is irreplaceable?

Let's go to the landing in North Africa. When we landed there and spearheaded that at Arzew, I had a sense of anticipation, or looking forward to it. I was thinking, "Well, this is what I've been training for. And so, come on." But before the next invasion I was a little more apprehensive, 'cause I knew what was in store. And every landing thereafter got more difficult. So I don't know how else to explain it. It went from a feeling of anticipation to a feeling of "Well, this is it." You began to realize that if you did this often enough, there was going to be an ending somewhere.

Now, would you say that the officers who applied the sternest approaches in training really helped you with that stern approach, or do you think it didn't make a difference?

Our officers trained with us, under the British Commandos. They didn't train separately from us. So the officers were subject to the same weeding-out process that the men were subjected to, and the proportion of officers that failed was probably greater than the percentage of the enlisted men.

How about the officers in the British Commandos? Do you think that the ones that had the most stern approach really helped you or hurt you?

Oh, no, it helped. And there weren't many officers. Almost all of the people who trained us were the upper-echelon noncoms.

Let's go back to Scotland. I know that you were first sergeant of E Company. What were the circumstances by which Lt. Col. Darby decided to elevate you to battalion command sergeant major?

Well, I was filling that bill anyway. I was the first one, but I wasn't called sergeant major, because a battalion wasn't warranted a sergeant major. But somehow or another he got it done. So I suspect I'm the only one in the United States Army at that time who was a sergeant major of a battalion. I don't know that, of course, but I suspect it.

So on the basis of that position, you obviously were very close to Lt. Col. Darby. What were your first impressions of him and what were your impressions later on?

Admiration. Couldn't help but be, 'cause he went through the same training we did, and proved that he could do it. Sometimes I don't know how he could do what he did, but he paid the price to prove to us that he was as good a man as we were. He led by example. He was a good one.

Would you say he was the best leader that you worked with in your military experience?

Well, no. There were two or three of them, and another one was Col. Dammer. He was Capt. Dammer when I started, then Maj. Dammer, then Lt. Col. Dammer when he took over the 3rd Battalion. Then there was Roy Murray, whom you've probably heard of extensively. It's hard to rank them and try to determine which one was best. Basically they're all the same high quality.

All right, let's move on and talk about your first deployment and subsequent battle engagements. Why don't we start with November 8, which was the Arzew Algeria campaign. Do you specifically remember that campaign?

Very well. In fact, that's probably why I got to be the first commissioned officer from the ranks, I think, in World War II. My serial number was 0885703. 01 and 02 were ahead of me, but they were rear echelon in London. So I think mine was the first battlefield commission. We landed on November 8, and on November 10, I was a second lieutenant. One of the reasons for that, I think, was the fact that the colonel overlooked a landmark, and I called his attention to it. I told him he'd better go back and check with Capt. Schneider and Capt. Dammer, and they verified that we had passed the landmark. So he went back, and I think that that was the reason why two days later Darby promoted me to second lieutenant. That plus the fact that one of the lieutenants, and a company commander, lost his life. Gordon Cliffman lost his life, and so they made me second lieutenant.

Do you remember what happened to him? Were you there for that?

Yeah. We landed and we were completely successful, as you know, at Arzew. We were split into two forces, one to take the fort in town and one to take the fort on the hill overlooking the town. And then the infantry landed unopposed and started for Oran, but they ran into a little resistance and they got bogged down. So Gordon Cliffman went up with his company to see what could be done, and they broke the stalemate, of course, but he was killed in the process.

So when he died, did you assume command at that point?

Of the company? No. I just became one of the second lieutenants; I forget who it was that took over Gordon's place.

So some would advocate that the first major engagement that you had success with in North Africa was the Sened Station Raid. Would you agree with that?

Well, it wasn't our first success, but I think it was the first major success. You see, we landed and fought across North Africa into Tunisia and got into the Gafsa El Guettar area, and we gave them a pretty good whipping there. It was El Guettar that the Rangers had their first success, but I guess it wasn't success enough to be noticed. So then we were asked to infiltrate through the lines, three companies of us—A Company (and I was a platoon lieutenant in A Company), E Company, and F Company. And that was Len Dirks who commanded A, Max Schneider would have been commanding E, and Roy Murray would have been commanding F. So we infiltrated through the lines and then holed up on a hill, oh, I suspect 5 or 6 miles across the valley to the Sened Station. And we eyed them all that next day under camouflage and among the rocks, and evidently they didn't know we were there. That night was a perfect night for it because the moon didn't come up until about three or four o'clock in the morning. So we advanced across that valley in pitch dark and got to within 100 yards of Sened Station. And the guards that were guarding it, before they suspected that there was something going on out there, fired on us, but they fired over our heads. We didn't answer them until we got right in amongst them, with hand-to-hand combat, and I guess the mayhem is a matter of record. Then we took our wounded and carried them out. We actually had very few casualties. We got back to the French outpost about daybreak the next day, so we weren't wasting any time. And of course we were built that way. That's what we were trained to do. I suspect we were traveling at a rate of 5 or 6 or 7 miles an hour, in the dark, cross-country.

So as part of Ranger training, did they give you a lot of work specifically on reconnaissance as well as probing patrols. They spent a lot of time on that?

Oh yes, and night fighting was really our specialty. The fact that we were so good at night was probably the reason for our success.

Wasn't this the time where you had a close encounter and someone helped you out a little bit?

Yeah. You're talking about Little Tommy Sullivan. As we advanced that night and got in amongst them, I don't know how many I might have killed up until that time. But this particular night, as we advanced and this guy came out of the dark, and the flares were flying and I looked into his eyes. And I froze on the damned trigger. I couldn't pull the trigger, looking into that man's eyes. So I probably wouldn't be here except Little Tommy Sullivan thought my gun had jammed. That's what I told him had happened. And so he shot him. But he wasn't looking into his eyes. In fact, I dream about that, every now and then. Looking into that guy's eyes and listening to him as he was falling, "Momma mia, momma mia," as he was dying.

That probably was a very traumatic moment for you.

Well, hand-to-hand combat tends to have a lot of traumatic moments, more so than when you're shooting from this ridge to that ridge, because you don't really see who you're shooting. Or you see the shadows but you don't see the expressions or hear the words. Yeah, there's a difference. There's a difference in my own life.

For that event were you armed with a .45, or what did you have?

Yeah, I had a .45. It was a .45 I was pointing, but I also had an M1 rifle, because we had tried the carbines and they weren't adequate. So most officers refused the carbines and carried the M1s along with the enlisted men.

Did the officers ever carry Thompsons as well?

No, they had a Thompson machine gunner in every section, for that purpose. Our officers really would have no business with a Thompson, unless he was caught trying to defend something and that was available. I've used it. And there was a BAR man in every platoon.

Well, let's move on to the Djebel el Ank mountain pass. I understand that there was a key valley that was heavily lined with German troops. Do you remember that attack?

It was a pass, and it would secure the attack on El Guettar. They were coming through that pass, and the Allies were really outmanned and outgunned at that time. And we were the only real ground troops that we had in that area. I had been on patrol the night before in the valley to see whether we could attack them head on. Well, I reported that we couldn't attack them from the front. But Lt. Wojcik was the other one, and he went on the backside of the mountain and came up in behind, so the next night he led us that way. It was difficult, but the next morning at daybreak we came down off of that mountain screaming, right into the midst of them. As far as I know, we probably took a couple thousand prisoners, and we were probably four hundred men at the very most. So our surprise was complete, and they gave up in droves. I don't know how many we took, but it was several thousand. And that was the end of that, as far as the Germans were concerned.

Subsequent to that, my understanding was, the 1st Ranger Battalion was ultimately split into three battalions, so that the 1st Ranger Battalion consisted of C and D Companies; the 3rd, A and B Companies; and the 4th, E and F Companies.

Right.

From your perspective, how did this transition occur, from one Ranger battalion to three, why did they decide to do that, and was the conversion easy or did it take some adjustment?

None of the battalions that came after the original 1st Battalion were as good as the 1st Battalion. I think it would be easy for you to understand when you consider that here were two companies totaling 120 men that had to grow into a battalion of five hundred men again. So where did they come from, and how much time did we have to train them, and was our training as good, and was our supply of men as good? We couldn't weed them out, so every time that happened we were lessened.

So you had to train new replacements, and their training was not like the full-time training. You were fighting battles as well, and it's hard to get the same training in the field as you would have had in Scotland.

It sure is, plus the fact you don't have a chance to prove anybody. I mean really prove them. Now you can weed them out as far as their endurance is concerned, but you don't know how they're going to react to live fire. And it's amazing the different reactions you get, anything from blubbering, crying like a baby, to absolute maniacal behavior. Most Americans would eventually recover and do pretty well. But the first time you run into very serious combat, and if it's your first time in combat, it's entirely different. But it wasn't for us, because we were trained for it and we knew what to expect. But when they come in green and they don't know what to expect, it's a startling experience for them.

Do you think at that time you realized that deficiency? How did you get around that?

Well, I guess the basic formation would be the easiest answer there. In other words, we'd come back, and when we first started into the three battalions, we had to have three men to replace one. But we had no way of telling which ones were gonna be good, because size, build, athletic ability—none of that seemed to be worth a damn. It had to come from the inside of a man. Somehow he had control of his emotions, and when you first put men into combat, the first time they have no control. Now that sounds strange, but unless you are absolutely trained in specifics, you have very little control over a man who gets into serious combat for the first time. Especially if it's nighttime and hand-to-hand combat. And of course we were specialists at that.

Well, let's move on to Sicily. This was in the fall of 1943, and we could pick up with the Gela landing. Can you describe that?

Well, the 1st and 4th Battalions landed at Gela, and the 3rd Battalion landed at the same time at the sister port of Licata. The 1st and the 4th ran into more-serious resistance than the 3rd did, so as a result the 3rd just kept on going across the western part of Sicily, straight north to Palermo, leapfrogging down the north coast of Sicily. The Sicilian Campaign lasted thirty-eight days, and the 3rd Battalion fought all of those thirty-eight days. In fact, we said it was thirty-nine.

And I understand you were wounded during that campaign?

Slightly. It wasn't bad. It was the front of this leg and the back of this leg, right through here. It crippled me a little bit for a little while, but it wasn't serious. This one was hurt more than this one, because this went through the fleshy part of the leg.

Weren't you wounded a second time? In the helmet?

Yeah. That was the last day. We were supposed to take Cisterna di Latina and straddle the Appenine Highway, and we were 7 or 8 miles into their lines when we ran into a buzz saw. Instead of the headquarters of the Ramcke Parachute Brigade, we ran into five or six panzer divisions that had come in to strengthen their position, and they surrounded us. The battle was hot and heavy, and somewhere along there a shell exploded out here. I remember having given the order to shoot the guards, 'cause they had some of our men, and when that shell exploded, it went like this, and that's where all these scars came from.

No, I was thinking about after the Gela landing and one of your medics, Krise, helped you?

Ed Krise. I had several close calls, but wounded? I remember the incident, but I didn't get a Purple Heart for it. That was the time that the shell entered here and followed my skull around and came out the back, and that fist scar, all the way. That's still there to remind me of it. And if the weather is right, it's a good reminder.

Do you remember anything from the landing at Maiori? That was in September.

Maiori and Minori are twin cities on the coast. We landed relatively unopposed, about 5 or 6 or 8 miles away, and I suspect the height of the hills would have been 3,500 feet perhaps. But that was almost straight up from the harbor. We got up there and took them by surprise and took the Chiunzi Pass. So between Chiunzi Pass and Sorrento, we had our three battalions, or at the maximum, fifteen hundred men covering a front of 20 or 25 miles. So you know how thinly we were positioned to try to hold out. But we did. They attacked us every day, and we held them off for seven or eight or nine major counterattacks over a two-week period. The reason that they wanted out of that pass was because we overlooked the Apennine Highway. We had half-tracks with 75 mm guns on them, and we'd run them out of the pass and fire down on the convoys there and then come back by the time they could answer. And we didn't lose a single one of the half-tracks, but we sure caused a lot of damage. That's also where Little Tommy Sullivan was killed.

You remember that day?

Oh yeah, very well. By this time, I was a company commander and Tommy was first sergeant of one of my companies. I forget which one, but anyway he was on the right flank when they had a major counterattack. And during that time he was killed. I was within 100 yards of him. I was fighting in the same battle. It's just that he was hit and I wasn't.

Were you able to get to him fairly quickly?

Well, I didn't find out about it immediately, but when I called for him, then I was told. It was after the battle was over and we'd driven them off, and I wanted to know how we were standing. That's when I was told that he was killed.

Another disheartening moment, I'm sure, for you.

I had several of them, although you tried desperately not to get that close to anyone. But with Tommy Sullivan it was hard not to. He was my runner for a while, and he pulled my fat out of the fire even. He was with me as my messenger, and that was at a time that the radios weren't very trustworthy, so we had to have somebody like Little Tommy. I say "Little Tommy," but I suspect Tommy was 5 foot 8 or 9, with a stocky build. I called him Little Tommy Sullivan.

I know you lost a lot of your comrades throughout your campaigns, but it sounds like this may have been one of the ones that hurt you the most.

Well, there were three or four of them that'll be about the same. The one that bothered me the most probably was Ronnie Kunkle. He was my first sergeant. He was an Iowa boy, and he was always there when I needed him. When we got to where we had a lot of green kids we were trying to make soldiers out of, I would be at the head of the company and Ronnie was always bringing up the rear. Making certain that they weren't dropping out, because otherwise we'd lose them almost as fast as we'd get them, especially if it was the first combat.

I think he was hit at Cisterna, is that right?

Yeah, I was heading the company and he was bringing up the rear. I still don't know how I could get by where he was hit. It was a rather vulnerable place, and the tanks were coming in there. We were within machine gun range of the tanks, and it was the middle of a pitched battle. We were wiped out there, so it wasn't a picnic.

Right after the Gela landing, a Lt. Slim Campbell was also killed there as well? Do you remember that day?

That was at Porto Empedocle. The original ports at Licata and Gela were in such bad shape they couldn't be used. We couldn't supply the troops in those ports, and Porto Empedocle was probably 20 miles farther down the coast from there. It was a nice little port and, as far as we knew, was still intact. So we infiltrated through the lines and came in behind Porto Empedocle. But just about daybreak, about the time we were getting ready to hit, we were fired on, and Slim Campbell said, "I'll take care of it, Lieutenant." And he was killed in the process.

So as you moved on from there, the Venefro Valley was a pretty intense fight as well. Could you describe that battle, around Venefro Valley?

Well, I didn't think of Venefro as a valley. The valley of Naples opens up in a northerly direction, and it was a beautiful valley. The king's palace and playground was also in that valley, and it narrowed down to kind of a funnel shape. There were three high mountains that kind of plugged the funnel of that valley. So the Germans were looking down our throats, and we were supposed to take the area. Now, the infantry had been repulsed several times, so we climbed the first mountain and infiltrated in. But that's when we found out that there were two tops to the mountain. I don't know whether you know the story of Hans or not. That's where I met Hans. We were on this griffin 75 yards across. It was straight down here and straight down here. They were on one side and we were on the other. You'd have to be on top of a mountain to appreciate that, but voices carried up there, in that rarified atmosphere. You could hear a conversation from one peak to the other. So there we were, looking at each other. They couldn't get at us and we couldn't get at them, because they'd have picked us off like flies. But the same thing was true with them. They couldn't get at us. So there we sat, and Col. Darby asked me if I could go onto the next mountain. I said, "I don't have this one yet." He asked why, and I told him. He said, "Lieutenant, I don't give a damn what it's like up there. Take the other side of that mountain. We've gotta have it." I said, "Colonel, you better come up and have a look." He didn't come up, but he sent the company commander of the 509th Paratroop Brigade. So I was explaining to him where they had their strong posts and where they had their machine guns and what have you. And he kept looking over there and looking over there. And finally, with a great deal of bravado, he stood up and said, "Lieutenant, there's not a damned thing over there. Why haven't you taken the other side of this mountain?" And Hans stood up on the other side. Now, he didn't have to stand up, but he did. He stood up on the other side, nursing his burp gun. And he said, "He hasn't been here long, has he, Lieutenant?" Oh, boy, that colonel just went over backwards, like this. I'll never forget that. He said, "Now, I don't want you to tell Darby that." That was his reaction.

So you had a fairly good speaking relationship with Hans, didn't you?

Yeah, I kept trying to talk him into coming over for a steak dinner. I hadn't seen one in ages. Then I told him I'd introduce him to a couple of Red Cross girls. Now there again I heard we had them, but I hadn't seen them. But Hans was pretty cool. He knew what I was doing. He had a brother in the service, and Hans was being educated at the Hotel Management, Kellogg Center, at Michigan State. But when he went back home to see his folks, that's when he got called into the German army. He didn't have any choice because his brother and his folks would have suffered. So anyway, that's the story of Hans. Now, I had patrols in and around and behind, and I knew about how I could get to his position. But in doing so, I said if you can, take Hans alive. But, of course, in the middle of the night, how do you do that? And when daylight came, we had the other side of the mountain, but Hans was dead. So that wasn't a strange feeling at the time, 'cause you were dealing with death all the time, so I just promptly forgot Hans. You can't dwell on what could have been when you're in the middle of combat. You dwell on what's happening now. Now, I have to skip an awful lot of history now.

So after you were a POW and you escaped on the third attempt, you got over to Leipzig, Germany. Can you tell the story about Hans and his family?

They put me up in a room in a hotel in the headquarters. The headquarters of the 5th Army at that time was in a downtown hotel in Leipzig. So it didn't dawn on me right away, but then I got to thinking about it. Leipzig, hotel, Hans. So I got to digging and found out that when they took over that hotel, they bought it from an old couple who owned the hotel, and they moved out. I asked them to see if they could find out where they moved to. It turns out they were still in Leipzig, about three-quarters of a mile away. So I just took off on a scouting trip to see if I could find them, and I came across them in a little two-bedroom apartment. I knocked on the door, and here was this guy almost as tall as I was and very thin. And then she came to the door and she was just the opposite. She was about 5 feet 2 and about as big around as she was tall. They were quite a couple. So I started asking them questions, and they started asking me questions. Then, finally, one day Mrs. Shuller said, "You know something about our Hans, don't you?" So I explained the story, and then I felt badly telling them about it. But she came over and put her arms around me, and she wasn't more than a couple inches taller than I was, sitting in this chair. She put her arm around me and put her cheek down on my head and said, "That's all right, we understand. Thank you for telling us." The next time I went back they were gone, and I never have heard from them since. Of course they probably didn't have long to live, because Hans's parents would have been older than my parents. But that's the story of Hans.

Do you recall the San Pietro Campaign? I think that was where Earl Parish was hit.

Yeah, that was the mountains before San Pietro. We were attacking and had taken Hill 950. And we were advancing on Hill, let me say, 1250. It was twelve-something. They were lobbing hand grenades down on us, and one of them hit Earl Parish. But it didn't kill him, and I had two men carry him down to the foot of the mountain, but he was dead by the time they got him down. Earl had been my first sergeant at one time, and he got a battlefield commission. At that time we were giving the old-timers battlefield commissions because they were so much better than the new ones who were coming in there with no experience.

I believe you received the Silver Star for that action.

Yeah, we had to fight them back. We were under pretty heavy fire.

And I'm sure it was another hard loss for you to lose him as well.

It's hard to say that one was a harder loss than the other. Each time one of the old-timers left me, it was harder than it was the last time. Because the original five hundred men in the original 1st Battalion were becoming fewer and fewer. By old-timers, I'm not talking particularly about age, just about the original five hundred men. We were all still very young. When I came home after three years and seven months overseas, I was about to have my twenty-sixth birthday when I got married.

So that brings us now to January 22 at Anzio, and you were the company commander of E Company by then. Could you describe the Anzio landings?

The landings themselves were smooth as silk. I don't think we lost a man. If we did it would be accidental, something like a sprained ankle or drowning. And I had my company in the Apennine Hills overlooking Rome when they called us back. That would have been 20 miles back of their lines. But they called us back onto that beachhead that was never more than 8, 9, or 10 miles deep at any one spot. Since it was only around 20 to 25 miles along the beach, it was a very small area, with pretty concentrated troops in there. We were sitting ducks.

Did you have several firefights in the Alban Hills there?

No, we had none. We were completely successful. We were where we were supposed to be and had not been detected. We did our job and then we were called back, so we infiltrated back through the lines. We were still pretty good, even though by then the company was made up of probably two-thirds green men. But they had had enough combat by that time, so that I knew what I could count on.

Could you tell the story of the Little Angel?

Sure. When we were called back from the Alban Hills, we were a battalion, so they gave us an area that an ordinary battalion of fifteen hundred, two thousand men would cover. But we were probably at that time probably three hundred to three hundred and fifty men, with the casualties we had had. So we were spread pretty thin, and I was setting up my headquarters and deploying my men where I wanted them. I kept hearing somebody like a baby crying, but I thought it was one of my men breaking down. I figured I better find out what it was, so I went looking and came across this little girl, tear stained, trying to keep from crying, and she couldn't. When I picked her up, I guess that's all it took. She just put her arms around me and I was her security blanket from then on. The statue of My Little Angel, which is the only statue in Anzio, shows a little girl seven or eight years old, but Little Angel wasn't more than three or four at the very most. And a small three or four at that; probably more like two. But I became her security blanket.

How long did you take care of her?

A couple of days at least. And if I had to go to latrine, she went along with me. I washed her face, but even then she wouldn't let me put her down. So she was a fixture on me, in me, around me for those two or three days. It could have been three days, but it couldn't have been too long, 'cause we landed on January 22 and we were wiped out on January 30. So that gives you a time frame there that doesn't leave too much room for play. By then, the evacuation hospital had already come in and was being set up, so they sent a nurse up in a jeep to pick her up. I had told them the story, and they felt for the little girl. I can still see the nurse, but I have no idea what her name was. But she came up there in the jeep, and we had an awful time getting Little Angel from around my neck and into the arms of that nurse. She was still reaching out for me as the jeep went down the road. Well, that's one of those things you forget about. And then let's say fifty years later, we were back there for the fiftieth anniversary of Anzio in 1993. I walked down from the hotel we were in to that beach where we landed. There were probably twenty-five Rangers on this trip, old-timers. Now, by this time they had built a seawall up about this high, whereas it was just the beach when we took it. There was a cappuccino shop on that seawall, and so I ordered a cup of cappuccino and was sitting there. I looked across the road, and here was a statue. So I said, "I thought there weren't any statues in Anzio." The cappuccino shop owner said, "There isn't except for that one." So he told me the story, and I said, "Are you kidding me? Is it possible that that's my Little Angel?" And I told him my story. He said, "Well, that sure sounds like it is." So as far as I know, the only statue in Anzio was for my Little Angel. She was killed that night by an artillery shell, and that's why they built the statue to her and the nurse who came up to get her. I didn't know it until then. You know why I think that that's my Little Angel? Because how could those circumstances be the same and the statue be there? Of a little girl with peace doves flying around her head? And the sign says, "Angel of Anzio"?

So that brings us to Cisterna, and that's obviously a very traumatic period as well. The date was January 30, 1944. It's perhaps one o'clock in the morning and my understanding is that the intelligence had identified, from recon, an estimated division. But unfortunately there were a lot more German soldiers there than that. The 1st and 3rd Ranger Battalions were really sent out to infiltrate and secure Cisterna. Can you pick up the story from there?

Well, we followed the drainage ditch right up to the gateway to Anzio, and that gateway is still there. With all the shell marks and the pock marks. They've never taken it down. And Ranger Reel. Would that be "Road"? Ranger Reel runs right up to it. Right up alongside of it. So it's a place that I've seen since then, and they've preserved the gateway as it was when they wiped us out. Joey Larkin and I were the two old Ranger officers left by that time. We would trade off, so for one action I would be the lead company and Joe would be bringing up the rear, making certain there were no stragglers. Then the next time Joey would be the lead company and I would be bringing up the rear. So this particular day I was bringing up the rear when he radioed back. He said, "Bing, we're in trouble; can you help us out?" In retrospect, I've often wondered what would have happened if

I had done things differently. I was close enough to our own lines that I could have gotten most of my company out if I'd have gone back to our lines. But would I have been court-martialed for dereliction of duty in combat? Or if nothing else, censured for it? But I didn't even think of that 'cause he was in trouble, so I started passing everybody up. That's when I knew I had become the battalion commander, 'cause I passed Maj. Miller and saw that he had been killed and Joe was incapacitated. So I was in command of the company, and that's where all these scars happened. The shell exploded out here. It wouldn't have made any difference whether I lived or not. It was a hopeless situation. And so my receiving the wounds there that I did had nothing to do with the fact that we were wiped out there. We were completely, absolutely outgunned. I imagine there were a dozen tanks around us. How do you fight those with men armed only with a few bazookas?

And that's where Ronnie Kunkle was killed as well?
Ronnie Kunkle was killed there. There are two memories that I have, and Ronnie was one of them, when I was told that he was dead. The other one was when that shell exploded out here. I can remember falling to the ground, but I can never remember hitting the ground. So that's the most vivid memory to come out of that for me—my falling to the ground. The shell exploded out here. I remember that, but I could remember nothing after that for the next two or three months. They tell me I was walking around, and I have some memory of it, but only because they've filled me in with what happened. Not because I remember it.

And I understand the German forces were using Rangers as shields as well. Do you remember seeing that as well?
Yeah. They were using them as shields when the shell exploded, and in fact I had just given the order to pick off the guards. But in retrospect as I think about that situation, it wouldn't have worked because they had a new commander, sent in from West Point.

Do you believe that Col. Darby would have resisted attacking Cisterna, or do you think he was forced into attacking that position?
Well, none of us knew his S-2 was wrong, although Darby was nervous. He said, "Now, I'm nervous about this, because there are a lot more men out there than our S-2 says there is." But that's as close as I ever got to seeing him trying to second-guess the powers that be. He was a West Point man who followed orders.

You think that he was prohibited from doing his usually extensive recon of the area?
We didn't have the chance. Remember we landed on January 22, and you're talking about January 30. We didn't have time for much of anything except to follow orders.

And so I imagine with your amnesia, you don't even remember walking through Rome or anything?
I sometimes get the feeling that I do, but I think it's because I've seen the pictures of me walking with Chuck Shunstrom alongside of me. And it looked to me like I look normal. I might have looked dazed, but normal. That's the only picture I have of that time, and you've probably seen the same picture. That would have been outside of the Coliseum.

Do you think that there was a learning curve such that the more experience that a soldier had on the battlefield, the more they learned and the better tactics they had?
I think the most defining description of repeated battle exposure is the feeling each time that this'll be my last time. You get fatalistic, especially when all the men around you are being killed. So you get to thinking, "Well, my time has got to come. I've been lucky. I've been wounded several times. One of these time's it's gonna be serious." It's rather a relieving fatalism.

Now the question is, Does that make you more cautious, or does that give you that moment of hesitation that's critical?

I can't honestly answer that. I think that I became a better soldier as far as my men were concerned, but probably not as good a soldier as I was before all those experiences. You must understand, we've covered every battle of every campaign from the time it started in North Africa, until we were wiped out 10 miles back of the lines on Anzio. And there wasn't a battle that we missed. And so from days of combat, I doubt if there's anyone in the United States Army who has ever had more than I've had right now. So it's hard for me to answer some of those questions, because towards the last, I knew I wasn't gonna make it. In fact, the biggest surprise in my life was when I woke up and I thought, "Where am I?" I saw the slats on the bunk above me, and I didn't know if I was dead or alive. I was that confused. But then the GIs laughing and cussing off in the corner made me realize that I was still in this world.

Now, was that in the Stalag or was that on the train ride?

No, I was already in Oflag 64. I do not remember the train ride.

Do you think that it takes a while for you to respect a noncom or an officer, especially if there's a new officer that gets placed in the position and has very little experience?

Oh yeah, there definitely is a growing curve. Slim Campbell had a lot more respect after he was killed than he had before, 'cause he was relatively new. And one of the reasons he volunteered to take out that machine gun was because he wanted to prove to the men that he could do it.

So a good leader leads. What other attributes would you say would make a superior noncommissioned or commissioned officer, other than the fact that they're out there leading and they're doing by action?

I think that the most important attribute is control of emotions. Fear is gonna be there if you've got any sense at all. The realization that you're playing with death is going to be there. How you handle it determines what kind of an officer you are.

Any other attributes other than a confidence level and the calm, rational decision-making?

No, they come in all sizes. I've seen them from short to tall to pudgy to skinny. There seems to be no physical attribute that would define a good leader, although sometimes I think if you're in a position of command that your physical condition will lay the groundwork for respect or not.

You mentioned earlier Col. Darby, but are there any other leaders that you would like to focus in on?

Herman Dammer was not as colorful as Darby. Darby was a first-class showman. Dammer was a guy who quietly got things done. He was a reserve officer; he wasn't a West Point man. He came out of the same civilian life I did. He was probably two or three years older than I was, just enough to be a little more senior. Then there was Roy Murray, who if he was living now would be built about like you are. Max Schneider was built like you are. In fact, most of those leaders were not big, tall men, or imposing physical specimens. There was something else that set them apart, and I think it was their actions in their first battles and how they reacted under fire. When I stop to think of the men now, Max Schneider later commanded the 5th Battalion in Normandy. Roy Murray commanded the 4th Battalion that recovered from Anzio.

How about some of your noncoms? Would you single out one or two who were exceptional leaders?

Well, Ronnie Kunkle and George Kopanda stood out, as well as Earl Parish, who we commissioned from the ranks. They were men who could keep their poise under trying circumstances. I think poise was the main attribute of your good leaders.

Now, you were talking about the fact that the Rangers represented an elite force and continue to do so. Are there one or two things that you would say really makes you a Ranger?

I'm going to say that the thing that makes for a good Ranger is the fact that they don't know when to say, "I've had enough."

Tenacity?

That's a good word, because we've seen it so many times. When you get into combat, no matter how many times you've been successful in combat, there comes a time when some of your better officers collapsed, mentally and physically. That's quite a challenge, to lead a group of men when sometimes you know that you're gonna lose a bunch of them by a decision you make. That's not an easy thing to do. But you do it, and if you can overcome the desire to feel sorry for yourself, then you become a pretty good officer. But when you start feeling sorry for yourself, you might as well quit.

Do you think that a self-preservation mechanism for officers and leaders is to rationalize and say, "Look, I may lose a couple men, but if I don't do this battle, somebody else is going lose twenty or thirty"?

That often happened. All the time you're in combat, you're rationalizing. You're rationalizing, "Well, the next one might be me." And you get to the place where with me, when we went into Anzio, I wasn't afraid. I was beyond that. My only reaction to that was, well, this is it. And I'd kind of been waiting for it. I don't know whether you can understand that. That's kind of hard to explain. But there comes a time where fear doesn't enter the picture. There comes a time when you realize that this is what you've been working for, but a little more than you've been asking for, and you're not gonna make it this time. I think it's then you start becoming a good leader.

So at some point you just realize the inevitable: it is going to be my time, so the sooner I realize that, the better a soldier I'll be if I focus on my objective and stop worrying.

Yep. Because when you first get into combat, you don't expect to die. I know that's hard to believe. But you don't expect it, and then each time you realize that you've beaten the odds. And then it gets worse and worse. Then all of a sudden, the worry quits. I can't explain that time when all of a sudden I became nonafraid. I started out being gung-ho. Then with each action after that, I became more leery of the fact that I was pressing my luck. And then all of a sudden it kind of levels off and you don't give a damn, because you don't know anything else. There comes a time when you don't know anything else but kill or be killed.

So in a sense you've become emotionally numb?

Yes, that's it. You become emotionally numb.

I read a little bit about your POW experience at Oflag 64, and that was approximately in February of '44. I know that it was previously a girl's college, but it was an officer's camp and it had certain amenities that were nicer than some of the other POW camps. They had a greenhouse, a library, a tailor shop, a gym. There were personal exercises and guys played baseball, but there were pretty severe conditions as well?

Yeah, it was, but those things were because of the men involved. You see, we were all officers, and so you know that they had to be a little higher caliber. So in this officer rank, you would have a chaplain, which you wouldn't have as an enlisted man. You would have the captains that were leading companies, and the colonels that were in command. They were all leaders in their own right, and so just the fact that this type of man was all around you would have to be a rather motivating factor. Some of them were teachers, and I took the best physics course, far better than any I got in college, in a prison camp.

So you made the best of the circumstances. But the bottom line is, you had very tough conditions. You didn't have heat in the winter.

Oh, no. Your shower was just as cold as you could imagine it. And most of the time you didn't stand under the shower; you took a sponge bath. Now, once in a great while they'd give us enough fuel so that we could heat the water, and we could limit the time that they could take a hot shower. But oh, those were precious times. Once every couple of months.

And could you describe a typical meal for a given day?

They'd bring us into the dining room every day at noon for the one meal for the day. Once in a while they'd furnish enough oatmeal so we could have a dish of oatmeal, but the mainstay of course would be potatoes. If you got at the beginning of the line, you could get a pretty good potato. At the tail of the line, you probably got the peels, as you could imagine. That's why you always had a different head of the line each day. Other than that, the only thing we had were the Red Cross parcels, which had 7 pounds in them. There'd be a pound can of margarine, half a pound of cheese, a pound can of powdered milk. You get the idea. We were supposed to get them every week, but it wound up being more like one every seven weeks. It was unusual if we got more than two in a couple-month period.

Did they ever treat you nice on Christmas Day or anything? Did they ever give you anything special?
Well, we'd try. They didn't treat us nice. Oatmeal was a favorite and potatoes were a favorite. Those were the two things they seemed to have plenty of.

And I know you were in the camp on Christmas of 1944. Do you remember that? Can you describe what you did that day, on Christmas Eve?
Yeah. We had a stage play and a musical. We had a good orchestra, so we had a musical that night, and I sang in that musical. We had a pretty good time, and everybody enjoyed the show immensely. There were some former drama students who led and make us better.

Did you have a Christmas tree that Christmas?
No, no. And then the next day or so, we were marched out of the camp, because between then and the end of the war, it wasn't very long. The Russians were advancing, so they marched us cross-country on a death march. And it was from that that I finally escaped for good.

Was that was your third or fourth escape attempt?
Third. The one that was successful was the third one. My second one was my worst memory. It was Kenny Kerfoot, Tony Leibertor, and me. Kenny Kerfoot was a Oklahoma Indian, Tony Liebertor was from West Virginia, and then I was the third party. Our plan was to get to the Russian lines, but we knew we didn't have a chance of getting through the Germans in a pitched battle, since none of us could speak either German or Russian. So we holed up in a potato cellar out in the middle of a field and existed on raw potatoes. Then one day, a twelve- or thirteen-year-old boy jumped into our potato cellar to get potatoes for his family, and we scared the living daylights out of him. He jumped back out and ran and told his folks. But then he came with his dad the next day, and from then on, every day we got a hot bowl of soup that the boy would bring us. It would be potato soup, but it was hot and it was tasty and they'd have some onion and some flavoring in it. But then, wouldn't you know that the battle waged back and forth, and the Germans put their command post in our potato cellar. So there we were, and the boy was with us. So they rounded up the boy's family and lined them up in front of us and started one at a time. They killed the two girls first and the boy third. And the mother of course was raving. She wasn't with it, and she was on her knees when they shot her. And the father was a raving maniac first, then all of a sudden he got quiet, and they shot him. And to this day, if things are right in my life, that comes back to haunt me.

Do you know what town you were close to when that happened?
Well, I would say south of Danzig, about 50 kilometers. Out in the middle of a field. I don't know of any town close, but that would have been fairly close to Posen. It was spring, March or April probably. Close to the end of the war.

What would you say would be the greatest lessons you learned from your military experience?
To accept your vulnerability. I think it's something that most of us in this world do not do anymore. We don't accept our weaknesses. We fight them.

What comments or pearls of wisdom would you give future generations?
You need to have a physical and mental toughness. And I think the mental toughness is the greater of the two. If you can overcome fear, the emotion of fear and the weakness of fear, you can do anything.

I'd like to ask you about your recollections of Major (then Lt. Col.) Darby. Do you remember meeting him, and when was that?
Probably at the time I was being interviewed on whether I wanted to be a Ranger or not, in a Quonset hut at Carrickfergus, Ireland.

Do you think he asked some tough questions?
I didn't think they were so tough. He asked me if I thought I could take it. He asked me if I thought I was a good man. I remember my answer 'cause he laughed. I said, "How good do you want?"

So after that, you joined the Rangers and went through the training. Can you describe some of that training for us in Ireland?
Yeah. In Ireland they tried to run us through what they called speed marches. But they were nothing compared to what the British Commandos put us through. They were American speed marches, which were not as tough as the ones the British ran us through.

So the specialized training really occurred probably in Achnacarry, Scotland?
That's where it started, at Achnacarry.

Okay, and that was the British Commandos training center. You mentioned earlier that your leaders trained with you. They didn't train you but they trained with you?
They trained with us, that's right. Now, they lived in the Cameron Clan castle, and we lived in tents on the grounds. But otherwise they went through the same training and the same stamina drills. They had to climb the same cliffs and rappel down the same ropes, so the officers were weeded out. Probably a greater percentage of the officers failed than the enlisted men.

So it was not only exercising, but it was also cliff climbing, rappeling, amphibious landings, obstacle courses, swimming with packs. Can you describe how they taught you how to cross rivers?
Any damned way you could get across. Now, if you could run a rope from the top of one tree on one bank to the other bank, then it was easy. You could use your toggle rope and slide across. But other than that, you got across any way you could. In fact, the first death in the Rangers was a drowning when we were swimming with packs.

Now, when you were training, both in Ireland and in Scotland, do you remember what your typical gear was?
Well, that's where I heard the cutoff leggings began. Your full leggings up here would slow you down too much, so we cut them off below the muscle, and that became a trademark for the Rangers. The cutoff leggings. The Corcoran boots, the jump boots, came later. They caught up with us about Sicily. I'm guessing at that. I can't remember exactly where it was.

Did you train more in HBTs or did you train more in wools and M41 jackets?
Whatever we had. In North Africa we were in fatigues, 'cause they were summers.

Did you have full gear? Caps? Or did you have helmets? Did you have a full set of Garand belt and web gear?
Well, you can see pictures of us in the old-fashioned helmet. But we introduced the new-fashioned helmet too. So we had both.

So when you were in training, you could have been light in a given exercise, or you could have had full gear on, depending on the situation.
Whatever it was.

And were you issued Garands or carbines?
M1s, rifles.

M1 Garands? Okay, and .45s for the officers?
For the officers. And we had BARs, Browning Automatic Rifles. That was our automatic piece. We didn't have machine guns to begin with. And later we also developed a .30-caliber mortar section.

I know you were an athletic individual at the time, but do you think that the training that you got in Ireland and Scotland pushed you to the brink? Was it that severe, or was it easy enough for you because you had a history of being athletic?
The only time I personally felt pushed physically was the first speed march. And those where you would go as fast as you could march. Then you'd double-time for another quarter of a mile, which was a blessing because it eased your legs, because walking that fast tended to tighten your muscles. So that was the hardest part of the training, as far as I was concerned. The rappeling, the cliff climbing, and the obstacle courses were kind of SOP.

So how did your relationship with Maj. Darby evolve?
I guess my immediate reaction to Darby was if you can do it, I can do it. So that was sort of our relationship. I was a first sergeant at the time, and then when he was allowed a sergeant major, I became his sergeant major. As far as I know, we were the only battalion that's ever had a sergeant major, since I think they're regimental? But he had enough pull so he got a sergeant major. And I was it. When we landed in North Africa, he overshot the landmark and I was with him, so I called his attention to it. I said, "Col. Darby, you've gone too far." I still remember that look. I said, "Why don't you go back and check?" Max Schneider and Col. Murray were in the two companies back of us. The first team would have been Companies A, B, and C, and they landed at the fort. The second team was Companies D, E, and F, and they were taking the high ground. Darby was leading D, E, and F, and Schneider and Murray were the first two companies following us. I said, "Why don't you go back and check with Max and Roy?" So that's what he did, and he found out I was right. That was the night of November 8, and on November 10 I was a second lieutenant. But one of the company commanders had to get killed to make an opening for me. But that tells you that that night left an impression on him.

So did you have an immediate respect for him, or did it take a while for him to earn your respect?
What kind of respect do you have for any officer you meet the first time? You're going to thumb your nose at him. And I suspect I looked down my damned nose at Col. Darby. Maj. Darby at the time. The turning point was during training, when I found out he could do anything I could. I saw that he wasn't expecting his men to do anything that he couldn't do. It's a gradual thing. It isn't something that happens overnight. He was a good man, and the thing I liked about him was he didn't expect his men to do anything he couldn't do himself.

Did he have a high bar for his men? Did he expect a lot of discipline?
Oh yes. As evidenced by the fact that we started with several thousand men, and we wound up with five hundred men. So the bar was pretty high.

Was he really by the book?
Oh yeah, he was gonna make West Point a part of all of us. He was a strong taskmaster, and weaklings had no place in Darby's army.

So insubordination in any form would not be acceptable?
No. No. He was boss.

But if he knew that one of his subordinates was right about something, he would give in for the benefit of his soldiers.
Yeah, he'd make you a second lieutenant like he did me. I don't know how else to answer that.

So if you were right, he was a big-enough man to say that he was wrong.

There was nothing little about Col. Darby. Nothing little about him at all. I think he had some exaggerated idea of what was expected of him at the beginning, but he grew into his pants just like the rest of us did. And the British had no place for weaklings. You must understand that the British put the biggest and the best and the toughest Scotch trainers (and most of them were Scotch, not English) over us. They tried desperately to weed us out, and as a result we wound up breaking every record they ever set. They got hold of a bunch of guys who, when they knew what was expected of them, were kind of tough to beat. When we went back for the first reunion, some of those trainers were there, and they told us, "The thrill of our lifetime was training you Yanks. You were something special." And I guess we had to have been, to have been there.

Now, over time your relationship with Col. Darby evolved. And would you say that it was always strictly business, or did you or he ever go into anything personal?

We were never anything social at all. It was strictly Col. Darby and Sgt. Maj. Evans.

Did he ever ask your opinion about something? Did that evolve to the point where he respected you?

Oh yeah, but he did that with any of his officers. If they had a point, they could talk to him. He was not iron clad. He listened as well, but he made the final decision. For example, when it came time to go in at Cisterna, Les Kness and I, two former enlisted men, said, "Colonel, there's a lot more out there than you've been told. We have both had patrols out in there." And he said, "Lieutenant, those are my orders; those are your orders." And so we went to our demise. That's one of the times I was right and I wish I hadn't been.

It sounds like the decision was made above his level.

Yep, it was. There was nothing I could have done to change that. In fact, I tried. I told him there were a lot more troops out there than he had been told, and Les Kness backed me to the hilt. 'Cause I'd been in amongst them. Oftentimes as I've thought about that, I had the impression that he knew I was right but that he had been overturned. The same way that he was overturning me.

Can you recall going over the battle plans for Cisterna?

We landed in Anzio on the twenty-second of January, and on the thirtieth of January we were annihilated. So you see, in that time we'd been in the Alban Hills and back. We had several days of combat in our own area before we marched into Cisterna di Littoria. So you're only talking an eight-day period there. It sounds like a course of war, but it was only eight days. So you can't blame him. He had his orders, he gave us our orders, and I still didn't know what they were doing.

But unfortunately, instead of one division, there were several.

We were to take Cisterna di Littoria, which straddled the Apennine Highway that fed the Nazi troops at Cassino. It was as simple as that. But it didn't work.

Do you recall the weather conditions that day?

No. Must not have been too wet because we were going up a drainage ditch, and in that lowland it would have been flooded. So it must have been the dry season. That's as best I can tell you as far as the weather was concerned.

Was there any turning point in your relationship with Col. Darby as you went through the various campaigns in North Africa, Sicily, and, ultimately, Italy?

I think there was a legitimate exchange of respect. I think he had as much respect for me as I had for him.

You think that peaked in North Africa or Sicily?

Who knows where it peaked. All I know is that by the time that we got to the real fighting in Tunisia, we were almost on the same level all the time. He was the boss and he told us what to do, but he listened. And he knew that we knew what he knew. Except for the S-2 intelligence, which he had access to and we didn't.

So do you think he had a fairly open-door policy with any of his commissioned officers, to be able to come in and talk to him any time about issues?

I think the open-door policy would have been reserved for perhaps a half a dozen officers. Roy Murray, Max Schneider, Dammer, myself, and later on Les Kness. That might have kind of been the inner circle.

Did you ever see him ever bump heads with any of his subordinate officers?

There was no bumping heads with his subordinate officers. If Col. Darby said, "This is the way it is," that's the way it was. There was no arguing with him. Now, he would listen, but when he spoke, that was it.

Did you ever see him have to reprimand someone?

Well, I guess I came as close to being reprimanded as anyone when he said, "Lieutenant, those are my orders; those are your orders." That's the way it would come across.

In your leadership position, did you ever see your men question his integrity or his decisions?

Not out of the original 1st Battalion. There was none of that. He was one of us, and we knew he knew what he was doing. We knew he was good and he was a genuine West Pointer, which didn't brook a lot of argument.

Would you say he was very formal, by the book, ordered, calm, rational? How would you describe him?

West Point. That's the best answer I can give you. He was all business. Those of us underneath him never saw him in a lighter moment. Now, Col. Dammer did, Max Schneider did, and Roy Murray did, but none of the other officers ever saw him let down. If there was a social moment, like when Ella Fitzgerald came (he dated Ella Fitzgerald), Max and Roy were the ones who would be with him. None of the rest of us ever saw him at the lighter moments.

So they had a personal relationship with him? He would perhaps confide in them?

Well, he didn't confide in anyone. You put kind of a light touch on Darby, but there wasn't a light touch there. He was military. Everything he did was military. Everything he did was by the book, and if it wasn't by the book, it was by Darby. You didn't argue with him or question him. You might ask if that's all the information or something that was pertinent, but when he spoke his mind, you did what he said you were supposed to do. There were no questions asked. I knew that last day that we were going into a buzz saw. I'd seen enough of it, and Les Kness and I mentioned it that night. Darby told us, "Those are my orders; those are your orders." And that's all there was to it. There wasn't any psychological innuendos at all. That was all there was to it.

How about the military protocols. If he walked into a room, was everybody to stand up?

You snapped to attention, and you knew damned well he wanted you to come to attention. There were no ifs, ands, or buts about Col. Darby. He was all man, and he could back anything he did.

So there was a high level of discipline? If he saw a soldier with his boots unshined, or not dressed properly, would he come down on that?

Let me give you the other side of that. When Patton got us on the north shore of Sicily, he really read us the riot act because we were unshaven and dirty. Col. Darby stepped in and said words to the effect [of] "General, if you want to know how they feel and why they look like they do, get in their boots, not yours."

Did you ever see any other interactions like that with any other superior officers, where he had to stand up for his men or stand up for his position?

Oh, the Rangers were pretty fair that way. If you had a patrol out and they came back and reported to him, he went by what they did. And not by what you felt, but by the information they brought back. There was a deep respect for Darby, and Dammer, I might add. You haven't mentioned him. For we had just as deep a respect for Dammer as we did for Darby.

How would you compare and contrast Dammer to Darby?

Two entirely different personalities. Dammer was tall, lean, and very reserved. Darby was all up front. Two different styles altogether. If Darby had something on his mind, you'd hear it. And Dammer, you might not hear it right away. But Darby, no. When he had something to say, it came out.

Now, earlier you told me that one of the greatest features of a good field leader is to be able to maintain a calm state in a setting of severe circumstances. Do you think that Darby encapsulated that?

Oh yeah. I heard him lose his cool in a battlefield situation only once. That was the last day, when we reported that we were being wiped out. He cried.

You heard him cry?

On the radio, when he knew that it was all over with.

Who was the commanding general? Whom did he directly report to?

At the time, Mark Clark.

So we can assume that that's probably where the orders came from.

Yes. No other general in that area is gonna take over and tell Col. Darby what direction to take. It was probably Gen. Clark. It might have been someone else, but I wouldn't have known who it was. He was pretty strictly West Point, so he followed his orders like all the rest of us. But he wasn't afraid to speak his mind if he thought they were wrong. And because of his position with the Rangers, they listened.

Getting back to the incident with Gen. Patton, do you recall what Patton's response to that was?

Well, I wasn't there at the time, but I understand he took it, that's all. I think he felt he had it coming, from what I could understand. Now, I'm not talking from personal information there, that's secondhand information.

Of the core circle of four or five individuals that you said were fairly close to Darby, how many of those individuals were West Pointers?

None. Roy Murray was probably the closest to him of any of them. Max Schneider was a reserve officer out of the 34th Division. Come to think of it, Roy Murray was 168th Infantry commander, and that's out of the 34th Division. So some of his trusted officers came right out of Minnesota, South Dakota, and northern Iowa. Never West Point boys. I don't know whether that's just coincidence, but it makes you wonder.

So when you were encircled in dire straits in Cisterna and you heard him cry on the walkie-talkie, was that the last time you heard from him?

Yep. That was the last I heard.

If you were to describe Col. Darby, what would be the best adjectives that you could use as a combat leader?

That he didn't ask his men to do anything he couldn't or wouldn't do. There aren't many like that, not even in today's Army.

Would you use the word "decisive"?

Well, he was definitely that, yes. When he made up his mind, that was it. Right or wrong, that was it. And disciplined and tenacious.

Ordered?

I don't know ordered nearly as much as I think you imply, because I think that if he disagreed with the book, you'd hear about it.

Would you use the word "empathetic"?
No, he was strictly Darby. If his men didn't like what he was telling them, to hell with them. Empathetic is not the word.

Would supportive be a good word for him?
Oh yeah. He was supportive all the way with his men, as long as they were doing what he told them to do.

But you would not use the word "severe"? Harsh?
Oh yeah. He was severe, but who in his position wouldn't have been? He did what had to be done. It was simple as that. All these other things you're talking about came because he was doing what he thought had to be done, and to hell with West Point. To hell with anything else. To hell with his leaders. If it had to be done, he'd do it. That was his forte. He did what he felt was right at the time.

If there's something you could write for his epitaph, what would that be?
"He saw his duty and done it noble."

PART I PHOTO SECTION

British Commandos conducting training with US Rangers

US Rangers cooking "iron" rations

The weapons Rangers trained with, *from left to right*: 1903 Springfield with grenade launcher, 60 mm mortar, British antitank rifle, Thompson submachine gun, light machine gun, hand grenade, Browning Automatic Rifle (BAR), 81 mm mortar, and M1 Garand rifle

Rangers attend chapel in July 1942.

Rangers training in all conditions

Rangers and Commandos clean weapons after training.

Rangers practicing barbed wire infiltration.

Rangers training on opposed landing course

Ranger crawling through barbed wire

Ranger Instructor guiding Ranger training for Barbed Wire Infiltration

Ranger training with bayonet

Jumping from the 18-foot tower

Log drills

Scaling and stream crossing combined

Stream fording

Stream crossing under fire

Crossing with toggle rope

Opposed crossing under fire

Opposite below and above: Opposed crossing under fire

Opposed landing-under-fire training (the following pictures are from the same sequence)

Maj. W. O. Darby

Rangers in training camp

Rangers on speed march

Yet another speed march

Rangers charge across field in assault course during training in Achnacarry

Ranger battalion doctor

Rangers in daily formation

142352
2 E 387

Ranger sniper in North Africa

Rangers exercise aboard ship en route to North Africa.

Rangers rehearsing amphibious assaults before Operation Torch

Rangers embarking in assault craft

Rangers on a road march in North Africa

Rangers on training maneuvers in North Africa

Rangers training replacements in North Africa

Rangers training in North Africa

Rangers still do speed marches in North Africa.

Rangers conducting amphibious training in North Africa

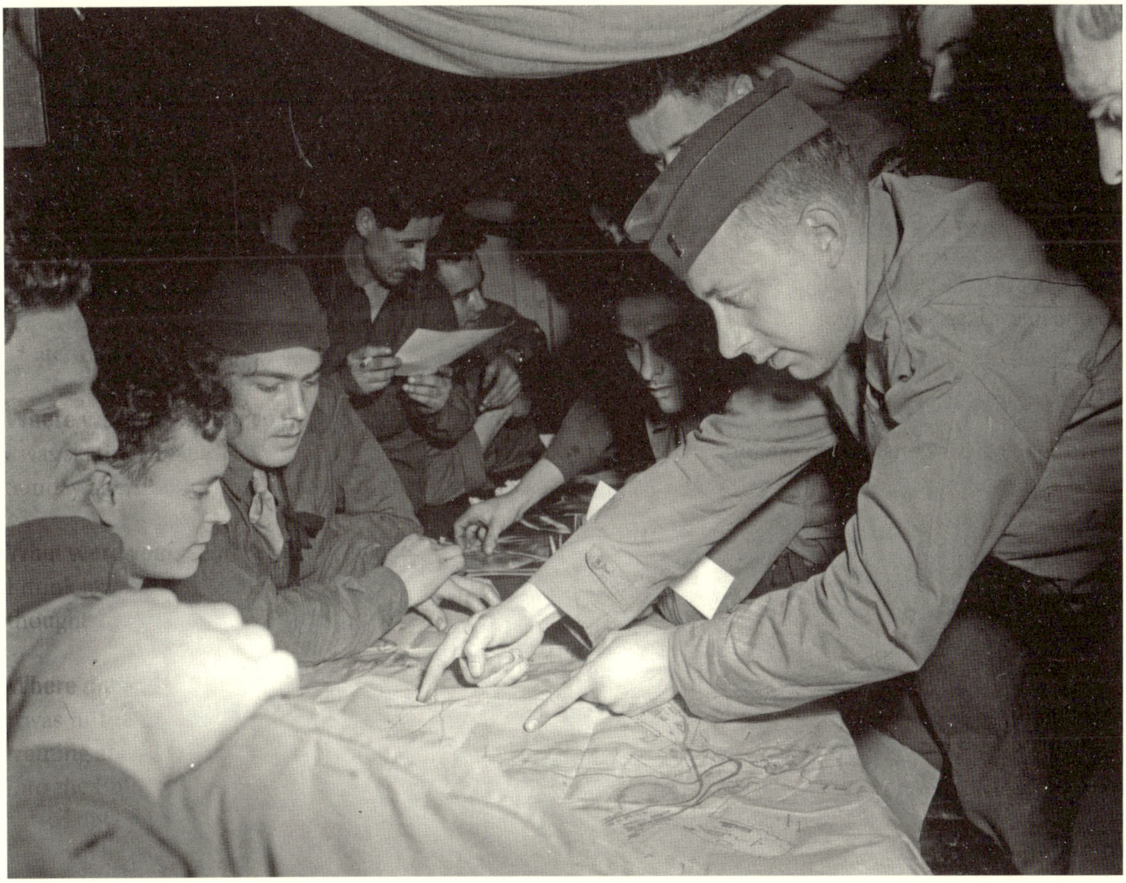

Rangers reviewing a map before Arzew

Rangers clearing enemy gun emplacements in Algiers

Rangers advance against German positions in Italy.

Ranger prepares to throw grenade at German position in Italy.

British Gen. Harold Alexander visits Rangers in Italy.

Rangers use local transportation in Anzio.

Rangers providing cover fire for an advance against Germans in Italy

Rangers advancing through an Italian village near Salerno

Rangers moving up in Italy

Rangers move to assault position in Italy.

Rangers attack German positions in Italy.

Rangers aboard LCIs in Baia, Italy

Brig. Gen. Teddy Roosevelt pins the Silver Star on Capt. Frederick Qaam as observed by Col. Darby.

2ND AND 5TH BATTALIONS

PART II

CHAPTER 7

RANGERS IN WESTERN EUROPE

On February 1, 1943, another Ranger battalion was created. Applicants from the 29th Infantry Division formed the battalion at Achnacarry, consisting of A, B, and HQ Companies. Interestingly, they were issued the new style of US paratrooper boot, which they were just as proud of as the paras. The new battalion commander was Lt. Col. Randy Millholland, who of course wanted this to be an independent battalion operating similar to the 1st Battalion. This battalion was designated as the 29th Ranger Battalion but was also referred to as the 2nd Ranger Battalion.

Soon after, another Ranger battalion was formed at Camp Forrest, Tennessee, on April 1. This was composed of A through F Companies and an HQ company. This battalion was officially designated the 2nd Ranger Battalion and absorbed many veterans of the 1st. Maj. James Rudder became their commanding officer, and they conducted training at Camp Forrest and in Florida before departing for Ft. Dix en route to the European theater of operations (ETO). When taking over, Maj. Rudder made this promise to the Rangers: "First, I'm going to make men out of you. Then, I'm going to make soldiers out of you, and, then, I'm going to make Rangers out of you."

The Army determined it did not need two 2nd Ranger Battalions, so the 29th was disbanded. The reasoning behind this choice was that the battalion in the US was trained better, which was questionable; both battalions were well trained. Many of the men who had formed the 29th Battalion kept their Ranger insignia when they returned to the 29th Division.

On September 1, 1943, another battalion was formed at Camp Forrest, designated the 5th Battalion. This battalion received more training in divisional-level exercises and physical fitness, similar to the paratroops. In fact, the requirements to join the 5th Battalion were the same as the paratroops. This required, among other things, being between eighteen and thirty-two years of age, with 20/40 vision, and the capability of "being developed into an aggressive individual fighter with great endurance."

The training at Camp Forrest was intended to mirror the training at Achnacarry. There was the usual obstacle course with live explosives and live rounds, 5- and 9-mile speed hikes, and 25-mile hikes on Saturday. If you fell out of a hike, you were out of the Rangers.

In November 1943, the 5th began its training at Ft. Pierce, Florida, as the 2nd Battalion had done. This involved training in amphibious operations and, interestingly, culminated with an "attack" on the town next to the fort. By December they were in Ft. Dix, following 2nd Battalion.

In December, the 2nd Battalion arrived in England to begin training for the invasion of Europe, which was planned for sometime the following year. On January 18, the 5th Battalion arrived as well. By April the battalions were training together, with the 5th being led by Maj. Max Schneider. Schneider was an experienced Ranger commander, having participated in the African, Sicilian, and Italian invasions. The training now included a focus on scaling cliffs. The Rangers also trained at the newly created US Army Assault Training Center, which focused on assaulting fortified and defended beaches. They also attached fire engine ladders to amphibious DUKWs,[18] giving clues as to what their mission would be.

In May, the two battalions were combined into one unit, designated Provisional Ranger Group, under the overall command of newly promoted Lt. Col. Rudder. They were assigned to V Corps for the upcoming invasion. On May 31, the Rangers were subjected to a German bombing raid but suffered no casualties.

DAY OF DAYS

By June 1944, the US and British forces were ready for the long-awaited invasion of Europe. The plan, dubbed Operation Overlord, called for landing at five separate beaches along the Normandy coastline. These were code-named Omaha, Utah, Gold, Juno, and Sword. Of the two US beaches, Omaha and Utah, the Rangers were destined to land at Omaha at a place called Pointe du Hoc.

Ranger Force B consisted of C Company of the 2nd Ranger Battalion, which was to land with the 29th Division at Omaha Beach. They would be at the right, or western, flank of the invasion beach, with the 29th division on their left, and the 1st Infantry Division on the left flank of the 29th, farther east.

Pointe du Hoc (referred to as Pointe du Hoe on maps at the time) was a prominent height jutting out to sea between Utah and Omaha Beaches. It was a key tactical position, and the Germans had placed six 155 mm guns there. This position allowed them to place heavy fire on both US beaches. They were well defended. The Pointe was accessible only from inland, since the seaward side consisted of sheer cliffs rising from the ocean. Scaling these cliffs and destroying these guns was a mission made for the Rangers. Ranger Groups A and C, under Lt. Col. Rudder, consisting of 5th Battalion and the remainder of 2nd Battalion, were assigned this mission.

For Pointe du Hoc, the plan was for Force A, consisting of 2nd Battalion's E and F Companies, to scale the cliffs and assault from the east while D Company assaulted from the west. They were to destroy the battery and then move inland to control the coast road between Omaha and Utah. Force C, consisting of 2nd Battalion's A and B Companies, and the rest of 5th Battalion were offshore as reserve.

To scale the cliffs, the Rangers would be equipped with rocket-propelled ropes with grapnels, rope ladders, and ladders borrowed from London fire departments. They had already been trained in climbing as part of the Ranger training regimen.

One June 6, 1944, the Rangers joined 120,000 other Allied soldiers for the assault on occupied Europe. The order of the day for the Rangers ended with "Good luck, God bless, and shoot to kill." One Ranger, in 5th Battalion S-3A (assistant to S-3 officer), overslept and almost missed his landing craft! He must have been the only man on the morning of June 6 able to sleep.

As can be expected, the landings did not proceed according to plan. C Company, at Omaha Beach, encountered the first of many problems when one of their assault craft foundered, causing the loss of several Rangers. Upon landing on the beach, C Company found itself in the nightmare that was Omaha Beach that morning. Unknown to Allied planners, Omaha was defended by the veteran German 352nd Infantry Division, not the second-rate units believed to be there. The 352nd had cut its teeth on the Eastern Front and made the most of the formidable defensive positions in Normandy. C Company landed at 0645 and within minutes suffered nineteen killed and eighteen wounded. Finding almost impassable defenses in front of them, the Rangers scaled cliffs on the western edge of the beach instead of heading directly inland as planned. They then destroyed a German position in a house that overlooked the beach, and over the next few hours flanked the other German positions. While C Company contributed greatly to the eventual if costly success on Omaha, at the end of D-day they were too exhausted and depleted in number to affect a linkup with the rest of the Rangers at Pointe du Hoc.

At Pointe du Hoc, there was a half-hour delay between the landing and the preliminary bombardment, enabling the Germans to be prepared for the attack. This also caused a change in the plan: all three companies would now land on the eastern flank of the position. The Rangers landed between 0705 and 0708. Against heavy German resistance, the Rangers scaled the cliffs and engaged the Germans in their defensive bunkers around the gun positions. Due to German resistance while the Rangers were climbing and the somewhat random position of ropes and ladders, the effect was that the positions were attacked from multiple directions by many small groups of Rangers acting on their own initiative. This resulted in the position being taken within thirty minutes despite fierce resistance and enfilading fire from defensive bunkers. However, the guns were not there—either they had been moved to avoid aerial bombardment or had not been placed yet; the exact reason for their absence in their emplacements has never been determined. The Rangers then moved inland to secure the Vierville-Grancamp road, the coastal road between Omaha and Utah. The Germans had not expected a cliff assault, but as the Rangers moved inland, German resistance stiffened, with numerous small-unit actions.

Force C landed at Omaha Beach, but farther to the east than was planned. Lt. Col. Schneider made this call as he witnessed the carnage inflicted on Task Force B. They absorbed the remains of C Company and moved toward Pointe du Hoc. Meanwhile, 1Sgt. Len Lomell and Sgt. Jack Kuhn of Force A had found the guns meant for the Pointe in a field, and destroyed them. Then they and the rest of Force A set up blocking positions on the road. Elements of Force C, specifically Company A under Lt. Parker, was able to make it to Pointe du Hoc, albeit with only twenty-three men. They were able to do this by crawling along the edge of the cliff between Omaha Beach and Pointe du Hoc, too low to be spotted by Germans, This, however, did not effect a linkup between the Pointe and the invasion beaches.

Force C fought off desperate German counterattacks that night at Omaha, where the remainder of the 352nd attempted to throw invading force back into the sea. However, they were not able to link up with Force A, which was forced to pull back from the road in places due to German pressure throughout the night.

The Rangers had succeeded in their D-day missions, contributing to the day's victory. In a battle totaling over 120,000 Allied men, a few hundred Rangers had made their presence felt.

By June 7, the Rangers had suffered so many losses that they began to consolidate units. The 2nd Battalion was composited into one group since the companies had been so depleted. A relief column from Force C moved toward Pointe du Hoc to effect the linkup, as Force A was attempting to get more supplies from landing craft over the cliffs at Pointe du Hoc. By June 8, the linkup occurred, and the Rangers started moving to capture Grancamp. Grancamp was so named because it was the site of the large campsite of William the Conqueror's army on its way to England in 1066, an invasion headed in the other direction. Now it was a town defended by the Germans and was the location of another heavy artillery battery, the Maisy Battery, which consisted of eight well-emplaced 155 mm guns.

On June 9, the Rangers, supported by half-tracks with artillery mounted on them, captured Maisy Battery. This time the howitzers were in position and firing on units moving inland from Utah. The Rangers eliminated this position in the morning with close small-unit actions and destroyed the guns. As part of this, 5th Battalion's A Company conducted one of World War II's few bayonet charges across open ground.

Soon after this, Col. Eugene Slappey was named CO of the Ranger Group; Lt. Col. Rudder became CO of 2nd Battalion. The group then went into reserve, pulling guard duty and conducting patrols.

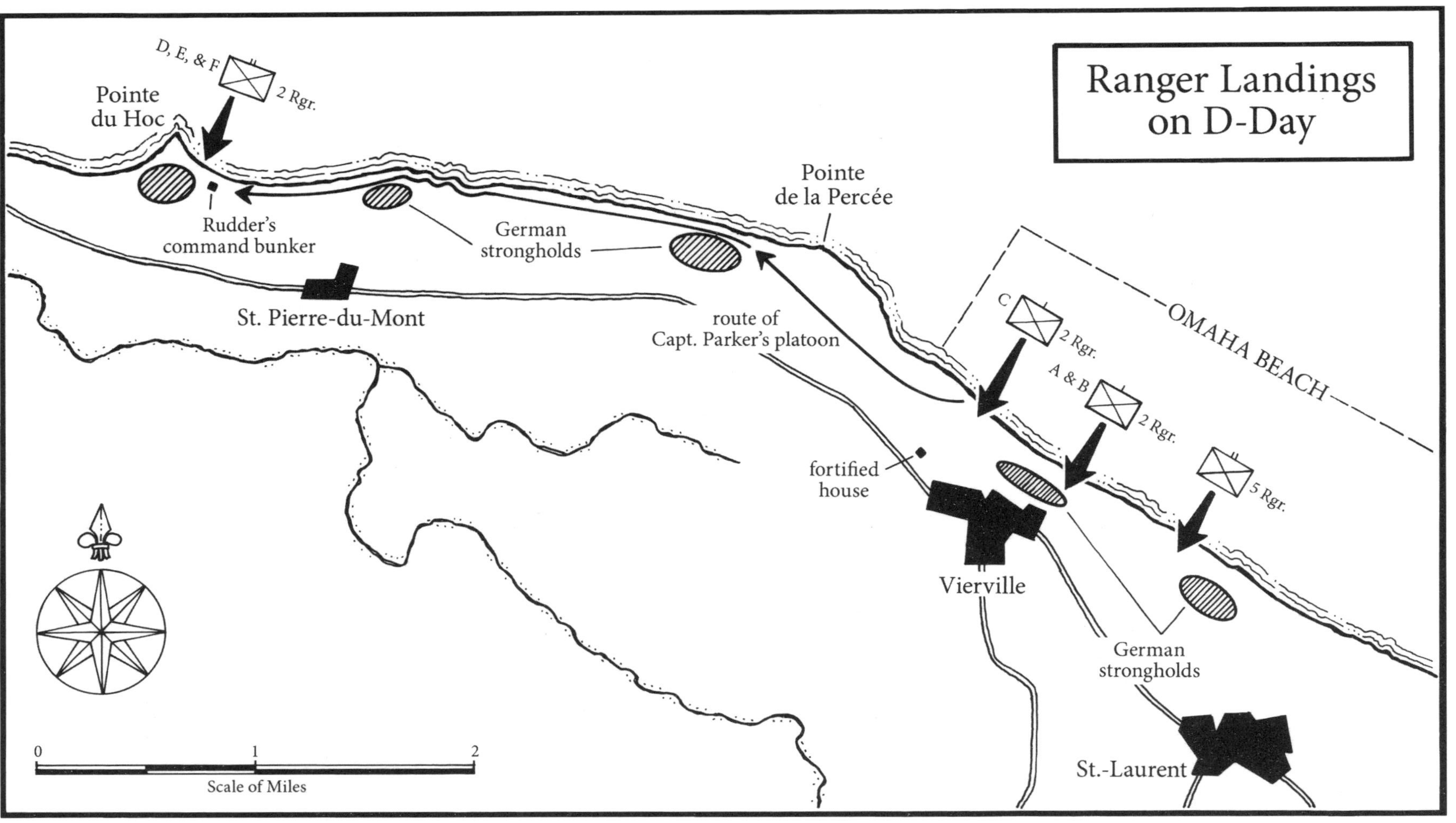

Ranger Landings
on D-Day
D, E, & F   2 Rgr.
Pointe
du Hoc
Rudder's
command bunker
St. Pierre-du-Mont
German
strongholds
Pointe
de la Percée
route of
Capt. Parker's platoon
OMAHA BEACH
C   2 Rgr.
A & B   2 Rgr.
5 Rgr.
fortified
house
Vierville
German
strongholds
St.-Laurent
0   1   2
Scale of Miles

Fortified stone house as seen from Dog Green beach near Vierville Draw

Closer view of fortified house, seen from the west flank of Vierville Draw facing south.

ASSAULT ON THE PORT OF BREST

On August 11, the Ranger Group was attached to VIII Corps for the assault on Brest. Brest was a major port in Brittany that the Allies needed to seize in order to reinforce and supply their invasion forces. The Germans were aware of this and defended the port and the peninsula tenaciously. To aid in this, the Germans had built several defensive belts on the peninsula, anchored on well-defended fortresses. Some of the opponents the Rangers would be facing were *Fallschirmjägers* (paratroops),[19] such as the famed "Ramcke Brigade" named for their commanding general.

The assault began on August 23, and the Rangers fought nonstop to break the defensive lines until September 18, when Brest surrendered. During this time, the Rangers mastered the art of combining artillery and air support to suppress the forts while they stormed them with improvised explosive devices. They also fought alongside the French Forces of the Interior (FFI), commonly known as the French Resistance. The Rangers captured Ft. Tolbrouch, Ft. du Mengant, Ft. du Dellec, Ft. de Portzic, Kergolleau Battery, and the Graf Spee Battery. After the seizure of Brest, the Rangers went into reserve.

HILL 400

In November, the 2nd Battalion found itself in Belgium, and then soon in Germany. Except for some patrolling, the battalion was mostly held in reserve. It was attached to the 8th Infantry Division, which was involved in the battle for the Hürtgen Forest. While in Belgium, there was an interesting incident where a Belgium family wanted Lt. Col. Rudder to take their son, who was sixteen, into the Rangers, because the family held the Rangers in such high esteem. Rudder urged them to ensure he received a good education in lieu of the Rangers. It was also in Belgium that 1st Sgt. Lomell received his battlefield commission. In general, the Rangers agreed that their time in Arlon, Belgium, was the best time they had. But they were soon back in action as part of the campaign to take the Hürtgen Forest.

The battle for the Hürtgen Forest was by any account horrendous. The forest was well defended by veteran German troops, and the terrain suited the defense, consisting of heavy wooded hills with few roads.

One of these hills, designated Hill 400, would become an epic Ranger battle for the 2nd Battalion. The hill was a prominent point in the forest, and its importance was not lost on the Germans. The hill was used as an observation point to call artillery fire on US units for miles around. It was defended by a *Kampfgruppe* (KG) of the 272nd Volksgrenadier Division; KG was the German designation for a task force and can be translated as "battle group." This one in particular was composed of troops and weapons specifically intended to defend the hill.

It should also be noted what a *Volksgrenadier* division is, since it is often confused with the term *Volksturm*. A *Volksturm* unit was composed of men or boys normally unsuited for military service, being too old, too young, or infirm in some way. *Volksturm* units began to appear in late 1944, as Germany depleted its manpower reserves. Conversely, a *Volksgrenadier* unit was an elite unit given the title of *Volksgrenadier* as an honor. Facing this accomplished unit would be 2nd Battalion's D and F Companies, with the other companies attacking other ridges in the area.

The assault began on 0730 on the seventh of December. The Rangers immediately came under artillery fire and charged up the hill, with some degree of anger propelling them. With this speed and aggression, they were able to capture the hill quickly. They found a number of bunkers at the top, which they quickly occupied, since the ground was too rocky and frozen for entrenching.

The Germans immediately counterattacked, but the Rangers fought them off with the assistance of friendly artillery fire in support. The Germans countered with their own artillery. Between the German and US artillery, Hill 400 was under almost constant bombardment over the next few days. Over the course of the day they received reinforcements in the form of more Rangers and elements of 5th Armored Division. However, losses in the Ranger companies were heavy.

On December 8, at 0700 the Germans launched another attack to recapture the hill, some of them being the *Fallschirmjägers* the Rangers so often faced. By nightfall on the eighth, the Rangers had only thirty men remaining to hold the hill. During the darkness, they were relieved by units from the 8th Infantry Division. Only twenty-two Rangers were able to move off Hill 400. Constant artillery and nearly constant German attacks had taken their toll, but the Rangers had captured and held the tactically critical Hill 400.

During this time, the 5th Battalion belonged to the 3rd Army and was involved in the general offensive into Germany at places such as Lauterbach.

The rest of the year saw the Rangers conducting small-unit actions on the line, while preparing for the assault on the vaunted Siegfried Line. Much of this time they were used in more-normal missions, reflecting the lack of infantry the US Army dealt with at the time. Also, it should be noted that by December, Europe was experiencing one of the worst winters in living memory, so the Rangers were fighting the elements as much as they were the Germans.

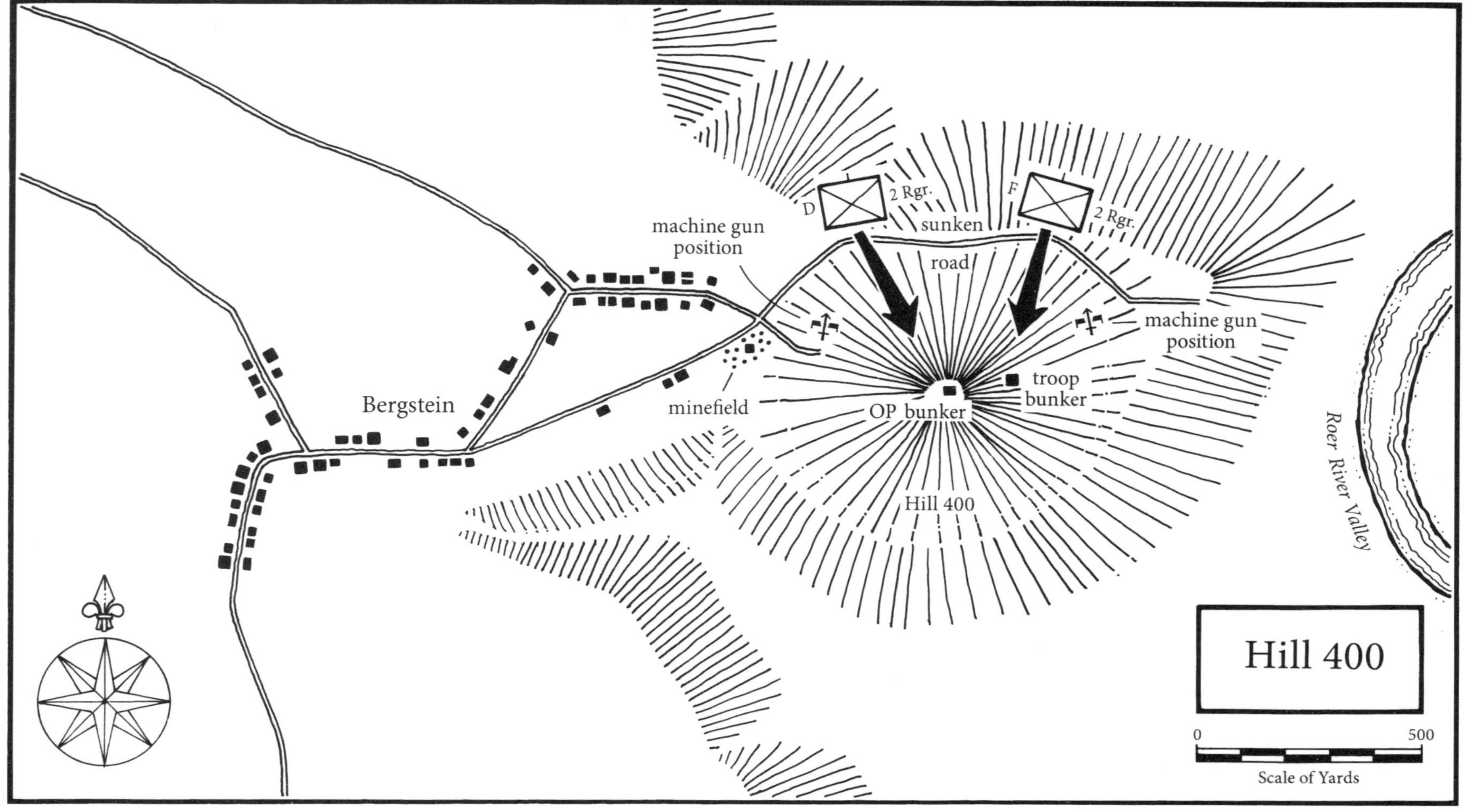

Bergstein
machine gun position
D
2 Rgr.
sunken road
F
2 Rgr.
machine gun position
minefield
OP bunker
troop bunker
Hill 400
Roer River Valley
Hill 400
0
500
Scale of Yards

THE IRSCH-ZERF RAID

The surprise German offensive in the Ardennes Forest, known as the Battle of the Bulge, delayed the assault on the Siegfried Line. But by February, the Rangers (2nd Battalion with the 78th Infantry Division, and the 5th Battalion with the 94th Infantry Division) were in position to begin the penetration.

The Siegfried Line was an imposing system of defensive bunkers and positions along the border of Germany. Fortunately for the Allies, the German failed offensive in the Bulge had cost them many of the men needed to properly defend this line. But it still would require fighting to breach, and the Germans who were there would fight with determination, since the Siegfried Line was the last defensive position protecting Germany.

The twenty-second of February found the 5th Battalion spread out in the 94th Division area of operations: two companies in Orscholz, two in Tabes, and two in Wieten. They consolidated at Tabes, crossed the Saar under the 94th Division cover, and prepared for their new mission under their CO, Lt. Col. Richard Sullivan.

By February 23, the 94th Infantry Division had broken the line, and the 10th Armored Division was prepared to exploit this success. However, the Germans still controlled a crucial network of roads on high ground that could allow them to cut off any attack by the 10th Armored. The solution was to have the 5th Ranger Battalion infiltrate enemy lines and establish blocking positions to prevent attacks in the flank of the armored division.

The Rangers crossed through the 94th's lines at 2345 on February 23. While their mission was to avoid contact, this was nearly impossible with the number of German units in the area. Numerous small-unit actions and German artillery caused some confusion and delay. Lt. Col. Sullivan attempted to reorganize the battalion on "Hocker Hill," a landmark on the other side of the Saar. The battalion moved out in two columns: C Company on the left under Capt. Jack Snyder, and D Company on the right under Capt. George Miller. The second echelon consisted of B Company under Capt. Bernard Pepper, and E Company under 1Lt. James Greene. As soon as the battalion was moving again, they were again hit by artillery. B and E Companies were separated from the rest of the battalion, and more time was consumed re-forming the unit. The plan was to move at night and remain hidden during the day. Since there was still darkness left, the battalion moved out in a square formation with the HQ element in the center. As they moved, they started to take a large number of prisoners, whom they kept in the center of the square. The rear of the square was attacked during the night, and B Company suffered a number of casualties. B Company was detailed to guard the prisoners, since it had lost so many men. This included a missing platoon and a half of Rangers who had gotten separated and whose whereabouts were unknown.

During the day of the twenty-third, the Rangers kept moving in order to make up for lost time. At one point they captured a German ambulance. The German doctor was shocked to find US soldiers almost 4,000 meters behind the line, exclaiming, "You can't be here!" After his initial shock, he began to competently treat the wounded of both sides.

The Germans knew there was a unit moving through their lines, but they could not detect the 5th Battalion. So, by the twenty-fifth, the 5th had reached the objective, the town of Zerf. Lt. Col. Sullivan sent F Company under 1Lt. John Neville to reconnoiter the town of Zerf. Finding it unoccupied, the Rangers quickly established blocking positions along the Irsch-Zerf Road. However, now that they were no longer moving, the Germans located them and started to bring heavy counterattacks on them by the twenty-sixth. Over the next day, German counterattacks grew in frequency and intensity while the Rangers waited for a linkup with the 10th Armored. Zerf proved to be a good place to block, but a difficult place to defend. This was made worse as the Germans brought up the 136th Battalion of the 2nd Mountain Division (*Gebirgsjägers*), an elite and experienced unit, in order to recapture the town.

Meanwhile, the 10th Armored was having problems of its own. The 10th, the 94th, and the Rangers were fighting the 256th Volksgrenadier Division and the 506th Panzergrenadier Battalion. Both of these units were still intact, having most of their authorized personnel and weapons. The *Panzergrenadiers* had some armor support composed of half-tracks and self-propelled guns. This combined with the winter weather and the hilly terrain gave the defenders distinct advantages. Tanks were road bound and therefore easy targets, requiring supporting infantry to dislodge antitank gun positions. This was the fight the 10th had en route to link up with the Rangers. To compound problems, much of the 10th's armored infantry was still trying to secure the tenuous bridgehead over the Saar, so there was not enough infantry to adequately support the drive to Zerf. Col. Walter Roberts, commanding Combat Command B, was driving on Irsch to Zerf with no infantry when he met up with 1Lt. Louis Gambosi, the platoon commander of the lost platoon from B Company. This mixed force moved on Irsch and captured the town, overcoming two Tiger tanks defending it. Soon arriving in Irsch was Task Force Riley, a force of armored infantry from 10th Armored commanded by Lt. Col. John Riley, detailed to link up with the Rangers at Zerf. 1Lt. Gambosi joined up with them in their half-tracks and moved toward Zerf on the twenty-fifth. Fighting throughout the day, Task Force Riley and 1Lt. Gambosi's Rangers were able to link up with the rest of 5th Battalion by the early hours of the twenty-sixth.

The Rangers held, though, and effected a linkup with the 10th Armored on the twenty-seventh, which allowed 5th Battalion to recollect elements separated on the first day. Having covered the flank, the battalion then joined the general attack until taken off the line on March 3. Zerf was the classic type of infiltration mission the Rangers had been trained for, and they performed it admirably.

During this time, elements of the 2nd Battalion had assisted in crossing the Roer River.

With the cracking of the Siegfried Line, the Germans no longer had any significant defensive positions to prevent the Allies from overrunning Germany. In any case, the constant pressure on them, including that of the Rangers, prevented them from organizing any defense. From March until the end of the war, while there were many sharp, violent small-unit actions, it was mostly a race to capture ground and round up prisoners. In this the Rangers provided a constant aggressive force to keep the Germans off balance. Mostly these missions consisted of patrolling and other "mop-up" operations. Usually the Rangers were paired with armored cavalry units, since they needed the speed of mechanization to pursue the fast-fleeing German forces. Eventually, the Rangers were relegated to guard duty of German prisoners until sent back to the United States after the German surrender.

The Rangers were slowly being prepared for additional operations in the Pacific theater when the atomic bomb brought the Japanese surrender. But their actions had secured their legacy and validated the concept of Ranger units. The US Army has employed Rangers in every conflict since World War II and continues to do so today.

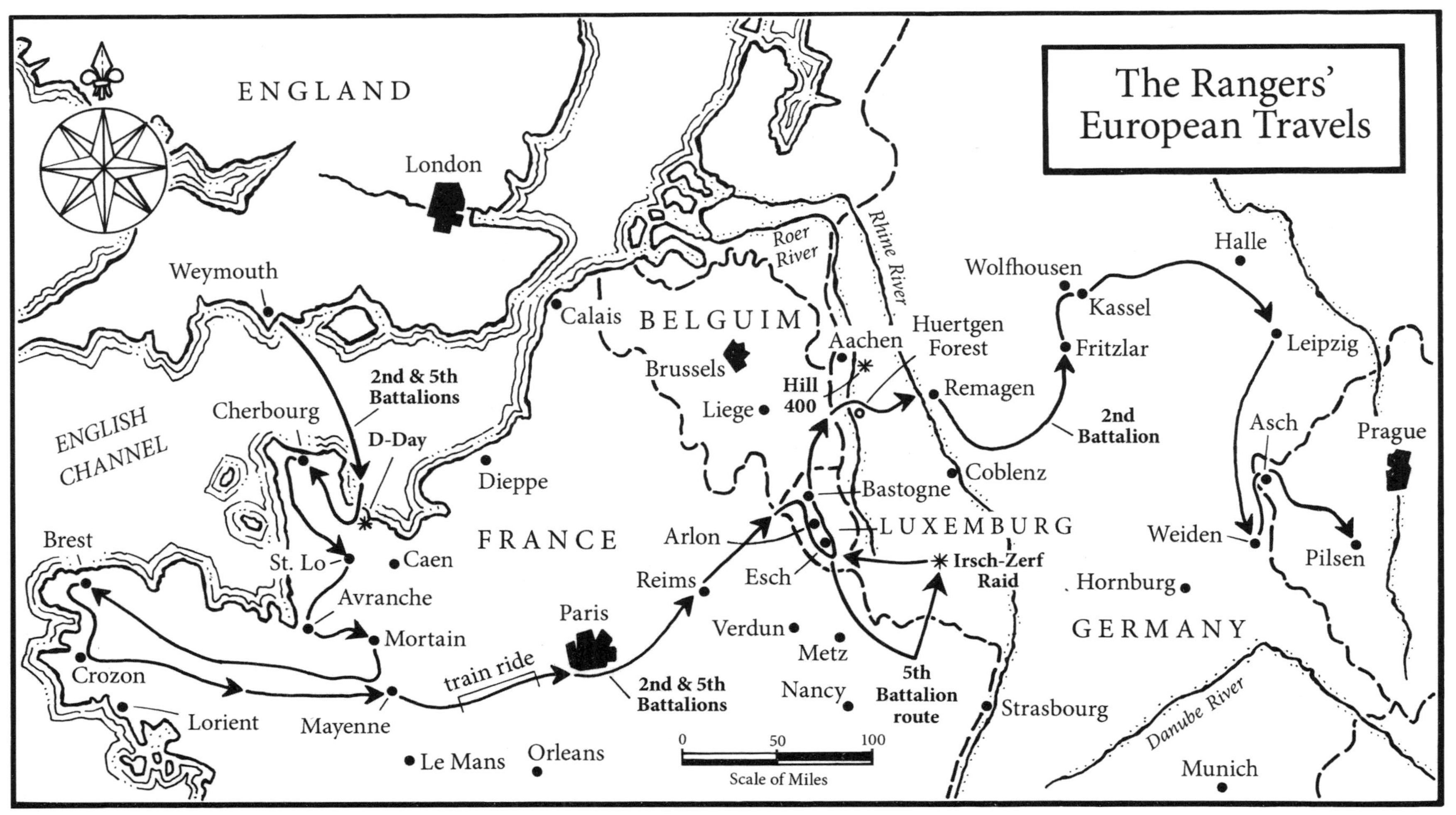

The Rangers' European Travels
ENGLAND
London
Weymouth
ENGLISH CHANNEL
Cherbourg
2nd & 5th Battalions
D-Day
Caen
St. Lo
Avranche
Mortain
Brest
Crozon
Lorient
Mayenne
Le Mans
Orleans
train ride
Dieppe
Calais
BELGUIM
Brussels
Liege
Hill 400
Aachen
Roer River
Rhine River
Huertgen Forest
Remagen
Coblenz
Bastogne
LUXEMBURG
Esch
Arlon
Reims
2nd & 5th Battalions
Paris
FRANCE
Verdun
Metz
Nancy
Strasbourg
Irsch-Zerf Raid
5th Battalion route
GERMANY
Hornburg
Weiden
Munich
Danube River
Wolfhousen
Kassel
Fritzlar
2nd Battalion
Halle
Leipzig
Asch
Prague
Pilsen
0   50   100
Scale of Miles

CHAPTER 12

THE INTERVIEWS

Raymond Tollefson

PFC RAYMOND TOLLEFSON

As a teenager before Pearl Harbor, what kinds of plans did you have for the future?

I was always active in sports, so everything involved a ball of some type or another, so once I finished high school in June of 1942, my thoughts were going to college and become a coach in sports in one manner or another. So that was my goal at that time. Beyond that, we knew there was a war on and so forth, and I knew that I would be going into the military. But beyond that goal, I didn't have anything further than being active in some manner in sports.

Sir, did you get drafted or were you enlisted?

I was drafted in March of 1943. I went to college in the fall of 1942. My mother invested twenty dollars for the first semester, and when I said I wanted to go in the service, she said she wanted me to get my money's worth, so I stayed in the first semester.

And when did you volunteer for the Rangers?

It was almost immediately after basic training. I was in Fort Jackson, South Carolina, in the 106th Division, and Col. Rudder came around at the time looking for volunteers for the 2nd Ranger Battalion, which was located in Camp Forrest, Tennessee. The reason I volunteered was because the 106th Division, it was a new division, and most of the fellows were youngsters. There were a lot of old ones too, but it seemed like most all of them were from New York or Philadelphia and they had always lived on sidewalks and so forth, and I wanted to be with an outfit that knew more about how to handle a gun, I guess you could say.

How would you describe the Ranger training you received relative to basic training?

Just so much more of everything. Well, first of all, you really learned all the weapons that there were. Some of them, you would pick up in basic training, but others you moved on, and so forth. Then there was the intensity of the physical abuse you took, if you want to call it that. But they told you ahead of time that they were going to put you through this, and if you wanted out, all you had to do was not participate in one of the things or fall out of one of the things, and you were out. So we had definite goals on what the Rangers were going to be doing and so forth. Whereas in basic, you just went through the motions.

So it was probably more intensive hand to hand, more intensive physical training, more intensive cliff climbing?
Well, initially, when you're first in the Rangers, they try to get you with the mental attitude of what it is to have tough going. Later on, the cliff climbing came in when they realized that maybe that was going to be part of the mission. We spent time in Florida at Fort Pierce, where we had jungle training down there and terrible rivers. When the tide went out, you were up to the waist or up to your neck in the muck and that there, and you'd be dragging boats upstream. There was no water, so you're just going through that, and this would go on for hours. You'd go day and night. There were lots of times you worked over twenty-four hours steady a day on things. So we practiced landings there. We were in Maryland. We practiced mountain climbing, and they had projects of all kinds. So me, as a young infantry PFC, I just wanted to stay in the Rangers so I just went along.

So do you think all that training paid off when you got onto the battlefield?
Well, yeah, to the degree that when we went in, we were going in for the purpose. We knew it was a numbers game. We had been on that ship for days out there, and we were kind of normal like, but that last evening everybody quieted down more, and it was a numbers game. But we had trained so many times of disembarking from the big ship and then to the smaller ones, the LCAs and so forth. We went through the same thing on the invasion morning, but everybody was quieter. There was no doubt why we were going in there. We had a mission to accomplish, and obviously we had been trained. That was it.

There was something you mentioned about a mission to get an enemy soldier from France?
Yes. When we came into England in November of 1943, we went down to Bude, which was in Cornwall, and we trained there for a period of time. And in January of 1944, A Company was transferred down to a little town that was the British Commandos' training headquarters just outside of Dover. I forget the name of the town, but we were assigned a mission where we were to go over somewhere on the coast. I don't know if it would have been in the Holland area; we never did find out. But there was a two-week span where the moon was not out and the tide was just out that these British Commandos were to take us across the Channel. There was an area where we were able to avoid the minefield and so forth and go there and go up through a pathway up on the bank or hill or whatever they had there. I can definitely remember when we got up on the top there; there was a trail crossing and we went left, and right around the corner a little bit was a sentry—a guard that normally walked that in the evenings. There were four of us in the squad, and we were to get him if possible, without causing any noise, and take him back as a prisoner. If we couldn't get him, we were to go further east, where there was a German barracks. And our assignment was to go in there, get one of those sleeping Germans, and bring him back to our silent ships out there. But that never occurred because the tides. Every day we would be ready for it, and we'd get the word from the Commandos that things weren't right, so we never did make that mission. We were told later on by Col. Rudder that because we had that mission, we would not be one of the ones going on to Pointe du Hoc. He felt we had had our chance there, and we were not pleased with the fact that we were not given the opportunity to go to Pointe du Hoc.

Now, when you were in England, were you in a barracks or a camp?
They put us in private homes in Bude. Harry Ward was the name of the party I was at, and I know it was on Chillerton Road. I still recall that, and I corresponded with the mother of that home. She lived to be over one hundred, and I have been back there since. Wherever we went, we were given ration cards and they had homes for us, and one time we were in kind of an old schoolhouse where, I think, there were about ten of us sleeping in a big room there. And we were on our own to eat and sleep, but we always had a designated area where we had to get together in the mornings, or whatever times of day. Many of our meals were in a pub, having a fish sandwich and a beer. That would be our rations for the day.

Did you like that experience?

Yeah, it was kind of neat, you know, rather than going to the Army regiment. Once we reached England, we naturally had responsibilities there, but we had quite a bit of freedom. In fact, when we went from one town to another, they would say, "Well, we got three days to get there. Here's your rations, your money. See you there in three days." So they didn't even say, "Well, get in line. We'll take you there by bus or car. You get there. Be there." In fact, they did that to go to this town by Dover. We had three days, so my friend and I stopped in London for a night on our way over there.

Did the English people you stayed with take good care of you?

They never did anything really, other than they provided you with a room. In some cases, you'd give them a ration card or money, and they would attempt to feed you with it. We were given money. So we usually had fish sandwiches and beer. But we always complained about the food, whether it was Army food or from the residents.

When were you first notified that you would be disembarking for the invasion?

We were in the area outside of Weymouth, England, and this was probably two weeks before the invasion, and we were locked in, where nobody could leave the premises any more. So once we were there where nobody could leave anymore, we knew the invasion was coming soon. But we were not told about where we were going until we were on ship. Maybe three days prior to the invasion, we were on the ship and they told us where we were going and so forth at that time. I think it was the first of June when we boarded the ship at Weymouth Harbor.

I see. So you were in Weymouth before then, before you boarded?

We were in the town outside of Weymouth. About 10 miles or so, I think near Dorchester. We had a big area there, and the Germans were aware of this because we were getting bombed by the Germans over there in that area.

So let's fast forward a little bit, and you're boarding the ship. You got on an LST, right?

We used an LCA, which is a small ship that brought us out to a bigger ship. I should remember the name of it. I don't though, anyway, but I think it was a Belgium ship that we had trained on many times prior to the real thing. Most of our battalion was on that ship, and there were two or three others as well. So once we got off the little ships, we climbed up the rope ladders, got on the big one. And we were there on that ship until it brought us over 10 or 12 miles towards the coast, when we took the rope ladders down again and got in our little LCAs.

Now, you said you were on those ships for about three days though, right?

Yep. We were just in the harbor area to start with. The invasion, as the world knows, was supposed to be the day earlier, and we actually did start to the coast of France. But then turned around and came back. So there we were again, waiting again.

What did you do for those two or three days while you were on the ship?

Well, we had a little bit of exercise, and there was a lot of card playing. A lot of fellows took it easy and that there, but I was not a big card player. We had been issued French invasion money, which wasn't very meaningful to any of us at that time, and we had all been issued candy bars too. I don't know why. But anyway, we had them and we got in a blackjack game, and I ended up with a good fortune where I took almost all the fellows' money, all that invasion money. After I had accumulated it all, I would sell the fellows . . . give their money back for candy bars and so forth, but I still ended up with a lot of money and that. So I put it in my pack sack. I had to rearrange my whole pack sack, but when I went in on the invasion, I was loaded with French invasion money and candy bars, and after I was hit on D-day morning, someone cut my pack sack off while I was laying [*sic*] on the beach. And sometime weeks later, maybe, I remembered I had all that money and all that candy, and someone along the line had to dig into that pack sack. What a surprise they got when they found that one.

You said you went out on June 5, but the water was pretty choppy out there, right? Were people getting seasick from that?

Well, not on the big ship. I mean, you could handle that easily on the big ship, but once we boarded the LCAs you were really bounced around big there, and some of the fellows always got seasick. One of our LCAs from D Company swamped and a number of the fellows drowned. Slater was rescued by the battleship *Texas*, along with a number of other fellows.

On June 6, as you were getting close to the time where you were going to get back on the LCAs, what was running through your mind? What were you thinking? Were you apprehensive? Nervous? Scared? What were you thinking about?

Everybody quieted down. There was a church service, and some of the fellows went to that. Some of us were writing letters. I had no desire anymore to write letters. My thought was what was coming up. But there was apprehension, 'cause we knew some of us weren't going to be around. We had gone through all this training together for over a year. We had been together, and finally we're going to go and do something. You keep getting these dry runs over and over and over. Well, how long are you going to have to do this? But now there was no doubt what our mission was, so let's get on with it. We know it's going to happen. Let's go.

So what were you personally thinking about?

Basically nothing more than that there. I mean, I can't remember saying that. Well, I used to think a little bit like, now over in New York, as we left we saw the cars going and everybody doing this and that there. I thought, "Now over there, they're going to be still going along, going to work, and so forth, and here we are going on this thing here." I can recall that, and also realizing that this was a major invasion, and that we were going to be part of history. You couldn't help but feel that way. But the safety of your own thing and that there; at that time when you're going in like that, you're still "I'm going," and we had our mission. That's what it was. Once I was hit and floundering around—at first I never dreamt I could ever survive, but then the thought came to mind that maybe I could survive this. The loss of blood I was getting from my injuries and that there—I didn't think I had enough blood to last a minute. But I was still alive trying to wash into the beach. Pretty soon then, the thought came that it would be kind of nice to survive. I was also remorseful and felt guilty really, since my goal was still to be with my fellow friends, and the thought that here I'm just laying [*sic*] here and everyone else is going on, but I'm not going to be with them. Well, I felt guilty and I felt bad because I wasn't going to be part of it. But I thought maybe after a bit I could get back with them. Well, I knew I was badly hit, but I thought one day I would be back with them. So that's basically my feeling.

Can you give me a little background on Capt. Cleveland Lytle? He was supposed to lead the Ranger forces on Pointe du Hoc, and I know that you discussed earlier that he had reservations and that? Can you give us some background?

He was my company commander all the way from when I came into A Company until about a week or so prior to the invasion, or maybe it might have been two or three weeks. He was assigned to lead the Pointe du Hoc attack, so he was in charge of D, E, and F Companies. So they each had their company commanders, but Col. Rudder assigned him to lead those three companies on to the Pointe, and he was going to be back with A and B Companies and really with the 5th Battalion, also going into Omaha. Well, I know two things, I guess, maybe. One, Capt. Lytle, our A Company commander; we thought was just the greatest. He was from South Carolina. He had an accent and that there, and when he had those steely eyes there and get to us that we're going to do this and that there. Man, you're talking about a Knute Rockne guy. Well, here's a guy here that could really get you going in that respect. And we really had respect for his knowledge and abilities. So anyway, what we heard later on is that he did not go to Pointe du Hoc, and what had happened, I'm told, is that they had been together, the officers, and I guess obviously they had been doing some drinking. But somehow the discussion got quite heated, where Capt. Lytle's thoughts were that here we'd been training for close to two years, and we just have a wonderful group of fellows that had the knowledge and the desire. And he felt sending them to the cliff would be just like sending lambs to the slaughter. That all of this training is going out the window. They're going to wipe these fellows all out and so forth. Well, obviously, the decision had been made above him that we're going to the Pointe, and Col. Rudder felt that rather than have him lead the group when he had negative thoughts about it, he removed Lytle and took the team to the Pointe himself.

So you get the orders on the sixth, probably 3:00 or 4:00 in the morning. Do you remember climbing into the LCA?
Yep. That night I don't imagine any of us slept too well. We knew this was the day, so the sooner we get going the better. And going down those rope ladders; we had done it so many times, you know. It was just another dry run for us. But again, you got on that thing and it was bouncing every which way. By that time, we got on there, and the thing I remember again was just the quiet resolve. Usually a lot of those times there's always small talk about this and that, and a little swearing and this and that. But this time here, there was a definite resolve that we're going, but it was quieter. And some of the fellows had problems with seasickness, and we had to use our helmets some to bail some because water would come over some. But then the apprehension came. "When are we going to hear from the Pointe? When we going to hear from the Pointe?" D and F Companies should have already been at the Pointe, and it was time for them to notify us to come on in. So everybody was apprehensive about that. But there was no word, and I can remember myself saying, "If I was the captain, I would go there." But military doesn't work that way; you follow the orders. So I'm certain that our fellows basically all had the same thought in mind. But as we went along there, we had quite a show with the bombardment. Once the bombardment started by the battleships and the rockets and the bombs and everything else, we just watched that. So by the time they stopped that and they told us that we were going in, in a way you kind of said, "This might be a piece of cake after all," with all that going on. If we can get in there soon enough, it might not be too bad.

You probably boarded about 4:00 a.m., and it took you a couple of hours to go down closer to the beach, and you were circling at that time?
Yes, so I imagine it was closer to 7:00. We must have waited quite a while beyond our allotted time where our captain would have had orders. By this time here, if you had no word, you went to the beach and your objective then was to get up on that hill and get over and help the fellows at the Pointe by coming in from behind the Pointe. That was our objective.

Were you climbing into a Higgins or an LCA?
An LCA. When our ramp came down as we approached, we had all this bombing going on, and we thought it was going to be okay. Well, we were a long way from shore when we realized that we were getting hit with everything. So eventually the two or three British men who were bringing this ship in there got hit, and we're floundering out there and we're still a long way from hitting the beach. Somebody lowered the ramp to get off of there, but as soon as that happened, machine gun fire came in there, and some of the fellows in front immediately got hit. Well, the rest of us realized that we couldn't get off that way, so we bailed off over the side of these LCAs. They were much lower, so it was easy to just roll right out of those things. Most of the fellows on my LCA bailed off the side; if we had kept going off the front, it would have just been suicide for all of us.

Were you closer to the back?
Yeah, I was close to the back.

You could see what was going on, as the ramp went down?
Yeah. We were getting off the sides and all ways, and we saw the British guys laying [*sic*] there too, you know, that were exposed bringing us in to where we were supposed to be. So off we went, and when I first got out of there, the water was deeper than I expected. I did go down and touch bottom and give myself a big bounce. I bounced a number of times before I got where the water was shallow enough that I could stand up, but I was basically half swimming and half walking. The waves were pushing us in from there.

Did your commanding officer tell everybody to get off the sides, or did you just all do it?
There was no command of any kind. Everybody did their own thing.

How many guys in the front got hit that you saw?

Sgt. Saul got hit, and I couldn't really tell, but I know at first there were a couple of them that got hit right off the bat as the ramp went down. And once the British fellows piloting the LCA got hit, that thing was going in all directions. So you just got off it. You didn't just want to sit in that thing, so nobody did. We'd been trained to do things. We weren't going to sit there.

So when you jumped off, obviously you were struggling for your life to get out of the water, but were you also looking forward at the beach?

Yeah, I mean, I was not concerned one bit about being over my head or nothing. We were used to that kind of stuff. There were no problems about drowning or anything like that. You're still looking where you're going, you know.

Can you remember exactly what you saw as you were going ashore?

The thing you saw most of all was the machine gun fire. Just solid tracers[20] coming along a flat surface, and still a lot of artillery of some type or another was banging up. Our Capt. Rafferty was off to the left. He actually made it to shore and came back and was trying to get the guys to get in there, when one of those shells hit him, and that took care of him. But I know when I was coming in there and seeing all that fire when I looked up to my left (which would have been east), and that's where the 29th Division was, up that way. It looked even worse than where we were. It was just solid tracers, so I was laying [*sic*] in the water and coming in that way, because standing up you'd get cut down. You hope that it doesn't hit you that way there, but I didn't get very far before I got hit in the arm and the leg. My arm was just about blown off. Somewhere along the line, one of the fellows came along and assisted me by taking his tourniquet or something and wrapped it around my arm to try to stop the flow of blood. And he wrapped it all up and that, and he tied my arm—it was just dangling—to my side and he left me. When I was in San Diego at a reunion sometime in the 1970s, I wrote my name on our log of who attended. Well, this fellow who helped me on the beach paged me, and he said, "I can't believe you're alive." And it actually was a fellow that I had known from before. But I was in shock at the time, and I never knew whoever did that until then. He said, "I did what I could and I went on my way." Turns out he was the radioman with Headquarters Company. But once he had me tied up with that thing, obviously that must have slowed the flow of the blood. At that point, all I could do then was to wash in with the waves, and I was able to have enough control to keep from drowning. So I floated in and I ended up next to two other A Company men. One was on his last few seconds. He was really shot up, and he was almost gone. The other fellow was Jim Slagle from Brookville, Pennsylvania. He and I were in the same machine gun squad at the time, and he had been hit in the back and was paralyzed. Somebody pulled him up so he wouldn't drown, and that man survived, and he passed away some ten years or so ago. So I had a lot of good times with him after. But I saw other fellows on the beach of ours. One fellow was cleaning his gun. Dorchek was his name. Obviously, he finished cleaning his gun and then up he went. My lieutenant, Stanley White, was actually in shock standing against a hill. Just staring, and that was the end of him. He never did come back to our outfit again. I don't know how badly he was shot up, but somebody told me that there was an aid station nearby. I had tried to walk in the sand and I was too weak, but there was a macadamized road up there a little ways, and I was able to struggle up to that. Once I got on that, I start walking down that road, and my thought was, well, any German could see that I wasn't going to hurt any of them the way I was, and I was sick enough that I took my chances by just staggering down that road, about 100 yards to an aid station. And that's when I saw my lieutenant over there. But those were the only ones I actually saw that I knew.

Who was the man that helped you, the radioman?

Bill Doyneuf is his name. He was able to place a tourniquet and stop the bleeding somewhat, and that allowed me get out. Basically what he did was, he tied it to me too, so that my arm stayed in place.

So that enabled you to get up and move to that aid station?

Yes. I was in the water when I got hit, and I probably had 100 yards to go before I would reach the shore. But the tide was coming in and the waves were coming in. So the waves each time would give me a nice boost, just like on a surfboard, you know. And another thing that helped me was that I wasn't standing up going through there, so the machine gun fire was going over my head, because I'm in the water. So coming in that way was helpful. I think this fellow, Bill Doyneuf, gave me a morphine shot, and that was a major, major thing because right away I thought I can run into shore. It didn't take very long for that to take effect, and the shock kind of went away from there. It gave you energy for a while, but I went into shock again, and I don't know how long it was—hours, I think—I laid [*sic*] there, and that's when someone else gave me another shot of morphine. They were probably the ones that told me that there was an aid station down there if I could make my way to it. So by then, I was coming to enough that I wanted to try to get help. That would have been afternoon by then.

So have you had nightmares because of this experience?

It bothered me, I'd say, the first couple of years. It bothered me. Another experience that bothered me was that evening, when I was evacuated onto an LST. When I got on there, I was having major problems, so they hauled me down to the inside of that thing, where they stored the tanks, you know. You're like on a big football field down there, and everybody's laying [*sic*] there. It was full of us down there, and then in the evening the German planes came over to bomb us. These here LSTs had some kind of artillery there, antiaircraft guns or something. And when they'd fire them, it sounded like somebody hitting sledge hammers on giant wash tubs, so you didn't know if you were being hit by bombs or what was going on. And here you were, sitting down there inside a piece of tin. And if one ever hit there, you know, that would be the end. So that went on for three nights or so before they had a convoy, I guess, to get us back over to England. So those nights were nights you didn't forget.

So it took you about two years, but after that you stopped having nightmares?

Yeah, and once in a while years later you'd be dreaming about that there, but it went on for years, or some would.

So D-day obviously caused probably some of your saddest moments in the military?

In my whole life, it was the most memorable, let's say. You wouldn't use the word "sad," you know. But you were there trying to stay alive. Initially you were there for a purpose, but once you'd been hit, staying alive was your goal after that. There was nothing else you could do, you know . . . either alive or not. So it was not like anything else I experienced in my life.

What was going through your mind when you were lying on the beach?

Once I was on the beach like that, I knew that I would do whatever I could to help myself out. But I wasn't thinking, "Well, will I survive or not survive?" You're still alive, so you're going to try to stay alive the best you can. When I got over to the medic station, I guess they must have had a lot of guys that were worse than me, because some Navy guy dug a foxhole for me right on the beach. So we were still getting shelled, you know. So he dug it deep enough so I had a little bit of protection so that I wasn't hit by shrapnel and all that. We were getting artillery a lot there. So once again, I just laid [*sic*] there and again I'm sick. You're really sick where you start coming to and that there stuff. So you're just sick, I guess, and you're just laying [*sic*] there patiently hoping that somewhere, somebody is going to do something to help you out.

What would you say would be the greatest lesson learned from your military experience?

It's unbelievable what a human being can do, what he can go through. The unbelievable courage. Like when I went in the Rangers, I wanted to get into something like that. And it was just unbelievable how these fellows had that dedication and how they just went through it, just went through it, just went through it. I mean, it's unbelievable what humans will do. And today, now here it is some seventy years later, and the reason we go to these reunions is because of that same feeling. We have that same feeling still to this day about each person, each of us. You had a friend and he was part of you, and that's what brings you to these things here, the respect we have for each other. These experiences are the last thing you want to talk to people about. But they're there with us fellows.

Is there anybody you'd give tribute to? A noncom, an officer in your group, a fellow soldier, anybody? Obviously the gentleman who took care of you? Is there anyone else you'd give tribute to?

Really it's Capt. Lytle. Of anybody that where you can say one person can control another person, Capt. Lytle had control of me from any which way you wanted to look at it. I don't think he said two personal words to me in all the while I was with him. Never talked to me. But he looked at me a lot when he was assigning things, and those eyes stared at me and I'd look him right in the eye back, you know, and he could understand that I went along with what he was saying. And he did that to many, you know.

So you had a great leadership role model, but it wasn't his destiny to lead you guys to the Pointe?

Yeah, I know that since then he did get the Distinguished Service Cross with another outfit, so the man was a professional soldier, and he eventually died in action too.

My last question to you is if you were to give some pearl of wisdom to future generations, what would it be? What would you tell people to aspire for?

I learned that teamwork got the job done. I found that out also in the business that I was in, over and over. Teamwork, teamwork. You have to work together if you want to get a job done, I don't care what type of occupation you're in. You get all cylinders going right to there and the way we did it in the Rangers, you're going to get something accomplished. You need a leader that you respect just like Lytle. I respected him. If you are in business and you get the right leader, you can come up with the right personnel. It's amazing what you can do with personnel that understands and gets your message. With that competitiveness, you're going to win.

SGT. WARREN BURMASTER

Let's start off by asking you what your aspirations were before Pearl Harbor happened. What were you planning to do with your life as a teenager?

Being the best ice man I could be. In my time, there was no refrigeration, and where I lived the road went 60 miles and you couldn't go any further. That was it. You had to turn around and come back. I delivered ice to houses. It was a daily chore except Sunday, and we would sell ice to the houses and go in and put it in their ice box, collect our money, and come out. I also provided ice for shrimp boats and shrimp industry with the boats. We'd fill the boats up with ice to go out and get their shrimp. It was pretty busy. I also had a service station that we operated in the winter, and happened to have a small sawmill where we cut cypress logs. So I was busy.

Warren Burmaster

Ranger Burmaster

Can you tell me where you were and how you heard about Pearl Harbor?

I think I was at a dance hall, out with a bunch of teenagers, and they made an announcement about us being attacked at Pearl Harbor. And we didn't know where Pearl Harbor was. I had never heard of Pearl Harbor. I was eighteen years old.

So when Pearl Harbor happened and you found out about it, did you think that would change your life?

Well, I imagined it would change all of our lives when I heard that Japan had attacked us. At that time, we didn't know the damage that had been done, but we found out pretty soon just what they did. They completely wiped us out as far as our ships out there.

So were you drafted or did you enlist?

All of us on the football team enlisted. Another boy and I enlisted in the Army because all the rest wanted to go in the Navy, and we didn't want to be in the Navy, so we enlisted in the Army. They also were drafting you at nineteen, and if you waited until you were drafted, they put you where they wanted. I took my basic training at Camp Hollis, Texas. I'd joined with this one boy, but I made buddies with another boy from Hammond, and after training for almost a year we happened to go to a town for a party somewhere in Louisiana. It must have been around Christmas. Anyhow, we went to that town, and while we were there, we got to talking to each other and we said, "You know, we're never going to get in the war if we keep training. They're fighting over in Italy right now, and Africa. Let's volunteer to go overseas." So the next morning when we got back to camp, I went in and talked to the sergeant, and I said, "Sergeant, we want to be sent overseas." The sergeant didn't say anything, but I knew he didn't like the idea of me leaving the company. I had just made sergeant, and here I was leaving him to go overseas. So one week later, they shipped my buddy overseas, but they didn't send me. Then a week later, he sent me out, so I think he was just making sure we couldn't go together.

And that's when you volunteered for the Rangers?

Nope. I went over to England. We got in a Quonset hut.[21] They wouldn't let us go to town, and we weren't busy doing anything. We were not training over there. There were twenty men in a Quonset hut, and after about two weeks of not getting out of the base or anything, we got word they were looking for paratroopers. So out of the twenty fellows, nineteen of us said we're going to join the paratroopers and get out of here. So we went and got in the truck, and they drove us up to where they were taking paratroopers. When our truck stopped, the truck ahead of us was the last truck of paratroopers that they would take. So the sergeant came in back of our truck and said, "Sorry, fellows, we can't use any more paratroopers. We got our quota. But if you go back up the road about 40 miles, they're taking Rangers." And one of the boys said, "Well, are they paying you $50 a month more?" He said, "No, you won't get paid any more for Rangers." We had heard about the Rangers, so we all said, "Let's go in the Rangers." So we went back and got into Ranger training.

What did you hear about the Rangers? What did they tell you about the Rangers?

Oh, we already knew about the Rangers, even before we went overseas, 'cause they showed pictures back home of Rangers. And I think it was the 1st, 3rd, and 4th that we heard about and saw news about.

Then you did your Ranger training?

We did ours in England.

Having been through basic training, can you tell me how Ranger training was different from basic training?

Well, to me it wasn't all that different, because I had hard training and I went there to learn how to be a soldier, so I never left camp for six months because I wanted to get the training. To me it wasn't all that much harder than regular training. Maybe it was different, but we were trying to learn how to climb the cliffs, how to get back down cliffs. They showed us how to handle explosives, but we didn't actually fool with them.

Did they have more hand-to-hand combat training?

Well, we had hand-to-hand combat before, and the Rangers had it too. It was a tough training. In fact, I'll tell you, they were trying to see if they could make us quit, and I found that out the first day. 'Cause this truck stops on a hill, and a fellow in the British Commandos comes to the back of the truck and said, "Fellows, this truck can't go up in that area, but the camp is only about a mile down. You all gotta just go on up to camp. You go on up the road and you run into the camp." And plenty of us that were wanting to get there, we went right on. But some of the fellows just dropped out and sat on the side of the road. They figured they had time to get up there. And when we got up there, they started talking to us, and these fellows come in straggling and they said, "Sorry, boys, we can't use you." So I found out from that day on they were trying to get rid of us. In other words, if you couldn't take it or didn't want to be there, they didn't want you.

So let's move on and talk about when you arrived on the Normandy coastline. I believe it was three or four days after D-day that you arrived on the boats?

We were on the boats on D-day. We tried to go on D+1 and the waves were too great. They said we couldn't get off the ship to get into the landing craft. We came back and then the next morning we tried and went out again, but they said it was too rough. That would be D+3. And on D+4 it was still rough, but we were able to get off of the ship into the landing craft.

And can you tell me what it looked like on D-day +4? Was it pretty much open? What did you see when you got off the landing craft?

Open beach. Some German soldiers near the base of the landing. We did not see any Americans, wounded or killed on the beach. They must have removed anybody that was killed by that time, and then we climbed up a cliff and went into the area.

Okay. And so as you entered, do you remember if it was a day or two later when you first entered combat, in terms of a firefight?

That night, the German airplanes came after dark and dropped bombs on us. Not as much in our area, but a lot of the boys would stand up and look around for the planes. And some of them were getting hit by the shrapnel that was coming from our fire or the bombs, whatever it was. They were getting hit, so we decided we'd better hide. We called them "Bed Check Charlie," and that was our first combat experience.

And then within a day or so after that, you started; did you have a firefight in the hedgerows?

No, I'd say we stayed there for four or five days. Some of the boys started shooting themselves either accidentally or on purpose. We thought it was on purpose because they would shoot themselves in the leg or shoot themselves in the arm. So this lieutenant says, "Well, I want to get all your ammunition." And some of the men started giving him the ammunition back, but the group I was with wouldn't give him the ammunition. We said, "No, we came here to fight."

So when was your first actual firefight in the Normandy coastline? Was it about probably five or six days later?

No, it would be quite a bit more than that, because we got to our base where the Rangers were, and we joined the Rangers. And then we got in with the regular Rangers and we took care of prisoners. We were handling German prisoners at first.

So what was your first firefight? Do you remember?

It was in the hedgerows. It was very dangerous, and a lot of fellows were getting killed.

And how did you usually go in the hedgerows?

Just climb over them and get going if you didn't get killed. Hedgerows was rough fighting, and at that time they hadn't learned to put that piece on a tank and bust the hedgerow with the tank. The tanks were busting the hedgerows later on. I've seen men lost in the hedgerows. I'm going to talk from my experience. When I first got there, I wanted to kill every German that was over there. That was my aim. And after a week of fighting and seeing men lose their lives and get so busted up you couldn't even pick them up, I believe I was trying to stay alive. My thoughts changed, to "I'd better see if I can stay alive."

So I guess at this stage, probably one of your most famous moments was, you know, the attack on Brest and the capture of the Graf Spee Battery. Can you tell me how you got in the Brest Campaign?

Well, we didn't get to Brest that quick. We went along the coast, and we were mainly trying to get the Germans that were along the coast to give up or, you know, fight them a little bit. And we were pretty lucky in getting the men that were still left in these places to give up and to get them out of their hiding places. They would come out with a white flag, and we'd take a white flag with us. We had a four-man patrol, and we would walk with our white flag. They would walk with their white flag, and we did that about four or five times. One time when they put their flag out and we put our flag out, we got about halfway out and they got about halfway to us, and this American tank fired at them, and when they fired at them they hit the ditches and we hit the ditches at the same time. It was almost dark, but when we hit the ditches, then they scampered from where they were and fired two rounds of mortar. This one round hit to our right, but it didn't explode. One round hit to our left, and it didn't explode. And we could see them sitting in the ground. They hit and got in the ground, but they didn't explode. We waited until dark, and we got back out of the trench and then went back to camp. The next morning we tried the same thing again, and it worked. So that was one that we were trying to get that could have cost our lives.

Okay. Now can you tell me about that patrol that you had with the Fabulous Four led, I guess, by Lt. Edlin? Can you tell me what your mission was and how you started off on that, and then all the events surrounding that?

Well, that morning our mission was to go forward towards the Germans and find the minefield that was in front of the fort. We were told that there was a fort up there with four big 14-inch guns on it. When we got there, to an open area, we could see the minefield they were talking about. This was a cleared area, no trees or anything, but to get from where we were to the base of a cliff (or a mound of some sort), we would have to walk through the minefield. Courtney, Dreher, Edlin, and I were on the patrol. And Courtney said, "I believe I see where people have been walking from here right on through there." We figured it was either the Germans coming out at night trying to get to town, or Frenchmen going in and trading with the Germans. Anyhow, Courtney said, "Wait a minute. I think I'll try it." So he walked in and he said, "Yeah, this is pretty well walked on." So we followed him in and we ended up at the base of this mound. It looked like a good-sized incline. Anyhow, when we got there, we didn't have a firefight, but six or seven Germans were in a trench, and the minute they saw us they stood up and surrendered. So we captured six or seven Germans, right at the base of this thing that we were attacking. And two of the men in there spoke English, so they talked with Edlin and we found out that we were right at the fort where these big guns were. Now, we had experience with the big guns before we got there. We were so close that they just put the guns down level, and they were firing over our heads, and when a shell would hit the ground, it would travel and make a trench 10 to 12 feet deep before it exploded. And it was covering up the men's foxholes and the places where they were, and they were dying by suffocation. So you were safe once you got under the guns. But if you were in front of the guns a little further out, you were getting covered up with the dirt after they exploded. One of these men showed us a house where a German officer was hiding. So Courtney and Dreher said, "You all stay here with these prisoners. We're going to go back and see if we can capture him or find out why he was there." So they went back through the minefield and got into the building. To get in this building, you had to take a German that was dead hanging by his neck, and push him on the side to get to the door. So Courtney and Dreher went in and captured this German officer.

Was that the commanding officer?

No, he was a German officer, but he wasn't a commanding officer. They brought him back with them, and he was the man who led us into the fort.

Now, of the first six that told you to go there to get that officer, did you have to get that out of them or did they just tell you?

No, they just volunteered. I don't think they wanted to fight us because they didn't fire.

So Courtney and Dreher brought the officer back, and now you have seven Germans for the four of you to guard? And then what did you do?

Well, between Edlin and this officer, we all walked into the fort. We still had our ammunition and our guns.

They didn't have any sentries there or anything?

Well, I don't know about that, but we got into an elevator and got into the fort. And when we walked in, it had an electric door and it was a hospital. It was on the ground floor of this fort, and they were operating on men in there. Might have been operating on some Americans if they had them. I know they were German. And this German officer we captured told whoever was in there, "Don't get excited. We're taking these men up." Courtney could understand and speak German, so he kept telling Edlin that everything was all right. We went up another flight and Edlin and Courtney went in a room, and they just let us walk around. We could walk around up there.

So you were guarding the seven?

No, we weren't guarding any of them. They were right where they belonged.

So you left the men?

No, they were in there with the rest of the Germans. They weren't our prisoners any more.

They weren't? You released them?

I don't know if you would say we released them, but when we walked into a German fort, I don't see how you could call them prisoners anymore. I never thought of them as prisoners there. You mean you think I captured all the rest of them?

Okay, so you and Mr. Dreher were walking around there. Lt. Edlin and Courtney . . . ?

Went into another room with some kind of commander. It must have been the top man. And all that happened in there, they did themselves. We weren't in that room with them.

You weren't. Okay. So you heard about it later what they did in there?

We knew when they came out. We knew that everything was all right.

I see. So from what you heard from them, what did they do in that room?

Well, I understand Edlin talking to see if they would give up, and the general or whatever he was said, "No, you're our prisoners." He said, "I've been told there's only four Rangers in this whole building." And he said, "You're our prisoners." I understand that Courtney told him, "No, we're not your prisoners. You're going to be our prisoners." And he reached over and got a grenade from Courtney. I don't know why he didn't have a grenade to start with, but he got a grenade from Courtney and pulled the pin. When he told the general or whatever rank he was, he said, "Either give up or we're going to blow the place up." And the general said, "No." And he said, "It's either going to be that way or we'll all die here together." And the general said, "No." And he said, "I'm going to count to three and I'm going to let this grenade go." And he said, "One. Two." And then the general said, "Okay, we'll give up."

He put that grenade close to his belly, didn't he?

Well, that's what they say. I wasn't there, so I couldn't tell you, but I could believe it.

And so at that point, did they come out of the room, and that's where you linked up again?

Well, when they come [sic] out they were still talking, and we started just walking around the place. I was walking just with the Germans and seeing what the place was.

But you didn't have them at gunpoint?

We didn't have anybody at gunpoint at that time.

I see. And then how did the rest of the German soldiers come out and surrender then?
Well, all this was happening over a long time. It didn't happen as fast as what I'm telling you.

So about how long were they in that room?
Oh, it seemed to me like a half hour and maybe even longer. But when they came out and everything was all right, I just started walking around. We were in a gun turret, and there was an observation room that fired the guns, and I just walked around and saw the charts on the wall, where, if you were in a rowboat 5 miles out, they could spot you on the wall. Get a number and fire a shot and put a shot in the rowboat if they wanted.

And that observation room was adjacent to where the commanding officer was?
It was in this room where we were standing, not in the room where they went.

So they went into a room adjacent to that room, then?
Yeah. I was told this place was twelve stories deep. Later on, I heard it was only six stories deep. And the bottom story had live animals on it. That's what they used for meat. And the other stories were for men.

At what level did you come in when you first came in?
We were on the bottom as far as I know. Now, the animals and stuff could have been further down. We were at the hospital.

The hospital, which is one of the lower levels?
It was ground level as far as I'm concerned.

I see. Okay, but there may have been one or two levels below that?
I think there were.

So they came out of the room, and then you walked around a little bit into the command area. Then what happened?
I don't know. We were in there a good long time before we found out they gave up. I mean, we were inside. We had nowhere to go.

And how did you link up then? Did you get all the Germans to come out of the command center and come outside, and then the other Rangers came in, but how were they taking prisoners at that stage, do you remember?
I was with Dreher and I got away from Dreher, so I was by myself just looking around, and I imagine it was two or three hours before we actually knew that they had given up.

I see. And what was Lt. Edlin doing at that time?
He was with this general. He and Courtney were together. Dreher and I were together, and we got separated. I ended up not being with Dreher, and Dreher was not with me. I came out of the place trying to find Courtney, Dreher, or somebody, and I never did find them. It might have been the next day before I found them, or that evening. I can't remember when I found them.

In essence, when did you link up back with your Rangers unit?
I imagine that night.

Okay. From your understanding, did the Ranger units come over and get all those prisoners out of there, or did you guys have something to do with getting them out of there?
I think the German officer made them all go out, and, according to the report I heard, after they all brought their weapons out and sacked them and gave up.

I think you received the Silver Star for that action, right?
Yes. They gave three of us the Silver Star, and Lt. Edlin got the Distinguished Service Cross.

Were you concerned that this could all blow up in your face and you could be a prisoner, or did you have confidence that you were going to succeed?

I thought we were going to succeed once we got in. I mean, I just went along with the flow of it. It was quite an experience, and I guess an unusual occurrence for us to get in there the way we did. We didn't go there to do that.

You were just doing reconnaissance basically?

Just to find that minefield. But we got through the minefield and ended up right at the fort.

Now, did you receive your nickname "Halftrack" that day?

No, that was when we were training to be a Ranger.

How did you get that name?

Well, I had already told these fellows about something that happened to me in the States when we were on maneuvers down in Louisiana. I had command of three jeeps with the heavy weapons, and my jeep,when I got in it, I asked the driver (his name was Hatfield), "What are you doing with that shell down there on the floor?" He said, "The lieutenant is going to send that to his mother as a souvenir to put on the mantelpiece." And I said, "Well, aren't you scared of it?" He said, "No." So we drove around about eight or nine days on maneuvers, and one day I picked it up and I was looking at it with the point down. It was painted blue. It was a 37 mm shell that had been fired by our men, and I figured it was safe. Then the driver hit a hole, and when he hit the hole, I dropped the shell and the whole jeep blew up. So I blew the jeep up with the shell. And one of the men said, "Well, man, you had to be half cracked to do something like that." And the fellow said, "Well, let's call him 'Halftrack.'"

So he said half cracked? And they somehow came up with Halftrack?

Well, nuts is what he meant. So one man took the name "Texas," and one called himself Montana, and we had one fellow in there I shipped overseas with from New York, and he had a chest full of medals. And I said, "Where'd you get all of them?" He said, "I bought them." I said, "Well, you were never in combat." He said, "No." So I told them that story about him, and they said, "Well, let's call him Combat." So that's how he got his nickname.

Well, you were fortunate that when you dropped the shell that it didn't blow you up as well.

I wasn't as fortunate as I just told you. That night I looked down at my foot because it was hurting, and I saw blood coming out of my shoe. So I decided I must have got some part of that shell. I took my shoe off, and I had a nice-sized gash in my foot. So they said, "You gotta go to the medic." So they took me to a tent. It was dark, at night. I walked into this medical tent, and when I walked in, there was a man lying on a stretcher. It was the man I joined the service with. And I said, "Clarence, what are you doing here?" He said, "Warren, I went to sleep under the ambulance." He was a medic. "I went to sleep under the ambulance, and the driver came and started it up and took off and run over me." Now you talk about putting occurrences together. Here are both of us hurt inside a tent with all these soldiers, and we're in the same tent. But he was all right. He never got hurt all his time in the service.

I understand that after that, you were involved in the Black Forest and you led a lot of patrols. Is that right?

Yeah. We went up to relieve B Company, which was stuck in a minefield, and they were getting their men hurt up in the dark. So we went up there to bring the wounded back by stretcher, helping out. Edlin picked up a stretcher with a man on it, and it was connected to the barbed wire, and Edlin got injured in the face. So he had to go back to the hospital and didn't come back to us for about a month and a half. And when that happened, then I had to get another lieutenant to be in charge.

Other than the time you were injured, was there any firefight that you remember most, or what was the most severe firefight you had after the Graf Spee Battery?

No, the only trouble was when I got blown up in a minefield working with another one of my men. We were laying the white tape out for the mines when the Germans started shelling us, and we got caught in the middle of it. Well, we all hit the ground and I heard my buddy yell, and I knew he had been hit pretty bad. I had another man with me that was just following us. He wasn't my man. He was just following us, and when the shelling stopped, we tried to pick him up so we could get him back to the camp. Every time we did, he would pass out. And this happened to be the boy whose nickname was Combat, so I told him to go back and get some help. He didn't want to do that, but I finally convinced him he better go back. So he went back to get somebody to come back up with a stretcher, and I stayed with my man. And he did get back and he sent a stretcher to pick him up, so we were able to get him back. When they picked him up, I finished putting the white tape out for the minefield. I had been out there with Edlin, so I knew where that tape went. And incidentally, that's the last time I ever saw Combat in the Rangers. I think he blew his top.

So that wasn't the time you were injured?
No. I didn't have a scratch.

Were there any other major firefights at Brest or the Battle of the Bulge that you particularly recall?
Hill 400.

That was one of the worst encounters you were on?
Well, it wasn't the worst encounter I was on, because D, E, and F, they were the ones who climbed 400. A Company was to the right at the base to keep the Germans from coming around, and B Company was on the left to keep them from coming that way. I knew where those two companies were, and the Germans never attacked and they never attacked them.

I see. Did you remember seeing the shelling that was going on?
Oh yeah. I guarantee you. Nothing but shelling.

One account I heard was that the reason why the Rangers succeeded is because they requested an artillery barrage that went in, and then they charged during the artillery barrage and attacked the hill during the barrage. Is that right?
That's the only way you can fight. You gotta attack and you gotta be ready to go. Our soldiers were laying [*sic*] down at the base where we were. You could see the Germans. They could see you, and the minute that attack stopped, they took off.

They attacked right after the barrage stopped?
Immediately. Maybe even going there when they knew it's going to stop. If you're going to try to save yourself, you better be there.

So you saw the fighting going on? You saw everything? And the D, E, and F Companies went up, charged it, and . . . ?
They went up, did a beautiful job, took the hill, and we let them down. We did not send anybody up to bring down the wounded. We were not doing anything. If they had asked us for some volunteers, we could have given them volunteers. But they didn't do that, and Len Lomell got very upset with his Rangers 'cause they couldn't get them down. They were up there trying to hold the hill.

So you could actually see hand-to-hand combat?
No, we couldn't see that. We were protecting the ground down on the side. Oh, you could see enough combat to know what's going on.

What was the most intense firefight you were involved with?
I'd say the 88s they kept putting in on us. Everywhere you went, there were 88s.

So those were the most-severe conditions?
Yeah. Never had to fight a tank. We could hear the tanks, but we never fought them. And we couldn't have done much against a tank anyhow.

But either in the Hürtgen Forest or in the Bulge, do you remember any specific firefights that you were actually involved in?
While that Bulge was going on, we never had any contact. They never attacked us. We never attacked them. And we were freezing to death. We were in about a foot of snow in our foxholes.

So the winter conditions were your biggest enemies during the Bulge?
I lost as many men with purple toes and purple ankles as you could lose.

But you don't remember any more very intense firefights in the Hürtgen Forest?
No, not while the Battle of the Bulge was going on.

It sounds like most of your intense fighting was in Normandy in the hedgerows?
Hedgerows was bad. Brest was bad. The 5th Ranger Battalion was with us there, and they lost quite a few men at Brest. I don't think we lost that many men at Brest.

Can you go over with me the day you were wounded in March 1945?
Well, we were traveling with the 2nd Cavalry Division. Rangers have no transportation. The cavalry was our transportation. We were with them for a week or so before I got hit. We drove up, and if you got in battle, fight a little while, but don't try and take them. Just see if you can get around them. When you know you can get around them, get on your trucks and go. You hit them again, fight them, go around. We did that for almost two weeks. This night we went into town and we fought them, and we kind of stayed to the side where we were, and they told me to take my two sections of men—twelve and twelve—and they told me to take them to this big warehouse. So I took them into the warehouse, and it was dark and that night there was no moon. I don't know why, but the moon wasn't out that night. And at 1:00 in the morning, a runner came in and told me to bring my two sections up, that we're getting on the trucks. So we got about halfway to the house where the trucks were, and one shell came in. There had been no shelling in this area. One shell came in. My first thought was an 88, but later years I figured out it was a mortar, and I know I heard that shell coming and I started down, and when I started down I got knocked down. The shell passed over my head and hit the man behind me, which was Johnny Lasor. I've been looking for where he came from for the last fifty years, and I can't find his family. Anyhow, all of them were knocked down behind me, and the last man was a medic. He came up and he had a broken arm, but he took me and brought me to the building. He said, "I'm going out and check on my men." So he left me and went to his men, and when he came back, I kept hollering, "Johnny." I knew I kept saying, "Johnny." It was the man behind me, and he said, "Johnny's dead." He said, "All the rest of the men are hurt, but they're not killed, but they are hurt." And I asked him about Johnny, and he said, "We can't find a piece of Johnny." In other words, he was gone. So they got ready to put me in the ambulance, and all of a sudden a lot of shells came in. The men who were trying to pick me up left me there and went into the house. When it was over, then they came back out, picked me up, and put me in the ambulance. I couldn't get up. I just laid [*sic*] there. We were in Germany, and they took me to a hospital in Belgium.

And that's where you got hit in the head?
I got hit in the head and hit in the arm and a piece in the butt. I had a German heat can that they heat their food with, and the doctor showed me the heat can, and it was all busted up. He said, "This is what saved your rear end." And he gave me three small pieces of shrapnel that he said "come out of your head." And it was in a little bottle, which I brought home. But I got hit March the sixth. I woke up March the eleventh in the hospital. I didn't know it was March, and I didn't know it was the eleventh. When I opened my eyes, there was a lady standing there. It was a nurse. I don't know if I realized it was a nurse. And I asked her what day it was, and she said, "This is Wednesday." And I said, "No, what's the date of today?" And she said, "March the eleventh."

I said, "That's my birthday." And I went right back to sleep. That's the only thing I remember when I woke up. And the next day, I woke up again. I don't know if I was in a coma. I don't know what I had, but I believe this is the sixth day that doctor's talking about.

So your guardian angel made sure you lived through your birthday?
Right. Now, if you want to know another thing that was interesting or funny, whatever you want to call it. When Edlin didn't come back, then I got another lieutenant. But when Edlin didn't come back and we traveled further up, you know going up into Germany, I got yet another lieutenant, and he told me, "You're going to lead a patrol tonight." I said, "That's fine. What are we going to do?" He said, "We're going to go behind the German lines and find out what that pillbox is made out of." Well, my first thought was "Well, shoot, they've been firing at us for the last couple of weeks. We've been firing at them. It's got to be made out of concrete." I thought it was a silly one, but I got my men together and there was snow on the ground, and real cold, so we put white cloths on. We were living in houses that were deserted, and we covered ourselves and our helmets with white cloth. Covered our weapons with white. And if you're all white and you're walking and somebody is a good distance away, they really can't see you. The white is the same as the trees behind you and everything else. So I got the men to get rid of anything that would make noise, and I told them what we were going to do. We had been watching the Germans in front of us, and they had been watching us. I didn't want to go straight across and try and find it. I thought if that fort was there and I could hear them firing, it was off to my right. So I had already made up my mind. There was about 1,000 yards between us and the Germans. I figured I'd go out about halfway into no-man's land, make a sharp right ('cause I knew that our lines were in that line), and say I hit our lines at a certain distance and see if I could find a way in behind their lines. Well, I did that and I came into a blacktop road. I ended up walking to the blacktop road, and when I got there I stopped and laid [*sic*] down, and of course my men behind me laid [*sic*] down too. I barely got down and was looking around when I heard clump, clump, clump. I knew right away that's Germans marching. Well, I was already down, and I looked up the road and here they were coming, and marching down the road. There was a little bend in the road right where I was. It made a bend, and I was right at that bend and I could put my hand on the blacktop. I said, "Well, my best bet is to lay [*sic*] right here. I'm all covered with white." They came there, and he gave an order to stop. I figured there were about forty men in there. He stopped them right there and gave a command to break up. Luckily, none of those Germans came on our side of the road. They all went on the other side of the road, and I couldn't figure that out. Why they wouldn't have some foxholes on this side. So I laid [*sic*] there, and actually I think it was the man in charge of them decided to come take a leak. He walked over to the side where I was, and he was pissing off the road. That was right where I was, and it was hitting over there and I was getting sprayed where I was. He went off and I crawled back and I asked the lieutenant, "What do you want to do?" He said, "Let's get out of here." And we came on back. Now, never once was I scared. I don't know why. I just knew I was there, and that didn't bug me at all. I did think that I might get to be a prisoner.

That camouflage really helped you out, probably?
Yeah. It was nothing but white sheets. And we went on back and that was it. That was the scariest one I had. But this lieutenant, it was his first patrol, and from that time on I made all of the patrols, but he never went out again.

So when you were with Lt. Edlin, he always went on the patrols with you?
He always went first. In the book, he is going to tell you he let us come in front of him. No way.

Would you say that that is what really makes a great leader? Somebody who takes the initiative?
Well, you look up to him a lot more when he's out in front of you. I was always the last man. He called me the runner. In other words, if he got in trouble, I was supposed to go run and tell somebody that we needed them, but I never had to do that. Then he always said I had a radio. We never had a radio. I don't think we had radios at that time.

What other characteristics make a person a great leader?

Doing a lot of training and learning all kinds of equipment and giving you good orders. Courtney always told us he was as good as ten Germans. I said, "Courtney, you might be as good as ten Germans. I think I might be as good as two Germans." And that's as far as I'd go. He wanted to learn everything about the German army, and when we got along the coast, we found a German tank that had been knocked out. He says, "I'm going to see if I can fire that thing." So he got up in the tank, and he used the hand crank and turned the gun towards the water. There was a buoy there, and he fired a round. I don't know if that was the only round, but he missed it. Then we found a German bazooka. He said, "I'm going to fire this thing." So he goes back away from the tank a good distance. We connected all these wires up. He laid [*sic*] down. He said, "Now watch out. I don't know what's going to happen." He fired it. He hit the tank, but when he turned around, his face was nothing but red blood. He did not have the screen that went on that weapon, so all that black powder came back and made holes in his face. He had to go back to the medical tent and get it taken care of. But that's the kind of fellow he was.

You were all very close, the Fabulous Four?

If you saw one, you saw the other three. Now, when I first got there, I'd never been on patrol. Courtney came in. We were all fresh, as green as could be, and he says, "I need a volunteer to go on a patrol. Stand up if you want to go." So I just stood up, and not one of my men stood up with me. So I automatically was the only one he could take, and that's how I started out with him.

What was the saddest moment during your military experience? Is that the day you got hit and the guy behind you was killed?

Well, when Johnny Lasor got hit, it happened so fast that I really didn't know anything about it. But we got a lot of shelling in the Hürtgen area, and one day we had already covered our holes up with wood and stuff, when they started shelling. I had my hole well covered and I could get to mine, but a boy by the name of Tex that I had a lot of trouble with, came by and got to his hole and there was somebody else in it. He was a pretty good-size man, and he didn't say anything. He just reached down there and pulled him out the hole, and he said, "That's my hole." So this other boy came over to my hole and jumped in and told us about Tex. A shell landed in Tex's hole and tore him to pieces. We had some German prisoners that we had there, and we got the German prisoners to pull the pieces out, and that's what they were—just pieces. And I think that was the scaredest I've ever been. I went back in my hole and I almost lost it. That was the one time that I was scared, and it was because I saw what they were doing.

Was that also your saddest moment?

No, my saddest moment ended up not being able to find Johnny's family. If you go to your computer and you look up "Rangers" and "Warren Burmaster," my picture will come up, and it will tell you I'm looking for his family of Lasors, wherever they are. If you could let me know, I would like to see his family. And his family would be two brothers. All three were from Yugoslavia, but they were American soldiers. Their mother was still in Yugoslavia. Johnny and I had decided we were going to join the occupation forces and go look for her. The Rangers ended up in Czechoslovakia, so that would have been easy to do. We'd have been right there. But I got hit and he got killed and that was the end of that.

What were the greatest lessons you learned from your military experience?

Learn everything you can if you're going to stay alive. That was it. Just be careful and keep up your equipment.

If you were to give the future generations some wisdom, what would you tell them?

Well, I'm going to tell you a silly thing first. Join the Navy. And you can get in the battleship and sail 3,000 miles away and fire to where you want to hit somebody. No, just be a good soldier or a good Navy man. Learn what you can.

SSGT. DAN FARLEY

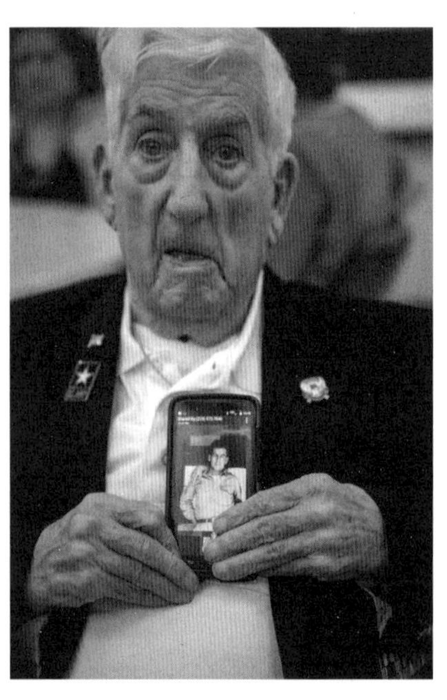

Ranger Farley

Dan Farley

Well, sir, why don't we start in the beginning. Where were you when you heard about Pearl Harbor?

I had just come back from church, and my father was listening to the radio. So he came in and said, "We've been bombed at Pearl Harbor and will probably have to go to war," and then we kept on listening and got more information. I was still in high school at the time. The following March, I told my dad I was going to go into service, and he said, "Hell, I don't want you to be a coal miner anyway." So I went into service.

You enlisted in March 1942?

In 1942. The Marine Corps made two mistakes. They turned down Audie Murphy, and they turned me down too. I was 127 pounds and they turned me down. My father was a coal miner who came out of West Virginia. I was a Golden Gloves champion boxer, and of course running around in the mountains, my father taught me how to make explosive TNT, black powder, and everything like that. Boring down, using caps to blow it up, squibs, or whatever. I knew all about ammo before I went into service.

So when did you enlist, and how did you enlist in the Rangers?

Okay, they came down to Fort Leonard Wood, and they were there to pick Rangers, and I had been reading about Roger's Rangers during the French and Indian War. And then I followed that and said, "Well, I'll go into that." So I volunteered. It was Rangers officers that interviewed you naked, just like you came out there. And asked you questions. I answered, "I was a Golden Gloves boxer. I did this, I did that, and everything like that." And they said you're excused. So I scooted and left and put my clothes on. And then it wasn't too long later when they said I'd been accepted. We went to Camp Forrest, Tennessee.

Was that in September? I think that's when the 5th started, right?

September of 1943.

Now, you had been to basic training at Fort Leonard Wood before that, right?

I completed the twelve weeks of everyday basic training.

How would you compare the Ranger training to basic training?

There's no comparison, because in the Ranger training, we used the logs, you know. You had one, two, three, four, five, six men here, and six over here, and you'd pick up these logs. You'd pick them up and throw them in the air, and they caught them with their arms and threw them back. And then we would go on the speed marches and a 25-mile hike at least three times a week. And you'd get up in the morning for exercises. The duck walking and calisthenics. Close-order drill. And then you went to the rifle range. In the regular infantry they trained you for gang fire. But we were taught in the Rangers aimed fire. Aimed fire. And that's where I think we were more successful than the regular infantry. We also had hand to hand, bayonet training, and everything like that.

The Fabulous Four

That was more extensive in the Rangers?

More extensive in Rangers and everything. I got knocked down plenty of times and got back up to try it again.

So do you feel like that training in the Rangers really prepared you for warfare?

Oh yeah. No question the training was more than what the regular infantry would get. And then we had more-than-average intelligence than the infantry. I think my ATG score was 118, and that was one of the lowest ones they got. But you only needed 110 to go to officers' OCS during World War II.

Did you get more training in Scotland, and when were you there?

Yes. We came into Scotland and were training with the British Commandos there and living in housing. And when we got there, this colonel, a Scots colonel with the Commandos, said, "Now listen, you're going to be dealt a lot of live firing up here, and there's sheep in the hills. If any of the sheep are killed, let us know so we can give the meat to the villagers." Then we said, "Why don't you take the sheep off the hill?" And this is true. He said, "The sheep are tied to the hill. If the sheep are removed from the hill, they would die and not reproduce. We cannot move the sheep, but you could pay us for the dead ones." And they did pay them.

How about cliff climbing they taught you there?

Yeah, cliff climbing and then we went on down to a resort town. And there was an engineer outfit in there before we arrived. They had been relocated so we could go in there instead of them. In the meantime, this engineer outfit from the 1st Infantry Division knew we were going to come in there, and told the citizens, "You're getting the Rangers in here, and they came from the prisons and they're nothing but criminals. And if they live through the war, they will be given pardons." So we go to this town, and when we would go into stores or restaurants and sit down and start talking, everybody there would leave. Then finally our chaplain said, "What the hell is going on here?" So he gets with the minister, and the minister tells him what the people told him. That's some of the things . . .

Tell me about the night of D-day now. You're on your LST,[22] and what are you thinking? Do you remember what was going through your mind that night?

No, I was so damn seasick I wanted to get on that sand. That's the God's truth. I wanted off that damned landing craft. Now, we did not go in on Higgins boats. The Rangers did not. We went in on Landing Craft Assault, and they were British. They had a real low silhouette. Now on the 5th, when they canceled it, a destroyer came by our mother ship where we were. They knew the Rangers were there, and signaled over to see if any of the Rangers wanted to come over and have lunch with them. I said, "Hell yeah, I'll go." So I got on that thing, went over, and got onboard. Turns out, the first guy I saw I went to high school with. Small world. But we got that food and came back. The next morning, we got up. Now, we did not go down the ropes. The landing craft was on the ship, and we loaded up on top and they lowered it down hydraulically. And the USS *Texas* was over there, and their bow was facing us and they put a full broadside to Normandy Beach. I thought that damn thing was going to sink. It went down in the water and came back up. It was fun to watch, and we could see those shells going through the air. And then we got in there, and it was kind of rough. Guys were getting seasick, vomiting and everything. I was too. And you know, this is the honest truth, I was glad to hit that beach and get off that boat. And I ran off of that beach and got over to the wall, and you could hear the bullets hitting on the sand between your legs and everything, but I wasn't seasick any more. We got to that wall, and then we reorganized, because it was mass confusion. That's when we went up to the ditch and went out to Pointe du Hoc.

Now, I believe you came in at Dog White, or were you farther down?

Dog White.

So you were probably just to the left of the Headquarters Company of the 5th Rangers?

Yeah, we were to the extreme left of everything. When we came in there, we blew the Bangalore torpedoes, blew the wire, and took off.

What do you remember seeing when you got off that ramp?
There was fire up on the hills, and the smoke and everything, where the firing had set it on fire. And I didn't see anything but bodies floating in the water. Legs gone and everything else. I wanted to get off the beach. That was our number one thing. The Rangers force job was not to fight on the beach. Our job was to knock out the guns, so we just kept on going. We were not to fight on the beach.

Would you say was there a lot of artillery at the time you got off the LCA? Was there a lot of machine gun fire?
Machine gun fire, cross gun fire, rifle fire, snipers, and artillery. Mortars.

Did you use the breakwaters for cover?
No, I just waded out of there, jumped up, and kept on going. I went to the seawall and got organized with Company A, with Ace Parker as company commander, and we took off.

Were you able to ascend high up onto the bluffs pretty easily?
Well, there was a drainage ditch there, which was quite wide, about twice as wide as this room. It was the drainage for some of the farmer's stuff. So we went up that drainage ditch, and the snipers were shooting down at us. And my friend from West Virginia, Bernard Strain, got killed right there right beside us. I mean, we got the sniper. We finally located him and we kept going on up in there and organizing at the chateau, which was our rendezvous point. Then we took off for Pointe du Hoc. One firefight after the other, gathering up prisoners, and changing the points. At one time, the point became the rear guard because they were circling around behind us.

So you went up to the coastal road and got to Vierville and kept going?
Kept going.

Was there any stage in that that was particularly bad in terms of firefight?
Particularly when you came across the hedgerows and everything through there. There were heavy firefights.

Was that after you hit the coastal road?
We left the coastal road soon after and got more to the beach side.

I see. So you did encounter some hedgerows on the way to Pointe du Hoc?
Yes, we did.

And were they a surprise for you in terms of how big they were, how tall they were?
Those walls had been there for hundreds of years, with dirt and the rock and everything else which was a barrier. And then they had an opening where the animals could go back or for farm machinery or whatever.

So they were probably a great defensive position for the German forces?
Oh yeah. They had crossfire.

How did you guys decide how you were going to conquer those hedgerows?
We didn't know anything about them. We just went straight across as hard as we could go. We ignored the hedgerows. We didn't get inside the hedgerows. Didn't get inside of the barriers, you know. We kept on going until we got to Pointe. That was what was our mission.

When did you get to the Pointe?
Two hours before dark.

Probably 8:00 or 9:00 at night?
I think we had double daylight savings time at that time. I believe it was. But it was before dark.

And whom did you link up with there?
An outpost for the 2nd Ranger Battalion. Someone said, "What's the password." And we hollered, "Talley ho." And they were sure glad to hear an American voice.

So I understand you were shot in the shoulder as you came up the cliff?
Yeah, I was clipped. Not coming up, but it was after we got up closer to the chateau; there was a sniper. We could hear him up in there because they had the bolt action. But if you could hear him when he fired a shot, you could run quite a distance before he could get loaded again. And it's hard to hit a moving target.

Let's move on to Maisy Battery.
That was on the ninth of June.

And that was probably some of your heaviest fighting as well, right?
Right. Five hours of heavy fighting. Constant gun to gun, weapon to weapon.

But if you were to say between D-day, Maisy Battery, and the Zerf engagement, would you say the Zerf engagement was probably the most severe?
The most severe I've ever seen in my life.

So in terms of the Zerf engagement, was the 2nd Platoon isolated behind enemy lines, and the rest of the company was with the other part of the 5th Ranger Battalion?
The 5th Ranger Battalion was assigned a certain defense area. A, B, C . . . whatever on up to F. And then D Company one time got in trouble, and we went up and rescued them in those bunkers.

You were in the 2nd Platoon, right?
Yes.

In the Zerf engagement, was it the whole Company A that went forward and fought behind enemy lines for nine days?
The whole battalion. The 5th Ranger Battalion. We were behind there nine days. We were told to close out the road to keep reinforcements by the Germans from going down to the Saar River and preventing the 10th Armored and the 94th divisions from coming in. And we were also picking up the Germans who were retreating and the Germans who were coming in trying to get down there.

During that mission, you infiltrated diagonally behind the German line?
We climbed up the mountain, and when we got to the top, there was a road where me and John Perry captured that medical doctor. Then we went down into a small village over there, and we went down and through a small road junction. They had farmers and everything down there, and they had some black bread, and in the fireplace we found a couple of hams to make some sandwiches.

Did they stuff them up the chimney?
Yeah, they were hiding them in there. There were a couple of young people there, and we made them get down, but we didn't harm them or anything like that, and that's the only thing we took of their food. We gave them cigarettes, chewing gum, and candy. The people wanted cigarettes. Then we went back and joined the rest of the A Company. We were just on a patrol down there and rescued them. Sullivan said, "Well, I'll go down there and use those houses for headquarters." Which might have been a mistake because I think the German artillery had them zeroed in.

So you would say that the Zerf engagement was the most intense?
Intense operation and constant. You didn't know where they were coming from; they were all around you. I got up out of a foxhole to go take a number one, walked around this tree, and there's a German standing there.

And I got a rifle and he's got a rifle. He dropped his and surrendered. Then on the day before we were relieved and they took us out of there, we were getting shelled, so we ran into this bunker. I had a bunch of prisoners and a Signal Corps 300 radio in there, and while I was guarding the prisoners, I stumbled and fell, dropped my rifle, and went to my knees. This German prisoner helped me up, and another one handed me my rifle back. The war was over for them, 'cause they wanted to go pick cotton down in Alabama or Georgia or someplace.

Well, you must have had difficulty sleeping during those nine days?
I don't think that I got twelve hours' sleep in two days. Then you're just completely exhausted. You were gone.

How did you function like that?
It was either that or get killed.

You were probably very hungry, too, with K rations and all.
K rations. I had twelve candy bars and two D bars, plus the sandwiches we had down there. We were hungry, we were tired, and we were thirsty. We didn't dare drink the water because we didn't know, and then finally relief came in there about the eighth day, when they took the wounded out. And the next day they came in and we got out of there. Twelve of us were left, out of seventy-two, and we were all D-day veterans. It was an adventure of a lifetime if you could live through it.

And your experience during the Battle of the Bulge?
During the Bulge, we were strictly a reconnaissance and combat patrol, protecting the flank of the guys going in to relieve the 82nd, at Bastogne.

So that wasn't as nearly as intense as Zerf?
No, no. There was nothing like Zerf. We were in a company. We were down to twenty-eight men at one point, and there were two hundred and some counterattacking us. And we stuck in there and with the artillery and running in and getting reinforcements from one company to another company.

At the Battle of the Bulge, you didn't have the firefights because the weather conditions were horrible?
Awful.

How did you survive the weather?
You know, they didn't have the proper clothes for us. That's where the Army screwed up during World War II. We did not have the proper winter clothing like the Germans did, but we survived. All the American soldiers suffered. Listen, it was so cold I didn't want to do number two because I didn't want to get in that cold to do number one. And then, if I had to do number two, it was so cold I'd do it and my pants would fall down and froze before they got to the ground. That's cold. The coldest winter in, what, sixty years in Europe, at that time. And your pants were green because you didn't want to pull that thing out.

Can you tell me about the day when you were, I guess, ordered by Gen. Patton to show the German civilians the concentration camps?
Okay, we were up there to help relieve them. There was also a black tank outfit there and black soldiers and a few others. Then Patton, Eisenhower, and Bradley were there. Eisenhower said to get some troops and go out and gather up a bunch of German civilians and walk them through here and see what they have to say. So Patton said, "I'll get the goddamn Rangers." So he did, and we went down and got these people. But we did not take any children in there. We didn't want them to see that. But I have some pictures. I've got one here that shows the oven. There were still some bodies that hadn't burned up inside the oven, and there's a stack of bodies laying [sic] beside the ovens. But there's a funny thing. I've often thought about this, and I've had nightmares about it. All the dead people had their stomachs slashed open. Was that a source of food for the living? Doctor, what do you think about that? I thought about that. The stomach area was opened up.

So all the dead bodies you saw had their stomachs open?
I saw several dead bodies, and their stomach was slashed open. And I'm saying to myself, "Is that a source of food?"

I'm sure that was one of the worst things you've ever seen?
Yeah. I seen a lot of heads blown off and legs missing and everything else down at the beach, and we even had a captain in the Intelligence Section of the 5th Ranger Battalion messing with a German bazooka. It blew his head off, 'cause he was messing with something he didn't know anything about.

Were there one or two particularly sad moments during your military service that you would want to mention?
Well, my friend from West Virginia (I'm also from West Virginia) got killed right there at D-day, and he's on that memorial that we have over here. His name is there. That was a sad day. Then another friend of mine got killed at Zerf when a mortar shell fell right in his foxhole. That got me. And then Portell, a good friend of mine, before we crossed the Saar River going to Zerf, got hit by an artillery shell. I took his BAR and cleaned it and gave it to somebody else. Those were sad moments when you're bunk fellows, you know.

How do you pick up the pieces and keep fighting in that situation?
I think it was here in the heart. The Rangers succeeded because we depended on each other, and I had somebody watching my back and I knew they were going to look out for me. That's what I believed, and still believe that. I think it was all in the heart.

What characteristics would you say made a good leader, whether it was a commissioned or noncommissioned officer?
Well the number one thing was, they were honest with the men and passed information down from their superiors. The other thing was that they didn't play favorites. Everybody was treated equal. The promotions were equal and everything else. As long as you treated me decently, I treated you decently, and that's what I believe made Ace Parker a successful commander. He played no favorites. If you deserved a promotion, you got it. And you know all of the time I was in the Rangers, our company never had a court-martial. Never.

So would you say your company commander, Ace Parker, was one of the best leaders you saw?
Yes.

Anybody else?
Col. Schneider, who later took over the battalion on D-day. He was another one. A good commander, and he was experienced and knew how to handle men. He was down on the beach talking to the general from the 29th Division, and the general stood up. Schneider was bending down but stood up with him. He was later asked why he also stood up, and Schneider said, "The general's standing up. I'm going to stand up too." And that's what I meant when I said Rangers lead the way and take off. That's what we did. When I was living in the Washington, DC, area, I used to go and read the morning reports and all the other information I could. And from that, I think the 5th Ranger Battalion saved D-day.

I'm sure you've seen some noncommissioned and commissioned officers that probably weren't very good as well?
They didn't last very long in the field. One guy got his stripes through the National Guard, and sometimes that family thing and the political thing and the National Guard before World War II was what got a lot booted. I don't think it is now true, but he got his promotion and he was a lousy NCO. And I'm not running down the National Guard. That's what I believe of this individual. He is dead now, and he and I captured that German doctor, and he then was a private. At one time he was a tech sergeant, and Ace busted him down.

Can you give me an example or two of how Ace Parker was a good leader?
Well, he did not put us into position without having the reconnaissance or doing something to protect us. If we ran across a bunch of Germans, he said. "You lay [*sic*] here and I'll fire the first shot when I think we're going to be doing it." And he took care of us and took care of the wounded. He's the one who put me on a damn landing craft and sent me to England.

Now, you were awarded the Silver Star?
And two Bronze Stars and I had two Purple Hearts also.

And the Silver Star was for what engagement?
Zerf. I pulled someone into safety, and the radio was out, so I became a runner and carried some information to communications.

So someone was wounded and you pulled them out?
Pulled them out of a minefield.

Did you do that on your own, or did someone order you to get over there?
No, I went and got him myself. Took me at least an hour to get to him because I was in there with a knife trying to find out if there was anything in there, and finally we got him out of the minefield.

Was that under fire?
Yeah. Not real heavy fire, because we had a crossfire there and they were protecting us.

And your Bronze Stars?
The Bronze Star was given for another communications system that I did. The radio went out, so I went and communicated stuff that Parker wanted done. Now, the second Bronze Star I got when Eisenhower ordered anybody who had a combat infantry badge and was a combat infantryman would receive a Bronze Star. And I never got my medals until back in the '80s or '90s, and I wrote to St. Louis and had sent them a copy of my discharge papers. It was like a 214, but it wasn't a 214. And they came back and they gave me the extra Bronze Star and said your medals are coming from the medal warehouse in Philadelphia, and they did.

What do you think were the greatest lessons you learned from your military experience?
The greatest lesson I learned is to learn to trust people and to be honest and straightforward. Don't lie to a Ranger officer or to another Ranger. If you want to bullshit somebody in a beer joint, that's all right, but don't try to lie to another Ranger or anybody like that.

When you think back to your military experience, I'm sure you get mixed emotions. Sometimes you're sad. Sometimes you're proud of what your Ranger buddies did. Is that about right?
When I think about what we did with the Rangers, I'm proud of what we did and I'm proud to have been a part of that. And World War II and D-day was the experience of a lifetime if you could live through it, and I'll never forget it. And for five years after I came home, I slept with a handgun under my pillow. I don't know why. My mother finally told me to get rid of it.

Did you have a lot of nightmares when you got back?
Yes, I did. I had nightmares for the first year, but not every night. My brother told me he came in there and woke me up a couple of times. That ended about the first or second year. But I still kept that handgun under the pillow.

Did you do anything to help that to end, or it just stopped on its own?
It just stopped on its own.

Do you still have some once in a while?

No. I haven't had a nightmare since I can't remember when. I get at least seven to eight hours every night. I get up in the morning, go exercise, eat a bowl of cereal or something, and then I go do caregiving for people with dementia and Alzheimer's. I get paid for it, of course.

Is there anything you would do differently had you had a chance to change your course in World War II?

Yeah, I think I could have kept my mouth shut and got higher promotions than I did. Sometimes instead of listening, we ran our damn mouth, and I had that problem for a long time. I guess it was because of the Scots-Irish, and my mother and my father encouraged me to speak my mind. They would say, "Tell me what you think, not what I want to hear. Tell me the facts."

Is there anything you really want to impart to future generations on the basis of your military experience?

Love your country. Fight for your country. Be ethical and be a good neighbor. Help thy fellow man.

Do you have any other things that we missed on your military experience that you want to tell us about?

The circumstances of armed combat must not be limited to leadership or charged with certain necessity that can be learned from manuals, studied, and practiced. Manuals, however, must very frequently be tossed aside. When you're in combat, you don't worry about manuals. You go do the job to save lives or to save your own. Changing conditions may come into play, dictating employment of split decisions on the here-and-right-now basis. Action by the enemy in World War II usually required the support of power, artillery, engineers, air power. All this was written into our training manual. But it didn't always work with us, because we didn't get the support that we were supposed to. Some of the generals in the divisions didn't know how to handle Special Forces and Rangers. They didn't understand since we were a small outfit, we could get in, hit, and get out. But we believed we could do any damn thing we wanted to do. We believed that, and that made us successful.

Now, the training had something to do with that. Don't you think it was the group of individuals that went into the Rangers because they wanted to be one of the best and the elite?

Of course. I agree with that. We wanted to be the number one best.

So it was your desire plus your training?

Plus the training and my desire. The Rangers had been criticized. We constantly trained; even when we weren't in combat, we were training. We had the sandboxes laid out of what we were supposed to do on D-day at Omaha Beach. It was laid out, and we studied that. Then they brought in these fire engines and ladders. We climbed the ladders and went over them and climbed back down. Did that every day. Then you did the calisthenics, pushups, log work, and Parker stopped us from doing something else. We'd go to the place where they had fish, get a grenade, and throw it in the water. The dead fish would come up, and we would have fresh fish. But he stopped us from doing that.

PFC DAVID OWEN

I'd like to start by asking what you were doing before America became involved in the Second World War. What were your career plans? What were your goals?

I had no career plans. My mother had some career plans for me, but she was getting more and more disappointed all the time. She thought I was on a criminal path, so she talked some people at a military school into taking me on a working tuition. Room and board and all, but I worked there to help pay the expenses, and she thought perhaps that I was going to be unhappy about that. But I was very pleased to be away from home. Very pleased to be at the school, and that was one of the turning points in my life. That's when it began, because I was on my own. I learned how to study, to be on my own, and how to make things happen my way.

David Owen

Did you follow news of the war in Europe and of the Japanese and Chinese fight?

I was in high school. It was the beginning of my second year at the military school. I was in my room studying and listening to a Washington Redskins game. I'm an Eagles fan, but all I could get at the time was a Skins game, and the announcement was made about Pearl Harbor.

Did you recognize the significance of that announcement?

No, I recognized the significance of the expression in the people's voices; the urgency and the seriousness and the excitement they were using to express themselves. Although I was in military school and I was set as far as a career path was concerned, we all pretty much knew by then that almost all of us were going to go into the service. Some of the guys weren't, but they were so brilliant that they were needed, after high school, if can you imagine, to work in industry with their brains.

Did the atmosphere of the military school change at all after the attack on Pearl Harbor?

No, no. We didn't get any lectures about being serious about this or anything. I don't recall anything of the sort.

Ranger Owen

Ranger Owen with camp sign

Did you enlist into the service or were you drafted?

I enlisted and did my basic training at Fort Benning. After my basic, I was assigned to the 63rd Infantry Division in Camp Van Dorn, Mississippi.

Did you stay long with them?

As long as I could tolerate it. I gave somebody a write-up about how I became a Ranger, and I cleaned it up and it's somewhere in your files now. I cleaned it up because I didn't want my kids reading about some of the things I had done. But I learned the machine gun from a really good machine gunner while I was in basic. I was really tight buddies with one of the corporals in the cadre, and I learned the machine gun from that sergeant and his corporal. And we used to go out and drink the whole weekend and go over to Phoenix City and get in fights and so forth. His name was Cooter, from Montgomery, Alabama. So in the 63rd, I drank a lot of beer. I did a lot of fighting, and I also did boxing exhibitions and sharpshooting for the regimental combat rifle team.

I pretty much had things any way I wanted them, because I was one of their show people. My captain, as I said, was a drunk. The second lieutenant was somebody I knew from military school, and he wound up there. And he knew what I thought of him, and he knew I knew what kind of a person he was. And I was not going to go into combat with these guys as my leaders, knowing he would want me dead and he wouldn't have a witness. All the little flyboys with their silk scarves were being dumped into the infantry, and they didn't want to get dirty. It was a woeful outfit. There was no one you could depend on, and I thanked God for allowing me to become a Ranger, because I knew that I could depend on whoever it was on either side of me, and I'd be damned if I was going to not justify their faith in me, you know.

How were you recruited into the Rangers? From the 63rd?
I was in the repo depot in France. The announcement came over the loudspeaker that the Rangers were looking for replacements. I knew ahead of time it was Rangers that they were looking for, and I said to my buddy, "Jerry, this is our chance. Let's go." So he went with me, and I was accepted but he wasn't. And the guy who accepted me was the guy I knew in the 63rd Division.

This was the machine gunner?
He wanted me for a machine gunner, but I asked him if he could use a BAR man just as well, and he said okay.

Why did you prefer the BAR to machine gunning?
I could move and set myself up where I wanted to be. Cover for the guys and move.

So joining the Rangers from a replacement depot, you had no opportunity for Ranger training?
No. When I came into the Rangers, they assigned me to a particular sergeant, a particular squad, but I was already in shape. I was in good shape.

The Rangers had a reputation as a tight-knit elite group, and you joined them as a replacement. What sort of friction did you face?
As an outsider. I don't recall any friction. Some of the older men, like the twenty-eight-year-olds or whatever they were, were less open armed about accepting, but it was a temporary thing. You can tell. It's a marvelous thing when you see all these sizes of these World War II guys and it really didn't matter. There weren't any specifications. It came from here and here, and they were a devil-may-care bunch. A careless bunch. Crazy.

Where were the Rangers when you caught up with them and joined their unit?
I don't know, but the first thing I remember when I got there was that we all lined up and went to a whorehouse.

Was that common as you progressed through the war, that you didn't know where you were?
Yes, that's true. I never paid any attention.

Is that the case with most of the other squads?
I don't think so, because if you talk to Dick Lemnitzer, he's a 5th Ranger and he always tells me where I was and what we did, and I remember some things. For instance, I can't recall being at Buchenwald until he told me I was there. I remember distinctly being in Weimar, but, you see, Weimar was a cultural center in Berlin and that's how I knew Weimar. From violin playing, from the life I had known before I went into the service. I got the Nazi flag down from the city hall, but that's all I remember. I think we were living, bunking in the city hall. I don't remember going to it to get the flag. I remember being in there and going up to get the flag. And Buchenwald was close by. So Dick tells me I was at Buchenwald. I'm Jewish. All of my mother's side of the family are Hungarian Jews, and they spent some time in concentration camps. I don't know whether that had anything to do with it.

Describe your first battlefield engagement.

It was a recon into the woods and [we] picked up some Germans that were shaving with a mirror against the tree trunk and collected them and brought them back. That was the first mission. I went behind the lines, picked up some guys for interrogation, and brought them out.

Do you feel that your training from military school or in basic training prepared you for the action you faced in Europe?

No. It didn't prepare me for anything. It helped me get grown up. It helped me become something different than I was. I don't know to what extent you can prepare anyone for some of the activity we were involved in. I know how to shoot a gun, and I was good with the guns, but I have a son-in-law out there in Utah who likes to shoot deer. I don't get it, but anyway he likes to shoot and so forth, but it doesn't mean a thing to me.

Did your fellow Rangers help you adjust to these combat experiences and situations?

Well, I don't think so. The only thing I do know is that after I came out of the service, it took maybe five years or so after I was discharged for me to fit into civilian life and mesh in there a little bit better than I had been. I realized that I was coming down, readjusting. As I say, I wasn't interested in being sensible or sweet or tender or understanding or anything. I figured if I was an animal, I would survive, and that's what I was.

What was your impression of the noncoms and officers in the Rangers?

Our platoon sergeant was an intelligent German-speaking American, and he was a wonderful guy. I tried to get his picture to give you, and I talked to his widow. She should have sent the picture, but he was an intelligent, excellent leader. I think he was twenty-three when I was eighteen, and that's a lot of difference in experience between a dumb eighteen-year-old kid and somebody twenty-three. He was a good leader. He confessed about ten years ago when we were talking, that the time he was leading us through the woods, he really didn't know where he was. He was lost. But you would have followed him anywhere. He was a wonderful guy. All the noncoms were absolutely firmly competent.

So you would say the Rangers met your expectations?

Oh yes. My company commander was a guy I knew in the 63rd Division, and he was a West Pointer. There was no "Lieutenant, sir!" stuff. Everything was on a first-name basis, and that was because everybody was responsible for that mission. Everybody knew what was going on. We didn't know it at the same time because it came down from one echelon to the other, but when it got to us, we knew the whole thing and what everybody was supposed to do.

And these qualities were lacking in the infantry units?

There wasn't anybody that I could depend on in the 63rd. I had a couple of buddies there, but I'm not sure I could have depended on them.

What major battles did you participate in?

No major battles. I was in raids, skirmishes, surveillance, reconnaissance. That's all. I came in right after Zerf as a replacement.

You mentioned frequently not knowing where you were. Did you know when you were inside German territory when your unit had penetrated that far?

Oh yes, oh yes. Before we went across the Rhine, we were in the state of just a blank space. We were moving and then we weren't doing anything. And the word came that we were waiting to get over the Rhine. And then the word came and Dick actually saw the planes, but we were all going to go. According to our colonel, we were going over in L4s and L3s to Rangers to a Piper Cub and get dropped on the other side in the Cubs. Then they were coming back for some more of us and taking us over, and we were supposed to jump out of the Piper Cubs. There was another guy in E Company, whom [sic] I knew had been a paratrooper, and I went to him and said, "Oh, Bob, how about that?" He was a sergeant. I said, "Maybe I can make corporal, because they'll want to know how to do some of the things, and I'll have to run some of the classes. I could teach the guys how to not get hurt, so they'll be useful when they hit the ground." But then they got the bridge at Remagen and we didn't do any Piper Cub activity. I think it was just another idea they had, as they were trying to figure out what to do.

So you had some training in jumping?
Oh yeah, I was a paratrooper, after the 63rd.

Did you consider staying with the paratroops at that point?
Well, the people that I was with had finished jump school, and we were told that we were restricted to the area because we were going to get shipped out on Monday. So I said to my buddies, "Well, if we're getting shipped out on Monday, let's have one more party." So I stole some passes from the company clerk's desk, and we all went off and partied in Atlanta, Friday, Saturday, and two of them got back to Benning and shipped out with the paratroops, but the other guy and I got into a discussion with the MPs and were not able to catch the bus.

What was the result of this discussion with the MPs?
We were finally handcuffed and taken to Fort McPherson, and from there we went by train handcuffed to Providence, Rhode Island, where we were fingerprinted and then put in the stockade, which was another one of the great experiences in my life. I wouldn't have traded that experience for anything in the world.

How so? Why was it a great experience?
Because folk literature was being written in the stockade while I was there. I also got into great shape there, since from the time we got up, fixed our bunk up, and went to breakfast, from 8:00 until 12:00 every day, seven days a week, we marched. Then we had lunch in the mess and then we were out marching from 1:00 to 5:00. Eight hours of marching a day, seven days a week. And what really pissed me off was when I heard "sound off" that the fruity air corps was singing. "Sound off, one, two," you know. 'Cause I was marching in the stockade, and it was an absolute thing of beauty. We were maybe 80 percent black. Every one of the groups that was marching had a wonderful marching commander or drill sergeant or whatever you want to call them, and they all had gorgeous voices. They would sing their songs while we were marching, and we would sing the second line each time in response. And they'd make up all kind of things, which was wonderful. It had nothing to do with the crap that these flyboys were singing. I called them Jody songs because they were all about Jody. Jody was the guy who was screwing their girlfriend while they were in the service. Jody was the guy who was doing whatever it was he was doing. Of course, it was stuff that they wanted to do. He wasn't in all the songs, and I don't remember all of these. I just remember two of them. The one was "Every time I get an allotment," and then we would sing, "Jody gets a new apartment. Sound off, sound off." But we did all of their military commands, left flank, right flank, reverse, oblique, skip a beat. And you doodled a couple of steps so that you syncopated your marching and everything. You're looking at fifty, a hundred guys doing this absolutely perfect marching order, voices all over the stockade. It was inspiring. The one I liked best was "If I die in the combat zone, box my ass and ship me home. Sound off." But that's the kind of stuff they did, which was not what the air corps was doing. I don't know what their songs were, but they weren't Jody songs.

It sounds like you had a better sense of camaraderie there than you did back at Fort Benning?
Oh, I was absolutely thrilled, and I was accepted, you know. I had my overcoat on, tramping up and down.

There were no prejudices?
None, none whatsoever. I never noticed anything, and I got along well there. I was from Philadelphia and I was a jitterbug. I danced, danced, danced. I used to go to Harlem and dance in the Savoy Ballroom on Saturday nights. So there was no adjustment for me with the black people, and they were accepting of me. I never had any problems one way or the other.

How did you get from the stockade into the Rangers?

Well, that was the point. After I was court-martialed and put in the stockade, then we were cannon fodder to be sent over there, and I was in the repo depot. I didn't want to wind up in another 63rd Division.

So, as you advanced farther and farther into Germany, did you find the resistance was growing fiercer or was it starting to slacken?

I think you could sense that things were falling apart a little bit. Now, a lot of stuff I never found out. I just did my thing. There were two squads in our platoon, and we were not together. The one squad was one place and our squad was another place. E Company sometimes was spread out over a 50-mile area.

Do you recall German resistance stopping you, and the announcement that Germany had surrendered?

I recall unexpected opposition, and I recall feeling sympathy, pity for these feeble people coming out to oppose us. They would shoot all their ammunition so they could surrender. And these old guys and these poor children, ten, twelve years old, could hardly carry any weapon, and they didn't want to fight. I never met the Hitler Youth with the Panzerfaust. I didn't know anything about them until I read about them.

What was your saddest moment during your time in military service?

Well, we lost guys after the war was over, and that was an unhappy thing. Now here I am, eighteen years old, and I'm telling you we had this sweet young boy in E Company, and you wonder where the hell I'm coming from. But he had a very nice face. He had a tenderness about him. He had innocent blue eyes, red hair, and he was just a nice kid who was starting out. He went swimming and drowned. We also had a guy who got electrocuted on the top of the metro. He went to France and wanted to travel first class on top of the subway instead of in the car, and got electrocuted. One of my friends there, Blackie, shot himself in the foot. He and I were collecting schnapps to celebrate VE-day, and the morning I got up to celebrate with him he went out to a truck and shot himself in the foot so he could get back to the States faster. So those are the things that made me feel confused and unhappy about what happens to people. Before, I didn't care, because the war was still going on. I didn't care about anything until after the war ended.

You mentioned being at Buchenwald concentration camp. What are your recollections?

Hardly any. Dick Lemnitzer asked me if I remembered being in Buchenwald, and I said no. But then the more he talked about it, I remembered some of the things. I remembered the gray buildings. I remembered the gate. I remembered some bodies and some people. We had a Polish kid in our outfit that we had to restrain when we weren't doing any activity, because he wanted to shoot Germans all the time. And I understood that, because my family, as I say, were all Hungarian Jews. I have to say something else that I did know as clearly as I learned recently. Northern Germans are Lutherans. Southern Germans are Catholic. Northern and central Germany are industrial and naval, but that sort of stuff was not found as much in southern Germany. So as we went farther and farther south, it was almost like coming out of a make-believe war movie. A lot of the people in southern Germany, I think, had to give up a few things, but as far as bombing and artillery shells hitting their homes and house-to-house fighting, they didn't see that. I fit right in there. As I say, I got friendly with this person and that person. I started learning the German language, and I would not speak English unless they taught me German. We made a deal. Interestingly, when we were in France waiting to get back, I went to Paris a few times, and I could not speak French. I could speak German, but I never found a Frenchman who spoke German. They didn't know the language.

Before the war, you said that Germany for you was Weimar; Deutsch culture. After the war ended in Europe, did you have an opportunity to experience any of this great German culture?

I didn't do that kind of sightseeing in Germany or in France on the way back. I went to drink beer in Hitler's beer garden where he started the putsch. I enjoyed going to that beer garden in Munich, and I went into Bavaria and the area all around there traveling and seeing, but I didn't go and see any other landmarks in Munich. And they're everywhere. I went to the beer garden, drank beer, and sang German songs, along with the other Germans. And I went to Paris while we were waiting to come back. Oh yeah, I saw this, I saw that. But I was interested in neighborhoods rather than tourist sites. I never went to the Louvre. I saw it from the outside. I saw Notre Dame from the outside. I saw a lot of other things on the Champs-Élysées. I got a kick out of being at the Place de la Concorde because that's where they set up the guillotine during the French Revolution. And I went to restaurants and the underground nightclubs for entertainment.

You lived with a German family for a while. Is that correct?
No, this family invited me to their house and I ate dinner with them. I don't even remember how I met them. I think maybe it was because I knew they were musical, and I told them I played the violin. Anyway, I remember eating dinner. I remember playing on the violin on this side of the piano. The girl sat at the piano. The mom and dad were singing the songs or playing other instruments. But I do know the piano player and the violinist were in tune. Later on, I used to hitchhike, and I traveled with groceries in my shelter half. All I had to do was put up my thumb and the next jeep picked me up. I went all the way up to Berlin from southern Germany. I went to Nuremberg and Erfurt. I tried to get into Hungary, but I didn't get too far into Austria before I couldn't go any farther. I returned to that area because that woman that I was with was very athletically inclined, and we had a lot of fun rolling around everywhere. Her child was in the other room, and I never saw that child. She was happy to see me. I'd give her the groceries. I'd go over there once or twice during the day. I'd go down and visit the old couple below, and the old couple said that if I stayed in Germany, they would make sure I got a good education. I said I'd love to go to Heidelberg, and they said, "Then you can." And I stupidly said, "Well I gotta go back to America and see my mother." And I should never had done that. I should have stayed. I was going great guns in the language.

What were the moments of greatest happiness during your time overseas?
Becoming a Ranger. That's about it. I didn't have any exhilaration. I was happy the war was over in a sense, but you understand there was no realization that I was going to be out of the service. I fully expected to be recycled into some other combat unit and go to Japan. And I felt that until the war ended in August. But I was Regular Army, so I still had time to serve. I wasn't out of the service, at least from my standpoint. When we came over in October, every couple of weeks I'd get a telegram saying, "Your TDY has been extended. You will be notified where to report in a future communication." Then sometime in January, they told me to report to Fort Leonard Wood.

What were the greatest lessons you learned from your military experience?
I'm a free spirit. I won't do something just because you tell me to do it. My mother used to try to tell me to do things all the time, and I got so sick of it I wouldn't do anything. And it probably isn't my nature anyway. And I became a completely independent person due to my time in the military.

Would you recommend military service for people today?
I recommend it to everybody. As a teacher, I recommend it to my students. I recommend it to their parents. Absolutely. If I was the dictator of America, I would not allow anybody who was sixteen or over to do anything without serving his country for a minimum of two years. It doesn't have to be in the military. They can work in the hospital. They can build roads. They can do anything. Male and female must serve their country and must not serve the country by working for dad on the truck. Somewhere else entirely different from where they are, so the circumstance and what they know about humanity and life is new. Absolutely required. Paraplegic kid works in the hospital. He can run his wheelchair up and down the halls and help other people.

What comments or pearls of wisdom would you provide for future generations on the basis of your military experience?
Well, you and I almost touched on this when we were talking. Our purpose in this life is to become as good as we possibly can be, serving others. That's exactly what I think. If you're not doing something for somebody else, you're a pretty damn sorry excuse. I'm serious about that.

CPL. FRANCIS COUGHLIN

Ranger Coughlin

I'd like to start by asking what you were doing and what your plans were for the future before America became involved in the Second World War.

Well, I was just getting out of grammar school and going to high school when things got going over in Europe. We'd never thought we'd ever be back into a war again after the first one. And as time went on, I went to high school and then I got inspired by a guy, and he said, "Why don't we join the Army?," and I said, "If I ever did that, my father would kill me." But he said, "If we go to war, sooner or later, we're all going." I said, "Well, let's wait. It may be a long time before we get that far." And the war did break out. I went so far as to get out of school and try to go into the service, but at that time there were so many people trying to get into the service that they had a backlog. Then I went to work for a shipyard company where my father worked. They were building minesweepers for the US Navy. I got a job there with him until I was called up into service, and I never told my mother or father what I'd done. The notice came for me to go before the induction board, and that's when I had to tell them that I was going into the Army.

This was before the attack on Pearl Harbor?

No, this was right after that. Anyhow, I went up to the selective service bureau and reported in. They said, "This is the date that you come back and go over to the auditorium. The doctors will be there, and they will give you a physical and everything." So the following week I took a day off from work and went up to the auditorium where the doctors were, and they give me a good physical examination and I passed. Six months later, I got a call from the Army telling me to report for induction. I went up and filled out all the reports and everything that was necessary. I went home, told them what I'd done. My mother started crying. My father came home from work. She told him and he blew his cork, and I told him, "Dad, everybody's going. We're going to war. We just got attacked by the Japanese." So anyway, I went into the service and I spent the next three and a half years and I joined what was one of the elite forces in the Army, the Rangers.

Before you joined the Rangers, where did you do your basic training?

My basic training was done in Fort Rucker, Alabama. I was with an engineering outfit, and we were building bridges and roads and such things at Camp Rucker. It was quite a chore trying to get everything squared away, because the sand was so light that even running a bicycle over it changed the pattern of the way you run on it. Anyhow, I wanted out of the engineers because I knew I wasn't going to get any place, since my superior officer and I didn't get along. I got the dirtiest jobs there were. I don't remember crossing him, saying anything back to him or anything, but we just did not hit it. So when the Rangers notice was put up on the bulletin board at retreat one night, I signed up right away and I tried to talk my three buddies into it, and they thought it all over and they said, "Nah, we're going to stay here." But lo and behold, two days later, before they took the notice down, two out of the three signed up. But I was the only one who passed the examination, physical and everything, and I said to myself, "I thought I was the stupid one." In school, they were a little bit better than I was, but I think that they were mostly scared of going, thinking about what they'd done. They knew that the engineers were going to be okay, and so they decided to stick together. I guess they probably figured out just about what the Rangers were, and they decided they didn't want to go into them. But I was never sorry the day I moved out of there and into Tennessee. I did what I wanted to do, which was to get away from the engineers and the officers I couldn't get along with, and I made a good mark for myself by doing so.

Where did you go for your Ranger training, and what was that like?

We started out at Camp Forrest, Tennessee, which was just outside of Tullahoma, and when everybody got into the camp, the six companies were formed and then we started training. The biggest thing was walking. We had to learn to walk, which we did. The first day we only walked 12 miles. The second day was 26 miles. And then we learned how to walk faster, cover more ground in less time. And honest to God, at the age that we were, we could walk almost twenty-four hours a day, because that's all we did was walk. But then when that part of the training was over, then we started on the rest of it: the running, the takedown of people who were shooting against us, and everything. We learned how to fight under combat conditions. Of course, it was all dummy ammunition and blanks they shot, but it gave us an idea of what a gun looked like and felt like when they're firing directly at you. It changed our lives quite a bit. I felt more secure.

How did the Ranger training compare to basic training?

You couldn't even compare basic training to what we went through. We not only walked, we ran. We did most of our work at night. We would leave camp about 4:00 in the afternoon and be gone all night long. We came back in the morning and slept until about noon, when we would get up, clean our equipment off, and get ready to go back out again around 4:00 in the afternoon. That's what we did for three weeks, and it got tiresome after a while. Our sleep was getting less and less, and the training got more and more severe. But when we got overseas, we really found out why.

So you would say that the training you received as a Ranger adequately prepared you for the battlefield?

Definitely. That's why we were trained the way we were. We were preparing for battle and what to do in battle, and we had a certain air about us, you know. Like the Marines used to have. They were the best in the world. Well, we were the best in the Army at the time. None of us ever really wanted to quit, but the idea was we were still being tested. People were getting dropped out. They couldn't keep up. They couldn't do this. They couldn't do that. And all it was, was the training. You were getting worn down. And I guess that's what they wanted. They wanted people who could go like heck twenty-four hours a day, seven days a week. And when we took our training in England, we used to walk 20 miles a day, every day.

What was your impression of your NCOs and officers? Did they have the respect of the men immediately, or did that have to be earned over time?

No, because most of the officers and the noncoms started with us right at the beginning. We lost very few of the regulars who first started in the States and went overseas. We all stayed together and trained together, and we only lost a couple officers and maybe about seven or eight noncoms. And the noncoms were taken out of the line because they were hurt. As soon as you got hurt, if you were out more than two or three days, they didn't want you anymore. They shipped you out and got a replacement. And the replacements that came in at the time were pretty good because they knew what they were getting into. It took a few weeks, but they fitted right in. So the training that I had was filtered down through the ranks and into other units. They saw how good we were, and they trained just as hard as we did.

You mentioned crossing over to England. Do you remember roughly when that was?

Oh yeah. February 2, 1944.

Did you have more training in England?

We did most of our training in England, Scotland, and Wales. We went from the middle of England into Scotland and trained up there. Some of the companies trained with the commandos of the British army. We trained with the equivalent of the Navy Seals, since we had to learn how to be in the water and on land at the same time and fight that way. And it took a few days to get adjusted to what they wanted, but once we got the know-how and everything, we were almost as good as they were. We really put a lot into it because we wanted to show them that we were just as good commandos who really showed us what it was going to be like in battle. Because when they were practicing, they were shooting live ammunition, and they shot pretty darn close to us, to let us know what it sounded like and what it felt like to get almost shot. It was great.

Did the British Commandos respect the Americans and treat them as equals?
Oh yeah. It wasn't too long by the time we got ready to go into battle in June of '44 that they really came down and said, "Boy, you Yanks aren't bad. You're almost as good as we are." You know, to throw a little dirt in our face. But they respected us because we did everything that they told us to do. And they showed us how to do it because they had more experience doing it than we did, since they got into the war earlier than we did. And we respected them a whole lot. Man, I'm telling you even afterwards, when I got out of the hospital and was floating around waiting to be reassigned, I was in the pub one time and I had the Ranger tag on. Then a couple Commandos came over, took the table, slid it away, and they said, "Okay, Yank, let's go." They wanted to fight right then and there. And then they laughed like heck. They said, "You guys are Rangers. Man, you're almost as good as we are." We sat down and started drinking. But we couldn't outdrink them.

What was your task in your unit?
I was a rifleman. I was in Headquarters Company and worked with the S2 and S3 officers. I would go out on patrol with an officer, an S2 or an S3, whatever the guy was at the time. We used to go out at night, and I was behind the lines three times in four days, picking up information. And we spent maybe six or seven hours behind the lines, letting the Germans walk within 20 to 30 feet of us. We couldn't do anything but just lay [*sic*] there, because there were only the three of us against fifty or sixty Germans. Besides, our job was to gather information, not to engage the enemy.

Do you remember crossing the English Channel?
Oh yeah. It rained like heck and it was windy. We had waves of 10 to 15 feet, and they had to call the invasion off and go back to England because it was too dangerous. We would have lost more men overboard that would ever probably hit land. So they brought everything back. We were in the harbor aboard ship, and we never got off the ship once we got on it and started, 'cause no leaks. We had patrol boats riding all through where the ships were, making sure that nobody went anywhere. If they caught you in the water, they didn't put you back on the ship where you were. They'd just take you with them and dump you off someplace else, and then god knows what the hell happened to some of the people they picked up. And all they wanted to do was go to town and have a good time. But they never came back. It was a scary thing the way the English operated. Man, I'm telling you, we were more afraid of them than we were of the Germans. But yet they gave us good training. Oh yeah.

On the sixth of June as you were on the boats approaching the shore, what was going through your mind?
What to do when I got off. I had a job to do, and my job was to get the priest up to the road, you know, onshore. I had to get him up there, and we were the last two off the boat. Everybody else went off and then we went off. But the priest stopped, instead of going on like he was supposed to. There was a guy laying [*sic*] over there on the left-hand side of us. Down, you know, his arm outstretched and everything. He was dead, of course, but the priest rolled him over and started praying. Giving him the last rites of the church and everything and anointed him and then he ran up to the next guy. And I kept hollering to him, "Come on, we gotta get up to the road. Come on, Father." And the major was hollering like hell at me to get him up to the roadway. So the priest said, "Francis, you take off and go up there and tell him I'll be there when I get there. I have a job to do." And that's the last I saw of the man until 1953 or 1954. Never saw him from the time I left him on the beach, which was D-day, June 6, about 8:00 in the morning, for another fifteen or twenty years. Where he went, I don't know. I do know that he caught up to the outfit someplace in northern France, and he was gone for almost three weeks. Nobody knew where he was, not even the major. But the whole time, he was out doing his job. Nice man.

Describe stepping on to Normandy Beach. What did you witness?
A pool of water about 4 feet high and a boat trying to come over the top of me. You know, when we jumped off the landing craft, most of the guys got in just with water up to their knees. That's about as far as it went, but by the time that they got out, our boat drifted a little bit with the waves coming in. So when we jumped off, we landed in bomb craters, where the shells came down and blew a big hole in the water or the sandy beach and it filled with water. And the priest that I was taking care of was a short man, so when he jumped into the water,

it was way up to here on him. So I turned around and helped pull him out, and that's when he started running to those guys who were laying [*sic*] on the beach. Dead or hurt, wounded or whatever. He gave them the last rites and anointed them and everything. That was his job, and he didn't care who was hollering, the major or the colonel; he was going to get his job done.

I guess he answered to a higher commander?
He sure did. And that's exactly what he said.

When you went up to the road above the beach, what was the terrain like?
Well, first we got up to the roadway that led across the beach from one little village to the next, about 4 or 5 miles down the road. You got up over the top of the roadway and it went right up a sandy hill. And you could see walking paths that the Germans made. Down and up. We always thought they used this prior to putting shells in it, you know, booby traps and everything. So they looked good, and I guess we were pretty lucky because we walked up their paths and nothing ever happened to any of us. No booby traps went off, no nothing. So we must have been in the right area at the right time. When we got up to the top of the hill, we were in people's yards. The houses were only 50 feet away. You could hear people hollering like heck inside the house, and of course they didn't bother us and we didn't bother them. But we left people there to guard them in case anybody came out. We got through that town with about twenty-six men, and that's as far as we got the first day, because we waited, to try to get everybody together. But it took three days before we ever got the full extent of the battalion together.

Were the Germans shooting at you at this time?
Only for a short time. They didn't stay around long. They were laying [*sic*] on the ground shooting right down. In fact, when we were on the beach, you probably could have seen them up there shooting at you. Maybe not directly at you, but at somebody. By the time I got up to the roadway, they had moved back across the yards where they were in, behind the houses, across the road, and on up into the woods again. By the time everybody got together, we took the same paths they used and went right after them. But we never did catch up to them. God knows where they went.

As your units consolidated and your numbers picked up, where did you go from there?
We went east on the highway that ran across the paths there through the homes, and we ended up in another town, and that's where we were stopped. Actually, we should have stopped long before that because we only had part of B Company and part of Headquarters Company. That's all we had going in from the beach up to that road. We didn't have anybody else. We had to lay [*sic*] there and wait, and the Germans were raising hell with the people who were behind us. And we couldn't do anything about it, since we had no mortars with us. I was a rifleman, so the only thing I could do was shoot my rifle when I saw somebody up in one of the houses move. And then we were running low on ammunition, so the major and the colonel decided we would stop here. So we regrouped for one day, and the next day was Friday. I went on patrol with the officer that I worked with. We knew the Germans had left, so we went through the town and about 2 miles beyond it. That would be toward Saint-Lô, and you could hear the church bells ringing, but we never had any contact with anybody. We couldn't even find an American. All the Americans went up that road, but we couldn't find anybody. So we turned around and went back to the rest of the company. Never did see any Germans.

After the beach area was secured, what was your next major engagement?
Let's see, Tuesday, Wednesday, Thursday, Friday. Friday morning, right after daylight, we went on the road and we walked through this town. Walked through the town, no Germans, no nothing. Kept right on going, walked around the outside, got up the road about 9 or 10 miles before we were engaged, and that only lasted a short time. And it turns out the Germans were trying to delay us. They would put up a lot of firepower, and they didn't care whether they shot you or not. They just wanted to keep you locked up some place. It gave them time to get farther away from us. That night, we were just outside of Saint-Lô, maybe 4, 5, or 6 miles, something like that, and the lieutenant came around and said, "Okay, Coughlin, let's go." I said, "Where to?" He said, "Up

there." And he pointed to where the Germans were. So we went on the night patrol, the three of us—myself, another fellow, and the lieutenant, and we scattered around. We were doing the job that we were trained for, scouting around. Then the lieutenant said, "We'll make one sweep and then we're getting the hell out of here." Which we did. And backwards we went. We ran across the open field, and then the moon started to break through. It got worse, but nobody shot at us. We thought somebody would shoot, but they didn't. So we got back to the company about 4:30 or quarter to five in the morning. The lieutenant reported into the major and they made plans for the next day. And the next day was Saturday, and everybody was more or less taking a breather and getting more ammunition. They started using two belts instead of one around their bellies so they'd have enough ammunition with them and things like that. There were three French 75s laying [*sic*] in a field, pointed our way, so the major said to me, "You and you, get some grenades and put them out of action." So we went down and threw the grenades down each of the barrels. Well, the grenade on this side of me went off, and the one on that side of me went off, but the grenade I threw down the middle one didn't go off, so I didn't bother asking anything. I just took out another grenade, pulled the pin, put it down, and then slowly walked away. All of a sudden those two shells went off. I got hit in the leg. Another guy got hit in the head. Another guy got hit in the shoulder. And a guy that was laying [*sic*] in the woods also got hit. So there were four of us hit for one stupid mistake. As it turned out, that was the last I ever saw of the Rangers again.

Did you split the barrel of the cannon?

Yeah, the whole breach. When the shell went off that was inside, it blew the whole damn thing apart. When it went, it made a hell of a noise. It happened so fast, I didn't even know I was hit. And as I turned, I fell, and when I rolled over, I looked at my leg and said, "Oh, Jesus." Then I started to holler like hell. They got me into an ambulance, and when I got back to England, they operated and I stayed in England for six months. I went in on June 11 and came out on December 27. When I got out of the hospital, I went back into Europe again.

So when you were hit, it was probably a piece of the cannon itself?

That's what it was.

When you were injured, how long was it when you were on the ground there before you received medical attention?

About five minutes, and then an aide man was there. We had good aide men.

What did he do?

He made a big slit in my pants and looked into the wound. Then he got this probe out and went down there probing, and I hollered. He had touched the piece of metal that was in my leg, and that hit a nerve or something. That's when I hollered. He said, "You'll be all right." He bound it up, and ten minutes later I was in the ambulance on my way to the beach. They laid me on the ground down at the beach. The doctor came over, looked at me, and then told two guys to put me on a boat that was going out just then. That was on a Saturday. Sunday about 4:00 in the afternoon I was operated on in England. They took the metal out of my knee and then they shipped me to another hospital inland, where I stayed until December.

Did you have the full use of your leg by then?

Oh yeah. I had the full use of my leg long before that. I was ready to go anytime, but they kept me there.

When they shipped you back to Europe, did you rejoin your Ranger unit?

No. I went to the repo depot, and then I got into Paris and was in another repo depot there. I asked the guy, "You know if there are any Rangers around? Most of them will have a diamond patch with a blue background and gold lettering on it." He said, "There's three or four of them down there." Which there were. I met them and we talked. I said to them, "If you're going back to the unit, I'll go with you, 'cause I just got out of the hospital a week ago." So they said, "Yeah, we're going back." I said, "Okay, where do you want to meet? What time?" So we decided we were going to leave at 6:00 in the morning, when it was still a little dark. Well, I went to the place where we were supposed to kick off. I never did find any one of them. Then I got picked up by the MPs, and they said, "What are you doing?" I said, "I want to get back to my unit." Yeah, they took me right back to the unit I was in already, you know, at the repo depot there. That's where they took me. They said, "Get inside. We gotta talk." So I went inside and the captain questioned me, you know, for all this and that, and I told him, "I was only trying to get back to my unit." He said, "But you're not qualified to be with your unit, and you're not going back into combat anymore." And I hollered like hell. I said, "What am I going to do?" He said, "I don't know, but you're not going back into combat. You'll probably go to some other unit." And I ended up in an ordnance outfit. I got so stinking mad, I wouldn't do anything, and they said, "Well, you know how to drive a truck?" I said, "I never drove a truck, but I can drive a car." They said it was the same thing, only bigger. So I drove a truck. I went all over Europe in that truck, and every truck I had was brand new, and on the canvas covers, I used to put "Ranger 5," which stood for the 5th Ranger Battalion. Somebody asked me, "You think anybody will tell you where your outfit is?" I said, "I don't know. If they're truthful and know where the unit is, I'll just leave the truck and go with them." I was ready to do anything to get back. But I never made it back to them.

What was it about the Rangers that brought such loyalty out of you? Why was it that you wanted to get back to that unit?

It just grew on you, once you were part of them. And a lot of guys did the same thing I tried to do. Oh yeah. You just wanted to get back over there because you knew how good they were, but you didn't know how good these guys were. So you wanted to go back to where you knew. Some of them made it. Most of us didn't. The MPs were on the lookout, and they picked you up.

If you had the full use of your leg and were recovered, why do you think they told you that you could not serve in a combat unit?

I have no idea. That's one thing I couldn't understand. I was playing basketball, running, jumping, doing everything. And yet I couldn't go anywhere. I was still, as they say, limited service. But I drove a truck and toured Europe. Every place I went where there was a soldier, I said, "Do you know where the Rangers are?" But most of the guys in the companies that I went through didn't know who the hell the Rangers were, you know, and I couldn't understand that no how. A couple of times I even asked an officer from some unit wherever the hell we may have stopped, but nobody had ever heard of them.

So you never caught up with them?

Never caught up with them.

Did you have any interesting experiences as a truck driver when you were going around Europe?

No, I couldn't do anything except follow the guy in front of me. I had to keep the front of the truck right on his ass, you know. It was comical a lot of the times. You got a big laugh out of driving a truck and seeing what some of these guys did.

Were there any moments of comfort or happiness during your tour of duty?

Oh hell yes. We had a lot of fun. Most of it was after I got out of the hospital, not back with the Rangers. That was all business. We were happy among ourselves, the Rangers, both the 2nd and 5th Battalions. We never caught up to the 2nd Battalion because they were in a different area, and the only time that they ever came close to one another was when they were in Germany. That's the only time the two battalions were close to one another. But the rest of the time I never saw them, never heard from them. And no matter where I went when I was driving the truck, I'd mention the 2nd or 5th Battalion, 'cause I didn't care which one I run into. I knew if I got to one I'd get back to my own unit. But nobody ever knew anything about the Rangers. I thought, "Well, I guess we are a secret bunch." But I don't know, it was a good life and I still run around with the Rangers. I'm still with them. That experience changed my whole perspective of life, I guess. I wasn't a kid anymore. I was a grown person, and it really made me feel good. Even to this day I'll talk Ranger. I'll go anywhere that they want to go. If they want to jump overboard, I'll jump with them, because it's still within you.

What were the greatest lessons you learned from your military experience?

To be patient, for one thing. And to analyze exactly what you want to do and how you want to do it. That helped me a lot when I was working as a fireman. I learned things and I said, "This is what I was thinking about twenty-five, thirty years ago." What I would do at such and such a time, and I still live by that. My whole life changed actually in about five days, from the time I landed on that beach until I got wounded.

Do you have any words of advice or pearls of wisdom for future generations, on the basis of your military experience?

Be as good as you can, and if you say you will do something, do it with your whole heart and your whole body. Pay attention to those around you, because that's what it all meant to us. Work very closely with the guy next to you. You save him. He'll save you. That's the way it is yet today.

Would you recommend military service to young men today?

Everybody should have to go in military service and serve a year or two. You bet your bippy, because that's the only thing that's going to straighten this country out. 'Cause you get these guys who are against war, they're against this, and they're against that, you know. It's great to be against the war. I was against the war too, but if I didn't help do something about it, I may not have such a good life as I'm having right now. So anything could have happened. But I've had a good life since the service, and I respect everybody and I want them to do the same to me too. I hang out with people who I have judged and they have judged me, that I know. And we get together and we trust each other. I would do anything for them and they would do anything for me, and that's the way it's been for the past forty years.

Is there a fellow soldier, fallen or otherwise, that you would like to mention now and acknowledge who maybe didn't get the recognition he deserved in the service?

Yeah, but he's dead. He was a guy from Illinois, and right now I tell you as good as I know him I can't even remember his name. I can see him. I can picture him standing right there, right now, but the name. But he was a very good friend of mine, and in service, we used to run around together. We kept in touch after the war, and then about four or five years ago, somebody sent me a letter with a few lines written on it and said that he had died, buried so and so. His name was Carroll. John Carroll. I remembered his name. He was a great guy.

PFC LEWIS HAIGHT

Lewis Haight

I'd like to begin by asking what were your plans and what were you doing before the attack on Pearl Harbor.

Well, I was still in high school when the war broke out. Of course, my dad and mother said I had to graduate. So I graduated and then I went down and tried to get in the Marine Corps. My brother was in the Marine Corps, and back then you had to be 6 foot something and perfect. But I had one eye that was a little bad, so I went down and got in the New York State Guard for a little while. And then I told my folks that I was going to enlist. So I went down to the city on the train, and I got to the enlistment area. They were taking the guys in that were draftees, and I said, "Where do I sign up?" They said, "Here, but you have to have permission." They gave me a form to take back to my parents to sign, but I had a letter from them that said, "We as parents authorize . . . you know." So they accepted that, and at that time you could pick the branch of service you wanted. Whether you could keep it or not, I don't know, but he said, "What branch of the service do you want?" I said, "The infantry." He said, "You want the infantry?" I said, "Yeah, the infantry. My grandfather was in the infantry in the Civil War. My dad was in the infantry in the Spanish-American War, so if it's good enough for them, it's good enough for me." So anyway, they put me in the infantry and I wound up in the 98th Division in Camp Breckinridge, Kentucky, and that was where I took my basic training. But I didn't like the outfit from the onset. The straw that broke the camel's back was this first lieutenant executive officer. We were going on a hike, and he said, "Nobody is going to drop out." So a guy dropped out. A lot of guys there were over thirty-five years old and were draftees, you know. Hardly any volunteers. Anyway, he told the sergeant, "Kick him. He'll get up." So the sergeant was kicking him, and he got up and he didn't go too much further. Anyway, to make a long story short, I was a corporal then, and in the noncom meeting, something popped. I said, "If you want your noncommissioned officers to treat their men like this, you can have these stripes." Of course, I had them sewed on pretty good, but I went through the motion. He told me to shut up and sit down. And I told him I'd shut up when I got done. And he said, "I'll have you busted for insubordination." I said, "You can't bust me. I already quit." And needless to say, I got busted. So after that, I got all the crappy details. A little later they came around looking for volunteers for the Rangers, so like a good boy I went to the officer and saluted him and said, "I'd like permission to go up and see about getting in the Rangers."

Did you have any idea, at that time, of what would be involved if you became a Ranger?

I knew it was a special outfit, and I figured sure enough I'd see combat. So anyway he told me, "Permission denied, and besides they wouldn't take you." So I went anyhow, and the sergeant did the same thing. The sergeant tried to get in different outfits, and the officers tore up his application. They wouldn't let him go. So he went over with me. We were both accepted. They wanted to know why I wanted to get in, and I said, "Well, I joined the Army and volunteered for the infantry, but I don't think we'll see any combat." And that's the only division in the United States Army that didn't see one day of combat in World War II. They were made a training division. So I got out and I got into the Rangers.

Where did you do your Ranger training, and what was that like?

Camp Forrest, Tennessee, and it was more or less endurance. Like 7-mile speed marches and a lot of calisthenics. A lot of exercises like getting a log up and over your head and then down and then up and over, as a group. Then we started working with our weapons. In the infantry, I was a rifleman. Well, here I wound up being a rifleman as a scout, but I had an OD BAR. I had to more or less qualify with it. I had to know every phase of the mortar crew's job, from the bipod to the guy out spotting where they land. The whole nine yards. The machine gun crew, you trained for all three jobs, and it helped out because one time we had taken this fortified area in Brest. And we were supposed to go over there because the Germans wanted to surrender, but when we got over there, they started firing at us for a little bit. We found out afterwards that they were just taking life easy because they were waiting for us, and the Free French came up there and opened up on them and they thought it was going to be us. So anyway, Capt. Lueker said, "Fix bayonets. Nobody fire a shot until I give the order." And we just started walking forward. At that point, all the Germans surrendered, and we took the fort without firing a shot. But then the town of Le Conquet, we got a little counterattack from there, and they caught us with our pants down more or less because we were eating the German chow. So we had a lot of stuff coming in, and I said, "We can't sit here like this." I climbed out, ran across, dove behind a machine gun, kicked the traversing bar off, and I wasn't about to sit up behind it or anything like that. I just started to give it a good burst and then move it and give it another burst and then move it and so on, across the whole perimeter, and it cut the fire down. Of course the Air Corps came in, and they bombed and strafed the place.

Do you feel that your Ranger training adequately prepared you for actions like you were just describing?

Oh definitely, definitely. You might even say we were brainwashed, because we figured we were special and could do the undoable. And a lot of times we did things that normally a sane person might not do. I mean, some the antics we pulled, and it worked out for us.

Were there things when you were in action that your training did not or could not prepare you for, and you could learn only in combat?

Oh yeah, I do believe so. One time I got hit, and I wrote a letter home to my dad. I said, "You always told me to keep my head down. Well, I kept my head down, but still got hit. I got hit in the butt." In Scotland, we made so many landings and things like that. Day landings and night landings and landings under fire and this and that sort of stuff. And on D-day, I knew those guys weren't shooting over our heads, but for some reason or other, I guess, a lot of us were prepared for it. I never dreamed that I'd even get hit, you know. Hell, I'm going to get in there. We're going to do the job. And unfortunately, several of them didn't get in there, like Lt. Anderson. He was my platoon leader and he got killed on D-day. Our first sergeant got wounded and died later, but you might as well say he got killed on D-day too.

What are your recollections of D-day from the beginning?

Well, we trained with the British navy, and we didn't have to go down the ropes and things. We just went to our boat station and got into our assault craft. They swung us out and lowered us down. I guess it was about 4:00 in the morning. We just circled and circled and circled. Then we started to go in. We all had upchuck bags, and I daresay an awful lot of us were seasick, especially just going round and round and up and down. It was rough, and going in, the 2nd Ranger Battalion was to take Pointe du Hoc, and they were given a certain amount of time to take it. Then we were supposed to go into the same place. If they didn't take it, then we had to work back to Dog Green, and, as it worked out, it took them longer than planned. So we had to go down, and Col. Schneider saw the backup on the beach at Dog Green, so he diverted us over to Dog White. Unfortunately, the Navy was doing a pretty good job with the destroyers, going along there shooting along the bluffs. So we took a lot of incoming fire, but it wasn't like we were bottled up. And a gentleman from D Company was the one who broke through the barbed wire with a Bangalore torpedo. He blew a gap so we were able to go through. But I didn't even get past the seawall. I got a minor wound going across the beach, and I laid [*sic*] down behind the seawall. They took me back to England, patched me up, and then I rejoined the outfit outside of Cherbourg. I was with them pretty much into Germany. During those times in different battles, we'd lose men, your good buddies, you know. Some would get maimed and some would get a clean kill. It just started to build up. I was the first scout and Norman was the second scout. When he got killed just before we were going to take this hill, I went to get help, and Sgt. Cliff said, "We're moving out." That's where we were going to use walking fire, so we were each given two extra bandoleers of ammunition and we formed a skirmish line. We started to walk forward. Bang, bang, bang. Took clip out, put another clip in. Bang, bang, bang. Like that. We got across the road and up into the woods before we had to stop and take cover, and the Germans took a lot of casualties. But in the interim, Norman got hit. This Kraut got him, and I got the Kraut. I think if he saw me and Norman at the same time, he might have surrendered, but he didn't see me. Well, Norman was going forward and this Kraut got up and nailed him, and he didn't have a chance to reload before I got him. So it was about ten minutes to 9:00. I could see the steam coming out of Norman. I knew he was probably going to go, but I still had to try to help him. I went back to get Clanton to see if he could get somebody to give me. He says, "No, we're moving out." Which we did. So he said, "They'll find him. They'll find Norman." And with that, we moved out, and I guess I was pretty good until it seemed like we'd dig in, and then at night, looking back I could see Norman laying [*sic*] there.

Which battle was this?

What was the name of it? We had gone into Belgium, Luxembourg, and back into France, and we went down into Germany. This was around the first part of December. I got put out of action and missed 90 percent of the German campaign. That's another thing that bothered me so much. I found out what happened at Irsch-Zerf, where the company was given a forty-eight-hour mission and they got miles behind the German lines and took this road junction. They had to fight their way in, and they were supposed to hold it for forty-eight hours. Nine days later they were relieved from being surrounded, but they held it. I had a gut feeling that I should have been there, and this was after I had gone back to England, after I had gone AWOL, and everything else with the MPs. I still kept thinking, hell, I was a Ranger, I shouldn't have cracked. I'm still embarrassed. I should have been too tough to let anything like that bother me, but I guess there were other guys in my outfit who did break down and had to be taken off the line. It just ganged up on me, I guess, and the old mind and heart and soul or whatever it was just couldn't take any more of it.

I see that you were awarded the Purple Heart. What were the circumstances?

Well, that's where I got hit. I didn't get the Purple Heart for what happened during the invasion. They missed it. I got it for when I got hit in the butt over in Brittany. But again, I was lucky. It was just a hunk of shrapnel that got my hip, and I went back to the Aid Station, where they pulled it out and patched it up. Then I rejoined and that's when we took that one pillbox. It ended the Brest campaign. Capt. Luther wrote an article. It's in the archives here. "How to Take a Pillbox." Sgt. Clatt went up with a patrol during the Zerf thing. There was like a little trench going down to the underground quarters where they had a periscope. This was a solid steel dome with apertures, and they had this periscope up there. He found out where the air vent was for the underground, and while we were up there, we got chased off the hill. That's when Manifol and Stryker got killed. So that night they went back up again. Well, the Germans figured we would be back, so they were prepared for us, and when we got there, we got done and set our charges off. We couldn't do too much except for the one that Dusty Raymond put on the door going into the underground there. I guess they pounded on the door and tried to get them to surrender, but they wouldn't come out, so they put the satchel charge up in there and we blew the ones up on the top. They blew that one and we all got out of there, but when they blew them they must have been prepared. We heard chump, chump, like that, and they had these mortars, which there were thirty-something up in the air. The guys down in the bottom there said, "There's thirty-some up there," and they probably exaggerated some of it before the first one even hit the ground. I guess these mortars were only about like that, but they killed Stryker and Manifol. But we had to run through that going back down because we had to get the hell out of there, and none of the rest of us got hit. When we got down to the bottom, the captain's report said everyone that came off that hill was suffering from concussion. Well, not too long ago I put in for hearing loss. I didn't know I had hearing loss until I put hearing aids in and take the damn things out. But my daughter worked at a VA hospital in Nashville, and she told me I should go over and see about hearing because I was always going huh, huh. And I thought I could hear good. Anyway, they turned me down. They said it was probably because I worked in a printing shop that I lost my hearing. So I appealed it. I was supposed to go to Washington, DC, but I couldn't do that. So I went to Winston-Salem, and I was telling them about this, that, and the other things, and he was there shaking his head. He said, "You'll be hearing from us." So a little bit after that, I got a 10 percent increase for hearing loss. But the irony of it is when I first got out of the service, they gave me a disability discharge with a 50 percent rating. It was fifty dollars a month, which was a dollar per point. I carried that up until I got down here to North Carolina and my daughter again. So about a year after I got out, I got a call to go back for reevaluation, and they knocked me down to 30 percent. But they eventually put me back to 50 percent.

So overall you feel that you were eventually treated justly?
Oh yeah.

I want to ask you about the Silver Star that you received.
Well, that's for one time I was on the patrol and I had Sgt. Ziba, a new sergeant. I was patrol leader, and we were in hedgerow country. They had slots in them, you know, where you go from one hedgerow to the other to move the cattle through. This one section was blasted out with a shell, and I was laying [*sic*] in that with my binoculars. I was trying to see somebody moving, and all of a sudden I heard this crack and dirt floating in front of me. This sniper took a shot at me and missed. I got out of there real quick, and for some reason Pop started walking down there, and I said, "Watch that opening, Pop," and with that he took one right here. He went down, and we got him out of there and dressed it the best we could, but he started to go into shock. Well, I took my jacket off and wrapped it around him, and then I took my shirt off and put it around him. Davis was my BAR man. I used to take a BAR man when I went on patrol because it was light and we had some good firepower if we had to get out. So Davis left the BAR and went back to get help while I tried to figure some way to get him out of there. I took my britches off. I tried tying knots in the legs, but nothing was going well. He had it in the belly, so you couldn't very well throw him over your shoulder. At any rate, I'm down to my shorts, and Davis comes out and Lt. Ross with a door. They ran out with a door. And with that, I wrapped up my pants to put under his head. So I took his tommy gun. I had my rifle, the BAR, and I knew they couldn't get back fast, so I told them to wait. I started firing in the general direction where some machine gun fire was coming from with a BAR. Gave a burst here, a burst there, like that, and again going back and forth. Well, they got him out. Then it dawned on me. In one of the books here, they said, "The Almost Naked Hero." And they got a drawing in there of me in my shorts running with a BAR in one hand, the rifle across my shoulder, and the tommy gun in the other hand. So I stayed there while they were getting him out. We dressed the wound and I didn't leave him.

Did he survive?

He died four days later. That's the one I got the picture of. His nephew came down to one of these reunions, and we got together and he sent me some pictures and things of his uncle.

You at one point ended up in the military police?

Well, that was after the last time they sent me back to England. No more combat, you know. So they sent to the hospital, and I guess it was a psycho hospital. Anyway, about three days after I got there, came in here and started giving us that truth serum? Sodium pentothal. They give me one shot of sodium pentothal that day. The next day they gave me two shots. The next day, three shots, up to ten shots. And then they brought me over to another area, and I was put out completely for three days. That's what I found out later. I think it was sodium pentothal. Anyway, they gave you up to ten shots, and then they gave us a big breakfast. We had talked to some guys across the way, 'cause we could see them walking up and down the hallway. But they didn't make any sense, 'cause they said, "Oh, they'll put you to sleep for three days." So I guess they would talk to you, interview you, try to get you to tell them what's bothering you, and I would have bad dreams and wake up. Sometimes I'd wake up crying. Sometimes I'd wake up hollering. After they decided I was well enough, they sent me down to MP school. I said, "Well, I'm here in England, so there's nothing much I can do about it." So I got the MP training and they shipped me back to France, and when I got to Marseille there was a guy by the name of Philby. He was in the glider troops, and we were the first two ex-combat men to be assigned to this unit. So we had to go before this Capt. Faust. We gave him a salute, you know, and he told us we were in the MPs now. The 65th MP Company, you know, and what our duties were going to be. Then he got around to "I see you got that blue piping around your hat, from the infantry. You have to take that off and put your green and gold" (whatever the hell the MP was). And then he said, "We're not assigned to any specific unit. We don't have any insignias, so you're going to have to take your insignias off here." I put my hand on the Ranger patch and I said, "There ain't no SOB that's going to take this patch off my shoulder." And with that, Philby put his hand on his airborne patch and said, "That goes for me too." I can see him today with both hands in front of him, "Now, now, now, settle down, settle down. I'm sure we can make arrangements so you can keep your insignias on." But I just couldn't take that being an MP, so just one day, I just packed my gear and started out. One of the guys said, "What are you doing?" I said, "I'm getting the hell out of this. I'm going to try to find my old outfit." Now that shows you how irrational I was. I mean there must have still been something wrong with me, because here I was going to leave and go out there and try to find the 5th Ranger Battalion. I was going to go back to them, you know. But anyway, I got several different rides and ended up with two officers from a tank retriever outfit. They took me just outside of Marseilles, where they let me off, and they said, "Well, you can't stay here because they will probably be looking for you around this area." So I got another ride to Dijon, and there was an airborne outfit there. I went down to see the officer and told him what I was doing, and I said, "Maybe I can tie up with you guys." He said, "You can't do that. You're AWOL." So he thanked me for my offer, but he said, "You better get going." Anyway, I got as far as Stuttgart, and after about a week I was getting kind of scroungy. I think the only outfit there at that time was the MPs and the railroad battalion, so needless to say I got picked up pretty quick and I got brought into headquarters. They told me, "I'll let you go, and you're not too far from the front, but you'll never find the 5th Ranger Battalion." And he told me the best thing for me to do was to turn myself in. So anyway, that's what I did. I got sent from Stuttgart to Heidelberg and then from Heidelberg back up to Paris in the big stockade. There was a colonel who must have been from the 3rd or 4th Ranger Battalion, and he was in charge. And he said, "Ranger, what in the hell are you doing here?" More or less he saw my patch. So I told him, and he said that the war had ended. "If I give you a provisional MP pass, will you promise to go back to Marseilles?" I told him yes. So he gave me a provisional MP pass. The sergeant put me on the train and told me not to get off the train until I got to Marseilles. So when I got back there, I reported in and no court-martial, no nothing. I found out that psychos or something like that, they wouldn't court-martial you. So at any rate, I was there a few more days at this replacement pool. They were sending guys back home, so I asked if there was any way to get into one of the outfits going over to the Pacific. And they told me that I was going to the Pacific, but I was going as an MP. So I said, "That's what you think." I went out and I got stinking drunk, and the next thing I know, I woke up; both my wrists were raw. I was on a mattress with just my shorts on. Nothing else, just me in my shorts and a mattress. And I thought, "Uh oh." The next thing

I heard was the door unlock, and a guy came in with the trays. I didn't mean to scare him or do anything like that, but I just said, "What the hell am I doing here?" I must have startled him or something, 'cause he laid the tray down, went out, and locked the door. The next thing I know, here comes him and another two guys and a nurse. They laid me on a sheet, took it over my arms, tucked it underneath, wrapped more sheets around me, then poured ice water on me. I guess that guy went back and told them I was violent [or] something. Then nurse said, "Will you behave yourself if we take you out?" I said, "There's nothing wrong with me. I just wanted to know what I was doing here." So they unwrapped me, and she told me that a doctor would be in to see me maybe tomorrow. And then something popped. I said, "I don't want to see a doctor. I want to see a chaplain." So a chaplain came in and he said, "What can I do for you?" I said, "Well, I volunteered for the Army. I volunteered for the infantry. I volunteered for the Rangers. I was wounded twice and I got the Silver Star and the Purple Heart, but I don't have enough points to go home." He said, "Don't worry, son; you're going home." Needless to say, the next thing I knew, I was on a hospital ship going back to the United States. I went through more stuff there. Actually I got a tape of some the stuff we went through. They showed it to me there. I don't remember these group things too much. But they had these group things, and the first thing was an interview by this doctor. The next thing I know, I'm playing the guitar. Played country western. But I didn't want to bother with this stuff, so I dropped that real quick. Anyway, they let me out with a 50 percent disability. "Psychoneurosis," back then.

So being in the stockade didn't prevent you from receiving the Good Conduct Medal?

No. I evidently got the Good Conduct Medal way before, just like I had the Silver Star and the Purple Heart, and then here in May I found I was getting the Bronze Star. I got a thing in the mail. I think anybody that's got the Purple Heart and Silver Star is supposed to get a Bronze Star too.

Can we step back a little bit, sir. What was the most intense firefight you were in? Would you say it was D-day, or would you say it was Brest?

Well, I guess D-day was, 'cause I had to lay [*sic*] there behind the seawall. I was out of action, but there was an awful lot of stuff coming in, so I would say that was one of the worst parts. And there were a few other places, like I said, in this wooded area. I guess we got too far ahead one time when we were assigned to this recon unit in Germany. I think it was their first combat, and we had to go ride along with them. We must have got ahead or something like that, because my company, E Company, was cut off. So we dug in and we were taking what must have been artillery fire from some railway guns, because you couldn't hear them going off and then all of a sudden you heard "whoosh, whoosh." I mean, a loud noise going through the trees "crack, crack, crack," and the shell would hit something solid and go off. So we were getting a lot of tree bursts, and some of them were getting down to the ground. They would really shake you up. I mean, they almost knocked me out of my hole a couple of times. They were just that close. Bill Boyd was a sergeant. He's here now and he had me digging holes. We had two-man foxholes, and I wound up with him, so I had to dig the foxhole. So we were in there, and, like I said, there was snow and rain. We were wet and cold, and they told us not to fire for any reason. Unfortunately, I think the BAR man at the time (it wasn't Davis) had to take a leak or something. So he got out of his foxhole and started across somewhere. Another guy jumped out of his hole and shot him. And that screwed everything up. A few times the Germans got out, but if they came up they were allowed to go through, because we were told not to fire at them. I guess they figured if one got close enough and there weren't too many of them, you could put him down with a knife or something like that, as long as there was no noise. I don't know if anybody had to do that or not. But it seemed like during the daytime when we were active, I was all right. But then nighttime came along, we would dig in again, and just laying [*sic*] there, I could see Norman. I can still see Norman, and finally I guess I started talking to Bill about Norman: Why did I leave him? It just finally caught with me, and they sent me back and said, "No more combat."

You mentioned several of the people that you served with. Are there any others that you haven't mentioned that you would like to pay honor or tribute to right now?

Well, one time Frank Lockwood was supposed to go out on outpost, and he was sick. So Campus went out for him and he got a direct hit by an 88. That shook Lockwood up quite a bit. And then there was Reams. He was a scout in the 1st Platoon, and he mentioned to me one time that he wasn't coming back, and he didn't. They nailed him. We would move into an area, and a lot of times, especially in the hedgerow country, Lt. Austin would say, "Lew, see how far out you can go and come back." So I might go one, two hedgerows. One hedgerow and I don't see anything, I go to the next. Well, I wouldn't walk right across the thing. I'd hug the side and then cut across about midway, and then I'd get up and look around like that and then go back, get to the side, roll over maybe on the other side this time, and start up that way. And if I didn't see anything at the second one, I'd go back. Usually our patrols were no more than five at the most for reconnaissance patrol. And then if we did find a good concentration of Germans in a position where they were going to be, we'd go back and at night we'd go out with a combat patrol. Most of the time I'd leave my rifle and take a Thompson submachine gun. It had one clip, and another one taped on to it the other way. It would be up to the sergeant to decide if we would try to disperse around the area. The sergeant would give the word, and then we all threw our hand grenades in first. And then open up and run like hell to get out of there. You didn't necessarily have to see anybody. You knew they were there, and you just saturated it with Thompson submachine gun fire. And of course, some of them you would see, but it was night and it wasn't always pitch black, and you could see them moving around. So you would try knocking one down. It was just part of the Rangers operation.

What were the greatest lessons you learned from your time in the military?

Well, I guess one of the major things is believe in God, and that we were all put here for a purpose. I just felt after a while that if I was going to get it, it would be God's will. And every time we'd do something and we'd come back, I'd say, "Well, He wasn't ready for me." Not that I'm an overly religiously Southern Baptist, but I mean I do believe that there is a power up there looking out for us, and he's going to decide the outcome of this world. And it doesn't look like it's going to be too far away.

I can't begin to imagine the trauma from these experiences. How did you cope with these battlefield experiences?

Well, I would just go along with it, you know. I mean, again, at that time not that I was overly religious, but I mean I felt bad about Pop, who wound up being killed. I guess I just accepted it. It's war and it just happens. Like I said, later on down the line, that's when it did finally catch up to me and I'm in hell. I mean, I just went bananas.

Did you have help from the military in trying to readjust to civilian life?

Oh yeah. Like I say, in the hospital they tried to tell me that you're going to be all right more or less. But I still had the dreams and stuff. I still do. I still do. And I tell the guys in our group there. Since I've been here, I got two guys from the Vietnam era who are starting to tell some of the things that they didn't want to talk about. I said, "You gotta get it out of you; you gotta get it out of you."

Do you find that you have similar feelings and experiences with the Vietnam veterans?

I tried to understand that they had a worse time coming home than they did on the battlefield. They were "baby killers." They were spit on. Well, a lot of them I guess were taking drugs. A lot of the boys were, let's say, drug addicts, and afterwards they talk about themselves and getting drunk all the time. Drinking to take drugs. And another thing is that the Korean War, that seems to be the forgotten war. Hardly any mention. And in the VA, I think John's got about six or seven groups like I'm in, and he said, "I think there's only two from the Korean era, and they don't want to talk about it anymore." It probably would have helped them, 'cause they went through some hard times, especially in the Krozon Peninsula. They took a beating up there.

During your time with the Rangers, did your noncoms and officers automatically receive the respect of the men because of their rank, or was that a process that had to be earned over time?

Well, I think we learned it fast. I mean, we did respect them. But you might say we admired them for what they were and for what they were trying to do.

What are the characteristics of a noncom and officer that make a good leader?

Well, the best thing I can say was, they wouldn't tell you to do something that they wouldn't do themselves, ninety-nine times out of a hundred. I was a point man and a scout, and when I was a point man (which wasn't a very good position to be in sometimes), the lieutenant would be right there with me. Meaning he wasn't way in the back there, letting his guys go forward. He was right up there with them. The noncommissioned officers and the officers were right with their men. That's why we lost a lot of officers.

Do you think that was unique for the Rangers, or was that the noncoms and officers for any division?

Well, I would have to say it's the Rangers upbringing. I mean we did respect them, and we had a lot of respect for them.

You said you were on point a lot, and as a scout did you get that specialized training or were there certain attributes that you had that made them say, "Well, I'm going to bring him out in front"?

No, I just kind of went that way. As a matter of fact, when the sergeant got wounded, Lt. Ross wanted to know if I'd take over the section. I said, "No, I'm happy with what I'm doing." Stupid me. It was just something that I was meant for.

Do you have any comments or pieces of wisdom or advice for future generations, on the basis of your time in the military and service in the war?

Well, I tell people to respect their country, and it gets me all upset when people . . . I mean war. I don't like war, but these people say, "Get them out of there." Well, if they bring all those guys out of Afghanistan and Iraq there, they would have all died in vain. All those guys gave their lives for nothing. So when we start something, don't do like we did before, which was quit and move out. Well, we wound up losing Vietnam. I mean, Vietnam is under one rule now, and I guess Korea is still divided.

Did you make any lifelong friends in the military that you still see?

Oh, Bill Boyd, Sandy out in Missouri. We've met a few times. And Sgt. Miller, Victor Miller. He was our poet. He wrote a lot of poems and things. He wrote about the pillbox. There's a poem about the pillbox and how it was taken, and as long as our children and great-grandchildren go back, it will still be there. As of now there are five known guys from my original company. We do keep in touch.

Is there anything I haven't asked you about that you think should be mentioned?

For the young people going into the military today, to be proud of what they're doing for their country. Well, I'm glad I was able to do my part, but when the war ended, I still feel I should have been in the Rangers instead of an ex-MP.

1LT. FRANK KENNARD

Before Pearl Harbor, what were your aspirations when you were growing up? Did you have any plans? What was in your mind at the time before the war broke out?

Well, I didn't have any aspirations that I can recall except going to college. I had two brothers, and we all were in college at the same time, and I think I wanted to go into the business world or something like that. But I'd had a very happy home life, childhood, did a fair amount of traveling with the family, and had really just enjoyed life. I was the youngest of three boys, and I had a sister. Life was a bowl of cherries, and you just picked the ones you wanted to eat.

Ranger Kennard

Well, can you describe where you were when you heard about Pearl Harbor?

I was in the start of my third year at Yale University, and I remember when we heard about Pearl Harbor, we all went down to the president's residence and we were getting fired up. We were threatening to burn The Neck, which was a bar that was of some ill repute, but otherwise the president calmed us down, and we didn't do anything that riotous in nature. But that was December 1941, and I was not quite halfway through my junior year in college.

I see. Did you have an impression that the attack on Pearl Harbor would be an earth-changing event?

No. Actually, the only predetermination I had was that my father insisted that all three of us must take military training wherever college we went to, and whatever we studied. He had been in Europe in 1937 and was convinced that there was going to be a world war. And he wanted his kids to be officers instead of cannon fodder. He'd served on the Mexican border with the 7th Regiment in New York and in the Navy in World War I, and he just felt that military training was essential. So when I entered college, I enrolled in the ROTC program at New Haven, which meant I never had to register for the draft or for enlisting. It also meant that I could finish my education before I went into active military service. So I had three full years of education in college, and then our fourth year was truncated. So we had six calendar months' less education than we would have had if we had gone normally from September to the following May. I graduated in December of 1942, and we had orders to report to Fort Sill for the officers-training course in field artillery at the beginning of January 1943.

January 1943. I think your initial division was the 106th Infantry Division. Is that right?

Yes, and after completing the battery officers course, a bunch of us were assigned to the 106th Division, which was in Fort Jackson. That was a training division, and I was assigned to the C Battery of the 591st Field Artillery Battalion. I don't really have many recollections of what we did or didn't do, but after a few months I was getting itchy to get overseas and pestered my commanding officer to be transferred. So eventually, in September, orders came through for me to go overseas as a casual, rather than going overseas with a unit, because the 106th Division was simply a training division. It would get recruits in for thirteen-week cycles and then get another cycle, etc. So I went overseas and sailed out of New York in October or November of 1943.

And how did you join the Rangers?

Well, I was a casual along with a bunch of other casuals. We went to a replacement depot in Shrivenham, England, which was on the west coast of England. And I got notice with maybe forty or fifty other casual officers to report down to a rec hall, and Col. Rudder, who was the commanding officer of the 2nd Ranger Battalion, was there. He introduced himself to the assembled group of officers and said he was looking for some recruits. And if we were interested, stick around, and if we weren't interested, we were free to go. So about five of us stuck around, and he picked me and another officer by the name of Harry Wynans. So that's how I joined the Rangers. For the invasion, we had assigned half-tracks with 75 mm guns on them and referred to it as a cannon platoon. Since I was an artillery officer and knew how to shoot the cannon, I got elected. Plus I volunteered. Incidentally, I went to Fort Sill with fifty of my classmates in college. Ten of us went to the 106th Division, and five of us went overseas on the same boat. I am the only one who volunteered or had the opportunity at that time to volunteer. The other four were all dead within six months of the invasion. And they have a saying in the Army: keep your bowels open, keep your mouth shut, and never volunteer.

After you joined the Rangers, did you get further training at that point?

The only training I had was unit training, and we were initially stationed in Bude, Cornwall, which is on the west coast of England, and we had exercises of one kind or another. We didn't get the guns until sometime later, so most of it was physical training. Since we didn't have the guns, we couldn't really maneuver them with a platoon or company of infantry. Otherwise, I was a flunky for the adjutant of the battalion, whose name was George Wilkins, and I admired him. He was older than I was. He was higher in rank than I was, and he had a bigger job. He was seriously wounded in the invasion and never made it back to the outfit.

If I'm not mistaken, you were assigned to Headquarters Company for the D-day invasion?

Our platoon was assigned to the Headquarters Company, but we had what I would call two cannon platoons. I had two half-tracks, each with a gun, and there was another officer, Epperson was his name. He had the other two guns. Basically, there were three aspects of the Rangers' mission. First mission was Pointe du Hoc, which was scaling the cliffs. The second mission was knocking out the strongpoint at Pointe Ile Percée, and those two missions involved Companies C, D, E, and F. A Company and B Company and Headquarters Company were landing on Omaha Beach. The arrangement was if the assault on Pointe du Hoc was successful, then the 5th Ranger Battalion would land at Pointe du Hoc. If it wasn't successful or it wasn't accomplished in a timely fashion, the 5th Ranger Battalion and Companies A and B of the 2nd would land on Vierville. Their mission would be to proceed westward along the Normandy Peninsula to Grandcamp and Isigny, which were geographically inland from Pointe du Hoc. The idea was that if the Pointe du Hoc mission was accomplished in a timely manner, the 5th Battalion and the two companies of A and B would get up the cliff, using these special London Fire Department ladders that had been mounted on LCAs for that specific purpose. In fact, they never worked, and because the assault wave of D, E, and F was at least a half hour late in getting to the proper point for disembarking, this caused problems. Although the mission was accomplished, there was no radio communication available. Nothing worked, so the message that the mission had been accomplished never got to the main force, such that they could be diverted to land on Vierville Beach.

So what was running through your mind at that time right before the invasion?

I'd have to say I don't really remember. I don't think that we were particularly thinking about getting killed. We weren't scared as far as I knew. Our training had been, I thought, very vigorous, and the whole invasion process was so huge and the support for it was so tremendous that there wasn't anything that was going to stop this force. And the organization for the invasion was so thoroughly and really so successfully planned and so coordinated that everything went like clockwork. We were in the marshaling area for a few days or a week beforehand. There were never any enemy aircraft overhead. There wasn't anything to disturb the tranquility of living in tents in the marshaling area. The English roads are very small and narrow, but they had carved-out niches in the side of the road, and the niche was labeled with a number. It corresponded exactly with [*sic*] the number of the landing vessel that you were going to ride on, and the niche was big enough to exactly accommodate the boatload. In our case, two half-tracks, or really four half-tracks and one jeep as I remember. Two of the half-tracks belonged to an antiaircraft air-warning unit and two were mine, and at the appointed hour we pulled out from the niche and started down the road, and gradually the convoy built and built and built. So when we got down to the harbor, there were hundreds of vehicles there waiting to load. They were all loaded in an orderly fashion, and we went out into the harbor because this was the third of June, which was two days before the actual invasion. It was raining, and we were lying on the deck of the LCT with no shelter, but there wasn't any enemy action of any kind. I don't mean to say that we were on a yacht, but there wasn't anything to scare you, and the operation was so well planned and so well carried out that there wasn't any reason to be afraid. As a matter of fact, for the invasion itself, which, of course, was postponed one day, we were in a column of ships that extended from horizon to horizon. On the left-hand side there was a column of ships extending horizon to horizon, and on the right-hand side there was a column of ships extending from horizon to horizon. And overhead was a fleet of airplanes with special markings on them that we'd never seen before. We're sailing toward the beach, and the analogy I make is that it was like a slinky, which is a spring that the kids play with, and it will go down the stairs. There wasn't anything that was going to stop this huge spring that was coiled and was going to expand on to the beach. In the morning the horizon was a ball of fire, as far as you could see. Just a ball of fire because of the bombardment and the bombing, and it was only after you got in close to the beach and you started toward the beach (10 miles out in the water) and got close to the beach that you got bracketed with enemy fire. Now all of a sudden you got scared. But there wasn't anything that was going to stop us from going in.

Did you climb aboard the LCA about 4:00 in the morning?

Well, from my experience, I was on the LCT. I got on that off a dock in Weymouth, and I landed on Omaha Beach on the same boat. We actually made three landings before we could drive the vehicles off down the ramp, and we weren't in a bomb crater.

What time was that?

Well, we were supposed to land in the sixth or seventh wave; I forget now. Nine to nine-thirty we were supposed to land. I have no idea now what time we did land, but it had to be an hour to an hour and a half later because we backed up, went in, dropped the ramp. The water's too deep, so we backed up, ran in, dropped the ramp. The water was deep enough, so we did offload, and you got on the beach and you couldn't move because it was jammed with vehicles and people and dead bodies and all the rest of it.

What sector did you land at?

Well, now you asked me, so I have to remember. I don't know whether I wrote it down or not. But I was originally supposed to land in Vierville Beach exit. But I think we ended up landing closer to Les Moulins, which was another exit, but still we were supposed to go out the Vierville exit.

So you were probably farther east from there?

Farther east.

So that's probably where the 5th Rangers were?

I don't know. I did understand that Epperson and his LCT landed nine times before he could get off the boat because of bomb craters. Now, whether it was nine or not I don't know, but in any event you landed in the wrong place. And the other thing that always sticks in my mind is that there wasn't a single radio that worked. There was absolutely no communication available unless you personally went to find out who's here and find out who's there. There was absolutely no communication available.

Can you describe the beachhead where you landed?

Where we landed, the beachhead was probably, I'd say, 30 yards deep, which would mean that it was high tide. Extreme low tide was 7:00 in the morning. At that point in time, the beach was about 400 yards wide, and all of the beach obstacles that the Germans had put on the beach were exposed. At high tide, they're totally underwater. The tide came in at the rate of a foot every ten minutes. So anybody that stopped halfway across the beach behind a beach obstacle, if they were wounded, were going to drown. The only way you survived was you got off your vehicle and you ran, and you didn't stop until you got to the beach wall at the back of the beach. The normal military maneuver is to advance and stop behind some cover and then advance again, stop behind some cover, advance again, and so forth. But if you did that, you were going to drown. When we landed, the tide was in full, and the beach was maybe 20 yards wide.

Was there carnage on the beach in front of you?

There was bumper-to-bumper traffic of vehicles and a lot of carnage, a lot of dead bodies. The escarpment behind the beach was about 90 feet high, and where we landed eventually, the escarpment was honeycombed with German firing positions. You didn't know where the fire was coming from, but some was coming, and the beach exit at Vierville was blocked. You couldn't get out the beach exit, and you couldn't move along the beach.

So how did you get your men off the beach?

Well, eventually I took a Bangalore torpedo, and we blew a hole in the concertina wire that was on top of the beach wall, and there was an antitank ditch behind that. But one of my vehicles trying to drive through the hole in the concertina wire lost its ability to move and got stuck in the sand. Whether that was an axle or the clutch, I don't know. My other vehicle was hit by either a mortar or an artillery shell of some kind, and it burned up. So I had no vehicles, and basically because I was an ex-artillery man, I realized that staying on the beach was an invitation to not surviving. So I took the men through the wire, and we went halfway up the escarpment. Then we were in the position of being in front of the people who were still on the beach. They didn't know who we were, and we didn't want to do anything to attract fire. We had no way of communicating with them, and at that point we ran into a stray part of a platoon of the 5th Ranger Battalion. So we stayed together, and there were a couple of other strays that we had picked up. The next morning, we assaulted over the top of the escarpment and captured about eleven Germans. Then Maj. Street, who was from the invasion command vessel, the *Ancon*, found us and urged us to go down to the beach, commandeer an LCA, and go up to Pointe du Hoc. Which we did. And I guess there were ten or twelve men in the cannon platoon. None were wounded. I did lose two men who were killed on the beach, and the 5th Ranger unit was maybe fifteen or twenty men. Something like that. We basically had an LCA boatload, which would hold around thirty men. So we went up to the Pointe and spent the rest of the invasion there. The men were spread out around the perimeter of Pointe du Hoc, waiting for the main body to come up from the beach. The mission had us getting into Grandcamp and Isigny by the end of the first day. We got relieved by elements of, I think, the 29th Division, on D+2, which was the third day.

So were you at the top of the cliff at Pointe du Hoc?

Yeah, yeah.

How did you get to the top?

We climbed up the slick rope, or the ladders were there. By that time, assaulting the cliff was over, and there was a rope and these scaling ladders that you assembled. They were in 3-foot sections, I think, and you could put them together like an erector set to make a ladder. You could get up the cliff, and there wasn't any opposition. And the command post was there.

What was the typical composition of a cannon platoon?

Well, you had a driver and you had a unit. Either I was the unit commander or you had a sergeant or a corporal or whoever was in command of the other unit. You had a gunner, an assistant gunner, and you had maybe three guys to load the cannon. So that's why I said I had ten or twelve men. It wasn't a platoon like in an infantry unit, which may have one or two hundred men in it. Our platoon had thirty men in it, and sixty men in the company.

From your perspective, what was probably one of the more severe battles that you were involved with?

Well, first place I was not in a foxhole in the forward line, wherever that might be, because Rudder designated me as adjutant of the battalion. Which, as I kind of facetiously say, I could read and write and I'd graduated from college, so ergo I could do the paperwork. I'm being rude. But that meant that most of the time I was either at the rear echelon of the battalion or at the forward command post of the battalion. Occasionally I would get up to one or another of the line companies that were deployed somewhere. So I didn't have any, what I'd say, real combat action. I was there, but I wasn't the same as a machine gunner who was up in a forward position. I think that the most-memorable things in my mind would be in the Hürtgen Forest, when it was so dark that you couldn't see your hand in front of your face as soon as the sun went down. It was just pitch black because of the foliage, and in order to move from where you were to some other position within your group, you needed a string that was strung between the two points. And you'd put your hands on the string, and that would take you from point A to Point B. Otherwise, you stayed in your hole until it got light. Okay. In Hill 400, which was the high ground outside of Bergstein, Germany, the battalion headquarters' forward command post was in the basement of a building in the town of Bergstein. And I went up there a couple of times: one time to present George Williams with his Oak Leaves when he was promoted to major and put in command of the battalion, and the other time was to go up and bring out several of the people who were going home on R&R. Lomell, Fitzsimmons, and I forget the others. There were five in total. The criterion was twice wounded in action or twice decorated for bravery, and we sent five men home on the first boat. But getting them out was an exciting experience. The other time, and this is just an anecdote but relates to Bob Edlin, who was a platoon leader in A Company. At the time that he took the surrender of approximately eight hundred Germans in the battery there in Normandy, the company commanders wrote him up for a Bronze Star for heroic achievement. I personally took that recommendation to the 7th Corps Headquarters G2 who was a World War I retread, full colonel. And I handed him this recommendation for Edlin and the colonel; I won't mention his name. I will forever remember he read it, he looked at it, and he said, "Lieutenant, this has got a drip of blood." And he handed it back to me.

So he rejected the Bronze Star?

He rejected it for Edlin. And you notice they gave Sgt. York a Medal of Honor for capturing seven hundred Germans in World War I.

That's extraordinary, isn't it?

At Hill 400, one of the times that I went up to the forward CP, they really were in desperate straits. I don't know how much Lomell told you when he was here. He's one of the heroes of that situation. I went back to regimental headquarters, and it was at night, and there was a comment: "Oh, there's a Ranger lieutenant here." So they wanted to talk to me, and I told them, "We sent a hundred and fifty men up that hill and we got fifty left. We need ammunition. We need supplies. And we need more troops." And the commanding officer looked at me, and he said, "Lieutenant, you go back up to Bergstein and you tell Col. Williams to hold that hill at all costs." And back I went.

Were you there when they attacked Hill 400?

Yeah, but the closest I was to Hill 400 was in Simmerath, and the only time you could get into Simmerath was in the dark. The other time in the Bulge, the 2nd Rangers were deployed on the north side of the "V" that would describe the Bulge. I think I have some towns wrong. Hill 400 is Bergstein, and Simmerath was in the Ardennes on the Bulge. I'll have to look at a map. But we got some replacements and we had thirty men. And I had a sergeant from each of the six line companies. The replacements were fresh off the boat, so we shook them down as far as extra stuff and loaded them up in a 2½-ton truck. I personally took them up to a road junction outside of Simmerath, and we had them organized in groups of five. I had a sergeant from A Company and five men, a sergeant from B Company and five men, and a sergeant from C Company and five men, and we walked down the road. We were supposed to be met by company guides, but no guides were where we were supposed to meet. So I went up into the town of Simmerath and into the headquarters, which was in the basement of one of the buildings, and got the guides there. The guides went back to get the guys who were the replacements. One man was missing, and I never knew what happened to him. Never knew.

Getting back to Hill 400, some have suggested that part of the reason they were successful was because not only were they were aggressive, but also their charge was made during an active artillery barrage. Is that true?

I have no way of knowing. I know that as a generalization, the Rangers welcomed special deals, and for the most part the Rangers had a lot of information, which we passed down to the rank and file. That way, everybody knew what you were supposed to do, where you were supposed to be, and so forth. And if you carried your assignment out, why, it would be successful. But I wasn't ever on that hill. Sid Solomon was the company commander of B Company, and it is my understanding that B Company screened. That is to say, they went ahead and then D Company passed through B Company to assault the hill. And I heard Sid Solomon talking to a sergeant from the other division, asking directions or instructions of where the target was, and this guy was just totally, I'll say, shell shocked. He couldn't give Sid any information, which Sid desperately needed in order to deploy his men properly. I don't fault the guy. Who knows? Sid was the platoon leader that actually assaulted the cliffs at Pointe Ile Percée. Now, they climbed those cliffs with their bare hands. They didn't have any equipment. There were nine of his platoon that got to the top of the Pointe Ile Percée, of which seven were wounded. They accomplished the mission, and that was typically the attitude of every guy who was in the 2nd Ranger Battalion and probably in the 5th Ranger Battalion and maybe in the 1st, 3rd, and 4th. A little bit different than the average GI. And actually I think the 2nd Ranger Battalion (and I was not a part of it at the time when they trained at Camp Forrest, Tennessee) probably went through over fifteen hundred Army persons to end up with five hundred keepers.

Can you describe the severe weather conditions during the Battle of the Bulge?
Yeah. It was cold and snowy. We didn't have winter clothing. Your normal uniform was a field jacket. Maybe you had a sweater. You had wool pants. You didn't have any snowshoes or galoshes or whatever you call it. The ground was frozen and there was snow. It was difficult. Actually, in our case, my men and I dug a hole in the ground about a foot deep, and we were all frozen. Then we put some logs together above the ground, so it made sort of a hut. And then we built some double-decker bunks in the inside, and we made a stove out of a 10-gallon can of cooking oil. And we used a number ten baked beans can or something like that to make a chimney, and built a little fire in the tin can stove. That's the way we kept it warm inside the hut in the forest in the wintertime. 'Cause we didn't have winter clothing.

Did you recall exactly what you were doing on Christmas Eve or Christmas Day in December 1944?
No. I remember the huge effort that the Army made so everyone had a traditional Thanksgiving meal on Thanksgiving. And so a Thanksgiving meal was delivered to us in the Hürtgen Forest, and we all enjoyed it and all had diarrhea the next day. 'Cause we hadn't had hot food, cooked food, and so forth for a month or more, and our systems couldn't take it. I've often thought in reflection of the huge effort, the huge effort to do that and the immediate result.

Was that a turkey meal?
It was turkey, mashed potatoes, dressing, cranberry sauce. The works.

They didn't do anything for special for Christmas, right?
I don't really remember. I'm hard pressed even to remember where we were on Christmas.

Were you awarded the Bronze Star?
Well, they tell me, but actually I understand that anybody who participated in the invasion is awarded the Bronze Star. Now, it happens that my brother, who was in the 1st Marine Division in the Pacific, was awarded a Bronze Star for valor. Recommended by Army troops that he had helped save by registering shellfire on himself and away from the Army troops. But we didn't have a Bronze Star in our organization, except for valorous service. But a Bronze Star was a medal, and it represented points, and points got you home at the end of the war. I never even knew that I was eligible for a Bronze Star until about five years ago. But because of my brother's situation, I just feel that being awarded the Bronze Star for having participated in the invasion was not appropriate. There were so many guys who did heroic things, some recognized and some not.

If you were to pinpoint one particular thing that your platoon performed with exemplary action during your military experience, what would that be?
The action, in the way that you're using it, as far as I was concerned with the cannon platoon, was limited to the beach, and essentially there was no action there because we couldn't get off the beach. Now, the men were dispersed among the different line companies, and it would be up to their leaders to identify things they may or may not have done, but I wouldn't know. You see, it depended on your perspective. If you were in a foxhole

in the front line, you were really in action. If you were back at the forward command post, you had it easy, and if you were at the rear command post, that was heaven. And if you were back at Regimental, my God, that was luxury. It may have been a distance of only a few hundred yards, but it all depended on where you were.

I guess those lines of demarcation broke apart in the Battle of the Bulge, where all of a sudden everybody was in the action, right?
Yeah. But I have an interesting anecdote there about the 106th Division, when I was in it as a training division, in the 591st Field Artillery Battalion. During the breakthrough by the Germans, the 28th Division and the 106th Division were basically overrun. I subsequently visited the 106th Division as it was then post-Bulge composed. The battalion commander was still the same as I'd had in Fort Jackson. The battery commander had been a junior officer in the battery when I was there. The 591st Battalion, I understood, had one casualty in the Bulge. Col. Rudder was promoted to bird colonel and put in command of one of the regiments of the 28th Division. I don't know which one. It was my understanding that Rudder's regiment suffered the least casualties of any of the regiments in the 28th Division, which was otherwise overrun. But volunteering for the Rangers, I think, saved my life, and I just don't think of it any other way.

What would you say would be one of the saddest moments during your military experience? I'm sure there were a few.
If there were any, I don't remember them. I really don't. Take England, for example. We were billeted in private homes. I had a wonderful relationship with the landlady and her family. When we were on the Isle of Wight, I happened to be billeted in Titchfield. It was in a private home on the mainland, with a man and his wife and two children. I babysat for the kids and had a terrific relationship with the people. I don't know of any hardship or really hard time that I experienced. I had a wonderful relationship at home. Every male member of our family served in the military in World War II, either in the Air Force, the Army, or the Navy. None even got a scratch.

What would you say would be the greatest lessons you learned from your military experience?
I don't know how to answer that. I mean, I always had no difficulty accepting orders. I didn't smoke. I didn't drink. I had a sweetheart at home who I subsequently married. I just didn't have any bad experiences. I assume I was much more mature when I came out than when I went in. I really was a young kid. I graduated from college when I was twenty years old. I went to a terrific university. There were a lot of advantages that I had had which a lot of other people didn't have. I didn't grow up in a rural area where there was no electricity. I just had lots of advantages.

Are there any pearls of wisdom that you would provide for future generations?
Well, I don't know whether you can solve anything by negotiation. If that's a pearl of wisdom.

You're saying that sometimes military action is the only option?
Unfortunately, I think so. What intrigues me is that when I was in high school, I was on a debating team, and our issue we were debating was war is inevitable. And I think one of the things that I remember from that is that between 1918 and 1939, there had been a conflict of some kind somewhere in the world every single year, despite the war to end wars.

2LT. LEONARD LOMELL

To start our dialogue, can you tell me what your aspirations were right before Pearl Harbor?
After high school graduation prior to Pearl Harbor, I was interested in a college education, and I was preoccupied with how I was going to achieve this goal. My father was an immigrant and a house painter, but we had no money as no one could afford to have their houses painted at that time. So I had to get an education on my own and take care of my immigrant parents. That is what I was confronted with. Then along comes World War II. So at that time when I was seventeen or eighteen years old, I figured, what the hell, if I have to go war, I

Leonard Lomell

might as well get an education out of it. This is before the war started. So I decided that I would go to West Point. I went up to West Point, and I took the exams and received a favorable response from West Point. When I submitted my application for admission, I submitted a baptismal certificate. However, despite a favorable reply and encouragement, one thing that I didn't know was that the baptismal certificate is unacceptable, it has to be a birth certificate. So I came home and after unsuccessfully trying to get my birth certificate, I hired a local lawyer whose secretary happened to be my sister's daughter. She went home and asked her parents, "What is Bud doing at my boss' office trying to obtain a birth certificate"(my nickname was Bud). What I found out from all of this was that I was adopted. I don't know where I came from or who my real parents were. But I learned from the first time that when a mother loses her child, they never get over it. Mr. and Mrs. Lomell lost a boy at seven years of age who died, and my two sisters were working in a

Leonard Lomell

Leonard Lomell

Ranger Lomell

department store in Brooklyn. One of the young sales girls who worked with my sister was seventeen years old. She became pregnant by an older man who then took off, and she had a baby. Then Mr. and Mrs. Lomell then adopted that baby, and that was me. And for the first time I learned at the age of eighteen that I had been adopted and that I couldn't get into West Point. So again, I had a baptismal certificate, and I couldn't get my birth certificate in time. I was then drafted, went to war as a draftee, and the rest is history.

You had mentioned earlier that you were with the 76th Division, how did you join up with the Rangers?

In the 76th Division, I was assigned to the 417th Regiment in which I rose in the ranks to a platoon sergeant in headquarters company within the intelligence and reconnaissance platoon. And that was my job as a platoon sergeant in the 417th Regiment. At that point in time, no Ranger Battalion was created in America. However, because the Scottish Commandos were so famous and successful from what they did earlier in World War II before America was in the war. Col. Darby was over in Scotland with the American troops and the higher echelon decided that was what we needed, what Scotland had, our own special forces volunteers. So the decided to organize three battalions, the 1st, 3rd, and 4th battalions as organized by Col. Darby. Of course at that time, I was a private back in the states in the 76th Division. So the Rangers were started and the powers to be or higher echelon came back to America and decided to create two additional battalions, the 2nd and the 5th in the states. And those two that were about to be created, sent out their advanced parties, and 2nd battalion starting recruiting volunteers. And a group of high ranking American officers came to the 417th Regiment when I was the acting first sergeant. I went into my company commander and notified him that there were a group of officers from a special unit called the Rangers that are seeking volunteers and the would like to meet with you. So I brought them in to his office and then they called me back in and told me that they had investigated me and they were interesting in enrolling me as a volunteer that was to be the first Ranger battalion to be created in the US, the 2nd Battalion.

What occurred in approximately June 1943?

Yes, it was early in 1943. They asked me if I had any questions, and I said to them, "Gentlemen, I have a question. How much does the job pay? I have to get the highest buck I can anywhere if I gotta serve, because I have an elderly mother and father to take care of." So the higher-ranking officer told me it was the highest pay that was possible to be paid for that position. So I became the first sergeant of D Company of the 2nd Ranger Battalion which was to be the first Ranger Battalion organized in the US which landed in Pointe de Hoc.

Did you think that the Ranger training at Camp Forrest was more extensive and prepared you better than the regular basic training?

Oh sure. You see, Rangers were all volunteers. They gave you a chance, but if you didn't hack it, you were out of there as quickly as you came in. In other words, you wanted to be the volunteer you presented yourself to be in going for such a unit, and if you didn't shape up, you're in and out before you know it.

So the Ranger Training was more intensive?

Yes, and I survived it.

At that point you were then deployed from Camp Forrest to the ETO?

Ultimately, yes. And we obtained further special warfare training with the Commandos, they were the experts. And we tried to be better than them.

Did that include cliff climbing?

Oh yes, everything they knew, they taught to us. And everything that we received in training that they were supposed to be the best at, we tried to out do them. It was a contest between the "would be" Commandos and the "Old" Commandos.

Can you recall what your thoughts were the night before D-Day, or when you were on the ship?

At that point in time, I was still a first sergeant in D Company of the 2nd Ranger Battalion, so I had a lot on my mind. My thoughts were to be the best first sergeant and having the best company out of the Rangers at D-Day. So I didn't think much about myself personally. I just devoted myself to working with my company commander and the senior officers of my battalion to make sure we were the best of the best.

So the night before and when you were on the ship, that's what you were focused on?

Yes, I was not thinking about am I going to live or die. I mean, I had a lot as a first sergeant to think about, and the lives of those friends of mine. I don't know how else to explain it to you, but I didn't have much time to think about myself.

Did you climb down into the Higgins boat or LCA or did they lower the LCA into the water with you in it?
It was a landing craft assault that was built in England that we climbed down into from the side of the ship.

What was the water like that night?
The sea was running rough and was high, and it was raining, it was nasty.

And did you get into the LCA at around 4 a.m.?
Yes, it was the early morning hours. And about twenty-two to twenty-four men were loaded into each boat.

And then you went out, and it probably took you a couple of hours to actually get to the shoreline?
By the way, these LCAs were English built, and we were aboard an English troop ship, and it was English sailors that operated our landing craft. And on our way to get to Pointe du Hoc, they got lost. There were those of us who recognized that we were going the wrong direction. Fortunately, most of us and our colonel also came to the same opinion and told the British crew. And that delayed us by about an hour. We ultimately got back on course and got to where Pointe du Hoc was, but we landed late. At that point in time, my B Company was supposed to land alone on the far west side of Pointe du Hoc to climb the cliffs. Whereas all the rest of the Ranger LCAs were landing on the other side, in mass. But because we were late, I decided the hell with this. I thought the delay would be to my disadvantage, so I deliberately ordered my LCA sailor to ram the boat right in with the other boats and find a place to jam us in, between two other LCAs. Which he did, and we landed among the first. We were among the first to reach the top of the cliff. I was the first one wounded as soon as we landed. I received a shot through the right side over the hip, through the muscle. But I was up the cliffs, among the first up the cliffs even while wounded. And to tell a story which is true, the day before, I had an argument with one of my men, another sergeant, and when I got shot, I thought that he shot me. So I turned around and was ready to kill him, but the guys yelled at me, no Len, he didn't shoot you, the guys up on the cliff shot you, so I gave up on that since I didn't see where that shot came from. And to make a long story short, that man and I became the closest of friends and we served together the rest of the war.

When the ramp went down on the LCA, can you describe the conditions when you went out?
Yes, we were soaking wet. We had been bailing with our helmets to try to keep our LCA afloat. We landed in the low surf on a narrow beach, directly under these 100-foot cliffs, which you had the following dangling down: pure rope, maybe 3/4-inch, or a toggle rope hanging down or a rope ladder or sectional metal ladder hanging down or a metal ladder sectional. In our case, we ran over and chose the straight rope and started up the ropes. A lot of them were shot off. The Germans were dropping grenades on us and shooting us off the ropes as we were trying to make it up. And we can't fight back while we were climbing. So we're nearly to the top, and we're about 2, 3, 4 feet from the top. I'm the first sergeant acting as a platoon leader because my actual officer had been assigned to headquarters. But my radioman said, "Hey, Len, help me, help me. I have no more strength." And I said, "Bob, I can't help you. I'm in the same boat. What we'll do is we will hold on to the ropes, throw the rope around one wrist so that it will hold you there. I'll look for somebody to help me." And as good luck would have it, along came Leonard Rubin, one of my men from B Company, who was perhaps one of the strongest men in the Rangers. It would take a half dozen of us guys to put him down when we trained in hand-to-hand combat. Well, he came over, dropped his weapons, and he got the radioman over. And I'm screaming, "Watch the antenna jostling, you'll draw fire on us." I figured I'd get shot because whatever was going on excited me to give me a spurt of energy, and I could hop up with my submachine gun and start shooting the Germans who were trying to shoot us off the cliff's edge. Incidentally as a side story here—I knew nothing about it at the time—this moment I just described to you was described by other men who saw it who were top officers. Years later, I found some outfit that paid for photographers to go over there and reenact that scene. So now I have a large painting on my wall in my home of that scene. My radioman Bob and I were strong, healthy young guys. We were on the verge of dropping off a 100-foot cliff onto the rocky bottom down below, but we survived, got over the top, and carried out the mission and ultimately found the guns and destroy them.

So when you got to the top, did you meet heavy resistance at the top?

Oh sure. We had to fight the Germans who were up there. They were trying to shove us off the cliffs or shoot us off the cliffs, but we prevailed. We drove them back as we came in, and we had a three-part mission. The first and most important part of the mission was to find the five howitzers, the big coastal guns. Those were the famous guns of the Nazis. The second part was to set up a roadblock to keep the Germans from moving up and down the tops of the cliffs along the coastline. And the third part was destroying all the communications that the Germans had. Well, we got up there, fought our way to where the guns were supposed to be, but there were no guns there. They were just telephone poles sticking out of the gun emplacement, which looked like the big gun barrels of the 155 mm howitzers. So the important part of our mission was a failure at that moment, because the intelligence the Army gave us was erroneous. So we fought our way in anyway and created the road block so the Germans could not get up the coastal road. I had started with twenty-two to twenty-four guys, but I was down to only about twelve, since all the rest had been wounded. And we still had to set up the roadblock so the Germans couldn't get up the coastal road on top of the cliffs, and we still had to send out patrols to cut all the communications for the Germans out along the coast there. But number one, we still hadn't found the guns or destroyed them. So I told my guys, "You take care of the communications; you take care of the roadblock. Jack Kuhn (the platoon sergeant) and I are going to find those GD guns." So we went up to the shore road with only twelve guys, looking for possible places. So Jack Kuhn and I started looking for possible places for the howitzers. And on the top of those cliffs, behind them, were roads that went down into the meadowlands, where there was water and little creeks. Now in the US, hedgerows are about three feet high at most. The hedgerows over there were like twelve feet high, some were a little lower. So Jack and I decided we'd go down that road in back of the top of the cliffs. We saw a road going across the meadows and the hedgerow on the side and trees, and thought that maybe the guns were hidden down there, along a hedgerow behind some trees. Well, we did this leapfrog, and I dove fifty yards, and he dove over and leapfrogged. And it came my turn and I looked over next to me, and lo and behold, there were the five big guns all ready to fire, ammunition all open and ready to use. But E Company of my battalion had satisfactorily attacked the facility that the Germans had built on the actual point of Pointe du Hoc, on the cliff's edge. And that would have been used to send back firing orders to any of their guns along that part of the coast of Normandy. But since E Company had them so bottled up, they couldn't get messages back to their gunners at the big-gun positions so they could fire accurately. So while E Company was battling the Germans there, nobody was bothering to fire those guns that we had luckily happened upon. So I thought this was my opportunity. "Jack, get up on that ledge, and you make damn sure nobody shoots me. I'm going in there and destroy those guns." Jack went up on the ledge and got into position with his submachine gun to protect me as I went into the gun position. Now, all we had was a thermite grenade each, which was only enough to take out two of the guns. But there were five of them, so I put the grenades into the middle of the traversing and elevation mechanisms of two of the guns. I laid one grenade right in the middle of this and pulled the pin. There was no noise, no explosion, but when the air hit the contents of the grenade, it melted everything around it. So the guts of that part of the gun just melted into a ball of melted metal. As it cooled, it hardened up, and so the guns were useless. But that took care of only two of them, and there were five in all. So Jack and I decided we'd take a chance and run back behind the other hedgerows, and maybe we'd be lucky enough to get to our guys at the roadblock up on the top of this cliff. So we got several more thermite grenades from the guys at the roadblock. Back we went with several more grenades, and Jack took up his position to protect me while again I slipped into the gun position, took the rest of them, and placed them in the traversing and elevating positions of each of the other three guns and destroyed them as well. In the meantime, that part of my platoon had gone and destroyed all of the communications that the Germans had along the top of the cliffs. We'd destroyed the guns, and the roadblock stopped the Germans from moving on the coast, so we had completed the mission. We were the first ones to complete our D-Day mission in World War II, so say the record keepers. So a few days later, we were relieved. We had had heavy casualties, and a lot of guys died, but we were the first unit to be successful on our D-Day mission and we saved a lot of lives because if those guns had been permitted to fire, they had all the targets they needed. They would have been able to fire on all of our invasion craft and transports during the landing and many soldiers of the 29th and 1st Divisions would have been shot up badly. Thousands of lives were saved by our good fortune. I received the DSC, the Distinguished Service Cross, for that. Jack got the Silver Star. I got my Purple Heart for my wound.

You just ran across these guns, right? You didn't know where they were?

No, they weren't where they were suppose to be, where intelligence had told us we would find them. It would have been a piece of cake if they were where they were supposed to be, but they weren't. We lucked out looking for them, and we had no information that these guns were there. Once they weren't where they were supposed to be, Jack and I looked at each other and said, "Where the hell are they then? We've got to go out and find them." And we lucked out. To survive the situations that the Rangers and every combat man were faced with, you had to have a lot of luck, and we were a bunch of lucky guys.

Well, that and perhaps somebody was guiding you from above?

Well, I hope so. I think so. I'm a religious man, but I also got to give credit to the guys because the Rangers were volunteers. They were not forced to become a Ranger. And what I liked about them was, they were thinkers. They were bright boys with high IQs, guts, and clear thinkers. On my LCA, I only had twenty-two or twenty-four of us, so we had lots to do. And we lucked out and did it. You have to have luck, you know.

I understand you went through the entire ETO with the 2nd Ranger Battalion, which battle would you say involved the worst conditions, D-Day or Hill 400?

Well, of course, D-Day was the worst. There was so much to do, little time to do it in, not enough firepower, and not enough men to help. So I thought D-Day was perhaps the worst of my experiences in combat. Although I got the Silver Star at Hill 400, that was a different situation. That was an attack on a hill or mountain or whatever you want to call it, where we were to catch up to fight German firepower and put them out of action. Which we did.

Can you describe your involvement in Hill 400?

What I think you are asking me is what I did to earn the Silver star. At that time, we had lost a lot of our officers that had been shot, wounded, and killed. At that time, I was the 1st Sergeant, and I had to take command, organize patrols, and win the battle. We lucked out and did. In battle, you never know from one moment to the next what will come up, close combat or hand-to-hand fighting. So Hill 400 was part of the Hurtgen Forrest ordeal.

So it was your leadership role at Hill 400?

Yes, that got me the Silver star.

I understand that Hill 400 was a key strategic outlook point for the German forces and that an entire division attempted to take it without success. Can you describe how the 2nd Ranger Battalion achieved success to complete conquest of this critical Hill?

Luck, in a word. Luck… Now you must remember this was more than sixty years ago. I do remember that we were so persistent in the attack and that despite most of the officers that were either shot up or killed, we rallied to the cause, took their positions, and did what they would have done. We were successful and accomplished our objective without our officers. I was not the only one decorated for bravery, but others like Sgt. Secor, a very quiet D Company Ranger. I recall that since he was out of ammunition and did not have a functioning weapon, he improvised by obtaining German weapons to fight against the Germans. He ran them down and did a wonderful job in a tough situation. Another Ranger, SSgt. Sigurd Sundby, took a machine gun nest out by himself. Some men rise to the occasion and do unbelievable things. These are just a couple of the many men that solved the problem.

It is my understanding that the initial charge by the 2nd Ranger Battalion on Hill 400 occurred during an artillery barrage. Was that part of the reason for success but perhaps also led to many casualties?

Yes, that is true to some degree. But we were great with our guns and that in part led to our success.

Would you like to comment on the conquest of Brest France?

That was another battle, and I was in some many battles in World War II. I was wounded three times in three different battles. At this late date, I am unable to provide you with the specific details of many of these battles.

I am sure that there were many sad moments during your military service. Can you describe any of them?

Listen, the Rangers were brothers. I have two brothers, but the same is with the Rangers: we were brothers. When we lost a Ranger, we lost a brother. When a close brother is badly hurt or dying, and you can't help him, it's upsetting.

So as 1st Sergeant, did you have a father role?

Yes, I did.

So anytime you lost someone in battle, was that a bad moment?

Oh, sure.

What do you think is the most important attribute for a commissioned officer or non-com to have to be able to effectively lead their men?

He needs courage and a lot of it! He needs brains to apply his courage properly. He needs the ability to control his troops. The Rangers are special fellows, as far as I am concerned. They are volunteers, and we sometimes say that there has to be something wrong with you to volunteer for some of the battles we were in. That may be so. But I think it is sort of like when you are playing football. You know who is going to work the hardest to lead you to victory and so it is with Rangers: they will work harder for victory.

Who would you say was exemplary as a fine leader during your military career?

To begin with, our leader was Col. Rudder. He went on to become President of Texas A & M University after the war. A great guy. We had two or three so-called prospective leaders for our 2nd Battalion before Rudder came to us. Several supposedly experienced, intelligent, and well-trained leaders came to take us over and failed. For some reason, the powers-to-be decided that they were not qualified to take over the Rangers, and that we had to have better leaders. Then along came Rudder, and he shaped everybody up. They would do anything for him. There are some guys that are born with leadership ability and with brains that are the kind of men that can encourage you to achieve the best performance of your duties. And Col. Rudder was this kind of leader that brought out the best in his men. And his men would die for him. He was a great guy.

What characteristics of a Ranger make them a more effective soldier? Was it the training, was it the inertia, or was it the energy that drove someone to volunteer for a special operation unit?

I think that it relates to how you are brought up. I always wanted to be on winning teams, and I generally was on a winning team. And when it came to war, I wanted to be with the best, and I thought the Rangers were the best. Those were the guys I wanted to be with. I think that most men, when their life is involved, want to be surrounded by the best men available. Men that can be depended upon, men that would die for you, and that is what Rangers do.

We know that the training helped to prepare you, but do you think that the experience you gained in the field played an important role on how good of a soldier you were?

No question about it. There is so much training that you need. When we were boys, I don't care how good of a football player or athlete you may have been, you gradually realize that you need to be better to be the best. And so Rangers are always striving to be better or the best. That is the way I was taught. And if you were not willing to give your all, we don't need you. We can find guys that aren't willing to give their all.

What battles would you say that the 2nd Ranger Battalion excelled at during World War II?

Well, I thought we did exceptionally well on D-Day. The battle of the Bulge was successful—our efforts there were successful. Quite frankly, wherever we were in battle, whoever urged us to be with them and for us to lead the way for them, we did. I'm sure you have heard of the 1st Infantry Division, a great outfit, and the 29th Division, another great outfit. Well, those two divisions chose our Battalion to be their leaders—to be out in front. We have 500 men in our Battalion. They have 15,000 soldiers in their respective divisions. Our 500 men went out as a point for those 15,000 men to lead the way. And you have all of those thousands of lives depending on you if you are one of those Rangers out in front. Your part is such that you want to do the best that you can humanly achieve and to protect those who are depending on you as you are the point out in front--taking the battle on yourself. The 15,000 behind you will roll up there and take up what you have accomplished since you will not be able to hold your position since there are not enough of you, so the regular division will have to take over the rest of the effort.

What were the greatest lessons that you learned during your military experience?
Up until the point where my life was on the line, I think that I was already trained by my parents, by my former coaches, and by my outstanding officers of the Rangers. By the time I am facing the enemy, and it is either his life or my life, he is going to have one hell of a tough time killing me if I don't get him first. It's how competitive you have become and how deliberate you are. I wouldn't want a Ranger after me--that is all I can tell you.

What emotions are you left with after your experiences during the war?
Well, let me tell you that sixty-five years after the war I must have at least three communications per week at my home, either hearing from my Ranger buddies over the phone, by letter, when they come visit me, or when I go visit them. So we have all been very close all these years since World War II. My children were teenagers before they knew that Uncle Steve and Uncle Joe were not their real uncles but daddy's Ranger buddies. To this day, the Rangers are an important part of my family as we are all part of each other's family. We are just loyal family men. And we are special that way. I don't know of any other groups that are as close family-wise as we are.

Are there are any comments or pearls of wisdom that you would leave for future generations?
Just be honest and hard working. That is about as simple as I can make it.

Are there any other comments you would like to make or any other experiences you would like to address?
Your first training starts in your home with your parents where you learn a lot about leadership. Then comes the war where you enter the service and meet specialists. Along that road, you tried to be the best of the best and mirror the way your best leader was. In my life, I have always felt that I was a good leader because my mother and father were good leaders, and my brothers and sisters were good leaders. Then in school I had good leaders. And then in the Army I had good leaders. And I wanted to be a good leader. And to do that, you have to work hard, whether it is in school, in the Army, or wherever you are. If you don't work to be a good leader, you will never be a good leader. It is as simple as that.

Let me also comment on the difference between the German people and the Nazis. We hated the Nazis. The German people were nice people. Do you realize that most of the ancestry of our Rangers were German? I had Scandinavian ancestry but most of my Ranger buddies were Americans with German ancestry. I can tell you that in the Hurtgen Forest, we were so dirty living in the forest with all of the fighting and rain. One of my company commanders told me that we would be leaving this area soon and going into a dry, sunny area, take a patrol, and see what was around this area. So I got some of my best Rangers who spoke German and told them that this was what we were going to do: We are not out to attack or kill anybody, but we are out to observe. And if we can find a place where we can take a bath and shave, then we can leave this area in decent shape with cleanliness. So we found a nice German structure where the front half was a home and the back half was a barn. And as we exited the forest, it was sunny, and there was a nice woman that was sixty or sixty-five years old and a girl about fifteen. It was such a lovely, peaceful scene with animals and no soldiers. So I told my Rangers that I don't speak a word of German, but that they should go over and see if they could sweet talk them. So low and behold, they trusted us and we trusted them, and they allowed us to go into their barn and take a bath. We got cleaned up and shaved while they washed our clothes. When our clothes were clean, they brought them to us and after we got dressed, they had a great Thanksgiving meal for us on the front terrace. There were six of us and two of them, and it was wonderful. We ate, and it was delicious. Then suddenly, both the mother and the daughter started to cry. We found out that they were worrying about whether or not their husband and son who were German soldiers would recover from their wounds and make it out of the hospital. There were good times and bad times—good people and bad people. You had to take chances—we were at war. Some took chances and got killed. If I had to do it all over, I would have done it the same.

The rest of my life turned out beautifully. The same guys that I fought with are still my great friends, and we will always trust each other as we took care of each other, like gentlemen should. War is war, men are men, and you've got good guys and bad guys. Life would be great with no war. Trust me, I am a retired lawyer, and I have been through so many battles. Seeing the way some people live today, some of them are bad people while others haven't learned discipline. They are not trying to do the right thing. Well, we knew how to take care of the people around us that were doing the right thing. They learned to do the right thing, or else.

Before you destroyed the howitzers on Pointe de Hoc, could those guns have been used to take down D Company?

I suppose they could have.

How many times have you gone back to Europe and visited those areas?

Several times. And I have had some of those people visit me. Some of those people come to our Ranger reunion and, afterwards, stay at my home. When I am there, I stay at their home, and it is so wonderful.

Do you remember what you were doing on Christmas Day, December 25, 1944?

I don't remember, but I can assure you that my troops and I would be respectful of Christmas Day and why we have a Christmas Day, and somehow we would manage to have a Christmas. We should always have respect for Christmas Day.

Let me ask you a question. Would you have done anything different?

I would try to emulate your service.

Right. But the point is, we don't tolerate guys that don't think like us or try to act like us. And we are pretty tough in our discipline. We take care of the tough guys in the way they should be taken care of. I am very proud of the Rangers, and I am very proud of their success in civilian life. Their self-discipline shows why they are successful business men. The guys you see at this reunion are old men, but they are honorable. And that's the whole thing in a nut shell. Good luck to you guys, and I hope your book turns out well.

THE FOLLOWING PERSONAL ACCOUNT OF THE ACTIONS AT HILL 400 WAS WRITTEN BY LT. LOMELL

Hill 400: The Hurtgen Forest

December 7, 1944

Lt. Len Lomell, 2nd Ranger Bn, D Co., US ARMY

My name is Len Lomell, and I was the lieutenant of the first platoon of D Company. Late on an evening of December 6, 1944, the 2nd Ranger Battalion, boarded trucks and under the cover of darkness and by the circuitous back roads through the Hurtgen Forest, were taken close to the town of Bergstein, Germany.

Hill 400 or Castle Hill loomed 400 meters high (1,312 feet) at a 45 degree angle, thickly wooded with evergreens. The German observation post on the summit enabled the Germans to control their artillery fire against the Allies in the Roer River Valley's approach to the Rhine River crossings. For over two weeks, the American 5th Armor Division and the 8th Infantry Division had tried to take control of Hill 400, without success. Companies A, B, and C were assigned to defend the town, which was still partially occupied by German troops while Company E was kept in reserve for reinforcements. Companies D and F, just 130 men were to take and defend Hill 400.

Our battalion commander, Lt. Col. Rudder had assigned a special mission to D Company—to supply a patrol to investigate the possibility of assaulting Hill 400 located on the outskirts of Bergstein. The patrol was to discover evidence of pillboxes, bunkers, and enemy troop strength and position, but through all of this time the patrol was to go undetected. I set out with my reconnaissance patrol at 3:30 a.m. at the right flank of Hill 400 and returned with the desired information to the battalion forward CP at 6:00 a.m. The plans were quickly reviewed. E Company would be kept in reserved for reinforcements. D and F Companies assembled near the church and the cemetery in the partially sunken road that paralleled the base of Hill 400 about 100 yards away. F Company was at left, D Company was at right. The assault was to begin at 7:30 a.m. sharp.

A German artillery barrage started just as I lead the first platoon of D Company across the 100 yards of half frozen mud and snow. Yelling and shooting randomly, we were at a dead run, facing small arms fire with creeping enemy artillery to the rear. Sigurd Sundby took out the machine gun nest. My C.O., Capt. McBride, was wounded and evacuated at the time. D Company's First Platoon was the first to reach the top of the hill. Sam O'Neal and I as well as several others of the first platoon were the first to reach the top, quickly followed by the second platoon. Sgt. Harvey Koenig and his patrol chased Germans over the crest, almost to the Roer River, before returning to deploy along the forward crest. Meanwhile, Sam and I neutralized an enemy troop and weapons bunker by throwing a grenade through its forward aperture; this was later used as a temporary hospital shelter. At this time, the CO of F Company, Otto Masney, arrived with the two F Company men and assigned them with two D Company men to remove the German prisoners and return them to the rear. It was just 8:30 a.m. We had captured the hill in just one hour.

The men of both D and F companies found great difficulty in digging foxholes in the rocky terrain. The hilltop was covered with large evergreen trees except in the area of the observation post or bunker summit. The almost continuous artillery shelling was devastating as the shells detonated immediately upon hitting the trees, causing the trees to come crashing down along with a shower of shrapnel, killing and wounding many men. It was horrendous. The heavy German artillery barrages would lift from time to time to allow German ground troops to counter-attack the Hill. The German attacking forces numbered in excess of 150 men. The first counter-attack came about 9:30 to 10:00 a.m. The fire fights and assaults were at close range and from time to time resulted in hand to hand combat. The almost continuous artillery shelling detonated against the trees, raining shrapnel.

Near the top of the Hill, the large enemy troop and weapon bunker was put to use as a hospital for the many badly wounded Rangers, as well as some German casualties who were unable to withdraw. Unfortunately, it was a hospital without medical supplies, all medical supplies having been used up early in the day and no supplies were getting through the rear. Some of the Rangers were out of ammunition and forced to use captured German weapons to fight with.

By 11:30, my left index finger was hanging on by a tendon, so I cupped it in the palm of my hand and steadied my submachine gun in the crook of my arm. I was later wounded in the same arm and was also bleeding from concussion, as were many other Rangers. Some were bleeding from their ears, nose or mouth from concussive effects of the constant shelling. At times, Hill 400 felt as if it were trembling, as though an earthquake was taking place.

Shortly after noontime, the C.O. of F Company, Capt. Masny was captured by the Germans, which left me the ranking Ranger officer in charge. By then, radio communications, hit by shrapnel, were out from the top of the Hill to battalion and company headquarters, necessitating the use of D Company runners in mid-afternoon to keep contact with the rear and try to bring ammunition, medical supplies and reinforcements up the Hill. Often the Hill would be surrounded by German combat patrols and the runners would have to infiltrate. The afternoon attacks resulted in many wounded men. No fighting reinforcements arrived the first day. Although we were spread very thin to cover the perimeter of Hill 400 with only two or three Rangers in any given position, we were able to ward off the German attacks by constantly evaluating the points of attack and reinforcing those locations by pulling men from other locations.

At about 9:00 p.m. several E and C Company men reached the top of the Hill to help in the evacuation of the wounded. Since many trees had been felled, crossing one anothers' trunks and stumps made evacuation by litter extremely difficult. At times men had to be dragged on the ground on a shelter half for a considerable distance under trees that had fallen. I sustained another shrapnel wound and was evacuated by 10:30 p.m. Sixty-five D Company men had started the assault; fifty-five made it to the top of the hill; only fifteen walked away. I was one of them.

We lost more men there than on D-Day, June 6, 1944 when we climbed the cliffs of Point du Hoc during the Normandy Invasion. However, December 7, 1944 was my longest day.

Originally, D and F Company were to be relieved within twenty-four hours, but it was not until forty hours later that they were relieved by the 13th Regiment of the 8th Infantry Division late on the afternoon of December 8, 1944. On December 16, 1944, the Germans retook Hill 400, using this observation post to protect the flank of its army during the Battle of the Bulge.

PFC RICHARD LEMNITZER

I'd like to start by asking what you were doing and what your career plans were before America became involved in the Second World War.
My career was to get into the service as fast as I could and get into the war, as was everyone else within two blocks of me. And then everyone in high school was leaving.

So even before the attack on Pearl Harbor, you knew that the war was coming and that America would be involved?
Yeah. We thought so.

Where were you and what were you doing when the Japanese attacked Pearl Harbor? Do you remember hearing the news?
Yes. I was at the Palace Theater in Marion, Ohio, and they stopped the movie and turned all the lights on and told us what happened at Pearl Harbor. Then they closed the movie house down and we went home. Everybody was all excited.

Did you rush off to enlist in the military after this incident?
No, I was too young.

When did you enter the military service?
June 6. The same as D-day, 1944.

Did you enlist at that point or were you drafted?
No, I was drafted for immediate induction.

Where did you do your basic training?
Well, I started out at Camp Stewart, Georgia, and then I was moved to advanced infantry training at Joseph T. Robinson in Arkansas. And there I completed all my firing weapons, expert in most everything, passed the OCS. I was supposed to go to Jump School. Some chap from the Rangers came along, and a couple of us were accepted, and bingo, we're gone.

Did you have any specialized Ranger training in the United States?
No. I did pass the Expert Infantry Test, which was fairly easy for me at that time. I fired Expert in all the weapons except the .45. And I could take a .50-cal. apart and put it back together blindfolded.

Do you recall the journey across the sea to Europe?
Yeah. We went to New York and got on the British ship *Aquitania* and landed at Glasgow, Scotland. Got off the boat there and rode a train all the way down to Southampton and got on a landing-craft infantry to Le Havre, France. That was in January of 1945.

Where were the Rangers when you caught up with your unit?
They were outside Metz, France.

Now, as a replacement you were joining an elite unit of men, and they had trained together and bonded. Were you treated as an equal?
Well, in the particular platoon that I was assigned to, there weren't many left. Most of us were replacements. I think there were probably two or three sergeants and a couple of enlisted people, but even they were replacements. My sergeant came D+5. The captain came in on D+10, something like that. So there was only one chap in our company, his name was Arthur LeBlanc, who made D-day and was still there on VE-day. But Arthur got hit a couple of times, so he went back and forth. But they transferred other noncoms and people in from parts of the other companies. There were a lot of replacements going on.

What was your impression of your NCOs and officers?

Well, no one had any insignia on, so we didn't quite know who was who. You couldn't distinguish an officer from a noncom until we got acquainted. They put a blanket down, made us take the weapons apart blindfolded, and put them back together. We got acquainted very quickly with people's voices while we were blindfolded. On-the-job training.

Where did you go from Metz?

Luxembourg. We did some extensive training, and then we were mopping up on this side of the Rhine, which involved various things, not too important. We had a couple of interesting things that did happen, which I didn't find out about until the war was over, when we had a reunion. I noticed one time when we were down by the Rhine River and there were a lot of L3s and L4s in back of us (this small airplane), and a lot of artillery. And then we left. In 1980, we had a reunion in Las Vegas, and I asked our captain what was going on there. He told me that the battalion was going to cross the Rhine, and the L3s and L4s and our company were to be the assault company. And we were to be the first platoon and the first company to put the Rangers in an L3. They were going to go across the river and land, and then they were going to bring the artillery, and as we got everybody over there, they were going to build a bridge to us. But that didn't happen.

Were you diverted someplace else?

Yeah, I don't know where. We got across the Rhine and took off.

What was your first combat engagement?

Well, we were mopping up a little bit before we got to the Rhine, since we had met with some resistance. And then immediately after we crossed the Rhine, we got into some firefights there.

Did any particular action of these firefights stand out in your mind?

Well, some of them. Yes. And we were one of the first troops into Buchenwald concentration camp.

What did you witness there?

Horrible. I can still smell it.

What was the condition of the prisoners that you witnessed? Were these Jewish prisoners?

A little bit of everything. There were some kids that were captured in the Bulge down to 85 pounds. American prisoners, French, British, and there were some Air Force prisoners in there. We were separating them and getting them out as fast as we could. And we left shortly thereafter. They destroyed all the after-action reports there. As I told them there, the captain put six SS troops in a little building and gave each one of them a rope, and they didn't hang themselves. So the next morning we put them away.

The SS men were executed? I can't imagine witnessing the atrocities at concentration camps. Did this change your attitude about the war and what you were fighting for?

Yes, because I didn't know it. My world was so small. That's the first time I really found out what they'd done to the people. It was very tough on you when you're eighteen years old and you've never seen anything like that.

How long were you at Buchenwald?

I don't think we were there more than three or four days at the most. I marched the people in town out and made them haul the bodies out and so on.

The German civilians?

Yes.

You put them to work in the concentration camp?

Yes.

What was their reaction?

Aw, they denied it and said they didn't smell it. But you could smell it for miles around. They claimed they didn't know it was there. After that, we were riding point for the Cavalry and the like. We were taking jeep, go out in front, and we'd keep trading off with the jeep. We had a .30-caliber on that and a wire cutter, and then we'd keep changing off back there. We'd go back to a 6 × 6 and back to armored cars and back to the tanks, and sometimes we'd be out 8 or 10 miles or 5 miles back in front of everybody, taking little towns and various small firefights and collecting prisoners.

Witnessing the atrocities at Buchenwald, did that change your attitude about the German people?

Yes. I think so. And I came from German extraction. I was raised in a German area in Columbus, Ohio. It was called Germantown in Columbus. My family were all still writing before the war, but then we couldn't find anyone after the war.

I'm surprised to find that there were Allied POWs in the concentration camp.

In the concentration camp. Yes.

Was this just a random assignment? Were these Jewish POWs?

There was Jewish too. There was a little bit of everything in Buchenwald. They figured there were twenty thousand left there, when we were there. They were dying at a rate of about two hundred a day.

Was there anything you could do to help them?

No, there was not much we could do.

Where did you go after Buchenwald?

We were riding point for the cavalry, light tanks and away we go.

I understand your unit was involved in an action at the bridges to secure Regensburg?

Yeah, we were near Regensburg. That was on my nineteenth birthday. We were at a firefight there. 88s were firing at the tanks, and I didn't know why it didn't hurt the tanks. They were ack-ack 88s, and they were shooting at the tanks and the armored cars, and we had to eliminate them. They had them protected by a lot of infantry, and firefighting occurred.

Were they on the other side of the river?

Oh, no. That was different. This was outside the river. There were two bridges across this river, and the one river when I was going across the railroad bridge went up. And there was an SS trooper underneath trying to blow a bomb, but they got him out. I don't think I want to tell you about that one, what happened to him.

By this point, you had been involved in quite a few combat engagements. Did you feel at this point that your training up to now had really prepared you for this?

Yes, very much so. I was very comfortable in the military. It was easy for me.

As your unit penetrated farther and farther into the German Reich, what kind of resistance did you encounter?

Well, it slackened, but there was still some Hitler Youth that were firing at us, and SS troopers, and they were hiding, and when the war was supposed to be over, the SS troopers were hiding out with the Wehrmacht, so we would just take their shirt off and find the guys with the tattoos and take them out.

Once you separated the regular German army soldiers from the SS troopers, what did you do with these two groups?

Well, what would you have done with the SS troopers?

That answers my question. Do you recall where you were and what you were doing when you heard that Germany surrendered and the war in Europe was over?

Yeah. We thought it was going to be over any day, and it was a nice celebration. But there were still an awful lot of cleaning up to do, and a lot of displaced persons to deal with. Then for weeks we helped transport people around with trains. Interesting fact: Gentry (another Ranger) and I were lying on this little beach by the lake, and I'm laying [*sic*] facing the road like this, and he is watching the water and hundreds and hundreds of displaced persons were going by the road. These were people from the concentration camps or whatever, and they were in different rags, pushing a bicycle, riding a bicycle, pushing a cart with their clothes or belongings. And I watched these two chaps who had been in a concentration camp put their bicycles down real slow, and they were looking at a fellow that was swimming with his family. All of a sudden they took off running by Gentry, and I turned around to watch. They jumped in the water and drowned him right there. Dragged him out, took his shirt off, and he was an SS trooper at the concentration camp they had been in.

Was he trying to escape?

Well, he was evidently not in uniform. He didn't want to be caught.

How did the German people react to your presence after the surrender?

Well, very friendly. I think they were happy it was over, 'cause they'd been through heck too. I mean, it was not a very pleasant experience for most of them.

Where were you stationed after the surrender?

A little village called Mark-Graffing [*sp.*] south of Munich in the foothills of the Alps.

I understand the concept of unity, strength, purpose has been especially influential in your life. Can you describe that?

Yes, well I came from a very disciplined family in the Depression, and discipline was there. When your father or mother told you to do something, there were no questions asked. That's what you did. I think that plus the war and the discipline that we experienced with the Rangers was a great bonding spirit that we had. Many of us are still very close. But it did help me in my career. I went to college after the war at Bowling Green State University in Ohio and then articulated up with some various business opportunities.

And the discipline that you learned . . .

Oh yeah, hard work. Seven days was the way you did it sometimes.

Were you wounded?

No.

How about any of the men in your squad or platoon?

There might have been some, but they were light wounds. We only lost three Rangers after we crossed the Rhine. Killed in action. Their names are in the book there.

After the Germans surrendered, did your Rangers continue in this effort to try to track down SS troopers?

Yes, that went on for some time, and then we started getting back in shape and training because we didn't know where we were going. There were some that felt that we were going to the Pacific very quickly, but that didn't happen, thank heavens.

The controversy these days was the decision to drop the atomic bomb in Japan. Was that the right decision to make?

Yes.

What is your view on that matter?

I think it saved 100,000 lives at least.

After the German surrender, did you stay on an American military base?
Well, we moved around a little bit in Austria. Then the battalion came back intact in October after being in Le Havre. And when we hit Camp Miles Standish, near Boston, we unloaded there, and they told us we couldn't go to town. Then the colonel called us out and told us at such and such a time we're going through that front gate together and go to town. We were surrounded by MPs, and we took our own and came back in.

What was your impression of the state of German cities and infrastructure at the time of the surrender?
They were pretty well destroyed. Most everything. A lot of churches left though.

To what do you attribute that?
I have no idea, but that's how I found out about a lot of my relatives, through the churches. Back to the 1700s of my family in Germany.

Did you witness any exceptional acts of bravery, courage, or sacrifice?
I think most any Ranger had a little bit of that at some place along the line.

Are there any individuals that you feel deserve to be mentioned now and maybe they didn't get mentioned before?
My sergeant had two Silver Stars, and he was a fantastic combat man.

What was his name?
Snead, and he has passed away now.

What was your role in your unit? Were you a rifleman?
Yeah. 745. I was the first scout, 1st Platoon.

Were there any moments of comfort or happiness during your tour of duty?
You mean during the war, not after the war. Yeah, when it was over. And we had some relapses back to Paris, which were nice.

What things did you do with your fellow soldiers during the downtimes?
Played a lot of cards, pinochle. We had a lot of good times. There were never any squabbles. It was a well-bonded unit.

After the Germans surrendered, did you have an opportunity to socialize with the German people?
Yes.

You mentioned they were friendly. Were there any particular instances or experiences that stand out in your mind?
Well, we gave them a lot of our supplies, food, candy, and whatever, and they were very happy to get it. And we got along very well with them. It worked out quite well.

Did you ever encounter any Russian soldiers, or did the news of the Russians affect your actions either before or after the Germans surrendered?
No. We saw a few of them when we were down by Pilsen, Czechoslovakia. We were reviewed by Patton, and there were a few Russians in the background. I don't recall ever any conversations with them or anything.

What were the greatest lessons that you learned from your military experience?
Discipline. Discipline.

Would you recommend military service to young people today?
Yes. Especially if you could physically and mentally qualify to be a Ranger, it would be an experience to look back on the rest of your life.

Do you feel the role of the military or the command of the military has changed since the Second World War?
Well, it had to modernize. Technologically, they were changed. These kids today, we couldn't carry their water bucket. They're good.

What emotions do you feel when you reflect back on your time in the military?
I'm very proud of what we did. I was proud to be accepted as a volunteer for the Rangers.

Did you consider remaining in the military and making that a career?
Yes.

What factors went into your ultimate decision?
They didn't want anything to do with us. I was in nine camps before I got discharged. They didn't know what to do with the Rangers. They'd find two Rangers in a camp, they'd ship somebody. No, I would have gone on and back to college and probably continued. One of my relatives is a general, and I would have probably stayed in, but they didn't know what to do with Rangers at that particular time.

What did you do with your life after you left the military?
College at Bowling Green State University in Ohio.

Did the discipline and skills you learned in the military help you in your education?
Yes. I was still a little bit wild, but we got through it all right.

Have you returned to Europe at any point after the war?
No. I have no desire to go to Germany and France. I have been to England a couple of times and Scotland.

Why don't you wish to go back to Germany or France?
Buchenwald would be enough.

Did your experience at Buchenwald still color your attitude about the German people and the German nation today?
Somewhat.

You mentioned Snead. Were there other officers and noncoms that made a lasting impression on you?
Our Capt. Green. He was fantastic, a good combat soldier, very fair. Listened to his troops. All the noncoms were good people.

Have you corresponded with the friends you made in the military? Did you keep these through your life?
Yes.

Do you attend reunions?
Yes. I was very close to my Indian friend, Arthur LeBlanc, at Sault Ste. Marie. He couldn't even buy a drink after the war. I'd go up to see him, and I'd have to pass it out the window to him. He couldn't buy a can of beer.

Why is that? I don't understand.
It was still against the law. You couldn't serve Indians alcohol.

He was an Indian?
Yes, chief of the Chippewas.

And they were still second-class citizens?
Oh yes, definitely. Now the reservation is great. I think I told you a little bit about that.

How did that make you feel that these soldiers laid their life on the line for the country?
Bad. And they couldn't even buy a can of beer. That's correct. Arthur went to see President Eisenhower. He had an audience with President Eisenhower. Some of the things changed for the better.

Do you generally like to discuss your participation in World War II with family and friends?
Not really. It's better if I can talk to my Rangers buddies about it. I can talk about some of the funny things.

Do you have any examples?
Oh yeah, one time we had a lot of cooties—bugs—and we were dirty. We got this brass tub, jacked it up, filled it with water, and built a fire underneath it, and we drew straws from one to ten. There were ten men in a squad, and who was going to go first got number one. So as you got closer, and it was cold, then you could disrobe more. And I got down to where I just had my boots on and my long johns, and something happened and we had to leave. So we were going down the street putting our clothes back on. The captain always laughed at us about that one. There were sure a lot of white buttocks running down the street.

How do you cope with your combat experiences and the atrocities that you witnessed?
Well, I think we've worked so hard to make a living and develop a family and your job and career and so on, you just put it aside and blocked it until we started to have reunions, and then we could sit down and talk to someone about it. But blocking it out was essential. It was survival. Making a living before the war and after the war was hard work.

You mentioned the funny incidents with the cooties. Are there any others that stand out in your mind?
There had to be some good laughs along the line, yeah. We were in this house. We thought we had cleaned out the town, and we were sleeping downstairs and looked up the stairs, and here come some German guys down with their hands up in the middle of the night. It was funny. Snead started laughing. How did we miss these people? But some of things were funny.

At that point, it seems that the Germans were probably very eager to surrender?
Oh yeah. It was about over. That was pretty close to the end.

Do you feel that the government has taken care of you and any issues you might have faced as a veteran?
Yeah. I've been under care of the VA for certain things, and it has been very adequate. Got hearing aids and my medicine.

I see that you have material in front of you. Is there anything else?
Oh, I think we've covered this pretty good here. It was interesting to see all the people we were transporting. We had trainloads of displaced persons, and we had to go on the train. We had a car for the Rangers, and Snead took four or five of us, and we'd take this whole train and transport displaced persons to Nuremberg and so on around Germany. That lasted a few weeks, and it was quite interesting to help somebody to get back to where they belonged. It made you feel good.

When you returned to the United States, did you get a special welcome or homecoming?
My family was glad to see me. My mom and my dad and my cousins were there.

Anything official?
No. We immediately got forty-five days' rehab. Didn't count as a furlough, and I think I got the flu. My doctor friend said, "You've got the flu. You can't go back." So he sent a wire and I got another seventeen days. Then I got to another camp, and I'll tell you about that one later, but I got out of there all right to come back.

Can you tell me now?

Well, it was funny. I just tried to kill time, so I went on sick call and they asked me, "Why are you going on sick call?" I said, "I think I've got piles." So I got in the hospital, and they finally found me a week later 'cause I was hiding out pretty good, having a good time playing ping-pong. The food was good, and you could go to town when you wanted to. They came up and shaved me and wheeled me down to these two doctors, and they busted out laughing. They said, "What are you doing in here?" And I said, "Oh, I thought I had piles." "Get out of here," they said. So then I went back to the company clerk and I said, "I've never had a furlough." So they sent me home again and I got sick again. Amazing how you caught the flu when you went home. So I got another extension on my furlough. We were trying to get out. And they were shipping us all over. Another Ranger and I ended up at Camp Polk, Louisiana. I think it was quite hilarious. This is really funny. They had a lieutenant giving us a demonstration of the M1 rifle. Well, I sat down with my back to him on my helmet with my M1, and I'm just watching the birds fly over. So all of a sudden somebody whacked me on the head, and I jumped up and it was a one-star general, and he said, "What are you doing?" I said, "I'm getting ready for hunting season when I get home, sir." And he said, "Why aren't you paying attention to the lieutenant?" I said, "Sir, general, he can't take that thing apart and put it back together. He doesn't know what he's talking about." He said, "You're kidding." I said, "No. Why should I pay attention to him? He can't take it apart. He can't put it together. He doesn't know anything about the M1." "Get out of here and pay attention." So I ran into the general again. Gentry was on guard duty, and he fell asleep down at this big motor pool at Camp Polk. So they arrested him, and they came and got me and just told me to go down to motor pool. And they didn't give me directions or what I was supposed to do. This was Sunday morning, and I knew that general came by at daylight, and I'm sitting down at the post. And he drives up and gets out of the command car. Walks over to me. I get up and salute him. He said, "What are you doing here?" I said, "I don't know." He said, "What do you mean you don't know?" I said, "They woke me up and told me to get down to motor pool. They didn't give me instructions or general orders of the day." He gave them to me and he said, "You stay right here." And he went and got the camp commander. Well, needless to say, I was in Camp Atterbury two days later getting my discharge, so I did get out.

Did the general recognize you from the shooting incident?

Oh yeah. He knew what I was doing because we were writing letters to our congressmen and trying to get the heck out.

MAJ. GEN. JOHN C. RAAEN

Let's start off by getting your perspective of when you heard about Pearl Harbor. Where were you and what did you think? Did you know it was going to affect your life and the world?

I was probably a yearling (sophmore) at West Point, and it was a Sunday, of course. I had gone to the movies with a couple of friends, and as we came out, another friend ran up and said, "Hey, fellas, the Japs just bombed Pearl Harbor." "Oh come on, Scottie, knock it off." He says, "No, it's the truth." So we all rushed back to the barracks and got out our little BP-10 radios, and sure enough the Japanese had bombed Pearl Harbor. I had entered West Point in July of 1939, and World War II began on the first of September. I had been there only about three months, and here was war already. Now in 1941, war had come to us personally, and being at West Point I knew we'd be commissioned and go right out into the war. So there was actually great elation in one sense because we knew that we now had a real mission instead of a peacetime mission.

So when you entered West Point, were you planning to be a military man?

Yes. I entered on the first of July of 1939, and my father was an Army officer. All my uncles were Army officers, and that was exactly what I intended to be.

Did you realize before Pearl Harbor that that was imminent? Did you get the impression that we were probably going to go to war?

Yes. Yes. I think everybody knew that we were going to war. There were still a few people who thought we might

John Raaen

Gen. Raaen

go in on the side of Germany, but they were mostly the *Volksbund* and people like that. But I think all of us were absolutely convinced that we would go on the side of the English.

Could you describe your basic training, or you didn't have basic training?

I never went through what you would call basic training. Of course, West Point itself covered all of that by the kind of training that we received. When I graduated from West Point, I was a Corps of Engineers officer, so I went to Fort Belvoir for a quick refresher course, which must have lasted about six weeks. What we did mostly was build bridges, do scouting and patrolling, and worked with wire and demolitions. After that, they sent all of us new second lieutenants of the Corps of Engineers across the street to the Fort Belvoir Replacement Training Center, where we ran basic training as platoon leaders in the Engineer Replacement Training Regiment, and we spent about six weeks there. That was where I found out that Americans really don't like to build things; they like to blow them up. We had much more attention in the demolition courses that we did in the carpentry courses. Let's put it that way. Essentially, that was my military training: West Point plus those two stints at the engineer school. From there I went to the 10th Armored Division and was initially in the bridge platoon of the 55th Armored Engineers. And I think that being a bridge platoon leader just meant that I built pontoon bridges for the Armored Division, and I got to know that particular end of the business. We then started on maneuvers in preparation for the Tennessee Maneuvers, and because our S-2 was away at school, they took me, a brand-new second lieutenant, and made me S-2 of the battalion, which was fascinating. They had many other people. In fact, I had a couple of first lieutenants working for me, but I was still the S-2, and there I learned one heck of a lot more about how one plans bridges and things like that. I learned a tremendous amount about mapping. Mapping had been one of my hobbies since I was in maybe the fourth grade, so with all the facilities that an engineer battalion had, I really learned about mapping. Then immediately after that, they gave me the engineer reconnaissance platoon, which is the cream job for an engineered armored lieutenant. You not only have an engineer platoon, but you have four extra quarter-ton reconnaissance vehicles, with four extra noncoms, and you really get to run around with all those wheels. In the Tennessee Maneuvers, I had even more fun because Corps immediately took away the armored reconnaissance battalion of the 10th Armored Division, and that made me division reconnaissance officer. So I was the guy that had to go out and lay out the screens that ordinarily a whole squadron of cavalry would do, with my four little jeeps and a couple of 2½-ton trucks. Actually, I had an armored scout car. It looked like a half-track but was on wheels. So with those vehicles, why, I had to act like a whole reconnaissance battalion, and believe me, I got a lot of experience. I got a lot of chewing out from infantry colonels, who said, "Mister, you gotta remember what your goddamn mission is," and so on. So I learned a lot. But before that, I found myself really not liking the armored engineers. I don't know why, but whenever I hit a roadblock, I became an infantryman. I'd dismount four, envelop, and build a base of fire in front. Pure infantry tactics. Whereas the Armored will step on the gas and burst right through. So I said I'm not suited for armor, because my attitude is considerably different. So I just stewed over it and didn't do anything about it. Then one day they announced they were seeking volunteers for a Ranger battalion, and I said, "Whoa, there's a chance to get back in the infantry." So I volunteered and was interviewed by Maj. Carter and a captain from the 1st Battalion, and probably Col. Trevor, the British commando. I got accepted because they needed an engineer officer to handle field fortifications, minefields, wire, and demolitions. So I became an infantry officer, and instead of using me that way, I was immediately assigned to C Company and made a platoon leader. I was a platoon leader probably for six weeks, maybe even more, and one of the other officers was not doing well on the staff. He was a fine combat leader, but he just wasn't suited for staff work. Since I came out of West Point, they said, "Well, you will be able to do staff work." So they made me an assistant S-3 (Training) of the Ranger battalion. I proceeded from there. When we left Camp Forrest, one of the company commanders was not meeting the requirements, but he was a good officer so they moved him back to a platoon. They moved the Headquarters Company commander over to take his company and moved me up to take over Headquarters Company. So that's how I became Headquarters Company commander, and I kept that job until after the Brest Campaign.

So that was perhaps in September 1943 when you joined the Rangers?
The first of September 1943. As a matter of fact, that first night I was the B Company commander because no B Company officers had showed up yet. So I had to be responsible for the wild monsters that turned into B Company.

Did you get any additional training, either physical or educational, with the Ranger group?
The Ranger training was derived directly from the commando training in Scotland. And it was run by the 2nd Army initially. When the 2nd Battalion went through, they actually were in what was called the 2nd Army Ranger training program. By the time we got there, I think that the Ranger training program had been transferred down to Corps, so we were working for Corps, and they had a very specific program. There was physical development, confidence development, and a tremendous amount of map reading, in the sense of you are here, get there any way you can, but be there in one hour and twenty-seven minutes or less. I did a lot of rifle marksmanship, qualified on all of our weapons, and began to do the elementary things. We had the death slide. We had the bull pit. We had the telephone pole exercises. Everything that you see in the Ranger course down here at Ft. Benning, we had, but we didn't have any cliff climbing or rappeling or anything like that, because the requirements to be a Ranger were such that you be Airborne qualified in every respect, except you would not be required to jump. So we were all good physical specimens, and we went through very rigorous physical training. We speed-marched. We did all kinds of things.

Having gone through that, do you think that initial training really made a difference?
Oh, absolutely. It developed men who never asked why. They went and did it. Ace Parker told me once that he had read a study that the Army made that concluded that although a squad was about twelve men, a squad leader or a platoon leader could only count on one or two riflemen to provide aimed fire in combat. The rest would fire their weapons into the sky or not fire their weapons at all or hold their weapons above them in a foxhole and just fire like this, but only about one or two men in that squad would actually give you aimed rifle fire. In the Rangers, we had assault sections of about eleven men, and the rifle squad of an assault section had about five men. You could count on every one of them giving you an aimed shot every time they pulled the trigger, and they would shoot away their ammunition a lot faster than the regular troops. So our training developed very, very qualified, dedicated soldiers. And since we used the buddy system from the inception, it developed reliance upon the other guy, and that developed into a responsibility for the other guy, and the wish almost that he would survive instead of me if it came to one of us. I mean, it just developed that kind of attitude, and that's why the Rangers were such good troops. At Brest when we first went into combat, one of our companies relieved an infantry regiment and then advanced 1,000 yards. If you can imagine a silly little Ranger company of sixty or so people replacing a three-thousand-man organization and advancing. It was a good bit of training and developed good soldiers.

You know as well as I that battle is fluid, and the ability to improvise and to adapt is critical. Do you think Ranger training instilled that in soldiers as well?

Oh yeah, because many times they were given problems in training and they had to solve the problem. There was no schooled solution. They had to figure out how to solve it. Some solved better than others, but in the process, all of them learned how to solve problems.

Well, let's move on and perhaps go to your first entry into the war and the combat on D-day. I know there was probably a lot of preparation, a lot of map reviewing, a lot of terrain reviewing, but you were well briefed for what you were going to anticipate for D-day. Could you go over some of that?

It was, of course, learn the plan, and, as plans are, they changed, but you had to learn the plan. Crucial. Now it wasn't just the officers that learned the plan. Every single Ranger rifleman knew the plan almost as well as the officers. The second thing that we had to learn was the terrain in front of us, and we learned the terrain from sand tables. For instance, when I got on the beach and had probably been there for five or ten minutes, I figured I had time to look at my surroundings. Up to then, I had been watching actions as the troops debouched and so on. As we made arrangements to find out what the orders for the battalion were. But somewhere around five to ten minutes, I began to look around and I looked at the seawall, and for the first time it registered on me. That seawall is wooden. Our seawall is concrete. I'm on the wrong beach. Where am I? I knew the terrain so well that even though it was a mile away from where we were supposed to land, I said, I have to be at the Les Moulins exit, where we have wooden seawalls and where we have these breakwaters. I knew within five seconds where I was. And when one of my sergeants asked me, "Captain, do you know the way to the assembly point?," I said, "I believe I do." Well, I damn well knew I knew. I knew exactly how to get there from where I was, because I knew the maps by heart. We also had wonderful aerial photos, which were not in 1:25 but were in 1:25,000 or even as low as 1:7,500, and with things blown up like that, you could place yourself practically on the twig of the hedgerows as to where you were. Well, that meant you knew exactly where you were going to go and how you were going to get there. We had marvelous map coverage and marvelous aerial photo coverage.

Let's take it back again to the day before or the night before D-day. What were you focusing on at that time?

Personally, I was focusing on the next scotch and water at the bar of the Prince Baudouin. Okay?

Were you nervous?

No, I don't get fidgety in the sense of excited. Fidgety in the sense of wanting to get in the action. It's like the first football play. You're not nervous. You're excited and you want to get into it. And the other question is fear. No fear. We had long since passed fear. We had long since decided that probably 50 percent of us aren't going to survive, but so what. You can't affect that one way or the other except by being a good soldier. So no, there were no problems that way. I didn't have a girl. I had a mother and father that I corresponded with, but I had nobody that was important to me other than they. And I don't recall thinking about anything, if you want the truth.

So let's say you're on the ship, and you're getting your orders on the LCA. What time was that?

Around 4:00 a.m. I don't want to say it was exactly that. The anchor dropped at around 3:30 or something like that. And we loaded into the boats at about 4:00, maybe 4:30, because the run in was 12 miles and the speed was about 6 knots, so that's a two-hour run in, and to be there by 6:30 you had to leave at 4:30.

As a junior officer, did you have any intelligence about what had happened before you got on that LCA?

You mean in the sense of the bombing, for example?

Bombing, or I don't know if there were any groups that even were on their way before then?

No, no intelligence in that sense. Absolutely none.

How would you describe the ocean? Was it fairly choppy that night?

It was worse than choppy. The seas were running out in the anchorage area I've read 10 to 12 feet. Certainly 8 feet, and so that is one hell of a chop.

As you entered your LCA and they lowered it down, was there a lot of water coming over the side?

No, there was a lot of water hitting the keel and smashing you into the side of the ship. Because of all those gyrations and things like that caused by the water hitting the LCA as it lowers the tackle jammed. You had to use axes to cut it away. We didn't have the axes. The Royal Navy crews had the axes, and they had to cut away the tackle so you could get down into the water. Once you got into the water, it was really quite calm, it seemed to us. Yeah, it was tossing around, but it wasn't anything like being lowered into the water and having that baby swing and smash into the side of the ship.

Did you have to counsel any of your company in any way, or did you give a word of encouragement?

Nothing. Nothing. No, they were all just the same way I was. They were all eager to get ashore. There could have been some fear in them, but I think mostly it was excitement. The attitude was so different from today's wars, particularly Vietnam. The entire country was behind us. Every single person in the country was behind what the US troops were doing. Particular landing in Normandy. We knew it and we were on a mission. It was our mission as well as the mission of the people of the United States, and you can't ask for greater motivation.

During the two-hour trip, I'm sure it was bouncy and people were getting sick.

People getting sick. Each of us were issued two vomit bags, and for those that got seasick, they got seasick early, and those bags were handed to friends or to anybody, as a matter of fact. They'd use them, and pretty soon they had all been used and we still weren't there. So then helmets began to be used. You'd take the shell off and vomit into that and then hold it up into the waves and the water sprays. It comes over to wash it out. Put it back on. Pretty soon the helmets had to be used for bailing because the pumps on the LCAs weren't sufficient to handle the water that was coming aboard. On most LCAs, not all, but on most LCAs, all the troops were bailing with the shells of their helmets.

So you arrived in Dog White Sector. What do you recall about your exact experiences when the ramp went down?

Well, somewhere around 500 yards out (very roughly speaking), we began to hear artillery fire. You don't really hear that much, particularly when you're down in an LCA. The engine is running. The seas are bashing the side, and, by the way, the seas were down to around 4 to 6 feet close to the shore. So there was a tremendous amount of noise, so you just don't hear much, but as you get in closer we began to hear the artillery, and we watched an LCM[23] hit by artillery fire with a great burst of fire and smoke. Then we began to be able to hear these small arms chattering, particularly a 20 mm antiaircraft gun. As we got in closer, we got into the obstacles, and the coxswain had to start maneuvering to try and avoid the telephone posts, called "Rommel's asparagus." That was most of what we had. There may have been some tetrahedrons, but most of what I remember were Rommel's asparagus. I can remember once coming down right on a Rommel's asparagus, and there was a big Teller mine and I was looking at it. I wasn't 10 feet away from it, and I remember distinctly saying, "Well, that's it." And instead, another wave picked us up and threw us away from the mine, so we got through that particular one. And as we came in, boats all around us were being hit by artillery fire. Most of the machine gun fire and rifle fire was reserved for troops already on the beach. But the artillery was firing at the big lucrative targets as they came in, and the biggest lucrative target that we had would be the Landing Craft Infantry, with about 250 aboard, or an LCM, which could have maybe seventy-five aboard or something like that, plus two tanks. So the artillery was shooting at the big targets in the water, and the small arms were shooting at troops on the beach. There was no point in the small arms shooting at the boats out in the water. First off, the ranges were too great, and second, it would be totally ineffective. And then again, there was no point on using artillery on the troops on the beach, because they were scattered and down. But those big boats coming in were lucrative. So it was very noisy on the way in. We finally ground down, touched down. I was the second man off the boat. Sullivan was first. He went left. I went right and didn't get the top of my boots wet, maybe just up to the ankles. It was the best landing I ever had, and [I] got across the water. I don't know how much water, but I would venture 20 feet at most, and then onto a beach. And it was not sand. It was more like gravel and shale and shale flakes. Frankly, it looked like hell because of smoke, flames, smells, noises. You could see bullets whipping up the sand. You could hear artillery impacting a boat 20 yards away, plus we had this ocean of small-arms fire coming down the beach on us. Got through that. Got up to the protection of the breakwaters (the retards), but

I couldn't get to the seawall. The seawall, which was about 4 feet high, was physically covered by men cringing to get out of the small-arms fire. Maybe two and three deep. I don't know how the men on the bottom survived. It was like a football pileup the way they were lying up there on the seawall. So we stopped out, but we had the retards to protect us. All the small-arms fire was coming in from the right. There was nothing from the left, and there were two reasons for that. One was that the Widerstand nest that covered the Les Moulins exits (there were two of them, one on each side) were around the nose of the bluff and couldn't see us. And the second thing that helped us was that there was a grass fire on the bluffs. Now the bluffs started about 150 yards in and went up very sharply about 130 feet. So the German emplacements on the bluff, which would have been individual infantry foxholes, tobruks for machine guns, and things like that, they were masked by all this smoke, which was so bad that I actually ordered my men to use gas masks. So you can imagine the German soldier there. He is almost smothered with smoke, and the flames from the grass fire are coming up and licking at him. First, he couldn't see us, so he couldn't shoot at us. And second, a brush fire is a pretty frightening thing when the flames are coming into your foxhole or right around your foxhole, so a lot of the Germans actually deserted their positions, and when they did, they left their weapons there. They couldn't take an MG34 with them or an MG42, so they abandoned their automatic weapons, and when we met them inland, they had only rifles and Schmeissers and pistols to fight us with. So the brush fires saved us from anything directly above us. What we got was stuff coming down the beach from the right, particularly from WN70, and the 2nd Battalion B Company, unknowingly, just to get to the top of the crest, went right through WN70 and wiped it out. And to this day, I think I'm the only one who knows that they did it. So when they managed to do that, the fire lessened considerably coming down the beach, but there was still a tremendous amount of small arms from the bluffs and from the forts down at Vierville, which were almost exactly a mile away.

I'm sure those breakwaters were identified in reconnaissance for D-day, but I don't believe that you had the perspective that they would really provide the cover that you needed?

Well, we didn't intend to go there. That's the whole point. We intended to land 1 mile to the west, and because of the disaster that happened to A Company of the 116th at Vierville, we were diverted by landing control to the Dog White beach. Our first wave consisted of A and B Companies of the 2nd Battalion, plus a headquarters boat. When they came in straddling that boundary between Dog Green and Dog White, they were hit by WN70, which was sitting right above them with all this rifle and machine gun fire plus all the German emplacements in between the Widerstand nests. So they took over 50 percent casualties on the beach. Basically, Col. Schneider was watching about 1,000 yards away when this happened, because there was about 1,000 yards between waves of LCAs. And he said, and I'm quoting from people who heard him, "I'm not going to lose my battalion on that goddamned beach." And so he got the English to turn to the left, and we went down another 800 yards to Dog Red and we came in there. My boat happened to be on Dog White, and there may have been a C Company boat on Dog White as well. But despite what the books say, the 5th Ranger Battalion, less maybe two boats, landed on Dog Red. And one or two boats landed on the edge of Dog White, right next to Red.

Your boat?

My boat.

When you landed, did you know about the carnage that was happening to your right on Dog Green?

I didn't. Sullivan, who was the senior American officer in my boat, ran a very strict boat, and he made people keep their heads down. And because it's a matter of discipline and things, for the most part I kept my head down. So I did not even know that we weren't coming into Vierville. I expected that we were landing at the Vierville exit when the ramps dropped. Yeah, I had my head up a couple of times as we came in. I saw the asparagus. I saw that Teller mine. I saw the tanks at the edge of the water and the infantry moving up the beach and things like that, but I didn't have the perspective of where we were coming in. I had no idea. I just assumed it was going to be Vierville, and then to look up at that seawall and find out that it was the Les Moulins wall, I knew exactly where I was, but it just wasn't where I expected to be.

Let's back up a little bit, then, and give us an overview of the invasion plan for the Ranger forces. What the original plan was, what the objectives were, and then what it evolved to?

Okay. For the invasion they established a Provisional Ranger Group, which was commanded by Col. Rudder. He drew his staff out of the battalions. Most of the staff he drew out of the 2nd Battalion, because he knew them, but he drew about ten people out of my company. None from the line companies of the 5th Battalion, but about ten people out of my company, and that was his headquarters for the Provisional Ranger Group. Now, underneath Rudder, he had Ranger Force A, which was a task force, and it consisted of D, E, and F Companies of the 2nd Ranger Battalion, and they were to assault the cliffs at Pointe du Hoc. I won't go into the details of that. Ranger Force B consisted only of C Company of the 2nd Battalion, and it was to land behind the 116th Infantry at H-hour. They were like a minute apart, and really they were going to land to the right flank of the 116th and decide either to follow the 116th (if the 116th was successful in getting through the Vierville Draw) or to move down the beach and scale the cliffs. No matter which way they went, either through the draw or up the cliffs, they were to attack the German positions at Pointe est l'Aras de la Percée (Pointe et Raz de La Percee). This was a substantial German artillery position with many, many guns. Ranger Force C consisted of A and B Companies of the 2nd Ranger Battalion plus their Headquarters Company, and in that boat was most of the Group Headquarters as well. Now, in the Group Headquarters, people were sort of dual. Sullivan, for example, was the executive of the Ranger Force, but he was also the executive of the 5th Battalion. And the way things went, he performed the duties of the executive of the 5th Battalion, because the Provisional Ranger Force didn't exist the way it actually happened. Anyway, that was the organization. I think I did not mention the fact that the rest of the Ranger Force C was the entire 5th Battalion. So that was the basic plan. The Ranger Force C was supposed to land at Vierville about H+45 minutes, follow the 116th through the draw, move overland, and then attack Pointe du Hoc 5 miles away, from the landside. In the Fabius exercises, they made two changes. First, we put orange diamonds on the back of our helmets after that, because we found that many Rangers were following the wrong leaders and ended up in infantry units of the 29th Division. So to make sure that you followed only Rangers, we put these diamonds on our heads—"2" for the 2nd, "5" for the 5th—and that particular change came after Fabius. The second change was that some genius said, "Wait a second. This is stupid. Suppose Ranger Force A is successful. Why put Ranger Force C 5 miles away? Let's have Ranger Force C follow Ranger Force A, if A is successful. If they're not successful, go back to the original plan and come in at Vierville." So that was the only real substantive change that we had in the plan from the very beginning. Now the missions. Ranger Force A, which stormed the cliffs, was to destroy the guns and then to move inland to the coastal road and establish blocking positions to prevent German reinforcements from the Grandcamp-Maisy area from being able to counterattack Omaha Beach, 5 miles away. That was their basic mission. If Ranger Force C also landed there, now instead of having three companies to perform this blocking, you have eleven companies. I don't know for sure because I was never brought into it, but I think that in that particular case, Rudder would take his full Ranger group less one company (he has eleven companies now), and he would go ahead and drive in on Grandcamp and Maisy and expand the beachhead that way. I don't know for sure. It never happened, so it never came to my mind. The mission of C Company was to attack Pointe et Raz. They did go up the cliffs rather than go behind through the draw, and they found themselves fighting WN74, which was the fortified house and all that stuff near the Vierville exit, but not at the Vierville exit. And they became so involved in that which was directly impacting on Omaha Beach, because all their fields of fire were right straight down the beach. C Company became totally involved in that fight. Goranson did take a patrol in the afternoon out to Pointe et Raz and found out that naval gunfire had destroyed all the positions of worth, so he came back and continued to fight around WN74. The Ranger Force C, as we came in to land at Vierville, we were warned off by landing control and told to land at Dog White. We went in, and actually B Company landed on the edge of Dog Green. A Company landed on the edge of Dog White, and that was where Schneider saw what was happening and moved us over another 800 yards to land essentially on Dog Red. Our mission was still to go inland to our assembly area, which was just southwest of Vierville. After the companies assembled there, we were to immediately start toward Pointe du Hoc to make sure that the guns were knocked out, and also to relieve the 2nd Rangers. So those were the missions.

I understand that the original commanding officer for the 2nd Rangers going to Pointe du Hoc was relieved of his command, and that's what led to Col. Rudder leading that force? If Col. Rudder had not led that force, he would have been perhaps with A and B Companies?

He would have been with A and B Companies. He would have been the first man off of that Headquarters LCA. The first man was killed, so Rudder probably would have been killed.

Let's move back to your segment of the beach. You were down at the breakwater. How did you move up the hill?

Okay. As soon as we got on the beach, I began to get the reports from the noncoms and my company of about thirty-five men were scattered in three of those bays. My noncoms reported in on the casualties and began to collect their men. And they might have one man over here. Well, they've got to get him back over there and that type of thing. So we were reorganizing. And we had to set ourselves up for a possible German counterattack. We didn't know where they were going to come from, but we set ourselves up for whatever defense we had to do. I reported over to Sullivan, who was in the next bay, and he told me to remain with the company because I was the right-flank unit, and to organize them for defense in case the Germans counterattacked down the bluffs. He went over to Schneider's position, which was another three or four bays, and got in on the orders, which were to proceed by platoon infiltration to the assembly area. He came back and gave me those orders, and I made sure the noncoms were aware of what we were doing. We were to stay together as a platoon and would move back to Schneider's area, where there was going to be a hole blown in the wire by D Company. The Rangers blew four holes in the wire. We had the right-hand one to go through and that we would move over there and wait for C Company to go through. Then we would tag on to C Company and go up the bluffs. And all of that was fairly easy. We did it without any casualties. I'd lost one man crossing the beach (wounded, not killed), and it was that simple. But as I was organizing the men and the noncoms, one of my dear drivers who was acting as an infantryman that day looked down the beach and said, "Hey, Captain, look down there at that guy." And here was this guy with a cigar, waving it and yelling and walking down the beach just as unconcerned as anything. Yelling at the troops up there on the embankments because he was beyond the seawall, and proceeding in our direction. We said, "Wonder what he is. Is he a reporter? Is he crazy? Is he high ranking and thinks he's invulnerable?" We just didn't know. We'd rather bet that he was a newspaper reporter and he'd gone silly. But as he approached closer and closer, it was clear he was going to come into our bay, so I decided I'd better go find out who the hell he was. So I ambled down to the end of the breakwater, and as he came around, I saw a star on his collar and I said, "Okay, Option 3." And so I reported to him, gave him a full snappy salute, and he returned the salute. I said, "Capt. Raaen, 5th Ranger Infantry Battalion, sir." And he said, "Raaen, you must be Jack Raaen's son." I said, "Yes sir, I am." He said, "Well, I'm Gen. Cota. What's the situation here?" So I described the situation that the 5th Ranger Battalion had landed intact over a 200-yard front. I was the right flank. The battalion commander had ordered us to proceed to the assembly point by platoon infiltration. He said, "Okay, thanks. Where is your battalion commander?" And I pointed out where Schneider was, and said, "I'll take you to him, sir." He said, "You will not. You will stay with your troops." Well, he was right. I was wrong. So he took off, but he hadn't gotten 15 feet when he turned around, and of course Rangers are interested in anything that is happening around them. So he had about thirty-five sets of Ranger ears tuned in on this entire conversation and my reporting and that type thing, and as he was going away, he looked back and he saw all these inquiring faces and he knew we were Rangers. And he looked at them and said, "You men are Rangers. I know you won't let me down." And then he took off for Schneider. And then I immediately followed behind him, and the rest is history. We went through the gap that was blown up the bluffs and so on.

So were you actually there when he said, "Rangers lead the way"?

No, I was there for his first version. His first version was "You men are Rangers. I know you won't let me down." In the next bay, there were more Rangers, and he said something different. And in the next bay, there were more Rangers, and he said something to them. By the time he got to Schneider, he was talking orders and he apparently said, "It's up to you Rangers to lead the way." And he was talking to Schneider. "It's up to you Rangers to lead the way." So that's where the motto came from.

How far were you from Col. Schneider's post?

Well, I was about three bays away, and at 25 yards a bay, that would be about 75 to 100 yards from him when I landed. So I moved over that 75 yards and waited for C Company to go through the gap in the wire, and tagged on.

You went through the gap and went up the bluff?

Well, first there was about 100 yards of flat area, and that's where today the beach villas are—in that flat area. There are a few up on the hill, but most of them are in the flat area. Then the bluffs began, and at the base they were not quite as steep as they were as you got farther up. We went diagonally up on a little path and got into the smoke. It was so dense, my men kept saying, "Captain, can we use our gas masks?" "No, damn it." And finally I had to give in. And at that particular point, I ripped open our gas masks, and the ones for the 5th Ranger Battalion were carried on the left leg. The 2nd Ranger Battalion carried the chest gas masks, but we had it on the leg. And I ripped the baby open, and of course my orange and my apple fell and went down the hill. My maps fell out and I had to pick them up, and I got the gas mask out and I took the helmet off, put it between the knees, put the gas mask on, took a deep breath, and damn near died. I had forgotten to pull the breathing plug in all of the mess of picking up maps and things like that. So I ripped the gas mask off, and, in the process, my helmet came out from between my knees and started rolling down the hill. I realized what my mistake was, put the gas mask on, pulled the tab, and took a deep breath. It was awful smelling, but at least it was air and it didn't have smoke. Sgt. Graves came up and said, "Here's your helmet, Captain. I caught it." So I proceeded two steps and was out of the smoke. I was so furious that I kept the gas mask on for another 50 yards. But that put me at the top of the hill, and from there I found C Company and found the battalion headquarters CP, which consisted of Sullivan, Schneider, probably Burns, Hefflefinger, and a few clerks.

Where was it that Lt. Dawson opened up some areas for your company to traverse with a BAR?

Well, he didn't do that. D Company blew a hole in the far right in front of Schneider and Cota. Elliot Reed and Woody Darman were the two Bangalore torpedo men, and they blew a double hole. Dawson, being the platoon leader, was the first man through, and of course he's carrying a submachine gun, so he is unencumbered in a sense. The rest of the platoon had to climb the wall and fight for position to get through the gap. There were strangles of wire sticking out and things like that. It was slow going, but Dawson rushed ahead like the bull he was, and he was halfway, three-quarters of the way up the hill. And he looked around to give an order to somebody because he saw something ahead of him, and there was nobody within 25 yards of him. So he had to wait until they caught up with him. Reed came up on him, and he had a rifle grenade, so Dawson ordered him to use it on a German machine gun position he could see. Reed hit it absolutely perfectly, but the grenade was a dud. At that point, Dawson just jumped up and began spraying the area with his submachine gun and killed everybody in the pit and then continued on. By now, he had his platoon with him, and in a couple of moments he would be in the smoke.

And you and your company were right behind him?

No, I was more than right behind him, because C Company was right behind him, and I followed them. And I have the impression that Dawson actually went more to the left, whereas we went more to the right.

You penetrated the top of the beachhead, and of course from there you moved west, went through Vierville up the coastal road. Were there intense firefights in that part of it?

Yes, there were, and it was unfortunate. It was the one error that I think Schneider made. But first, you've got to understand that every field had signs that said *Achtung! Minen!* in it. Now I would say that probably one or maybe two out of ten actually had mines, but they all had signs, and when you see an *Achtung! Minen!* you just don't barrel through. So we ended up as a tactic going essentially in column, because if you follow the man ahead of you and he didn't hit a mine, you probably won't, but if you go parallel to him and he doesn't hit a mine, you probably will. So we went in columns, and B Company was in the lead. B Company reached the coastal road, and Schneider did not want to go through Vierville. He figured there would be a fight in Vierville, that the Germans would defend. So he wanted to go south of Vierville to the assembly point. So the platoon leader was Bernard Pepper, and Pepper and I think Whittington started across a field which contained some kind of crop like wheat, which was 3 to 4 feet high. And so he started across this field and got about 50 yards into it, and a machine gun in the corner opened up on him. Well, good Rangers dropped to the ground, but in this case, when you dropped to the ground you disappeared in 4 feet of wheat. So they were able to actually maneuver even though they were caught in the open, because of this grass. Pepper sent two men down to cross the hedgerow and come down the other side, and he sent two men this side of the hedgerow. The far people got behind the machine gun and knocked it out. So they started moving forward again, and another machine in the other corner opened up. Well, now that's in the wrong direction. So Schneider, who happened to be right near there, ordered another company (I think it was E Company, but I can't tell you for sure) to deploy a platoon to attack the next machine gun. Well, that was taken care of, but then another machine gun opened up. Schneider ordered another platoon, and before I even got up there, he had the entire battalion strung out along the coastal road in the wrong direction. So that fight held us up about four hours. Finally, by the time he deployed his last platoon, he realized that he was never going to get to his objective. So since the machine guns were not along the road, he just bundled up the troops and we moved down the road. We had the protection of hedgerows along the road, and we moved into Vierville around four o'clock. So that's how we got there.

Is there anything you can describe that you hadn't anticipated would be a problem with hedgerows?

It was terrible. First you have to understand what a hedgerow is. Most people don't. We thought when we heard hedgerows, we were thinking of hedges, and England has the most beautifully manicured hedges you'd ever seen, so we thought that's what we were going to be dealing with. We saw them on the maps. We saw them on the aerial photos and we thought they would be hedges. They weren't. Hundreds of years ago, farmers began to clear fields of rocks, and they had to figure out what to do with the rock. Well, this is my field and that's his field. I'll pile my rocks up on the boundary between my field and his field. And as time went on, they piled up more rocks. But of course there was spoiled dirt, and that went over the rocks. So shrubbery begins to grow in there, and finally little trees start growing in among those rocks and among that dirt, and as they plow more and more, century after century, more dirt gets piled in there, more rocks get piled in there, the trees grow, and by the time we got there, a typical hedgerow consisted of perhaps 8 to 10 feet of rocks and dirt intermingled, going up perhaps 5 or 6 feet and then shrubbery. They weren't quite trees, but they had trunks that were maybe 6 inches in diameter, and they were growing up out of this rock mass. And the worst of it was, there were only breaks here and there for the farmer to get in and out. So you had to go over the hedgerow. But believe me, these trees were 6 inches apart, some of them, and you couldn't go through. You could establish a nice base of fire, but you couldn't go through them. Worse, the Germans would tunnel in the back of a hedgerow and dig a nice little cavern, open up just a single little fire port, maybe a foot by 4 inches. They would put an MG34 there, and they could shoot at you forever and you'd never know where they were. So that was what the hedgerows were like. Tanks couldn't knock them over. They were just too big. Our troops finally used the obstacles from the beach. The Germans had put in a lot of metal obstacles, particularly tetrahedrons, on the beach, and our troops made them into sawtooth blades that we put on the front of tanks. The tank would run into the hedgerow and then go right and left, and that would actually cut through the hedgerow, cut through all the roots, and with one or two runs they could get through and create a new opening in the hedgerow. But that didn't come until a week or two after the invasion, when some brilliant engineer decided that was the way to do it.

So before the tank came along to address the hedgerow issue, what would you say was the approach that had evolved for our GIs, especially Rangers, to get through? Obviously, they could bypass hedgerows, but at some point they would have to get through?

Well, I have no direct information on that because I was far enough down the column that those tactics had occurred far ahead of me. But what I believe happened was of course you concentrated on getting through the existing openings. You also examined the hedgerows to find a place where a man could get between the trees, and there were lots of these. I mean, they weren't all 6 inches apart, but there were probably lots of gaps of 2, 3, 4, even 10 feet. So if you stayed down, you had pretty good coverage as you tried to go across the tops of the rocks or dirt, and you could work your way down a hedgerow there. And if while you were doing it you didn't get fired on, great. There wasn't any enemy out there. Then you could work to the bottom of the hedgerow, and staying below the level of the wheat or whatever the crop was, you could probably move along that hedgerow unseen by any enemy. So that's the way I think it was done. It was tough on infantrymen, but then again it wasn't as tough as open battlefield, because you had the cover of 180 degrees of the hedgerow, and you had at least visibility cover of the crops in the field. We were lucky that it had not been harvested yet, because those open fields averaged about 200 yards by 200 yards, and that's an awful good rifle range.

Going back one step again to D-day, although Col. Schneider made the command decision to divert to Dog White and Dog Green when he saw what happened to A and B Companies of the 2nd Rangers, it was actually someone else who made that decision?

The actual plan was that the Ranger Force A would land at H-hour, which was 0630 hours, British Double Daylight Time or French Standard Time. It may have been French Daylight Time. If they were successful, they were to send us the message "Praise the Lord." That meant success. If they failed, there was a single-word message (which I don't remember now) that meant we had failed, and divert to Vierville. If we did not get a message by H+30 minutes, which was 7:00, we were to automatically divert. So we circled halfway between Pointe et Raz de la Percée and Pointe du Hoc, and we circled and we circled and we circled. The attitude aboard the boats was that we want to go in and help them. We do not want to divert, but the plan required that we divert. Schneider did not divert at 0700 hours as he was supposed to. Now, I think I know what you're getting at this point. At approximately ten minutes after 7:00, there was a Royal Navy captain who was in charge of the big ships and was, in fact, in command of our landing craft until we touched shore. At about ten minutes after 7:00, he gave an order, which he regretted in his after-action report. He said, "I didn't want to do it, but I could see no profitability in continuing offshore." He gave the order to his LCAs to divert to Vierville Beach and follow plan B. Most people will give Schneider credit for having given the order, and in fact he may have. If he gave the order, the flotilla commander would just say, "Commodore, do you have any objection if I follow Col. Schneider's order to divert and follow plan B?" That may have been the way it happened, but the official order was given by the captain of the *Prince Charles*. It's just like Rudder as he was going in and he saw Pointe et Raz de la Percée in front of him instead of Pointe du Hoc. He said, "Turn right." And the coxswain turned right. Well, the coxswain can't turn right without the sublieutenant aboard saying, "Turn right." The Royal Navy is very tough on that kind of discipline. So even though he said, "Turn right," it probably was the sublieutenant who said, "Turn right." Or rather, he would have said, "Starboard."

I wanted you to comment on your perspective about how the German forces, perhaps to their fault, did not regroup, and basically allowed themselves to handle the attack on Normandy with small-unit actions rather than regrouping and having a strong approach.

The first point is one that very few people know, but the German higher headquarters believed that the threat was Pointe du Hoc. They believed that Omaha Beach was contained, and they had all sorts of reports from their WNs, particularly at Vierville. "We stopped them cold in the water. There was not a one of them that got to the foot of the bluffs yet." So that's what the German high command believed. And that was the reason why Pointe du Hoc had company- and battalion-sized counterattacks on D-day night and on D+1 night. Because that was the threat as far as the German command was concerned. They did not bother to send their troops down to Omaha, because they thought it had been contained. They thought they had won. Now, the second point is that the German tactics had been very successful since 1939, and they were always attacking concepts. Now just think about the deployment of machine guns. In the attack, your machine guns have narrow fields of fire. They are constantly moving forward, and again, narrow fields of fire. In defense, you really need to have final lines of protection, and you've got to have interlocking machine gun fires. You've got to support the next guy's front, which they did on the beach. The whole concept of their forts was you don't protect yourself in these forts. You protect the front of the next guy down to your right and the next guy down to your left, and it's their job to protect your front. So the German organization on the beaches was great, but once we got into mobile warfare, the German doctrines were narrow fields of fire from machine guns constantly going forward. But that didn't work, because the penetrations were to your right and left and the machine guns were useless. So in that sense, we "out-tacticed" them quite badly. I remember thinking of this and figuring it out in Normandy, that it was those narrow fields of fire that they were using. Except in tobruks and positions like that. They just didn't have the idea. In fact, they were firing from bipods, and a bipod is a narrow field of fire. Our machine guns were light machine guns mounted on tripods, and so when we went in defensive position at night, we set up final protective lines and fired with impact areas in front of the adjacent troops, even with light machine guns. So I think that our tactics were just better than theirs because we were doing the attacking and they were trying to defend with offensive tactics.

I know you were injured in the latter part of December, but you were obviously part of the Ranger campaigns when you were at Brest or the Saar Campaigns. Is there one of those that you would like to pinpoint and discuss a little bit about your active involvement in the firefight or one of the most severe conditions other than D-day?

Well, Brest was more of infantry action for me. By the time we were in the Saar, I was the S-4, and my job was to find supplies and push them forward. So that was totally different there. I didn't even get close to a firefight in the Saar region.

Were there specific events within the Brest Campaign that you could describe for us?

Yes; when the 5th Battalion went into Brest, the first orders that we got were to attach three companies to the 2nd Division. I think he was still a captain at the time, but Hefflefinger was the battalion exec and S-3, and he had command of those three companies. Sullivan retained command over headquarters and three other companies. The mission was to take the right flank of the 29th Division and close on the water and, in the process, knock out the German forts that were along the coast. There were approximately five of them. It was called "straightening out the lines." So the very first fort we went into was Toulbroch, and in a sense we were almost fighting platoons. The battalion was fighting the platoons, in the sense you would call down the company commander and say, "Send your first platoon over there to support C Company at such and such a place." So that's the way we were doing the fighting, and in the process of attacking Toulbroch we got our little fannies whooped the first day and had to withdraw all of our attacking forces back about a kilometer. The situation was so serious, since we had committed our battalion reserve, that I was ordered to convert Headquarters Company into a Ranger company, and to hell with headquarters functions. So I pulled in all the cooks, all the drivers, most of the mechanics, even the commo people, the malingerers around headquarters, the wounded who really couldn't be sent back to their companies yet. That type thing. So I made two rifle platoons out of them. We may have even had a couple of machine guns, but I think we were mostly rifle and formed them into a company and made that the battalion reserve. We moved right up behind the line companies. On the second day, we operated as the reserve. Maybe I better go back for just a moment. The artillery ran out of ammunition in the early days of Brest. They had gone pell-mell along the Brittany peninsula and just completely outrun their supply lines. So we had no artillery to support us the first few days of the Brest Campaign. We sometimes could get smoke, but smoke is not very good in reducing forts. I don't recall that we were ever able to get HE, although Bob Black has some Corps artillery reports that may tell us how much artillery we did get, but we couldn't get much. And as a result, since the Germans outnumbered us ten to one, it was pretty hard to attack them. The second day when we attacked Fort Toulbroch, we got ourselves a squadron of fighter planes, and they were dropping 500-pound bombs, although the first two passes missed Toulbroch completely. We finally tried to fire smoke, but that didn't work. They were duds. So they fired white phosphorus and actually marked Toulbroch, so on the third pass they (I think they were P-47s) just pulverized Toulbroch. Then the infantry attack was through the smoke and debris of the bombing, and the Germans hadn't even looked up when they suddenly found themselves with bayonets in their necks. So Toulbroch was taken very quickly as a result of that. The next day we attacked Petit Minou, a much-smaller fort. I think D Company and Headquarters Company were the attacking companies. So Headquarters got to actually be a part of the attack. I was leading the attack, and when I reached the line of departure, and the sergeant came up and said, "Captain, they want you back at headquarters." And I said, "Sergeant, look, I got two minutes to jump off here." He said, "I don't give a damn, Captain. The major wants you back at headquarters." So I called my motor officer over, Lt. Nee. I thought he was better qualified than Lt. Van Ryper, and made him company commander for the attack. I went back to headquarters, and they didn't need me at all. Either Sullivan was trying to save my life or Sullivan wanted to go up and do a hands-on command of this battle, and he needed me to be back at headquarters to run that, because Hefflefinger wasn't there. He was over with the other three companies, and I was the only one who was capable or competent to run headquarters. It was my job to run the headquarters, but not in the sense that he suddenly made me the senior officer. So he took off, and the next thing I knew he was out of communication. The Germans counterattacked, and I was the one who had to start fighting those platoons, moving them around to head off this German counterattack. But we successfully did it, and just about the time the battle had been won, Hefflefinger came up. He refused to take over from me. He said, "You know what's going on. Wait until

I find out what's going on before I take over." So I continued to fight the battalion, and that evening the other three companies came back and rejoined us. So now we had a full battalion doing what it should, with Hefflefinger at the command post, Sullivan out front, and me just running the headquarters operation.

Did your company have heavy casualties?

No, we did not. It was a very quick action. Again, aerial bombardment and 500-pound bombs will change a good soldier's attitude into that of a bad soldier. And most of these were not necessarily army types. These were coastal defense, which were navy types in the German army, and they were not accustomed to fighting like infantry. So they had a tendency to surrender when faced with what they knew were impossible odds.

You were awarded the Silver Star in Normandy.

On D+1, I took a patrol and worked my way clearing the area north of the coastal road back to the Vierville exit, got in a firefight with a couple of Germans, and chased them off. Then I took the patrol down to Gen. Gerhardt's headquarters and finally convinced them that I truly was an American, not a German in an American uniform, and got in to see Gen. Gerhardt, who also knew my father. So he knew who I was. I gave a report as to what we were doing, and he asked if there was any way he could help. So I said, "Well, we're out of mortar and machine gun ammunition, and we're running low on rifle ammunition." He turned to his aide and said, "Take Capt. Raaen down to the beach, find a jeep for him, and load it up at the ASP." So we did that, and now my driver Sharp and I were driving back into Vierville, and the town was empty. It was real spooky. If there was an American soldier around, you didn't worry. But if there wasn't an American soldier around, it was because the enemy was around. So it was real spooky. We worked our way to Pointe du Hoc, catching up with the end of the column. We were picking up the walking wounded and suddenly we came to an area where I couldn't get through in the jeep. The hedgerows were low at that point, and there was German machine gun fire on the gap, so they could just blast the jeep. So my driver and I got out of the jeep, laid [*sic*] on our backs underneath the jeep, and manhandled it forward 50 yards through this gap, with bullets plunging into the ammunition boxes above us. But we weren't being hurt, so we managed to get the jeep through that way. Some people say, "Well, why didn't you just step on the gas?" But as I recall, the road was sufficiently broken and there were too many troops at the far end, so you couldn't stop in time to keep from hitting them. Believe me, we wouldn't have done it if we hadn't had to. Well, I did that. And another time on D-day, when the battalion was strung out, Sullivan said, "Find out where the hell our flank is, and come back and tell me." So I worked my way down the coastal road until I got to the end of where the Rangers were, and at that point I ran into a patrol from the 1st Division with two paratroopers in it and brought them back to the headquarters, and we made contact with the 1st Division now. My friend Ambrose always maintained that that was not the 1st Division, it was the 175th Infantry. They hadn't even come ashore yet. But anyway, that was pretty sporty running along all alone in a foreign country. At the defense of Saint-Pierre-du-Mont, Sullivan and Metcalfe (the 29th Division battalion commander) went back to Vierville and took all the tanks and left me in command of one infantry battalion almost. It was shattered. Two Ranger companies and one shattered Ranger company. So I had command of Saint-Pierre-du-Mont that night. There were a lot of things, I think, were included in the reasoning for the citation.

You also received three Bronze Stars, right?

At least three, I think. One was for that Brest company attack, which I didn't do. That's a good story too, but you don't need to hear it. One was an automatic Bronze Star for anybody who landed on D-day. I think that had a "V" with it. I'm not sure. And then one Bronze Star "V" I got in the Normandy Campaign. I don't remember what that one was for.

Would you say that once you had arrived in the battlefield, you would pick up certain things that you wouldn't have picked up in your training?

Oh absolutely.

So experience obviously makes a difference in that?

A tremendous amount of difference. And you could see it in the performance of the 1st Division versus the 29th Division. When faced with the disaster of Omaha Beach, the 1st Division's noncoms took over. When faced with disaster on Omaha Beach, the 29th Division stayed there. When faced with the disaster on Omaha Beach, the 5th Rangers (and the 2nd Rangers too, but I'm thinking of the 5th Rangers in particular) rallied around the officers, moved off the beach, and accomplished our missions. The experience of the 1st Division, and its noncoms in particular, was just unbelievable the way they handled the disaster they were faced with. They didn't wait around and look for somebody to take command. They said, "You man, you man, you man. Clean up your rifles and follow me." And that was it. They took off up the hills between the German forts and as a result were able to penetrate to the top. Then they came back on the forts from the rear and cleared the 1st Division beaches. They were into Colleville by the end of the day. But it was just combat experience by those noncoms and many of the officers. Most of the regular dog-faced infantrymen were probably replacements picked up in England, because the experienced men had become noncoms or officers. Experience is tremendous as a teacher.

What do you believe was a very important attribute that would make a noncom or commissioned officer an effective leader?

The first thing, I think, is sound technical training so that you can use the tools that you receive. That was one of the things the Rangers did. You didn't just learn the weapon that you were going to use. You learned how to operate every weapon in the battalion. And most of the enlisted men also learned how to operate captured German weapons. This was particularly important with the MG42 and the MG34. I don't think it was as important with mortars because I don't remember ever hearing that we used the German mortars. But we did use their machine pistols and their rifles and their hand pistols. So learning how to use the tools that you have is crucial. The second thing is developing the attitude of instant obedience. You do not have the information available to you that caused your commander to give you that order. You've got to understand that he has much more information, and if you had that information, you would probably make the same decision that he did. So you've got to learn to not resist it, but to understand that he has a better perspective on what's happening and to go ahead and do it the best you can. Always do everything the best you can. The third thing that I always tried to teach to people was (and it's mainly a Ranger thing, but it does occur in infantry) that by carrying out your orders to the best you can, you may cause yourself to be killed. But in the process you save that guy and that guy from being killed. Now, if he is also going forward, he is saving your life, and in the process, if you do it properly, do everything the very best you can, all of you are going to survive. There are going to be some who die. But all of you are going to survive in the larger sense, and most organizations do not have that mental characteristic—that I have to do the very best I can for my comrades because it will save their lives even if it costs me mine. And knowing full well that he is doing the same thing. Trying to save your life. That should be the credo of the infantry soldier.

So basically the third point is that you need to be out on the front frequently? And that's leadership? Leadership and not commanding?

Oh, yes.

Getting back to an earlier point, I think one of the advantages the US military had was their ability to improvise and adapt to the environment, whereas the German soldiers were very much tied to their orders and couldn't improvise. Would you like to comment?

They absolutely were. That is one of the toughest things that a soldier or an officer or a noncom has to do. Generally speaking, we always try to give mission orders, and if you give mission orders, you automatically have the authority (or your underlings do) to do what has to be done to accomplish the mission. If you tell a man how to accomplish the mission, you have eliminated any initiative on his part, and that is bad. That's why we always insist on mission-type orders as opposed to instructions on how to do things. You should be trained well enough to know how to do the thing. You don't have to have that in the order. What you have to have is what the objective is. So yes. When I was in Vietnam, I was flying with a division commander in the 9th Division, and it was funny listening on the radio. The division commander said to a radio station down on the ground, who happened to be a battalion commander, "I want you to take one of those companies and move it over to such and such a coordinate." And the battalion commander came back and said, "Will the unidentified radio station that just interfered with my conduct of the battle please get off the air. I am fighting a battle and I do not need any interference." And the division commander said, "Hell, that's a good battalion commander." But I will never forget that. "Will the unidentified radio station shut up?"

Did you think from that perspective that the German soldiers were less mission oriented when they would say, "You will not leave your position"?
That's right. But they did leave and they did give up.

But they were less flexible, right?
Well, that's right. They were trained to follow orders. They were probably better at following orders than the American soldier. Starting with the "Junkers," down through the history of Germany, they were taught to follow orders. We tried to teach our men to follow orders, but we tried to have those orders in the form of a mission assignment rather than an instructive detail.

What would you say were a couple of the saddest moments during your military service?
The saddest moment that I ever had in the military service was in the Saar. The doctor came down to me at the headquarters and said, "Willie Moody is in here." And I said, "How is he?" He said, "He's not going to survive." Now, Willie Moody was the man who led that two-man patrol on D+1 night, contacted Rudder from Saint-Pierre-du-Mont, and came back. He was in my platoon at Camp Forrest, and I considered him to be the best soldier in the 5th Ranger Battalion. So I went up and found him on a battlefield stretcher. He was obviously in extremis, and I sat there for an hour while he died, talking to him, stroking him, and that was, without a doubt, the saddest moment.

Well, at least he had a good friend by his side.
Well, he didn't know about it, but I did.

I know there were probably many other sad moments as well?
Oh yeah, there were lots of sad moments. The moment of learning that Dee Anderson had been killed on D-day. He was our Boy Scout lieutenant, a Mormon. He was the only man that everybody wanted to say goodbye to. You probably haven't ever read Buz Sawyer, but that was a comic strip in World War II. Buz was a Navy pilot, and he was assigned to probably the worst squadron commander in the entire United States Navy as the executive officer, and we went through all of Buz's trials and tribulations until he finally understood this squadron commander. One of the things he learned was that the squadron commander had a list, and on it was who was going to die next. And Buz got to look at it, and sure enough the first five names were the first five people to be casualties. And he said, "Well, who's the sixth name?" It was the squadron commander's name, and he did die. Well, we all knew that Anderson was going to be killed, and we all loved him. After we were on the ships, we took boats over to his ship just to say goodbye to him. I'm speaking of the officers. And there were probably a lot of noncoms who did it too, just to say goodbye to Anderson. He died on D-day, and everybody knew that he would be killed, just as the squadron commander knew who was going to be killed. We knew that Dee Anderson would be killed, and we all wanted to say goodbye to him, and we all did.

Did he get hit going ashore?
No. He was killed inland. There was a German machine gun nest, as I recall, and he went around the hedgerow around the edge of a building and threw a grenade, but in the process took one right between the eyes.

I'm sure there were moments in your service when you felt that you had a guardian angel. Can you mention some of those moments?

Well, I had to have a guardian angel on Omaha Beach. There is just no way that anybody could have survived Omaha Beach without some intervention. I don't have any specific things. I do know that in my little jaunt from the 29th Division ASP[24] up to the rear of the column that my helmet was hit on several occasions. During that trip from essentially the Vierville Draw out toward Pointe du Hoc in my jeep, my helmet was actually hit by rifle fire four times. That's my memory at the time. I don't remember it, but I remember at the time saying I was hit four times on my helmet by rifle fire. One of the times, it spun my helmet so much it fell off into my lap. Now, I don't know if there was a guardian angel that moved my head 1 inch forward so that the bullets would hit the helmet. But that was one particularly bad thing. In Brest, there was sort of a lull in the battle, and we needed a radio operator and somebody said, "Well, I'll go get . . ." I think it was Victor Fast, and I think he's here. I'd have to check to see whether it was Victor who they needed. But I said, "Nah, nah, I'll go out and get him. I want some fresh air." So I went out, and there was Victor Fast sleeping on a haystack with a wooden crate about 6 feet away from him. As I bent over to wake Victor by grabbing him on the shoulder, I saw something move out of the corner of my eye. And wham, a 10 cm German shell came down but didn't explode. It hit Fast on the leg, ricocheted away about 6 or 8 feet, and bruised his leg severely. It shattered the rifle stock that was underneath his leg. Now, how did I escape that one? Why was it a dud? That was that one. Another time at Brest, I was driving down the coastal road down to the water's edge, and I had a driver and two noncoms in the back. I was in the front right seat. The windshield was down, and we may have had a wire cutter up, but the windshield was down. And as we came down to this particular point, we all knew that it was under German direct artillery fire. This wasn't howitzer fire; this was direct gunfire. So you usually stopped or slowed down and collected yourself, made sure the road was clear, and hit the accelerator and went through the 50 yards or so stretch, which was really dangerous. As we did it, we were going as fast as we could. Again I saw an artillery shell. It came down, hit the hood of the jeep, shattered the windshield, went between me and the driver at about shoulder height, and between my two noncoms in the rear at about head height. I don't know where it went after that, but it didn't detonate near us. It may have detonated. In any event, the driver jammed on the brakes. The three of them went to the left into the biggest mud puddle you have ever seen in your life, and I went to the right and I hit the driest ditch you ever saw in your life. I got up, and here I am just as clean and dry, and these three monkeys got up and they were covered in mud. Faces, heads, everything just solid mud. I was not very popular. They almost took me and threw me into the mud puddle, but I think they realized that I would probably court-martial them.

Well, I think that your angel probably believed in tidiness as well?

Yeah, so that was that one. I'm trying to think of battlefield-type things and I can't think of any more, but throughout my life I've had so many warnings to stop what I was doing, and when I stopped what I was doing I saved my life.

On the basis of your perspective of leadership roles in World War II, who would you say were some of the greatest leaders that you have been able to attest to?

I'm going to start with Bradley. After Brest, we moved to Wiltz, Luxembourg, which became famous during the Bulge, almost as famous as Bastogne. In a sense it was suburban Bastogne, and we put the battalion in position there and laid out the companies in a nice defensive position. We were in reserve, and Sullivan was a superb battalion commander. He wasn't even settled in, and the companies were not even in position when Sullivan was out on the road contacting adjacent commanders, finding out who they were, what their call signs were, what their frequencies were. He wanted to know everything about them—exactly who was where and how to contact them, and for them to know how to contact us. And in the process he went forward to the very front of the battlefield, and he found an infantry regiment stretched out over about 15 miles. You've only got three thousand men. I mean, that's incredibly thin. And he was quite upset about that because between that regiment and us, there was nothing but quartermaster and ordnance and engineer units and things like that behind us. So he was upset. Now, because of the experiences that we had had, Gen. Bradley had given Sullivan absolute authority. "If you think you are being misused by any commander by whom you are attached, you have the authority to come see me at any hour of the day, any day, and you will be given immediate access. And if you have any other problems that you think worthy of my attention, you do the same." So Sullivan was upset. He went to Bradley. Now, I got this directly from Sullivan himself. He confided it in me. He went to Bradley and he said, "General, I don't know if you realize it, but you have this infantry regiment spread out just unbelievably thin. And there's nobody behind them except my little 5th Ranger Battalion, nobody between the Germans and Paris if they choose to come through that way." And Bradley said, "Damn it, Sullivan, I forgot about that. I should have known not to put you there in Wiltz. You're going to move to Arlon to get you out of the way, because we pray to God the Germans will come through that gap. They've done it twice before, and if they come through there once more, we'll catch them outside of the Westwall and we will win the war." So we got moved to Arlon the next day so that there would be no combat troops behind that infantry regiment. And guess what? On the sixteenth of December, they started right through that area. It was a different infantry regiment by then; they had been replaced by the 106th Division. The Germans came right through that spot, and we had the Battle of the Bulge, which, if you know your military history, was similar to the Battle of Cannae. In Cannae, there was a curve of the river, and Hannibal placed his heavy infantry right on the edge of the river before the curve and on the edge of the river before the curve over here. He placed light infantry in between, and as the Romans attacked, the light infantry gave way in the center because they couldn't have held them up anyway, and the infantry poured in through the gap. They got so crowded that men were crushed to death. They couldn't use their shields, they couldn't use their swords, but they kept plunging through this gap. And suddenly the light infantry threw away their weapons and swam across the river, and the Romans were caught by the Cannae River there. In World War II, I think it was the Moselle. The 101st was at Bastogne, and there was a complete gap in between. The Germans crowded in, and they couldn't use the road hubs at Bastogne, so their convoys got mixed and they had all kinds of problems. Just like Cannae. Then Patton came up from the south and just clobbered the hell out of them. It was like the Battle of Cannae, but on a grander scale of hundreds of thousands of men instead of just tens. I think Bradley, knowing his military history, had figured out that if only the Germans would do what they've done twice before (and it was very likely they would), we could catch them.

So let me take that further, because a lot of historians say that we were really caught off guard.
Not in the least. It was planned. But you couldn't tell the American people that I planned the battle in which I knew I would lose twenty thousand men. Now, if you didn't win that battle losing twenty thousand men, you'd lose a hundred thousand trying to go through the Westwall. But the American people don't react to that long-term thinking. The American people are short-term thinkers, which is why we had trouble in Vietnam, which is why we are having trouble in Iraq. They want us out 'cause they just aren't long-term thinkers. So anyway, I consider that Bradley was a great military genius. The second one obviously is Gen. Cota, who deserved a Congressional Medal of Honor. I don't know if Teddy Roosevelt deserved one. I personally think he probably did not, but I am not an expert. I've never studied Utah Beach. I don't know what his contributions were, but I know they couldn't have been a tenth of Cota's contributions on Omaha Beach. And if you want to read about Cota, there is Lt. Shea's report of Cota's actions on Omaha Beach. Pure Medal of Honor stuff from first landing to the end of D-day. Pure Medal of Honor stuff. He's my "number two" one. And the third one as far as great leaders, I'm going to come down to the battalion level and say Sullivan. When Sullivan went into a place, as I told you, he immediately found out everything he needed to know. Every after-action report will say we moved into bivouac at so and so and immediately sent out patrols to determine where the enemy was. Sullivan wanted to be with the troops. At night, when the battle had quieted down, Sullivan would go to different companies on different nights. And he'd lie down beside the riflemen that were at the forward edge of the battlefield, and he'd question them. "Who's on your right? Where is he? Who's on your left? Where is he? What are your fields of fire that you were ordered to protect? Do you know where the enemy is? Have you got an alternate position when they find this little slit trench of yours? Do you have another one you can go to? Who's your noncom? What's his name? How far is he? Where is he located? What kind of ammunition have you got tonight? Have you got tracers in there to give away your position, or do you fire in ball?" If he was a machine gunner, "What are your fields of fire? What is the impact area? Who's the interlocking fire from the other direction in front of you?" That type thing. And he would go down through a whole company at night, talking to every single Ranger on the forward edge of the battlefield. That's the way he spent his evenings, and if that ain't leadership . .

If you were to summarize, what are the greatest lessons you learned from your military experience?

Instant obedience, loyalty, and doing the very best that you can under any situation, no matter how odious it might be.

If you were to impart to current and future generations some pearls of wisdom, and perhaps a lot of them would be from your military experience, what would those be?

Well, those three that I just mentioned. But there is one other, and I used it on young officers, and I'll describe one occasion. And it was simply this. That every assignment is a selection. I asked this one candidate, "Now, Mr. X, you want such and such a job, and the supervisor here has three candidates, of whom you are one. Who is he going to pick? A man who is always causing trouble? A man who is always challenging him? Or is he going to pick a man who may not be anywhere near as well qualified but will do everything he says, and do his best to help him? Which man will he select?" And he said, "I guess he'd pick the man who's always going to help him, even though he isn't as well qualified. He'll get his job done a lot better." He was thinking the whole time. And he became the most cooperative labor agitator you have ever seen in your life. He straightened out the entire population in my command. When you're being selected for a job, it isn't the most qualified who always gets the job. It's going to be the one who will help the selector do the best job. I sat on two selection boards, and it was very useful to be able to point out that in every single case, if you do a good job and get a reputation for doing a good job, you're going to be selected for a better job. If you do a bad job and if you're always in trouble, you're not going to be selected, and you're just going to be another agitator. And it works. I've worked it on young officers. I've worked it on quite a few people who were giving me problems. The only reason I paid attention to this particular man was when he wrote his complaint, he wrote it in longhand instead of typing it. It was the most stunning handwriting I have ever seen. Every letter was perfectly formed. Artistic handwriting. So I called him in and I complimented him. I said, "The only reason I'm seeing you is because I know the discipline it took to learn how to write this way, and the discipline it takes to write this way. That tells me you have a great deal of self-discipline and that you could be a very useful man in this organization." And of course that didn't hurt either.

If you were to pinpoint one campaign in World War II that you would say was one of the most pivotal for the Ranger concept, which one would that be?

The pivotal one was the 5th Battalion landing intact on Omaha Beach, because if we had gone and landed at Pointe du Hoc or something like that, the 29th Division would have been chased back into the sea. There is just no doubt about it in my mind, and I've begun to convince British historians of that. They've already put out a couple of BBC shows that emphasize the point that it was the 5th Ranger Battalion landing intact that saved Omaha Beach. It's just absolute fact as far as they're concerned now. And with most American historians who concentrate on this, that that was it. But that wasn't the Ranger mission. We were not doing a Ranger mission. So when you're talking about the Ranger concept, the only part of the Ranger concept that was involved there was the discipline to do the job that had to be done. Because we completely changed the job that had to be done as we went off the beach. So that's that one. The one that I've been told for the 5th [that] was the best example of a Ranger mission was the Irsch-Zerf Campaign, which I know very little about, but I've been told over and over again by people who participated in it that it was a real Ranger mission, and it's the one that we should have been doing all along, even though the casualties were high. The infantry could not have done it. It took Rangers to do that particular thing.

A STORY OF THE BATTLE OF THE BULGE: GEN. RAAEN

In late September 1944, when the 5th Ranger Infantry Battalion left Brest, we did so in many ways. Some companies by truck, some by rail, and not all at the same time and definitely not by the same routes.

As for me, I was the advance party as usual. My orders were to proceed to wherever I could find it and obtain further orders at VIII Corps Headquarters. The trip by jeep was very sporty from the length of Brittany, up through Paris, and into the southern parts of Belgium. MP traffic control points were a godsend. The MPs knew where I and my men could get gasoline, water, a meal, and a place to bed down. They knew what routes were safe and also what routes would avoid those maniacs who drove the Red Ball Highway.

In the 600 to 700-plus miles I traveled, we had several narrow escapes, for in many parts of our trip, we were skirting the edge of the battlefield. In one such, my driver and I entered a French town. I could hear the sounds of battle on the other side of the still-smoking town. As we drove along the half-blocked deserted streets, we passed a US soldier crouching in a doorway. I told Eckern, my driver, to stop and back up. I then went over to the soldier and asked him what was up front. He calmly said, "Enemy." "Enemy!" "Yup, I'm point." "Why did you let me drive past you?" "You looked like you knowed what you was doing." And that's the way it was, sporty.

When we started out, I'm not sure if I knew where VIII Corps Headquarters was, but thanks to the MP checkpoints I learned soon enough. Past Verdun, Longuyon, Longwy, Arlon, and Martelange. And there it was, Bastogne. Traffic in the town was horrendous, as one might expect from Bastogne being a major road and highway intersection and a Corps headquarters. The headquarters comm gave me a small office with a desk and not much else. I think we slept there and took our meals in the headquarters messes, though we may have had C rations instead.

Someone in G-3 gave me my orders. The battalion was to locate on a wooded plateau just southwest of Wiltz, Luxembourg, a small village about 12 miles away. We refueled, picked up supplies, and took off for Wiltz. It was a beautiful drive, cool but not cold, fairly light traffic, road in good shape. We traveled through heavily wooded areas where the evergreens were planted in perfect rows a couple yards apart to break up an armored cavalry charge in the Middle Ages. No underbrush, neat as a pin.

Our bivouac area was much the same. Fairly flat, wooded with evergreen trees placed in perfect but staggered lines. The rows of trees were far enough apart to allow our vehicles to pass. I laid out the bivouac area, placing headquarters at the center of a circle of companies, and then camped out, waiting for the battalion to arrive.

While waiting, I drove down the hill into Wiltz and found it a lovely little place. As I recall, there was very little war damage, if any, but it's been so long that I really can't remember that.

The companies of the battalion finally began to arrive, one company at a time, and, as expected, the company commanders unanimously rejected my bivouac plan and rearranged everything. While they were still arriving, the battalion commander, Lt. Col. Richard P. Sullivan, was hard at work doing the things that good combat commanders do. He traveled. He visited every unit in the vicinity, setting up liaison procedures, exchanging call signs and phone numbers and the like. This wasn't as difficult as it sounds, because the MP traffic control points were like information centers, knowing the location of every unit for miles around. Sully traveled all the way up to the front, where the divisions were in contact with the enemy, and what he found horrified him.

First, the divisional infantry was spread out over enormous fronts, with huge gaps between platoon and company positions. Second, the 5th Ranger Infantry Battalion was the only combat unit backing them up. No other infantry or armored troops anywhere, as Sullivan put it, "between the front lines and Paris."

The two Ranger battalion commanders had been given permission by Gen. Bradley to visit him personally if they ever thought there was a misuse of Rangers by senior commanders. Sully thought the situation he saw called for such a visit, and he drove straight down to 12th Army Group at Verdun.

When he got in to see Gen. Bradley, he told him of the situation as he saw it, that the enemy could attack through our front lines like water through a sieve, and, good as it was, the 5th Ranger Infantry Battalion wouldn't be able to stop them after they shattered the weak front lines.

Bradley answered something like "Damn! I had forgotten about you Rangers. I'll have to move you immediately." And then he added, "Sully, we* just hope the enemy does just what you say. He's come through the Ardennes twice before, and if he does it again we'll be able to stop him and crush him outside the Westwall. That'll save tens of thousands of casualties."

Sully came back to the battalion with alert orders to move. He told me about his visit with Gen. Bradley in detail. At the time, I thought it was interesting, but we were so busy getting ready to move "out of the way" that I didn't give it much thought at the time. Only in retrospect, after the Battle of the Bulge was long passed, did I finally realize that Bradley had re-created the Battle of Cannae! I don't think Bradley realized the magnitude of the force with which the Germans would attack. After all, no hint of the German offensive was found through ULTRA, because no use of radio was permitted by Hitler in its planning and preparation. I also believe that Gen. Bradley did not *expect* the Germans to attack through the Ardennes, but that he *hoped* they would. [Note that in the previous paragraph, I highlighted the "we" with an asterisk. I don't know who "we" was. Perhaps Eisenhower and Bradley; perhaps it was a "Royal We." I don't know.]

Sure enough, the battalion moved out to Differt, a suburb of Arlon, Belgium, before all of the companies arrived in Wiltz. In the Arlon area, we joined up with the 2nd Rangers, began training and the never-ending search for volunteers to fill our ranks depleted by the battles fought in and around Brest.

SSGT. WILLIAM E. BOYD

First of all, did you enlist or were you drafted?

I enlisted. I was in the National Guard. I joined the 121st Engineers, A Company, of the 29th Division in Washington, DC, about June of 1940.

What were your interests or future career plans prior to you enlisting?

There wasn't too much of anything. Things were kind of tough, and I was kind of a free spirit. I didn't have long hair or nothing like that. I was young. My mother died when I was ten, and after that my life had changed. But I never did anything bad. I never was arrested or anything. The worst thing I did was stay after school after hours. After I enlisted, I went home to Jersey, Point Pleasant Beach, and I met a couple of guys. One I went to school with, and he belonged to Company G of the 114th Infantry Regiment of the 44th Infantry Division in Asbury Park in Jersey. So he talked me into joining. He said, "Hey, you'll make about a dollar every time we have a meeting." It sounded pretty good, so I went from there. When I transferred, this was around the middle of August, and then on September 16, 1940, the 44th Division was inducted in service as one of the first National Guard outfits in World War II. And then that winter, I got sick and they found out I was underage, so in May or June I was discharged. Then, after trying to find work and not getting along with my father too well, I went and joined the Canadian army. I went up to Canada for about ten months. After Pearl Harbor, my buddy wanted to volunteer to come back to the States.

So you were underage when you enlisted?

When I was in the National Guard. Then when I transferred to Canada, I told them I was nineteen. I jumped a year.

So where were you when you heard about Pearl Harbor?

Myself and a guy named Harrington from New York, and two Canadians. We were in what they called the enlisted men's canteen. On account of the English army, every [one of] the enlisted men in the Canadian army had their own canteen, noncoms back there. The officers back there. But we were just sitting there on a Sunday, drinking beer, talking, and the officer of the day came in. So we said, "What are you doing in here? Nobody called you." So he said to the bartender, "Turn the radio on." We didn't know what was going on. He turned it on, and all you heard was Pearl Harbor, bombed, this and that. So he bought us each a beer, and that's when I learned about Pearl Harbor.

What were your immediate thoughts after that?

Well, it took a little while to sink in, really. And then, this rumor came up that we were going to be able to transfer, and then it did happen. But that's when everybody was really interested in doing something. So I transferred and got sent to Fort Riley, Kansas, and I met some pretty interesting people in basic training. I met Henry Morgenthau III, whose father was secretary of the Treasury. There was a guy named Owens. He was married to Donna Reed. She played in the Christmas story with Jimmy Stewart (*It's A Wonderful Life*).

So where did you complete your basic training?

Well, I never finished anything in basic training. After I was in Fort Riley for a while, I got called in the first sergeant's office, and he said, "I got a new job for you. You don't have to do all this stuff." So I had to take care of the officer's horses every day, and that was pretty good.

So what position were you first assigned to?

Well, from there I was sent to Fort Benning, Georgia, to the 10th Armored Division and the 11th Armored Calvary, which was tanks. But I met a guy I joined the National Guard with a couple of years before, and he was an officer in . . . I think it was the 184th Infantry of the 10th Armored. He worked and got me a transfer, and then we went on maneuvers up in Tennessee, and we had just finished maneuvers and we were washing our socks and our underwear and stuff in a stream, and a couple of guys came by and said, "Hey, they're looking for volunteers to join the Rangers." Now, at that time nobody knew who the Rangers were, really. So I went and the first sergeant said, "No, you can't." So I went out of the tent, and it was just my luck that my platoon leader was coming in. He said, "What's the matter?" I said, "The first sergeant won't let me volunteer for the Rangers." He said, "No problem there. That's an order from Washington. Nobody can turn you down." So he went in and told him to make out the papers; that I was volunteering.

And you didn't really know what the Rangers were about? You just signed up?

I knew a little bit, being in the Canadian army, because they had the Commandos in England, and that's what we were, American commandos, actually. They called us Rangers. So about two thousand guys volunteered. Ten of us enlisted men and two officers made it, and we went to Camp Forrest, Tennessee, for training.

What additional training did you receive as a Ranger then?

Well, I guess a little bit of everything. Small weapons we had to learn. And later on, we did some mountain climbing, cliff climbing, running up and down the side of the mountain. We did the rubber-boat training in Fort Pierce, Florida. Our commanding officer was Maj. Carter, and we went over to England and then on to Scotland for training. The training in Scotland was good for us. We were cut off from everybody, so we learned to rely on each other.

How did your additional training as a Ranger affect your performance on the battlefield?

It was very important. Whatever job we had, we always did it in pairs and sections. I was a section leader. I joined the Rangers as a private; in the two months I was there, I became a section leader and went all the way up to staff sergeant. Everything we did, we did together. I was in E Company of the 5th Ranger Battalion and was quite proud. I still have contact with the four of us left from World War II. We started training in Camp Forrest, Tennessee, and we were quite close to one another. We relied on each other too. We only had one fight in the company.

Did your military training prior to when you actually got into battle give you a reasonable perspective on what to expect with the battlefield conditions?

Yeah. I'd say yes. I mean, we took care of each other. I always made sure I had my toothbrush and tooth powder, and a couple of pair of clean socks most of the time. And when somebody got hurt, we'd make sure that there was something being done, or if somebody got killed, we'd make sure that they were going to be taken care of, picked up or whatever. And we had a couple of friendly-fire situations, I guess you'd call them.

That's the term nowadays.

Actually, the strangest thing was both times it happened with the same man, and he was in my section. And it was just an unfortunate thing. We were getting ready for D-day, and they had just a couple days before they just gave us Browning Automatic Rifles, and we trained some of the guys. All our machine gunners were given Browning Automatic Rifles, which were more convenient for us. We were told to clean our weapons and get ready, load them and everything else. But the Ranger made a mistake and put the clip in and then pulled the trigger and hit four or five guys. But then things got straightened out pretty fast.

What did you think of your officers during training?

Very few of our officers didn't make it. We lost a couple in training, but most of our officers were leaders. I mean, we looked up to them and they looked up to us, I would say. Even in training, they did everything we did. On some of our early training, some of us got blisters on our feet from the speed marches. Our officers made sure that the guys who were next to us picked you up and helped you out, because if you dropped out, you were kicked out of the outfit. I was lucky in E Company. We had a Lt. Pepper from Minnesota, who was a tremendous leader. He ended up getting killed in Korea. Then we had Capt. Ed Lewis from Massachusetts. He ended up commanding the whole way through. And our platoon leader was one of the first officers of the 5th Rangers killed on D-day. He was a Mormon from Utah, somebody we all liked.

When were you first deployed to combat conditions?
D-day. June 6, 1944. That was our first engagement.

Was it similar to what you expected, on the basis of your training?
Well, in a way it was. After we got in the landing craft, it was a little choppy, but I didn't think it was that bad. But I was raised in Point Pleasant, New Jersey, right on the seashore. I was on fishing boats, and so I didn't think it was that bad. And our landing was pretty good. We were supposed to go in with the 2nd Rangers at Pointe du Hoc, but communications broke down because of the weather, and our battalion commander, Col. Schneider, changed our landing point and we went in to an area that was pretty good. It was a little rough, but not that bad. It was called Dog White at Omaha Beach. We got off of our landing craft, and all I remember was that Pvt. Marks was one of the littlest guys in the company, and he was having trouble with seasickness. We got him off and went forward, and there were things hitting all around us. Hitting the sand and whatnot. Then we realized—this was it.

Well you know the _Private Ryan_ movie was incredible, but that was just a movie as to what you all went through.
I saw that too, and only the first part of it was about D-day. But we from the 5th kid our friends from the 2nd Rangers, because they were mentioned in the movie. Some of my best friends are 2nd Rangers, and Leonard Lomell is pretty well known. He's in Brokaw's book _The Greatest Generation_. He went to school with my sister. I knew him when I was a water boy when he was playing high school football and baseball. I was about ten years old when I first got to know him. He lived in the borough behind us. And then another young fella, John Wortell, was a year behind me in school and is one of my best friends today. He was one of the first replacements in on D-day. I think we learned a lot in the Rangers, just being friends. And some of us did pretty good. Some did very well in life afterwards, and most of the ones who did very well never looked down at us. Because everybody has to work their way up, and some people have just a little more luck. So there are four of us left, and we keep in contact with one another. I think our training had a lot to do with it, because at our reunions I have met guys from other battalions, from the 1st, 3rd, and 4th, who were very friendly, and it all started with D-day. When we were going in on D-day, the only troops I saw, when I got up to this wall, there were two guys laying [_sic_] there, and they were soaking wet, and I said, "Who are you guys?" They were engineers, and they were clearing off the beach. And they said, "Have you got any cigarettes?" And I said, "Yeah, my cigarettes are dry." So I gave them a pack that I had opened, but I had a couple of other packs, and all they wanted was cigarettes. I remember seeing only a couple of planes overhead, but since we were there, I guess they couldn't do too much bombing on the beach, because it would have been a mess. And I was there when the infantry started to land. I saw some of the landing craft with two hundred men on them get hit with shells, and that kind of woke us up. Then we knew that this is it. As young and foolish as we were, these things started to sink in. And one thing led to the other. This general was walking down the beach, and our regimental commander of the 115th Infantry was named Col. Cunningham or something like that. He was wounded in the left wrist. I'll never forget he was smoking cigarettes like crazy.

How did your noncoms and commissioned officers handle the activities of your company or battalion?
I was a section leader, so I was in charge of eleven men, twelve counting myself. Every section took care of their own, in that we slept together, we ate together, we had friends in other sections of the company, but when we did anything, it was section to section. Each section had twelve men except for the mortar section, and they had six.

Did it take a long time to build that respect for your noncoms and commissioned officers?

I don't think so. Most of us had been through basic training before we started our training at Fort Pierce, Florida. But this was something different. This was expected of us because we were volunteers, so actually we couldn't gripe or anything. So once we started, we learned as we went along we had to rely on one another, and finally I think we just gelled. I mean, I brag about this to guys from the other battalions and other companies, and I say that's one thing about E Company. We did our jobs, and we did it together. We, not I. And that's the way I feel.

What kind of attributes would you say made your noncoms or commissioned officers so effective?

I don't know. I think it was the attitude. I remember one officer who had just graduated from West Point. He was a real southern boy, and we liked him, but we got lost a couple of times on patrols and things, and he just couldn't make it, so he was cut. The day he was leaving, he came up to our platoon and he practically had tears, because he was sorry he was leaving and because he wanted to prove to his family that he could. He had gotten the appointment at West Point, I guess, through political connections. And we kind of felt sorry for him, 'cause we realized how tough it was to make it. But we had some fine officers, and only a couple didn't make it. They all work hard, and they had to do what we did. In fact, they had to do just a little bit more, taking care of us personally. And we had good medics. Our first medic, I think, was a Mexican. He was a little guy, and every time we'd come back from walking on a day of training, road hikes, or anything like that, he wouldn't leave our barracks until he checked every one of us. He got hit on D-day and was out for a while, but when he came back, he was assigned to headquarters. But we all loved him. I mean, he was the best. And that's the way we felt. They had to do what we did, but they didn't carry a weapon.

Okay. What aspects of being a Ranger made you a more effective soldier?

When I was interviewed for the Rangers, they had three enlisted men from the 1st Ranger Battalion and Maj. Carter at the interview. We had just got off maneuvers, and I'm lined up with all these guys who went through a physical. So it was my turn to go up before this review board, and I told them who I was, and I saluted the major. And the major said, "Why do you want to be a Ranger? What makes you think you should be a Ranger?" I said, "Well, the Rangers are like the British Commandos." He said, "How do you know about the British Commandos?" I said, "Well, I was in the Canadian army." "You were in the Canadian army?" and back and forth, and this one sergeant who I became friendly with asked me a couple of questions. When I joined the American army, when I joined the Canadian army. And he sat there and said, "Major, I accept this man." So all of them accepted me. That's how I got in the Rangers. I considered that I had been in the Canadian army and had some years of service, and yet I still was a private. To me, becoming a Ranger was the start of everything. I think my life started to change. After the war, I learned about a lot of the things we did and the battles we fought. I think I contributed. One of my riflemen is still alive and is in close contact. I can say that I think I saved his life. He had broken down, and I had to take care of him for two days and a night while we were in combat.

And that's what you said before. That you took care of each other.

All he says today is "All I remember is the boys keep telling me every time we stopped, to dig a hole. And make it deep." It was raining, but that's the only way I could think of keeping him occupied while we were chasing tanks and other things. Then another time, I had my platoon sergeant and he got hit pretty bad. We were in a spot where we couldn't get him out, so I ran back and stole a jeep from D Company. It was on an outpost and they had three jeeps, and one of them had keys in the car, so I took it. I drove back and picked him and another guy up and drove. All I remember is driving and stuff dropping all around us. All I wanted to do was get out of there. We were pretty close. When I got him to the aid station, I just said, "Take good care of him." And he survived. Little things like that. But in my company especially, we never thought anything we did would be classified as "heroic." We did it because it was who you were, and that's the difference between the Army and the Rangers.

So being a Ranger, you really saw a difference than when you were, let's say, in the Canadian army or during basic training?

Oh yeah. I mean, it just gives you a little pride when somebody asks, "What did you do in the Army? What did you do during the war?" I'd say, "Well, I'd do everything they told me to do." "What do you mean? What kind of outfit was that?" I say, "I was in the Rangers." We found a lot of people who pretended who they were, and that seemed to be quite common. But we just laugh about it.

What were the major battles you were involved with, Mr. Boyd?

Well, I was in D-day, Normandy, and then I was in all the way up to March 3. The first time I got wounded was around September 3.

And what battle was it that you were wounded in?

That was in Brest, during the Battle of Brest. It was a pretty good battle. I got knocked out there.

How were you wounded?

Well, the 1st Platoon was running patrols for the 2nd Division to our left. My platoon was running patrols for the 8th Division to our right, and my company commander said, "Boyd, you run the patrols. We have other jobs to do." I had three men and myself. Well, one man always stayed behind in our little area, and we'd run patrols and things like that. And we didn't see much. We saw some of those poor infantry guys pretty well shot up, and a lot of them were killed in action. A couple of days after, we were going to jump off and attack these pillboxes. So we were leaning against this hedgerow, and they started throwing what we used to call jerry grenades. The Germans had a little mortar shell which was not much bigger than a tomato, and they just kept lopping them all around, and one of them hit me. And they told me to go back. And after that, Brest was good. I didn't see too much action then.

Did this event represent your greatest moment of fear when you were a Ranger?

Well, not really. The lieutenant said, "Can you walk?" I said, "Hell, I think I can run." Nothing bothered me until I got back. I got hit on the right side, and right above my wrist a piece hit me, and it just blew up my arm, and everybody said, "Hey, you got a million-dollar wound. You'll be going back." I thought it was broken. I still got it there. That was it. Then I came back and got in a couple of little skirmishes.

What was the most intense battle or firefight that you participated in?

I guess running the patrols. That was pretty intense. There were a couple of times on D-day, but we were lucky. The fighting was pretty intense, but the Irsch-Zerf Campaign was one of the big ones. I had just gotten out of the hospital, and they assigned two of us the job of going behind the lines and hold a crossroads so the 10th Armored Division could come up. That was pretty intense. When I got out of the hospital, I joined Battalion Headquarters, and they got orders to go up and help the battalion, but they were in pretty bad shape. So we took off and ended up with the 10th Armored Division. And after meeting a couple of people, I met one of my old company commanders, who was shocked when he saw me and I told him I was a staff sergeant. They assigned us to half-tracks, and I was assigned to one of the lead half-tracks and we took off. The tanks tried to go through the town of Zerf and they got blasted, but we got through and relieved the 10th Armored, and then we got to a certain point near where the battalion was, and the 10th Armored wouldn't go any farther, so we had to run about a mile to join the battalion. That was one of the worst ones, 'cause the battalion was beat up pretty bad. They killed about six to seven hundred Germans, I guess. It was one of the biggest battles in World War II of that type. In my company there were eight guys left. When I joined them, that made nine, and we had no officers, and I was the only noncom. We survived, but quite a few were hurt pretty bad. One guy who was with me the whole time was from Brooklyn [and] was pretty well beat up, but he made it. I saw him after the war. I don't know how to explain it. I remember the good times much better than the bad times.

So do you remember where you were on Christmas Eve or Christmas Day 1944?
I'm trying to think where I was. I do remember the night before Thanksgiving, we were in this little town. We had cleaned out all the Germans. The next thing I know, I found a house that was empty, went in, and I was dead tired. There was all kinds of cans and broken glass and everything. So I cleared a space in all this stuff. Then I fell asleep. A couple of hours later it was daylight, and a couple of guys came looking for me. They opened the door to come in. They were stepping on all these cans and everything. Then on Christmas Eve, we were just going into battle and then they called it off. I'm trying to think of where we were. A lot of the things I remember, and a lot of things I don't. All I remember is that we were pulled out, and they sent us a quartermaster outfit to pick us up. And they came right up to us, and as soon as they loaded a truck, they were gone. They knew where to go. I don't think it was twenty or thirty minutes, and all of us were on our way back for Christmas Eve. And we talk about this today, and some of the guys say, "Yeah, you remember that? We didn't even get a chance to light a cigarette, so to speak." That's the way it was—everybody did their job. As the Germans would say in English, "With the American army, there are no privates. They are all generals." They said it in a good kind of way. And when somebody got killed or anything, somebody took over. But there were a lot of good things that happened.

What was one of the saddest moments during your time in the military?
Well, I think the accumulation of all the guys that got killed. It happened so fast, you know, and then we had to keep going. But there were a couple of guys that I was pretty close to. One kid was from Kentucky, and in fact, his sister still corresponds with me. He was a replacement in the 82nd Airborne and he volunteered for the Rangers. I think it was just before the Brest Campaign. And he was assigned to me. He was a real redneck southern boy, and the Yankees used to climb all over him. His name was Larry Lambert, and for some reason we all liked him. He was brand new, and so I got him and I made him one of my BAR men. I had two BARs. Steve Reavis was the other one and had been with us since Scotland. So I had two good BAR men. And we went into this battle where we were going to take this pillbox. This was just after Zerf, and my section was told to take this area, and we had to go down a little bit of a road and then over this little open field and up to these woods. There were a couple of shots, so we stopped everybody. In the meantime, a person who was with the rest of the 2nd Platoon was going into this other area, mainly into a minefield, and a couple guys was pretty close to getting killed. One of them got his foot blown off. He was one of the good guys. Lambert was my BAR man. Now, we're laying [*sic*] shoulder to shoulder, and he said, "Hey, Sarge, I think I see some movement up there." I said, "Have you got a spare helmet or something? It don't look right. Shoot him, but make sure that you shoot him, because you know what the orders are." About a minute or two later, he said, "There he is." And he shot him. He said, "I got him." And then about three or four minutes later, one shot rang out, and he kind of rolled and touched me and he said, "They got me." And that was it. I turned him over, and he had a hole in his forehead and was killed right there beside me. Most of the rest of my men didn't get hit. But a couple of others, they got beat up pretty bad. And it was a very bad thing. We took everybody out except Lambert—he was dead. Two guys from Headquarters Company came up and got him. So that was it. And I kind of broke down a little bit, so they sent me back to the hospital. I was there for three or four days. Then our ambulance came in to get supplies. The driver was from Headquarters Company. He said, "I can't take you now, but I'll be back tomorrow." I said, "Well, get a uniform for me. Get some stuff for me." Which he did. I got back, and that's when I ended up with B Company. We were headed to the 10th Armored, and when we got up to B Company area, there were eight guys left. I went to report, and my company commander was in a bunker with Col. Sullivan. So I said, "I'm reporting I'm back. Well, since there are no officers and no noncoms, how about me being first sergeant or platoon leader or something?" And my battalion commander said, "What the hell do you mean? You just got back." And he said to my company commander, "Ed, I told you he'd be back." He bet $10 that I would be back. He said I would be back, and my company commander said I wouldn't be back. So Col. Sullivan won $10 on a bet.

Oh, that's great!
While we were training in Camp Forrest, Tennessee, I used to train the officers and the men on the English weapons because I knew them all from being in the Canadian army. I was a private, and Col. Sullivan was our training officer for Tactics.

What was your most important contribution to a given battle or in the aid of a wounded comrade?

There was that time when one of my men accidently pulled the trigger on his BAR and hit five guys from B Company.

Oh, this was the friendly-fire incident you were telling me about earlier?

Yes. I kind of jumped in. I don't know why, but I knew a lot of guys from B Company. I knew their first sergeant, and the company commander was mine at one time. And their first sergeant just happened to walk in. They just woke up when this just happened. And I ran and I hollered at them, "Constable." His name was Grant Constable. Nobody got killed. One guy got hit pretty bad in the groin area, and most of the wounds were in his leg and his arms, which was lucky. I have to say, and I don't know how to explain this, but I didn't get excited. I don't know why. I can remember details and everything that happened on that day, and all I was concerned about was to cause no trouble. I saw right away what could have happened. A couple of the guys from B Company were very popular. But I had a couple of friends that were in B Company. That really helped 'cause I thought that was great the way they helped me, and our guys took care of this fellow. We got him up on deck, away from everybody, and I'd say that's one of the big reasons. And when this other fellow broke down, I had to take care of him for two days and a couple of nights. I talk to him all the time. His name is Lou Hayes.

You told me a little bit about your feelings and your thoughts when you were wounded. Is there anything more you want to add about that particular incident?

The last time I got wounded was March 3, 1945. This was right after the Irsch-Zerf Campaign, and what happened was our platoon leader was Lt. Richard Aust. We called him the little guy. He was from Brooklyn, and he was one of the replacement officers after D-day. We got him and we really gelled. I mean, all the guys in my platoon were northern boys, and he was from Brooklyn, and we had some of the guys from A Company, and so the night came and they had us in big holes, and the guys went to sleep. So somebody woke me up and said, "Hey, Boyd, it's your turn." I said, "Okay." And Lt. Aust said, "Oh no, let Sgt. Boyd sleep. He's been up about three days and three nights." And I had just about fallen asleep, and all I remember was everything seemed hot. I didn't know what happened, so I jumped up. My left foot felt like it was on fire, and the bottoms of my left foot and the sole of my jump boot was blown right off, and a couple of other little ones, but the guys from A Company all got hit. Lt. Aust was just laying [*sic*] on his over the hole, and I went towards him and one of the guys from A Company, and somebody said, "Don't touch him; he's dead. He got hit." A rocket hit a tree about 5 to 10 yards in front of us, and the explosion hit him face on. He was one of the good officers.

Were there any individuals fallen or otherwise that you would like to pay tribute to or want to describe their impact on you and your company during a given combat engagement?

Well, our first sergeant got killed on D-day. I was with him. Our battalion commander was with us. Took two or three guys from my platoon and myself and met up with the company commander and the battalion commander. Sandy Martin was our first sergeant, and he was from Kentucky. The first sergeant was the top noncommissioned soldier in the company, and he was between us and the officers. And Sandy would go out with us to drink beer, but he would holler at us and give us hell when we deserved it. And he used to call me a damn Yankee, but he got hit on D-day, and everybody left him but me and two guys, three guys. We had to get him out of this area, out of this trench in the hedgerows. Some of them were shaped like a "U," and we were in there and that's where we started seeing Germans. We started shooting, and when they shot back, Sandy got hit in the back. So we got him out and sent him up along the road, and he said, "I'm all right. I'm all right." But he had a little hole in his back right where his kidneys were. An order came. One of the guys said, "Luther, they want you and Boyd." So they sent an aide to pick him up. So I said, "Well, he's hurting. He can't even walk." "That's the orders." So we had to leave. And Sandy said to me, "Boyd, I hate to say this, but I knew I could always count on you if something happened." Today, I'm still stunned by what he said. I was kind of like a free spirit. Every time I went to any camp or anything, I always found a way to get out without a pass. So that just made me feel good.

It was an honor for him to say that about you.

He was really something. He was a good first sergeant. And we had a lot of guys. We had Benahan, a guy whose parents were German. That's how they got him. Because he's fluent and he's hollering at them in German. One guy thought it was a German, and started shooting and hit his leg. He was a pretty good athlete. Even after the war. He used to be an outfielder in the Canadian American League. They switched him to pitcher. He played a couple of years while he was going to college. He lives in Minnesota.

Can you also describe for me a fellow soldier's struggle with combat, or one who had a great combat achievement that never received official recognition?

Yeah, I think a lot of guys . . . I mean, they often involved me, but I'd tell them I don't want to be in the story. But we had one guy Campos, and he was Puerto Rican. He was one of our football players, and he was the fastest man in the company. He could run backwards and leave somebody behind. But he was one of the good guys. So anybody who played football was considered one of the good guys. But Campos took a guy's place, and the guy . . . he just died a couple of years ago. We were up in Brest, and Campos got killed. To me . . . I mean, that's freedom. And he could have slept. It was this guy's turn. So, after the war, every time I was with this guy, he'd tell me the same. Why he, Campos, he didn't have to do stuff like that. There was so many . . . a ton of things . . . back there. He was a good soldier. We had one guy, Cecil Gray from Louisville. He was a rifleman. He got hurt or anything, and he couldn't train and he got kicked out. So he was the guard on our football team. And he got hurt in the last game. He hurt his knee and he couldn't walk. So we just went and got ahold of Lt. Anderson. He was our platoon leader. He was a Mormon, and he played on our football team. And we went to him and said we want to keep Cecil. Everybody liked Cecil. So after four or five of us got on top of Lt. Anderson, he went to the company commander, and I went to the battalion commander without telling anybody. And I went and I said, "Sully, I gotta talk to you." Sully said, "What do you want, Boyd?" I said, "I need a favor; one of our guys got hurt in football." He said, "Oh yeah, I heard about that or something like that." So I said, "We don't want him to get kicked out. We gotta keep him." And he asked, "Why?" I said, "Can't we make him company clerk or something like that?" "Well, we have a company clerk. Spurlock is company clerk." John Spurlock was our company clerk. He was a corporal. Gray was a private. He hadn't even made PFC yet. Capt. Luther and Lt. Anderson and everybody talked to the company commander. He went to Sully, and Sully told him, "I know all about it." He wouldn't tell where he got the source from. He didn't want to get me in trouble. So they called in Spurlock, and they said to Spurlock, "You're not going to be E Company's company clerk." And he got a little upset. He said he figured he didn't do anything wrong. Then they told him that Pvt. Cecil Gray was going to be company clerk. Spurlock was from Kansas City, and he ended up being a bank manager. And he said, "What about me?" So Col. Sullivan said, "You're going to be battalion company clerk. You're going to be in charge of all the company clerks. So everybody was happy. Everybody was really happy. Everything worked out good. We had something to do with it, and we're proud of him. That's the so-called Ranger Creed. But he made it.

What are the greatest lessons that you've learned from your military experience?

I think respect has a lot to do with it, 'cause you learn to respect your fellow man, so to speak, because he was a Ranger. You got to know each other. And some of our officers were well educated. I dropped out of school my freshman year, and I was lucky enough to even get into the Rangers. You had to have an IQ of a 100 or over to get into the Rangers in World War II. I think it had to do with respect and the love for one another, so to speak. Being men, we didn't say, "I love you" or anything, but the respect was there. Then I settled down after the war and got married, and then I started to learn you gotta listen first before you start saying anything. But being a Ranger . . . I thought that's all I can say, and that's enough. We knew what we did and knew what we could do, and that had a hell of a lot to do with my life. I did quite well in my life. I worked my way up to a supervisor. I got my high school diploma after the war. It took three months to get that, and then I went to college for two years. I didn't do too well because I had no high school education. I should have wised up and taken notes. But then, right after that, I started to question my actions, I guess you would say. Coming from a small town, it was kind of tough for a while.

What emotions do you feel as you've been talking for more than an hour to me about your past military experiences?
I don't know how to explain it. Sometimes I can almost close my eyes, and some of the things I said I can almost see. Yeah, it does bother me a little bit, but it's not as bad as it used to. But what really bothers me is this war business today, and the way it started and everything else. We go to Fort Benning every year. I go there sometimes twice a year for what they call the Best Ranger Competition in Fort Benning. It's probably in May this year. It has tremendous activities that these young guys go through to be a Ranger. You'd be surprised. And they make this event and break records and end up coming back to where they were before. Some of them get automatic promotions. And we have the 3rd Battalion of the 75th Ranger Regiment that's active today, and we can see them. We call them kids. They're twenty-two, twenty-three, twenty-four years old. And we sit down and talk about things. They tell us some of the things that really happens over there. They're not supposed to tell too much. Some of them are rough looking, but they're all nice kids. They treat us great. That's what I really enjoy. And they don't say anything bad. I don't think I ever hear them swear. I think that they learned respect for one another like we did, and I think it's like it was sixty years ago. When I see them, I look at myself almost and some of my friends.

What commanding officers or NCOs made a lasting impression on you?
Well, my battalion commander. The first one, 'cause he's the one who accepted me into the Rangers. I had respect for him, and he wasn't a Ranger. He was a lawyer, but he made our battalion on paper. So I always respected somebody like that. And Col. Sullivan was a captain when he joined. He was from Massachusetts, Boston, and he was the trainer and the executive officer. He was also the training officer that I worked for. He helped me out because of my Canadian background. I had a lot of respect for him, and I thought he was great. A lot of the guys didn't like him because sometimes he was a little straight laced, but he had to be because he was our battalion commander, and he sometimes had to make decisions that weren't too popular. He pulled his rank and stuff, but that's his job. I had a lot of respect for him, and some of the things he said to me and I knew that my company commander knew that he liked me. When I went to a new camp, the first thing I looked for was a way to get out without a pass. That was the hardest thing to do. I enjoyed the Army. I wanted to stay in, but I was discharged with 50 percent disability, and they told me I had nothing to say in the matter. You're out.

SGT. ALVIN RUSTEBAKKE

Ranger Rustebakke

Good evening, sir. I want to thank you for being involved in our project and allowing us to interview you, but also, more importantly, I want to thank you for what you did so many years ago to preserve our freedom. Thank you for being with us. What I would like to do is ask you any questions, and if you have trouble hearing them, I can repeat them for you, okay?
Okay.

Well, why don't we start off, sir, before World War II, before Pearl Harbor happened. What were you thinking about as a young man in terms of what you wanted to do with your life, and perhaps pursue a career?
Well, I finished high school and graduated in 1938. I stayed around home and I helped Dad on the farm mostly. I worked for a neighbor one spring, and I went to the CCC camp for one summer. I don't remember just what summer it was, but it was somewhere between 1938 and 1940. I wasn't really planning ahead at all. I had had a hard time going through grade school. I have a speech impediment, and the teachers were rather cruel to me. They thought it was stubbornness. I couldn't say some things and got quite a persecution for it. I really didn't have any plans other than staying home and farming the rest of my life with Dad.

Do you remember where you were and what you were doing when you heard about Pearl Harbor?

When I heard about Pearl Harbor, I was in the barracks at Fort Lewis. I had joined the Army in November 1940, and it was kind of chaotic around there. Everybody figured that the next time there were going to be some bombs dropping into our yard. It was kind of exciting. It was frightening, and I really didn't know what to think of it.

Where did you do your basic training?

I am the only man that ever joined the Army that took basic training about two to three years after joining the Army as a sergeant. After Pearl Harbor, I had been working in Force Headquarters in Fort Lewis, and after Pearl Harbor, they loaded up every able-bodied man that they could get loose and put us in a train and headed east. We had no idea where we were going. We wound up in . . . I think it was North Carolina for a little while . . . maybe a week. Then we loaded on another train and went to Florida, and I was assigned to the 110th Infantry of the 28th Division and I was initially put in F Company. It wasn't long until they found out I was accomplished in Army paperwork, so I was transferred to Service Company.

Now, when did you volunteer for the Rangers?

I went overseas with the 28th Division in November 1942. Col. Rudder came to do interviews about the middle of January 1944. Sgt. Williams was a personnel sergeant for the Rangers, and he came with Col. Rudder and Capt. Lytle to take care of the paperwork for the interviews. He had a lot of work to do the day before, and I was CQ in charge of quarters and residential headquarters the night before the interviews. Art came up there and he had a lot of . . . I can't remember what it was anymore, but I know we worked for about two, maybe three hours getting the paperwork lined up that he needed for the interviews. When he was about to go out the door, he said, "Did you ever consider joining the Rangers?" I kind of laughed at him, and I said, "No, I never intended in joining the Rangers." And he said, "I think you should." I said, "Well, I got a pass to go to London tomorrow, and I'm leaving on the train early tomorrow, and besides that, I haven't had a physical or nothing ready." He said, "Well, I think you can find a medical officer tonight. I can get you in for the first interview." He was kind of persuasive. So I went and looked up the medical officer, and he happened to be in the personnel office that night, and he looked at me and said, "Well, you've got the chance of a snowball in hell of getting in that outfit." And I said, "Well, we'll try it anyhow." He gave me the . . . whatever the form he had to sign. He okayed it. So I got in for the interview the next morning. The first thing Rudder asked me was "I see you're a sergeant. Why were you busted?" I said, "Well, I made sergeant in Fort Lewis running an office, publishing all the orders that the Army puts out, and after Pearl Harbor I was transferred to a line outfit, and they let me keep my stripes, but I wasn't qualified as a sergeant in the infantry outfit. When I was coming overseas, everybody had to have a spot, so I voluntarily took a bust because I wanted to go overseas with them." And he bought it as a good excuse. I don't remember what Lytle asked me, but that went in a hurry too. So I went and got on the train and had a week in London, and it was a lot of fun. Come back two days later, and orders come through to report to 2nd Ranger Battalion.

Where did you do your basic training?

When I left Fort Lewis.

When you got your specialized Ranger training?

Well, the Ranger training I got at Bude and that area. South of Bude a little ways was an obstacle course and a lot of stuff premade there, and we spent about a week or maybe two down there. And then of course there were highways going away from there . . . we'd get a little walking.

Do you believe having experienced both training, the regular infantry versus the Rangers—did that give you better preparation for battlefield conditions . . . the Ranger training?

I really didn't have any training for battle. I learned calisthenics.

You hadn't gone through regular basic training?

I never went through that.

But the Ranger training—would you describe that as quite rigorous?

That was quite rigorous, yes, and I never fell out of a march even though I was seeing stars when I was running at times.

Can you tell me that perhaps maybe the stern approaches with training paid off when you got into combat? Did you have a leader that was trying to get you really working hard in training? Did that pay off when you got to combat?

I didn't get into much combat. I got out of the landing craft and hit the waters and the Germans hit me. I didn't pass out right away, but I was standing by one of those ex–head sergeants. Henry Friar was a friend of mine in the Rangers, and he was standing by me, and he said that he had been hit too.

Before we go there, I would like to uncover more of the training. What did you do exactly in Ranger training? What kind of speed marches?

Speed marching was one of the most rigorous ones. Timing going through this obstacle course that they had . . . it wasn't anywhere near like speed marches.

And would you do 5 miles in forty-five minutes? How fast would that be in speed marches? How far were they, and how much time did you have to do them in?

We did 5 miles, and I can't remember . . . I know people called me a liar. But it was the fastest I'd ever traveled. They had the system of splitting the group into three platoons or whatever, and half of each platoon would go to the side of the road. When we started in the back, one would go to the center and run to the front, and when they took their position in the front, the back would go to the center and run to the front. And it got to the point where in your rest position, you were waiting for them to get to the end. You're going about as fast as you could run, and you had to put quite of bit of more steam to get there when you had to catch up and go to the front. That was the most rigorous of all.

And did they teach you demolition training as well with the Rangers? Demolition training, explosives?

Yes, there was some of that, yes.

And how about climbing the cliffs; they showed you how to do that? Climbing the cliffs?

No, I never got in on any of the cliff climbing, as that I was always assigned to headquarters. I should have been. They should have because I landed with C Company, and if I hadn't have got hit I would have probably climbed the cliffs, you know. It would have been my first time.

I see. Now let's move ahead and say, okay—this is the night before D-day, and you are probably sitting on a ship, right?

Yes.

What was running through your mind? What were you thinking about that night?

Well, I had come to grips with fear about a month earlier. I had been getting more upset and tight, and it was affecting my health even. And one day . . . it was a bright beautiful day, and it was probably sometime in April, and I just was working by myself loading the truck for a move, and I don't know why I was there alone or anything else. I don't remember now, but I stopped and thought, and I said, "I'm not changing anything by wrecking my health with worry. I'm just not going to worry anymore. I'm going to take care of every day as it comes, and I'm not going to worry about tomorrow. I'm not going to be uptight about anything." And I followed through on that. And it's kind of humorous a happening when we were in South End. Anyhow, we had set up headquarters in a hotel in the lobby, and I had a desk over in one corner. George Williams was over beyond the door that went into the rest of the hotel, and Pop Lemmon was straight across from me, and I was going over to Lemmon for something—I haven't any idea now—and Lytle came in, and he was mad. He says, "Why don't you guys answer your phones?" And I happened to be right in front of him when he started that, and I said, "Well, I've been here all day and the phone never rang and we didn't answer it." And he kept on stalling for a while, and pretty soon he believed me and turned on his heel and walked out. I went over to Lemmon's desk and got what I wanted and was walking back to my own desk, and George, he was actually the second in command in his battalion, and he said, "My God, you're a brave man." And he was afraid I would just back off and turn like hell on him. And when Lytle went out . . . I could see he was relieved.

Well, let's get back to the next for D-day. So you had pushed fear past you—what were you thinking about? Do you remember what you were thinking about before the invasion that night?
The night before . . . no, I wasn't really wondering about how tomorrow was going to be. I wasn't fearful about it. I know it was going to happen. I really didn't think in the terms of the death track. I knew that it was possible, but I didn't dwell on it. I just tried to take it as it come.

I guess they must have had you get into the LCAs, probably what, about 2:00 in the morning?
No, it was a little later than that. I think we had breakfast around 4:00, and there was just getting light enough so we could see the landing craft and things, but the sun was a long ways from being up.

So maybe you boarded the landing craft at 4:30?
Somewhere in there . . . probably that.

Were you in the LCAs when they lowered into the water? Is that what you were in?
Yes.

Were you in the Higgins boat, where you had to climb out the side?
No . . . now you ask me that, I'm pretty sure it was . . . we loaded hanging on the side.

Okay, they loaded up and then they lowered you?
Yeah, I was with the C Company, and I didn't know a soul in the boat.

Oh, is that right? Even though you were assigned to headquarters, you were in C Company's boat?
Yeah, and I really didn't have an assignment. If I hadn't've got hit, all I'd have done was follow the rest of them, and that's about all they were doing.

What rank were you then?
T4 . . . something like that. I'd have to look in the book 'cause I don't remember.

I see. You don't remember Mr. Charlie Ryan, do you? Did you know Charlie Ryan?
Charlie Ryan, no.

He was C Company, 2nd Battalion.
I know George Williams, because he was ahead of me and didn't know I was aboard. I was the last one.

So it was still kind of dark when you got in the LCA?
Yes.

And once they lowered you in, was the water pretty choppy?
It was real choppy, and we just kind of went in a circle waiting for everybody to get ready.

And was water coming in over the sides?
No, it wasn't that bad.

It wasn't that bad? You didn't have to bail any out with your helmet or anything?
No, I think the ones that had to bail out . . . it must have got a hole in it . . . something in the rear . . . something was leaking. There might have been some waves high enough for that. I wouldn't say, but I don't recall. We were sitting there dry.

But you were bouncing back and forth probably?
No, not too bad.

Not too bad?
I had the seat in the very back of the LCA, right next to the British driver or whatever he was called, and I sat there visiting with him while we were going in.

So you were probably getting in the boat at 4:30 in your LCA, and then you were going around for a couple of hours circling?
I don't remember. I don't think it was that long.

What time do you think your landing craft hit the beachhead? 6:00, 6:30?
No, we were late. I had a watch that wasn't waterproof, and it seems to me that stopped around 8:00. We were late . . . I know because the choppy waters . . . you couldn't go very fast through it, and there was only delays too. I don't know.

When you were in the LCA circling before you landed, can you describe that at all? Did you hear artillery in the background? Did you see anything on the beach when you were still in your landing craft?
There was quite a bit of activity on the beach, but I didn't really pay much attention to it. But the British guy . . . he said he had been in two or three landings in the Mediterranean, and he said this is the worst one he had ever seen.

Is that right? That didn't give you much confidence, did it?
No.

All right. So let's say we've moved forward a little bit, and we say now we're getting close, and you feel the LCA hit the beach and the ramp goes down. Tell me what happened at that point.
I think it went down before we hit the beach, and being where I was sitting, I think I was the last man out and George Williams was up a ways, and he was down low in the water, and probably white water behind him. I don't know how he was moving so fast. I didn't even try to go that fast. I was going as fast as I could, but you can't run very fast in 4 feet of water. I think that's about what we were in, about 4 feet of water to start with. And the bullets were hitting . . . I suppose the distance between bullet holes . . . every bullet as it hit, there was a geyser of water went up about 12 feet, so you could see where the bullets were going.

So about every 2 or 3 feet you saw bullets coming?
No, it was further apart than that . . . probably 10 to 15 feet apart. I'm sure it wasn't a machine gun. They were rifles.

Artillery shells were hitting here and there?
I didn't see artillery at all.

What was your field of view? What did you see straight ahead when you got off that ramp?
Well, off to the left I saw a stone house . . . I took it to be a stone house, anyhow. And there were some shrubs to the right, and I didn't really see anything particular about the cliffs. They were there.

They were to the right?
I don't really remember.

Okay, so at that stage you were running off the LCA. What else did you experience at that moment?
Well, I was going as fast as I could towards shore, and the bullet hit me just below the belt to the right side, and I was pretty close to one of these steel hedgehogs or whatever they called them, and I got over and used that to balance myself a little, and Henry Ferrari was there and he said he'd been hit. He didn't say how or where, but he died and I didn't.

So you got hit, and you went to the ground after you were hit on the beach?
I was still out in the water a ways. I mean, the water was beyond me, and I passed out standing up, caught with Ferrari by this obstacle. I had no idea how long. I woke up with my head above the waterline and arms, and I tried to pull myself out of the water a little bit, but I was so darn weak I couldn't hardly move, but I moved up a little bit and then I relaxed and then I went out completely. I didn't know another thing until . . . I think it was that night . . . I'm not even sure of that. I was laying [*sic*] on a stretcher pretty close to the water's edge, and when I got to the hospital I got a letter from George Williams, who I'd seen go in ahead of me, and he described what he had seen. He said that I had been running around the beach quite a bit that day. He said it looked like I was hurting. I didn't have a helmet. I didn't have a lifeline. I didn't have nothing. But he said that I was moving around, and all I know is what George told me.

You don't remember that?
That's a total blank. My mind is so blank that . . . normally you wake up in the morning it isn't coming out of a total block. This is coming out of an absolute black hole. There was no memory, no nothing, except for that brief interval when I woke up and then passed out in about ten seconds.

From the time you exited the ramp and the time you got hit, is there anything else you recall? Was it really misty or foggy or were you able to fully visualize it?
I really didn't notice much of that.

Did you see guys falling all around you?
No, I didn't. Probably because after I got hit, I wasn't focusing on much of anything.

So then you were off to the hospital. How long was it before you actually recuperated from your injury?
Well, they unloaded the landing-craft tank and turned it into a hospital. I think it was late on the seventh that they picked up all of us who were laying [*sic*] there, and they operated and cleaned up my wound probably about 2:00 in the morning. And they run out of anesthetic, so they did everything under local anesthetic.

So you remember being on that landing tank?
Yes, I remember the entire operation.

Is that right. Do you remember feeling a lot of pain during the operation?
No, I really didn't have much pain with any of it, but I could feel everything they were doing because I was still conscious.

I see, but you weren't having any pain?
There wasn't any serious pain, no.

From there, they probably evacuated over to the ship and then back to England?
We went back to England and there was a train waiting for us, and we went north . . . I think it was someplace pretty much between Birmingham and Coventry. There was a hospital built for D-day, and all the nurses and all the aides and everything were standing in their places. Here they come, I guess.

And how long did it take for you to recuperate from that wound?
I was under their care while at the original hospital . . . I was there for . . . it must have been September and then I was transferred to a rehab . . . they called it a hospital too, and that was set up like the infantry regiment, and I got the job of company clerk, and one of the men there was a first sergeant of that group, and we were evaluated by a doctor every week. And they'd give us . . . I forget the code numbers they used . . . but the last one was AX. We got the AX and we had to go.

So when did you get discharged from the hospital?
It was about the first week in December. I got the AX, and the guy—lieutenant that was in charge of the group—said I can get you another week if you want it, and I says no, I think I'll go now, and I went. You want to hear about me going back?

Yes.
I went across the English Channel in a small seafaring boat about the same as the *Prince Charles*. And there was a forty and eight waiting for us, and we all got loaded into that, and it was a long train. I don't know how many replacement tours . . . it was all replacements that were in it. We went on for, it must have been close to a week. We got to Fontainebleau, which is up by Paris, and we were there for a few days, and then a truck was going in my direction, so I got on that and I got to a little town in Culver Herberg on the fifteenth of December, and I stood guard with a fellow I knew from the 20th Division at Culver Herberg, and there was buzz bombs and V1s and V2s blowing over us all night. We thought something must be happening, but we were hoping that them guys that were shooting .50-caliber machine guns at them, they were right over our heads, would miss. The next day a truck came and took me through Herkenen Forest, where my Headquarters Company was, and that was the sixteenth, which was the day the Battle of the Bulge started. If I had taken that week . . . where would I have been? I would have died at Le Havre at that time.

So from then on, what were your actions? What were your combat actions with the Bulge?
The 2nd Ranger Battalion held the point, the old line and the new line. I really didn't see much of anything. Headquarters was in Herkenen Forest. Pivit was a little to the south and east of us, and we had contact with them, but I never went up there. And then of course as the war progressed, we kept traveling across. We really didn't see any hard combat.

Very few firefights?
Well, yeah, if you needed any extra help, he would ask for so many men from headquarters. We were kind of beyond it at that time.

In terms, what was your role in Headquarter Company during the Bulge?
Well, we didn't really pay much attention to it because it was beyond us.

Right, but what function did you serve?
Just the ordinary record-keeping reports and so forth.

Did you have to write any action reports, or did you just have more clerical work?
I really don't remember what I did. I know I was busy. There wasn't really that much out of the ordinary that would stick in my mind.

Would you say that you had a really good guardian angel?
I would say that I had a guardian angel from the word "go."

There were two major events with D-day and the Battle of the Bulge, and somehow you stayed out of harm's way?
For the Rangers, the Battle of the Bulge wasn't a big deal. It was Hill 400. 400 was worse than D-day. I wasn't at 400, but I've read the story. Bob Black has written about that and others, and that was . . . I have never even seen Hill 400, but I guess it's a sight.

When were you discharged from the Army?
When I was discharged, we had gotten to . . . we crossed the Rhine and we advanced through Germany. I suppose at 30 miles an hour we'd see German vehicles. I remember one German vehicle in the ditch, and there were six German soldiers sitting in it, all of them dead. And this is a common . . . it was not very pleasant.

I'm sure there were several sad moments during your military experience, but if there were one or two that were the saddest moments, what would you say those were? The saddest moments during your military experience?

Well, I was a good friend of Bob Lemmon. He had kind of taken me under his arm. He was the oldest man in the Rangers, I think, and he was a tough guy. I think he was from . . . I don't know what kind of a business, but I don't think it was law enforcement. But I loved the man. And Henry Ferrari was another friend of mine. He was a guy from Alabama, and I think he joined about the same time I did.

Were they both killed in action?

D-day.

D-day for both of them? Were they in your boat? Were they in your landing craft?

No, they weren't in my craft. Bob Lemmon, he was further east from where I landed, and the report I've heard is that he got out of the landing craft and he stopped at the site of the landing craft and was helping others get out, and he stood in one spot too long and somebody got a bead on him.

And Mr. Ferrari?

Ferrari . . . I really don't know what happened to him. He didn't tell me what his wound was or where it was or whether it was a fatal wound or if he got another wound later, but he was a big fellow from Alabama with a heart of gold.

So you had spent a lot of your training in the Rangers with both of them?

Well, Bob Lemmon . . . he wasn't in the training field. He was the sergeant major, and he had business that he was taking care of. He wasn't involved with the training. Others did that.

But you knew him through the Rangers. You were both Rangers—that's how you knew him?

Yeah, well, he was almost my direct . . . I was directly under him in my job.

I guess if you were to say having gone through that military experience, what lessons would you say you learned from your military experience?

I think I matured a lot. I wanted to do what needed to be done. I don't know if I could put a specific point on anything or not.

Did you have nightmares about your D-day experience?

No. I was too calm to get too excited about it.

So ever since that day you decided you weren't going to worry about it, after that you didn't worry about it, and you didn't have any nightmares or anything else?

When I got hit I really didn't . . . I knew I was in trouble, and when I woke up on the beach for just a moment, I remember the hospital morgue.

Your guardian angel took good care of you?

Yeah, I can't see that the Lord is handling the whole thing. In fact, just yesterday when I got up and went down to the airport, at one point I was asking the Lord for a guardian angel like he did me a year ago, and the first thing I found down there, I went to the desk and they took care of my papers, and I went and sat down, and there was a guy from Luster and his wife, and she was going to take the train to Arizona. She had a job down there, and I don't know anything about her other than that. Anyhow, I visited with them for a while, and then I got on the plane and got off at Billings, and I didn't really know where I was going to go or nothing. There was this gal that comes up to me. The first time I'd see her, and she saw I was a little bit confused. She took me and run me through getting my ticket verified and through the standing . . . I don't know what you'd call it. Got everything settled up, and she went and got on her plane and left, and I waited for mine, and that was exactly what happened. It was a different person and a different situation, but the same thing happened a year ago when I went to Cleveland. A gal . . . a total stranger I met . . . and she took care of me just like this one. And I don't think that was an accident.

What emotions do you feel when you reflect back on your military history? Do you feel any specific emotions?
Oh, I get emotional about a lot of things, and it's more pleasant thoughts. I don't have any regrets. How I got in. I didn't tell you that at the beginning. But better the fit now. I graduated from high school in 1939 and worked with Dad for a while, and then the local paper came out with the numbers of all the eligible draftees, and I was down the line quite a ways. I decided I would go to the draft board and I would be the first one. So I did that, and about three or four other guys did the same thing. So they threw our names in the hat, and they pulled mine out. I got the third selective service number in the state of Montana, and I went to Fort Lewis and was assigned to an engineer outfit, and I knew I was learning nothing about what they were doing or anything else, but the first sergeant came in and said can anybody type. Two of us raised our hands, and he said report to post headquarters this afternoon. I stayed there until about two weeks after Pearl Harbor. I didn't go through basic training or nothing. I got into the publications section. I was running it by the time I left. I had, I think, three civilian girls and three Army men helping me. My training there is really what carried me through the rest of the war. Every time I went anyplace and I took the letters I showed you. I found a mimeograph machine. It was absolutely unworkable. And I figured out how to put it together, where I could do it, and I was the only one who could even try to make it run. The guys from the outfit could write and draw pictures, and we had a lot of fun putting that little paper out.

Did you make any lifelong friends through your military experience?
Yes, in the 110th Infantry, I got acquainted with a fellow there. He was a close friend in the Army, and I kept track of him. I call him occasionally. He lives in New York City. He said he had cancer of the prostate, and he'd had it for ten years, and he was living with it and he wasn't too worried. And he is a nice fellow, and I wish I could go and see him.

I guess at this point, if you were to talk to future generations, what pearls of wisdom would you give them?
About the Rangers?

What would you tell future generations about your military experience, about your life and your experiences? What would you impart to future generations?
Well, there's some core problems with how they're being raised these days. The biggest problem is that Mom and Daddy are working, and the children are too much on their own. Some of them get in trouble and some of them don't. I've got grandchildren that have gone both ways. I've got one grandchild . . . he is small and one of the greatest guys you'd ever find. He is nineteen years old now, and he's still a small man.

You would say spend time with your children. That's what you would tell people, right?
I'd try to.

Are there any other recommendations or anything else you would tell people to make the world better or anything?
Well, find a way to the Lord and stay there. And going to church isn't the answer. Churches are being polluted too easily. Go to scripture and believe what you read.

Well, we appreciate you interviewing with us this evening, and we appreciate your service for our country, for our world to maintain freedom, and we thank you for that very much. Is there anything else you want to say?
Thank you for the interview. I hope that it is worth something to you.

It's worth a lot to me, and I think it will be worth a lot to future generations as well. Thanks again.

LT. COL. GEORGE KERCHNER

We're here with Mr. George Kerchner this evening, and we are interviewing as a second Ranger from World War II. Welcome, Mr. Kerchner. How are you doing?
Good.

Feel free to ask me if I need to repeat any questions, okay? And I will try to talk slowly with you. It is a pleasure to be with you, and thank you for joining us for these interviews. Can you tell us, Mr. Kerchner, before you heard about World War II and before you heard about Pearl Harbor, what were your interests? What were your plans in life?

Well, I was married. I had a child. At that time, the child was two years old and I was working in a family business in a store. I was manager of a luncheonette and ice cream store. I made for the times a fair amount of money. I think I was making about $40.00 a week, which wasn't bad back in 1939 or 1941. But I always had a yen to get into the military prior to when I was still in high school, and a recruiter came along . . . the ROTC. I tried to get in then. I was only sixteen and I couldn't have it. I wanted to be in the military, but after I was married with a family to support, it was a little too difficult.

I see. Where were you exactly when you heard about Pearl Harbor on December 7?

On the day of Pearl Harbor, it was a Sunday and I was driving to work. I worked on Sundays, and we had a radio in the car, and I was listening and I heard this about 1:00 in the afternoon, if I'm not mistaken. I heard the stories coming in piecemeal from Hawaii. Of course, I was shocked and all that, but I think I must have had a few feelings of anticipation about getting in the military. It might help me get in. That was a selfish thought—that I wanted to get into the military very badly.

Did you think that this was going to be an important turning point, Pearl Harbor?

In my life? Well, I hoped it to be, since I wanted to get into the military, and at that time I couldn't afford to.

And so, did you enlist or were you drafted?

Well, I had to sign up for selective service. I was classified 3A, I think it was. I was exempt from duty at that time because I was married and had a child. Of course, nothing stopped me from enlisting, except that I needed . . . it wasn't enough money in $50.00 a month to support a family on it, so I couldn't afford to go in.

So you did enlist though?

Well, I volunteered for what they called the Volunteer Officer Candidate Program, which enabled the people who were in similar situations like I was and couldn't get in because they couldn't afford to get in, but they wanted to get in. They had to be classified 3A to come into the program. We were interviewed by officers prior to being accepted to this, so you would pass a lot, and you had your physical and you had your AGD, your intelligence test . . . your IQ test . . . before you ever went in. So you had to be a potential officer in order to go into this program, which I don't know . . . maybe 50 percent of them passed or were accepted as officer candidates. The remainder of them went back to their civilian jobs.

So when did you actually go into the military per se?

I was inducted in June 1942.

After Officer Candidate School, where did you take your basic training?

After I had passed successfully, completely, the thirteen weeks training at Fort Benning here, I went to the 30th Infantry Division, which at that time the National Guard Division was down at Camp Landing, Florida, and I stayed in that unit from January until September of 1943, when I was sent overseas as a replacement officer.

And how did you enlist in the Rangers?

Well, the replacement depot where I was, was kind of a miserable life, and it didn't appeal to me. I tried to keep busy at the mail post. Every now and then a unit overseas was looking for additional officers and would ask to come in for interviews and have men volunteer. You had to volunteer for it. And the Rangers and paratroopers were the only ones who were accepting volunteers at that time. So Col. Rudder and his executive officer came and interviewed a number of officers at this replacement depot, and it was five officers who were accepted, and we went into the 2nd Ranger Battalion as reinforcement officers, not as replacements.

Did you get any specialized training as a Ranger officer?

Well, not so much as an officer, but as a Ranger, yes. We took the same training as the enlisted men took, and prior to that, I had never climbed a cliff. The highest hill I ever went up was a sand hill maybe 12 or 15 feet high. So we learned to climb cliffs. There was a lot of live-firing exercises, a lot of speed marches. You had to average 4–5 miles per hour while marching 20- or 30-mile hikes to see how much stamina you had. If you fell out of those marches . . . I mean, the other Rangers all went along with you. You had to keep up with them in order to be accepted.

Do you think that specialized Ranger training helped you?

Oh sure, sure. It toughens you up mentally and physically.

I see. Now, all the training that you had before D-day was, I assume, when you entered service. Did that training really prepare you well?

Oh, I think so. I was a pretty good infantry man. I had good initial infantry training as a recruit, and through the thirteen weeks at Fort Benning and the training that I had with the 30th Infantry Division prior to joining the Rangers . . . you learn military skills physically and mentally. You were toughened. But nothing like we received in the Rangers. The same training, but much more. We got a lot of live-firing exercises. I remember I was just a lieutenant, but I was encouraged by my company commander to carry my pistol with rounds to liven up the training to shoot over the men's heads and at their feet, or something like that that made them duck. To experience what it was like to have live rounds. And of course we received the same thing. We had live-firing exercises.

Let's move on to D-day. That was your first time in real combat?

Yes.

What were you thinking about the night before you went on the ship? What was going through your mind, you think?

Well, I guess most of all I was worried that I would be brave enough and tough enough to do my job. After all, when you're a lieutenant, you're a leader, and the men looked to you, and if you can't cut the mustard yourself, then they're not going to do it, so you had to make yourself able physically and mentally to take what came along.

Was that what you were fixated on right before you went into battle?

Well, of course you think about a lot of things. You think about your family and you think about yourself and you think about what might happen if anything happens to you. So you have a lot going through your mind, but uppermost and the primary thing is to be able to do the job that was expected of you.

At that stage, how old was your child on D-day?

My daughter on D-day was four years old.

Four years old. So I can understand what you would be thinking about then?

Well, you think about your child and you think about family. Somewhere in that stuff I brought along there, I show in there a copy of my first letter that I sent before D-day to my wife, and a copy of the first letter after D-day. I think it might have been D+3 or 4 the night I mailed the letter home, and it might be interesting to read those two letters. You might get a lot of my state of mind.

Now, do you know the approximate time? Did you enter in an LCA craft? What type of craft did you use?

It was before 4:00 in the morning when we boarded our landing craft. We were 11 miles offshore, and we were on British Landing Craft Assault . . . LCAs . . . British crew and our boats had approximately twenty-two to twenty-five men per boat. We carried quite a bit of extra equipment, launchers for our rope ladders, and ropes that were coiled up, as well as other metal ladders that we carried along in case the rope failed. We were loaded down with a lot of equipment, and up to the maximum weight that we carried. They couldn't put more than twenty-five men at the most. I don't think anybody had more than twenty-four or twenty-five men in the boat.

Oh, I see. So they lowered the craft with the men in. Do you remember the ocean? Was it pretty choppy?

It was very choppy, yes. It was a lot of up and down when you were being lowered into the craft. I would say the swells were probably 4 or 5 or 6 feet high.

I see. I would imagine a lot of your soldiers were getting seasick as well?

Oh, yes, yes. I don't remember myself personally, but none of them ate very much prior to going out there because everybody was worried about being seasick. Quite a few of the men were seasick. You had upchucking in the boat. They provided barf bags, but it would come on you right suddenly and you had to upchuck, so a lot of the men didn't get it into the bag. They got it over the fellow sitting next to him.

So those were not Higgins boats. Those were LCAs that you went in?

Yeah.

I see. Okay. I guess one of the big differences with the LCAs is that you can go only one man at a time in the front?

No. They lowered a ramp. We had a ramp that would cross the entire bow section. That ramp was lowered and you . . . as fast as men could get off. You carried your men in three rows, with a row down the center where they straddled the boat, and on either side were benches where the men sat. So you had three rows of men in the boat. One down the center and one down either side. Somewhere in that book I brought is a picture of one sitting on the beach when we were in France. You can get an idea what it looks like. They were good craft, and there were good seamen there.

Were your soldiers and your platoon . . . were they looking up to you? Were they looking up for encouragement?

It's difficult for me to speak for other people. I mean, you hope they were, yes. It's very difficult coming into a unit like the Rangers as a replacement officer or an extra officer when you haven't gone through the same thing the men went through. You're always worried about are you going to be tough enough or brave enough. I did, anyway.

So at 4:00 you entered the LCA. Can you describe the event after that?

Well, we formed up into . . . our landing craft . . . the twelve that were going to Pointe du Hoc . . . formed into two columns, six craft in either columns. And columns were close, one to the other. We had about 11 or 12 miles to go, and two hours expected. We loaded into the craft at 4:00, I guess, and we might have circled around for an hour or so . . . or for a half hour maybe . . . and then headed out . . . we were probably traveling at about 7 or 8 knots towards the shore. And about . . . I think it was probably about 5:30 or 6:00 when they started the bombardment of the shore. And we could hear the shells crashing overhead and see them landing on the shore. We were probably at that time 5 or 6 miles offshore.

So as your LCA approached the beach, can you describe those events when you got off, and what you experienced?

Well, first of all we had a lot of things happen before we ever got to the beach; one of the ships in our column of six had my company commander and another officer, as well as the battalion with three in it, and this boat sank about a half hour or forty-five minutes before H-hour, and instead of having ten craft loaded with men, we were only nine, and it happened to be our unit, and my company commander and my other platoon leader were in that craft there. So I moved up from being the youngest officer or at least the newest officer to be in charge of these men. So this was something that was very hard physically to adjust to. I suddenly realized I was responsible for all these men. Instead of just being responsible for my own platoon, I had the whole company . . . the remainder of the company anyway. This was probably the most difficult thing to accept as we were going in there. We weren't being shot at at that time. Our bigger enemy was the water. We were trying to make up . . . we knew we were running late. We were trying to get more speed out of these craft, and you could just only push them so far because water would wash over the gunnels, and that's what happened. The boats all started shifting water. We had to take our helmets off in our boat, anyway, and bail the water from inside the landing craft to keep that boat afloat. We saw . . . that's what happened after the boat sank. As soon as that boat sank, we knew right away that they weren't unsinkable like they told us. So we were very busily engaged with trying to save our skins, just trying to get ashore instead of worrying about being shot. We were worried about drowning.

It sounds like a very valid concern. By the time you got to shore, can you paint a picture of what you saw when you got off?

Well, of course we had received a very good briefing . . . a very thorough briefing on what to expect when we landed and what to expect when we got up to the top of the cliffs. We had sketch maps . . . every man had received a sketch of the terrain up there and where the guns were located, and we all had . . . every boat had its own mission. We had three guns located on the left side of the Pointe du Hoc that were our mission to destroy these guns and put them out of action. We were concentrating on the job to do, and that was our . . . rather than being afraid in my case anyway, I was more worried about getting my job done than I was about being shot . . . staying alive in order to do my job.

Do you remember what you saw when you went off the craft?

Yeah, I ran off first and I ran off the end of . . . they lowered the ramp. The water looked like it was maybe 6 or 12 inches, and we had landed on a large aerial bomb crater that was about 8 or ten 10 deep that was filled with water. So I immediately went in over my head and I had to struggle just to get ashore. The crater was probably 15 or 20 feet wide, and so I had . . . I was loaded down with gear and equipment, and I had to dog-paddle away to get to shore. I was the first one off the craft and the last one ashore because it took me so long. I couldn't . . . it was too deep for me to use my feet. I just had to paddle my way in. So I finally got out of the water. So I was pretty upset there. I was angry with the British, and I was angry with myself with not being careful that when jumping off the craft and trying to be in a big hurry to get ashore, and here I was still struggling to get out of the water, and my men were climbing the cliffs already.

So were you the first one off the LCA?

I was first one off and one of the last ones to make it up.

So once you got past that crater, then did you get up close to the cliff after that?

Well, my first action after I got out of the crater . . . I wanted to go down and find the battalion commander and tell him that the company commander and the other officer were casualties, and that I was assuming command of the company. This was military protocol. Chain of command within the unit; in case anything happened to a leader, there was somebody to take their place. So I told my platoon sergeant to take over my platoon, and I was assuming command of the company. So I went down to tell Col. Rudder this, and he told me to get the hell back there and climb my rope. Let him worry about those things. Which I did. When your battalion commander tells you to do something . . . you do it. Well, then . . . of course we were being shot at then. I landed . . . the only weapon I had was a .45 pistol I was carrying, because I had so much other things to carry: smoke grenades, thermite grenades, 536 Radios that I was loaded down with gear myself. So a machine gun opened up and hit some of the men right next to me, and it was a bad feeling when somebody is shooting at you a couple hundred yards and all you got is a pistol. So one of my men became a casualty, and I picked up his M1 rifle and took a couple of bandoliers of ammunition from him, and when I went up the cliff then I was carrying, in addition to my pistol, I was carrying an M1 rifle. The first thing I did when I got out of the crater filled with water, I attempted to use my radio. I was carrying a 536 Radio, which is a small, handy talkie, and I wanted to call the colonel to tell him I was taking over. Well, the radio wouldn't work because it had been dumped underwater, so that's why I had to go down in person and tell him that, or at least I felt I was supposed to. So I threw the radio down on the shore, and there went my communication for the rest of the day. So I picked up a rifle and got rid of a radio. I still had a lot of gear with me. I was carrying thermite grenades to be used to destroy the guns. I had smoke grenades . . . different-color[ed] smoke grenades. These were to be used for in case you were under fire by your own airplanes. You would use a smoke grenade to identify your position . . . either—I think the colors were green and red. One color was to signify friendly troops. The other was to signify enemy troops. So I had those grenades. I had thermite grenades. I had fragmentation grenades that I was carrying with me in addition to what I would normally have to carry. So I was pretty well loaded down, but I still . . . the pistol wasn't enough. I had to climb the cliff with all this gear on. That's the reason I carried the pistol instead of the rifle. I figured I could pick a rifle up when I got up the cliff. Well, I got one at the bottom of the cliff, and I climbed the cliff with the rifle.

How did you climb the cliff? On a ladder or a rope?

I went up a rope . . . a smooth rope. They were the easiest climbing. We had fired up toggle ropes. A toggle rope was ¾-inch-thick hemp. A toggle had a wooden toggle that ran every 2 feet. Also we fired rope ladders, which none of the men climbed because you couldn't go up them very fast. The toggle rope was a little faster, but the smooth rope was the easiest to climb because once you had acquired the strength of holding and pulling yourself up, you could move up the cliff faster. We could have climbed that cliff in thirty seconds with those ropes there, if we hadn't been loaded down with all this gear and being shot at the same time. It probably took us two or three minutes to get up the cliff.

I see, and at the same time were the Germans at the top shooting down and throwing grenades?

Well, you weren't looking up. I mean, we were being grenaded from up top, not very close. When we fired . . . every craft had six rocket launchers mounted on the gunnels . . . two with ropes, two with rope ladders, and two with toggle ropes, and these were fired way up in the air and smoke and flames coming out of the rear of them, and then they went down to the ground, so I'm sure that some of those Germans thought they were some sort of secret weapon, and they didn't realize what was going on. This actually served as a protective fire for part of us too. So that chased some of the Germans away from the edge of the cliff. The men being grenaded were generally before we started climbing the cliffs, before we fired our rockets up there. Once we fired them, that helped to give us a little supporting fire. And then a couple destroyers that saw the predicament we were in . . . see, we were nearly an hour behind time when we were supposed to touch down . . . actually forty minutes late. And all the protective fire had been lifted. We were supposed to land militarily under supporting fire, but the people doing the shooting didn't know we weren't . . . they weren't told we were coming in late, so they stopped shooting at H-hour, and we were forty minutes late. This gave the Germans time to get out of their holes and come out and see what was going on, and they saw the landing craft approaching, and they started firing machine guns and antiaircraft guns at us and throwing hand grenades too. That's when the Americans and the British destroyers—*Talybont* was the British and the *Satterlee* was the American—saw the predicament of the troops going in there; they came in close to shore . . . as close as they could come 'cause of the drift . . . and started providing us with cover fire, and that was tricky shooting because when you're shooting a 5-inch gun from a half mile, it's pretty much of a flat trajectory and you don't have much area to man that shell in, but they did a beautiful job. We'd have never made it without those destroyers firing their 5-inch guns that they had supporting us.

Did some of the preinvasion bombardment actually create some divots in the side of the cliff where you could use that to your advantage?

Well, actually in the side of the cliff it knocked some of the things down, but we were looking forward to have the shell craters up on top from the aerial bombardment, and the heavy guns next to us were firing 15-inch guns so we'd have holes to go from one to the other end. But those fires were lifted. We didn't have that fire. All we had was artillery coming in with flat trucks to get some fire. So it was ticklish firing on their part. I didn't even know it. I never realized it was American destroyers firing. I thought it was Germans firing at us. We could see these shells coming in. Couldn't tell what direction they were coming from. All we knew is that they were landing up there while we were crossing this point, so I was cussing at the American navy for not giving us supporting fire, and all the time they were shooting. The Navy did a beautiful job . . . those destroyers were great, the captains . . . they took their ships a lot closer than they were allowed to and fired flat trajectory. In other words, where they could see the target.

Now, you climbed up the rope, you got to the top . . . What did you do next?

Well, I can only speak for myself individually because every man . . . we only had one rope that all our men went up. Out of six, there was only one my men climbed. So you only got your men up on top one man at a time. But every man had his mission to do what he was supposed to do. He took off on his own. He didn't wait for relief. He moved on across this terrain up there, shell-torn terrain over to where the guns were, and they were supposed to put the usual demolitions on them. So I was one of the last ones up, and by the time I got up there, the men had already moved over to the gun positions, and they knew then that the guns weren't there. I was the last one up, because as company commander my job was to see that the men . . . get the men up on top of the cliff. That's when Col. Rudder made sure that I got up, but my job was to get the other men moving and take care of the wounded. We probably had half a dozen men wounded by the fire at the bottom of the cliff. The rest of them we had up, and when everybody moved across this 200–300 yards of terrain up on the top of the cliff over to where the gun positions were. When we got over there, we discovered then that the guns weren't there. So we moved out on our secondary mission, which was to move in and provide a roadblock up on the coastal road.

So that would have been farther west from there, right? Where you were supposed to secure that area by the road was farther west than Vierville?

Farther west . . . is that what you said? Farther in . . . south. We were coming in from the north and headed south. So it was farther south that we went in to block the road. That was about almost three-quarters of a mile inland from where the edge of the cliff was.

I see. And would you say that the top of the cliff was heavily fortified with German soldiers, or not really?

No, not with soldiers. And not really with fortifications, because the Germans didn't think anybody was going to climb that cliff. Their fortifications were all facing inland. The barbed wire and the minefields and the trenches that they had dug was to repel an attack from the landside. From the enemy coming in from the land. So this worked to our benefit to that extent. The fortifications we had to assault were facing the other direction, and it made it a little easier for us to get into the back of them.

Obviously you had your own event occurring over at Pointe du Hoc. Were you aware in any sense of the word that the A and D Companies of the 2nd Ranger Battalion were taking a lot of fire down on the Omaha Beach Dog Green Sector? Were you aware of that at the time?

Omaha Beach. We weren't thinking of those. We were thinking of ourselves. I figured they had all the supporting fire and everything going down there. We thought they were going to have any easy job of it, and it turned out that was the worst place to be.

Unfortunate. So after you got up to the top, you moved inland, you secured the road. Were there any major skirmishes or firefights that occurred in the next couple of days?

Within the next couple days . . . well, we got inland. We had to fight some Germans going across the terrain . . . ¾ mile we had from the edge of the cliff to the road. We were fighting some scattered Germans there, but we never had any organized attack against us until that night . . . D-day night was when we were driven back into the edge of the cliff.

So you were driven back?

Well, my unit wasn't driven back. The other two companies withdrew. We only had a few men left in our company, and we stayed where we were supposed to stay protecting this road, and the other companies withdrew and we weren't notified, so we were left out there. Actually, we were in a very heavily overgrown hedgerow . . . pretty well good defensive position of concealment there. So we were left there when the other troops withdrew, and we didn't get back until two days later at the remainder of D Company.

Now, do you think your Ranger training prepared you . . . your preinvasion training prepared you adequately for the hedgerows?

For the hedgerow itself . . . that was something new to us. All of them were fighting in the hedgerow. But pretty soon you learned to use what terrain you have to your advantage for the attack or the defense. When you were on the defense, the hedgerows were beautiful. It was when you were on the attack and you had to go against them they were so difficult. So we were on the defensive position, and the hedgerows worked to out advantage.

I see. I understand that you received the Distinguished Service Cross?

Well, this was a surprise . . . a big surprise, maybe, because I never felt I ever did anything heroic. I was trying to do my job of taking care of the men. I don't know why I got the medal, to be honest with you. The citation sounds beautiful, but that wasn't me.

But it was for your service during D-day, right?
I guess it was. Yeah, they figured it'd be assuming command, accepting the command, and leading the troops was what I got it for . . . not for the actual fighting.

I'm sure it was well deserved, sir. You also received the Bronze Star and a Purple Heart. The Purple Heart, I think, was a bit later in September, but was the Bronze Star for D-day as well?
The Bronze Star was something that came along at the end of the war, when anyone who was in a combat infantry that had actually been shot at and who didn't receive any decoration was awarded the Bronze Star. I think it was after this war was over before I got my Bronze Star. The Purple Heart I got when I was wounded, and I received that.

You were wounded, I think, on September 1 in the Brest Campaign?
Yeah, almost three months later.

So if we go beyond D-day, what would you say would be the next major battle you were involved with?
Well after D-day, we were up at Brest . . . fighting in Brest. We started the attack on Brest on August 25, and we were fighting for six days consecutively . . . fighting every day. So it was a series of battles one day after the other. Eventually, a man was going to get shot unless he was the luckiest man in the world. I mean, if you do your job, you got to be out leading the troops . . . they're going to be shooting at you. Sooner or later, somebody is going to hit you.

So after D-day, did you assume company commander at that point?
No, I stayed with the company until the remainder of that boat that sank on D-day, when those survivors rejoined us with the previous company commander. He resumed command of the company, and I went back to commanding our platoon.

So were there any particular significant firefights during the Brest Campaign that you recall or you would like to discuss?
I recall it very well. There was a lot of . . . every day we were being shot at by artillery, mortars, or rifle fire. So there were little battles going on.

I see. So your platoon and company would take a certain area, and then they would get pushed back, and then it would be back and forth. Is that the way it was in Brest?
Well, we had a mission to destroy some of the big guns that the Germans had, and we were headed down towards those guns during the period that we were fighting up at Brest. It was a series of small battles, but we were always headed down towards those guns, and eventually . . . after I was wounded . . . they captured them.

I see. And you actually were wounded on September 1. Is that right? Do you remember what happened that day?
Oh yeah, very well.

Could you describe that for us?
Well, the other platoon leader wasn't quite as aggressive as I was, and so I felt that my platoon was doing more than its share of fighting. So finally there was enough complaining going on that the company commander formed a composite platoon of half of my men and half of the other platoon and put me in charge of them, and we were sent on ahead to capture this road junction, which we did, and I was going back to notify the company commander that we were out there and our objective . . . we needed some reinforcements. As I was going back to rejoin my troop, the Germans had infiltrated behind me, and they fired. I was behind my own lines when I was shot by the Germans from about 20–25 feet away.

I see. Where was your wound?
I had a broken arm . . . big humerus bone in the upper arm was shattered. It went right through the middle of that humerus bone. It was a typical million-dollar wound.

Did you have a medic close by to help you?

Well, we had a company medic who provided first aid, and the American medical assistant and doctors and nurses who were attendants were the most wonderful people in the world. I have nothing but praise for all the American medical personnel that I ever came in close contact with.

I would assume once the medic took care of you, they took you to a battalion aid station?

Your first treatment is from your company aid man, who gives you morphine usually and stops the bleeding, stabilizes the wound a little bit with a sling, and then at the battalion aid station . . . all he did was check what the aid man had done and supplemented. And then you go back to the other installation, your collecting station, and you wind up back at the evacuation hospitals . . . M.A.S.H. hospitals they had in the Korean War. They called it evacuation hospital where they had the first surgical treatment. And those doctors and nurses were wonderful. They really did their job. They worked twenty-four hours a day.

Now, you mentioned you had very good training and you were prepared for battle. Do you believe there were things you learned in the battlefield that you never learned in your training that helped you as a soldier?

Yeah, you're never prepared for how different it could be . . . how bad it could be. I mean, unless you experience it. You don't know what a bullet is going to feel like until it hits you, and the hardest part of being the leader was to see your men become casualties. And the one thing you never wanted to have happen was for your men to ever think that you weren't doing your job to the best of your ability. After all, your job is to attack or defend—whatever it is—but the men look to you for encouragement and leadership. It is up to you to give it to them if you can.

From your battlefield experience from either D-day or Brest, what was the saddest moment of your time?

The saddest moment was when I got back after I was wounded, and I had been treated and was awaiting evacuation myself, and one of the nurses came up to me and asked me to go back and talk to one of my men who had been wounded the previous day. He had his leg blown off. And the medical people couldn't convince this man that he wanted to live. He didn't want to live. He wanted to die. And I went back to talk to him. He was a young kid. I remember him very well. His name . . . I remember the name of his girlfriend because they used to censor his mail, and he said to me, "Lieutenant, I can't go home to Ladette looking like this." That was his girlfriend's name. But he pointed down to his leg, and I couldn't convince him to stay alive, and he died two days later. If you were a doctor, you'd probably know what I'm talking about. But the will to live is awful important when you're suffering.

As you mentioned earlier, sir, frequently especially when a replacement officer takes awhile to get the respect of your noncoms and your other soldiers, were there certain things that one could do to get there with their soldiers? What things could an officer do to gain the respect of their soldiers and their noncoms?

Well, first of all, the word "leader" means to lead, and as a platoon lead you were supposed to lead. It was always "Follow me, follow me." So you were always as a platoon leader supposed to be the leader going out in front when they were shooting, to be shooting back and to be out in front there. It's the most important job and the hardest job in the military being an infantry rifle platoon leader, in my opinion.

Obviously from what you just mentioned, leadership is very important. Are there any other attributes that you would say would be good for a platoon leader? Any other attributes other than getting out there and leading? Is there anything else that would inspire the men?

Well, every man is a different man. In your own mind, you should know what's right and what's wrong, and you should set an example for your men. I mean, you always make sure they're fed first before you take anything to eat. You make sure that their physical condition is looked after; if their shoes are worn out, that they got good shoes to wear. If their socks are dirty, they should have clean socks to put on. So the physical condition of your men is all important, and setting a good example . . . you can be a good leader. I think that's the best way to be a leader is to set an example.

Obviously as a Ranger and perhaps as a paratrooper . . . those were the World War II elite soldiers. What do you think put the advantage on the Ranger? Do you think it was their training, or was it their spirit, or was it a group of men that had decided that I wanted to be in Ranger Special Forces that got them to be great soldiers?
A good Ranger is still the best infantryman. This is the whole thing in a nutshell. Your training as an infantryman is honed, and you try to be extra special good at what you're doing. You hiked farther, you hiked faster, you climbed cliffs that other people can't climb, you shoot straighter, you accept hardships—whether it is going without food or going without sleep or being under fire longer . . . all these things. It's just toughening of the mind that makes you a good soldier, and the Rangers are taught this through their training. This is my . . . I've always been proud. To me, there is nothing any prouder to be an Army Ranger in combat and do the job right . . . whatever is expected of you.

What do you think of your platoon and perhaps your company was the most important contribution to the war effort? Would you say that scaling the cliffs on D-day, or was it the Battle of Brest, France, or would you say . . . I know you weren't there, but Hill 400 in December?
Well, it all boils back to what I said earlier . . . to do what you were told to do and to do it well. Nobody willingly wants to be shot at, but you know you're going to be shot at, so to do it in your own mind, you got to do what you know is right and set an example.

Is there anybody in the past in your service or your company or in your platoon that you would want to pay tribute too . . . anybody that fell for their country?
Well, in my own mind, I think the bravest and best soldier I had was my company medic, Bill Geitz, although he wasn't supposed to carry a weapon and fight. He showed more bravery and strength in his mind in doing his job. To me, he was the ideal soldier. I know people might disagree with me, but if you have ever been in combat and you see what the company aid men can do and will do, you can appreciate what I'm saying. You could never do your job without those men.

Did he survive the war?
He lost a leg, but he survived the war.

What do you think was the greatest lesson that you learned from your military experience and your Ranger training? What do you think you could say you walked away with, or the greatest thing you learned?
Well, I mean, leadership, I think. Leadership applies in civilian jobs as well, and I think by setting an example you could be a good leader. I think that you carry this thing with you. If you were a good soldier, you should be a good civilian in whatever field you're in. That's my own.

So leadership was the most important thing?
I think so, yes.

And when you reflect back on your military experience, what emotions do you feel? Is it mostly happiness or sadness?
Well, you experience most of them. I mean, you have sadness because of the men you lose. You have happiness first of all because you survived, and secondly because you were able to do what was expected of you. I think most people who have been in combat feel the same way.

Are there any specific commanding officers or noncommissioned officers who you think left you with a lasting impression in terms of their excelling on the battlefield as leaders? As soldiers? Anybody who really stands out to you in terms of somebody who you thought was a great leader on the field?
Well, to me, I think the one I looked up to most is Col. Rudder, our battalion commander. He was brave. He was capable. He could inspire men to do what he wanted them to do, and he always set a good example in his job. I mean, a lot of people might disagree with me, but of all the military officers that I ever served under . . . in his own way, I think he was the best soldier.

And, most likely a major part of his leadership skills, he was able to lead the Rangers?
And to get every man to do his best is part of being a leader, I think, and he was able to do that.

Are there any comments or any points of wisdom you would give to future generations, whether they be soldiers, Rangers, or just civilians?
Well, to me, and this might sound corny, is if you're going to have to fight in the military, get into the best unit you can get into. When I say best, I mean the ones who are able to do their job best, whether it's a medic or, if it's a fighting soldier, get into the best fighting soldier and the toughest outfit . . . the paratroopers or the Special Forces or anything like that. I think part of being a good soldier is to have pride, and the unit that has the most pride or the one that does the best fighting.

Any suggestions for civilians or anyone in the United States, anything that you would impart on us as a future generation?
I'll reiterate what I just said. If you're going to fight, be in the best unit you can get in. Have the best men with you. It is going to be your best chance of survival, and the Rangers were.

So if I would paraphrase that for civilians to do the best you can in civilian life, achieve the most that you can?
Do the best you can with what you got.

That's right, and do the best you can even in civilian life. And be in the best institution, best hospital, best . . . ?
That's right. It's pride that makes you do your job better, I think. Pride in your job and pride in your companions.

Now, when you were evacuated and in the hospital, what do you think some of your thoughts were? Were you thinking back to your men when you were in the hospital?
Oh yeah. You feel a sense of guilt. I did. When I was wounded and I knew that I was going to go back, I actually felt guilty about being wounded. I was happy about it, but I felt guilty about it, and I can't say that I wanted to get back and fight again, because I'd be a darn liar to say that, but I mean I just wished my men well, and I was sorry I wasn't there with them.

Is there any other comment or anything else you'd like to tell us?
Well, not really. But, I mean, personal pride in what you're doing I think is the best thing you do. No matter what you're doing, do it to the best of your ability.

Well, we certainly appreciate you for what you've done for our future and for all generations, for freeing us and giving us freedom, and we also appreciate the fact that you were willing to interview with us today and help other generations in the future to understand what sacrifices you and your men made for us. Thank you, and we do appreciate it. Thank you, Mr. Kerchner.

THE FOLLOWING IS GEORGE KERCHNER'S RECOLLECTION OF D-DAY

In D Company of the 2nd Ranger Battalion, I was platoon leader of one of the platoons. This is when I left the coast of France. Things changed a little. When we arrived in Europe, I became the company commander at that time because of casualties suffered to the company commander and the other lieutenant in the company.

I guess I went overseas in November of 1943 as replacement officer. In December 1943, I volunteered for a tryout with the 2nd Ranger Battalion, who were then located in the town of Bude in Cornwall. I guess you know where that is. I arrived in this town of Bude where the 2nd Battalion was quartered early in December. I think it was the forth or fifth of December. Immediately, I participated in the training that the battalion was undergoing at that time. Very shortly after that, I think probably January 1, although we weren't told then, our battalion received its assignment for D-day. It was early in January that we began this intense training of climbing cliffs and working amphibious landings from assault landing craft. We moved around various parts of England. I think they had scouts out trying to find the highest and most difficult cliffs that they could find, and we would spend a few weeks here and a few weeks there. We left Bude early in January and went to a little town outside of Portsmouth called Park Gate. We were stationed there for several weeks. There was a British naval base—small naval base—where they had a number of landing craft just a few miles from there, and most of our training while we were at Park Gate was working with these landing craft that were manned by British sailors. They would ride us over to the Isle of Wight, and we would disembark from the landing craft and practice climbing the cliffs there. After a few weeks there at Park Gate, the entire battalion moved over to the Isle of Wight. We were billeted in the town of Freshwater, which is near Needles. They had some very lovely cliffs there to look at. On one side of the island they had these chalk cliffs. I guess they were 200 to 250 feet high, and we worked on those most of the time, and right around the point on the other side of island, these cliffs that were called Tennyson Cliffs . . . this was out of the birthplace where Lord Alfred Tennyson resided, and I think that's where they got the name for these cliffs. They were the tallest cliffs we worked on over in England. I guess they were about 350 feet high. We would . . . as I said, most of our training really from January 1 on was practicing climbing cliffs and working out of landing crafts and exercises. A lot of them were live-firing exercises that apparently were designed to simulate what we were expected to run into when we landed over in France. We spent two weeks up at the Assault Training Center at Ilfracombe . . . I don't know what part of England. It's over on the west coast. This is where I think all of the assault troops for the invasion underwent this training there, which was primarily designed as fire team assaulting pillboxes and fortified areas. From there, we went down to Swanage, which I think is in Dorset, and that was our last base that we operated from for any period of time. We were in Swanage for several months, and it was in Swanage that we received our equipment that we were going to use for the invasion.

There was a lot of very deep thinking that went into preparing equipment for us for our mission on D-day. At this time, I guess in May that we found out . . . maybe it was April that we received our mission for D-day. We received some very specialized equipment. We had had on the sides of these assault landing craft . . . these British landing craft . . . they were the equivalent of our Higgins boat and carried roughly twenty-five to thirty men. They mounted six rocket projectors to each landing craft. Each landing craft was equipped with two toggle ropes, two rope ladders, and two smooth climbing ropes. I would like to explain briefly just what the composition of our particular assault force was. We were . . . our D-day mission was to land at a place called Point du Hoe, or we called it Point du Hoe. Since then I understand that it is Pointe du Hoc. It was a typographical spelling. But we have always called it Point du Hoe, which was about 3½ miles to the extreme right flank of Omaha Beach and roughly about halfway in between Utah Beach and Omaha Beach. This was a small point of land that extended out into the channel, and there was supposed to be located on top of this cliff, which was roughly 100 feet high and rather sheer, six 155 mm rifled guns that had an extreme range of about 25,000 yards. We were impressed upon time and time again of the importance and necessity of our destroying these guns before they went into operation against the ships that were out in the transport area. We were told that these were the only guns that were in position to fire into the transport area, which was roughly 11–12 miles off the coast. So they were a very high-priority mission for D-day. In addition to our force, there was a lot of naval gunfire that was scheduled to fire on them, as well as light, medium, and heavy bombing that was to take place. But they didn't want to run the risk that this preparatory fire didn't destroy these guns, and that was the reason they decided to send the Rangers in to knock them out. Now, the force that was given this mission was composed of three Ranger companies, D, E, and F of the 2nd Rangers Battalion. We get together occasionally with various groups of Rangers, especially our force, the D, E, and F force, and talk about what happened on D-day, and we keep in touch with one another over the year. Anyway, this force was composed roughly of 225 men and officers. A Ranger company had sixty-eight enlisted men, and one officer assigned to it. So we had these three companies of Rangers plus some attached troops from the 29th Division, as well as some of our Ranger Headquarter Company troops that were going in with this force. We had ten boats that were working with this Ranger force. Roughly, the average boat carried between twenty to twenty-five men. My boat had twenty-two men and myself . . . a total of twenty-three Rangers plus the British crew. I think there were two enlisted men in our boat, and an officer as well. The officer who I think most of the credit for our training and any success that the group had was our battalion S3 at that time Capt. Harold K. Slater, who everyone called Duke Slater. Duke was a very, very fine officer, a very hard-nosed officer who demanded an awful lot both of himself and of his men, and everybody respected Duke very, very highly. But Duke was charged with designing, I suppose, a lot of the equipment that we used, and to a certain extent procuring it and screening out the equipment to see that it worked. Most of the things that we used over there . . . the specialized climbing equipment anyway . . . had never really been tested and used in warfare before. We did, of course, train with this equipment and tested it ourselves and managed to iron out a lot of the bugs that cropped up in it. But to get back to a description of this equipment, each of these landing craft . . . the LCA British landing craft . . . was equipped with these six rocket projectors mounted on the sides . . . the gunnels, I think they're called . . . with a wooden box directly in the rear of the projector. In this wooden box was the ropes that we were going to climb with. The two boxes to the front of the craft each had a rope ladder. The two in the center had toggle ropes, which is a rope roughly about an inch thick with a small wooden bar spaced through it about every 2 feet, and the furthest one to the rear was the smooth climbing ropes, which everybody preferred to work with because you could move up them a whole lot faster. It was a lot easier. However, if you ran into any overhang where you couldn't use your feet for climbing, then you almost had to go to the toggle rope or rope ladder. So each craft was equipped with the three types of climbing ropes because we weren't sure just what the cliffs were going to be like and where our ropes were going to go up the cliff. The way this would work, these landing craft . . . actually, if you could visualize them as a weapon . . . the landing craft was pointed at the cliff that we were going to climb, and when it was approximately 25 yards offshore at this particular place, or, I would say not over 75 yards away from the base of the cliff, these projectors were fired electrically, and the rocket would carry the head at a high arc. The head had a large grappling arm affixed to the end of it. Right behind this grappling arm was a lead wire of about 50–75 yards, and then the rope was attached to this lead wire . . . the idea because so the rocket wouldn't burn the rope, we had this lead wire. This was fired in a high trajectory. I guess it would go up into the air probably 300–400 feet and then come down, and the idea being to fire these over the edge of the cliffs so they would land 50, 75, or 100 yards inland, and then, as we would get out of the craft and go to the base of the cliff, pull the rope down until all the slack was out of it, and this would dig the grapple into the sod up on top of the cliff. We would give it a number of good tugs to make sure it was well seated, and then we would start climbing. Now we, of course, did this many, many, many times in England, and we could work in advance, in time so that a man carrying normal combat equipment and gear could scale equipped the height of which we expected to run into at Pointe du Hoc, and a real fast climber and good climber could probably get up there in under a minute. This was providing, of course, that he could manage to get some footholds. You could climb a sheer cliff fairly easy as long as you could use your feet to assist you in climbing up. Most of our training in England was conditioning training, in addition to learning the mechanics of this rope climbing, but in the course of the five or six months preparatory to D-day, I myself, who when I joined the Rangers back in December, probably couldn't climb 20 foot of slope on a rope ladder because of not having had experience or this particular type of training. By the time D-day rolled around, everyone of us who was going to go into there could climb these extremely high cliffs fairly easily just because of the conditioning and the training and whatnot. Anyway, starting in May, there was some full-scale exercises, some of which all of the assault troops participated in along the coast of England. One was a firing exercise in which the Navy participated shelling the area there, and the assault troops went in using the same time schedule that they were planning to have for D-day and it was a full-scale dress rehearsal. Of course an awful lot of things went wrong, and that was the whole idea of having the training exercise, was to iron out these kinks. In the latter part of June . . . it must have been just about the latter part of May and the first of June, we were sent to a marshaling area. This was the area right directly behind the southern coast of England, and at that time, I think, was just one vast series of marshaling areas. This was an area in which the troops were sealed off from the rest of the country and from the rest of the Army . . . those troops that were going to go on the initial waves. You were behind barbed wire. You couldn't contact anyone outside of it, and in the final phase of the last few days . . . I said June 1 . . . I guess it was about May 20, that we went in there. We had about two weeks in this marshaling area which ammunition was issued. The men were briefed at this time. The officers had been briefed a month or so previous. All of the men were given their D-day mission and assignments down to the lowest private. Everybody in our unit . . . this Ranger group . . . every man knew just what every other man in his particular unit, squad, team, or section had to do, so if a man became a casualty, someone else was expected to take over his particular job. The ammunition was issued, last letters were sent home. I don't recall that we received any mail there. Perhaps we did, but I know it was sort of a final breaking off from everything prior to the invasion. About June 1 or 2, we were trucked down to Portland, which is the port there in the southern coast of England, and we were loaded aboard our transport there. We were assigned to a former channel steamer called the *New Amsterdam*. This was a small passenger boat I suppose . . . 3,000–4,000 tons, that could carry several hundred passengers on the overnight trip from back and forth across the channel. It had small staterooms, and it was rather comfortable accommodations. It was a British ship and had a British crew. Very fine people, wonderful sailors. They treated us nice, and my only complaint was that there was a lot of food that the English thought was wonderful, but as far as I was concerned, it left little to be desired, and kidney stew was the one thing that sticks in my mind. Aboard this ship, we continued our training and our conditioning such as we could there. We would string these ropes up to the mast . . . the yardarms of the mast, and a lot of men would practice rope climbing up and down. We would do weapons training, weapons drills, a lot of the physical conditioning, pt, more briefing and assignments . . . individual assignments were gone over and over and over. We had time for a certain amount of recreation such as was available . . . playing cards. We didn't have any movies. We left Portland, I guess, about the third or fourth of June. We were one of the early ships to leave. I know a lot of the other ships were still in the harbor, and we started out into the channel. We didn't go directly across. They took us out there, and we more or less slowly steamed back and forth while they were forming the various convoys and columns of ships. The channel started getting rough on the evening of June 3, and on June 4 it rained and June 5 was D-day. This was originally when we were supposed to go in. I don't recall exactly when, but sometime on June 4 we were notified that the invasion had been postponed for a day. We were on our way over at the time, and this necessitated turning around, and we didn't go back to port, but we steamed back and forth. One of the things I recall then was that the British were saying they are going to have to run this thing shortly. We would have to go back because we run out of food. The food wasn't that good. It didn't worry us too much, I suppose.

On June 5, they definitely told us that the invasion was on for the sixth. So, remembering some of the things that we did on this last day that we were to be aboard ship, and the last day alive for a great number of the men there, I recall the Ranger group chaplain, Father Lacey from Hartford, Connecticut, who was not stationed aboard our ship, but he did come over to the *New Amsterdam* and conducted services aboard for the Catholics as well as for the Protestants. Most of the things that I have said, I am sure it was actually the way I thought at the time. When I was talking about Father Lacey, who visited the *New Amsterdam* and conducted mass for the Catholics and religious services for the non-Catholics, we were all very, very glad to see him. Father Lacey was a real wonderful man. He was sort of given to us just a few weeks before D-day. I know it was a surprise . . . I hope a pleasant surprise to him, but he hadn't done any of the strenuous training that we had had, and I know he was worried about being able to keep up with us. But one of the things that I remember him saying to all of us on D-day, at least the people aboard the ship, that has always stuck in my mind . . . he said, "When you land on the beach and you get in there, I don't want to see anybody kneeling down and praying." He said, "If I do, I'm going to boot you in the tail." He said, "You leave the praying to me, and you do the fighting." And Father Lacey, speaking to him just a minute, was a real hero. Father Lacey received the Distinguished Service Cross on D-day. He didn't land at Pointe du Hoc with us. He landed on the beach with the other three companies, but he constantly walked back and forth under fire, back and forth across the beach, dragging wounded men up beyond the high-water marks so they wouldn't drown, and he was awarded the DSC for this. Well, to get back to our particular group . . . on this day before D-day, I remembered the religious services. I remember we had entertainment among ourselves. One of the boys, Reggie Reggerio, was a tap dancer. I think he had done a little professional tap dancing before he came in the Rangers. He danced and various fellows would sing. I know we had a banjo or ukulele or whatever, it was aboard ship, and we did have some entertainment, I guess, just trying to cheer ourselves up. On the night before D-day, it was a constant checking of equipment and checking your men's equipment and making sure that everybody understood exactly what he had to do. One of our real big problems concerning equipment was, insofar we had to climb these cliffs, that weight was a very important factor to us. We had to keep things to a minimum. At the same time, we had to make sure that we carried with us what we were going to need. There was no way that we could be resupplied for several hours after the invasion. So anything that we figured that we were going to need for the first few hours of the invasion, we had to carry on our person. So we didn't carry any packs. We left our packs in one of the supply landing craft, but we had an assault . . . in our pockets and around our cartridge belt, we carried just about everything that we felt we would need. I recall some of the things that I had, not necessarily in the matter of importance, but my weapon . . . I only had a .45 pistol, and this worried me because I knew that you couldn't do a whole lot with a pistol when you got in there. However, I carried a 536 radio. I was carrying a thermite grenade, which was to be used to help destroy these guns that we were going in on. I had several smoke grenades that were supposed to be used to signal to friendly aircraft to keep them from bombing us in case they saw us inland somewhere. Of course your fragmentation grenade . . . we had several of these. I had a toggle rope. In fact, every man carried a toggle rope around him . . . the idea being that if we got stuck some way, you can hook these toggle ropes together. Each man had a length of about 6 foot, and we could make a rope out of ten or twelve of the men putting their toggles together. We would have a rope that we could use in an emergency to get up or down the cliff. Of course, I carried a map case. I think that I was the only one in the boat team that was permitted to carry a map. I also had the SOI, which is the signal-operating instructions, that we were under orders to destroy in case capture was imminent. The only food we carried was several D-ration bars. I had one canteen of water. Altogether, there wasn't too much weight compared to what we would carry later on. However, it still was a lot of weight on your back to climb a cliff. Because of this, we did try and keep things with weight down as much as possible. All this was checked over prior on the last day before the invasion. On D-day night, the last thing I recall doing before I went to bed . . . I played bridge with several of the men in my platoon. I was a very poor bridge player, but I think I did it just to keep from thinking about what laid [sic] ahead. I think I got to bed about 10:30 or 11:00. I got to sleep before 12:00. We slept just a few hours, and I think it was about 3:00 a.m. that we were awakened. The British crewmen had this job of coming around waking us, but I think everybody was laying [sic] awake there anyway . . . nearly everybody. We got up and dressed, and first we went down and had break-fast. Where we ate was in the forward hold, I guess you would call it, of the ship, and as we went out on the deck of the ship to go down to eat, we were anchored in this transport area, which was roughly 11 or 12 miles off of the coast. Looking toward the coast, we saw these flares up in the sky. They were very, very pretty. Of course, we knew that the paratroopers were going to precede us into France, and they were going to be dropping during the early morning hours. These flares . . . I think they called them channeliere flares that these planes dropped to help light the landing paths. But anyway, this was our first realization that the invasion was on. We could hear the planes going overhead . . . the transport planes with the paratroopers aboard. About 4:00, we were all finished eating, and we got our gear on and we loaded in the LCAs, the landing craft. These were carried in davits on both sides of the ship. There were, I think, on our transport six of them. This landing force of 225 men was divided between two transports. On ours, I think we had six landing craft, and we were lowered down. The sea was very rough. It was a little tricky letting go of the landing craft from the ropes supporting them as they reached the water, because of the waves going up and down on the side of the ship. However, we got away, got in the landing craft, and got away from the ship without too much trouble. These six landing craft that were in our group were in a column. My landing craft was the lead landing craft. We had a lieutenant commander from the British navy in our landing craft who was responsible for taking this column into that part of the beach where we were due to land. The other column from the other transport remainder of our assault force joined us on the way in. We were moving in two columns, six landing craft one behind the other. As we started in, it started to get light, I suppose around 4:30. It was before 5:00 that it was light, and I recall passing not too far away from some of the large warships that were preparing to deliver their supporting fires on the beaches. And just about the time we got a little past them, I recall that they started firing. This must have been about 5:00. The battleship *Texas* was among these, and I remember what a terrifying sound it was when they started firing their 14-inch guns. Of course, they were passing far over our heads, but we were close enough to hear and feel some of the muzzle blasts. I recall as we got perhaps half . . . well, not halfway . . . a little farther than halfway, and one of the rocket-firing craft that was off of Omaha Beach fired their barrages of rockets. This also was a terrifying thing. I think there were 1,000 or more of these rockets on these landing craft, and they fired in salvos of maybe ten or fifteen at a time. It was just one continuous sheet of fire going up . . . this rocket-firing craft . . . and thinking at the time and talking about it even there, I remembered wondering how could anybody really live on the beaches with all of this fire that was landing there, both from the warships and these rocket-firing craft. Our air force bombers were flying overhead at this time. We couldn't see them. There was a low overcast. It was a dull, gray day. I think the clouds were probably down to 1,000–2,000 feet, and of course all the planes, these bombers anyway, were flying above the clouds. But we could hear them dropping their bombs on the shore. We could see, as we got more closer to the shore, some of these things landing. However, as we found out later, practically all of the bombing was done too far inland to be of much help to those men who landed on the beach. They had all hoped . . . we were told that there would be so many shell craters on the beach that would offer cover for the men as they moved across the beach. I didn't land on Omaha Beach, so I don't know. But it was hearsay . . . I understand there were practically no shell holes or bomb craters on the beach. Well, anyway, our particular force . . . we headed off to the right. The other landing craft were heading directly to Omaha. We sort of went off on a tangent to the right. There was a British motor launch that had the assignment of guiding us in to make sure that we landed at the right place. This motor launch was some distance ahead of our two columns of our landing craft. Well, anyway, on the trip in, almost immediately after leaving the transports, we began encountering heavy seas . . . very, very heavy . . . and I guess the waves were 5 or 6 feet high anyway. We had been told that these landing craft were unsinkable. They had large air tanks along both sides that were supposed to support the craft even though the thing was holed by a shell. We weren't thinking too much of water shifting into the landing craft. The craft had a ramp on the front, and these heavy seas that would wash up and hit this ramp and wash right over the top of it, and very shortly we had 6 to 12 inches of water in the bottom of the landing craft. When we were, I guess, perhaps a half hour away from touchdown . . . we were due to land at 6:30 . . . I noticed that the motor launch and the leading craft in the other column started turning off to the right. We found out later that they made a mistake on the point that they were going to take us in on, and we actually were about 2 miles away from where we were supposed to land. Later on, this actually proved to be a blessing in disguise, but at the time it was almost a catastrophe. We were due to land at 6:30 on the dot. Backing up from 6:30 . . . forty minutes before 6:30, the heavy bombers were supposed to drop their bombs on Pointe du Hoc. Then the battleships . . . the battleship *Texas* was supposed to fire on Pointe du Hoc several hundred rounds. Then the next fire was to be taken up by medium bombers, which were supposed to come in and plaster the Pointe, and finally up to three minutes before 6:30 fighters were supposed to strafe the Pointe. All this of course was designed to keep the defenders pinned down, that they either couldn't see us approaching the Pointe or to keep them from the edge of the cliff, where if they could get up there while we were getting ready to land, they could cut our ropes before we ever managed to even get halfway up the cliff. So this fire support was very, very essential, supposedly, to our making a successful landing. Well, anyway, when we realized that we were heading for the wrong point and it was approaching 6:30, I naturally became very upset. I know the British lieutenant commander in our boat was all upset, because what this actually meant was that we were going to be late in landing at the Pointe when we were supposed to. So what we had to do . . . we turned to the right and we sailed roughly a half mile, I suppose, off of the shore at that point. It was all cliffs along there. We sailed parallel to the coast up to where we were supposed to land at Pointe du Hoc. I guess we traveled for a half hour or more. We sailed along roughly a half mile off the coast. We were brought under fire by the German antiaircraft defenses along the coast . . . small-caliber 20 mm and 40 mm guns were firing at our craft out there. Several of the craft were struck. One of them, I think, was sunk at this time. I know none of the men in my boat were wounded. As we were going in, one of our landing crafts . . . the one immediately behind mine, which contained the company commander of my company . . . D Company . . . as well as a large group of men that I was very friendly with. Some of them were from my platoon in this boat. This boat sunk not from being fired on, but from shifting all this water that I said before. This convinced me that these landing crafts were not unsinkable, as we had been led to believe. So we immediately began bailing with our helmets and managed to keep the water down, so that even though we were shifting a lot of water at this stage because we speeded up the boat being behind, and this made us shift more water. We managed to keep the water down. The other boats, I'm sure, were doing the same thing. There was this one craft with the men of D Company in it that sunk. There was another one of the landing crafts that was carrying some supplies and extra ammunition that was sunk at this time. Our column, then with the five landing craft, then steamed along parallel to the coast, and as we approached the Pointe du Hoc from roughly a half mile offshore, I was looking at my watch and realized we were far behind the schedule. It was 7:00 then. All of our preparatory fires had been lifted by half an hour. The Germans who were in the underground shelters on Pointe du Hoc were starting to come out and look around and see what was going on, and I recall as we turned to make our approach run into the beach looking up there seeing these Germans on top of the cliff, and my first thought was this whole thing is a big mistake. None of us are going to ever get up that cliff, because we realized how vulnerable we were going to be while we were climbing this cliff. The ropes were over the top of the cliff. We were on the side of the cliff, and all the Germans would have to do was stay back from the edge of the cliff and cut the ropes, and nobody could have got up. However, we turned and we went in and made our approach to the shore. The landing crafts all came in abreast. This was a change from the original plan, which was that three of the landing craft . . . the three from D Company, my company . . . was supposed to sail around the Pointe and come in on the right side. However, being late, this time we were almost forty-five minutes late, and approaching from the left flank to sail out and go around this Point would have taken another five minutes or so. It would have subjected us to additional fire, and at this stage, being as late as we were, I figured it didn't make a whole lot of difference where we landed then. The whole thing was to get in there.

Another reason, I could see the other landing craft making their turn in where they were supposed to, and I guess, seeking company, we decided to turn our landing craft in among the other landing craft that had this section of cliff assigned to them. This probably caused some confusion among the other landing crafts, because our two craft . . . that was all that was left now . . . wasn't supposed to land on this side of the Pointe. Anyway, we approached the beach, and about 25 to 50 yards offshore I gave the order to fire a rocket. All of our rockets fired. They were fired in salvos two at a time. I think out of the six ropes that we fired up there, at least five of our ropes cleared the cliff. This was a good percentage. Some of the other landing crafts had a great deal of trouble. Perhaps they fired them too soon, or perhaps the seas that were shipping over the landing craft had wet the ropes to such an extent that they were so heavy that they couldn't clear the cliff. Anyway, ours did get up, and immediately after firing the rockets, the ramp was lowered and we approached the beach . . . the idea and the hope and desire of all of us was that we were going to run right up on the beach, and we were going to make a dry landing. This, again, was not because we were afraid of getting wet, but because it would have kept that much less weight and that much more weight off of our bodies in climbing this cliff. As I mentioned before, weight was such a big factor in the climb. Well, anyway, hoping to touch down dry, and the British navy had promised they were going to put us down dry, we made this approach, and suddenly we ran aground with the ramps. They dropped the ramp and the British officer in charge said, "All right, everybody out." Looking ahead of the ramp, I could see at least 15 to 20 feet of water. The water was muddy. It was dirty gray. The ground along here was clay, and it had been our shelling and our bombing from the air. Both the bombers and the battleship *Texas* and I suppose some of the other supporting fire had practically all landed where we were supposed to. We had too many shell craters on our beach. They could have given a lot of them to the boys up on Omaha. Well, anyway, what we had done . . . we had run on the edge of one of these shell craters, as I discovered almost immediately. I figured the water was a foot or so deep, because the landing craft only drew about 2 feet of water, and when they went aground and they dropped the ramp, I thought I'm going to run through about a foot of water. So I hollered, "Okay, let's go," and I ran off the ramp, first one out. I immediately landed in about 8 feet of water. This was a large bomb crater, apparently from one of the very large bombs from one of the heavy bombers, and I know it was 6 or 8 feet deep because I couldn't touch bottom while I was swimming. I immediately went almost down to the bottom there under the water, and I thought, oh hell—here we go. My first impulse was I was angry, because they had made us run off this boat . . . had told us to go off . . . that there was shallow water there, and here I was in water over my head. I came to the surface and started paddling, doggy paddle, to try to keep my head above the water and swimming to shore. Well, the men immediately behind me . . . as soon as they saw me running off and going into water over my head, they realized what it was, and they filed around both sides of the shelf crater. Although they got their feet wet, I don't think any of them went in water as deep as I did. And instead of being the first one ashore, I was one of the last ashore, but I paddled in there with all this weight. Well, we were sure then. My first impressions of what happened immediately upon going ashore are a little vague. Some of the things that I remembered doing . . . I'll tell you. The first thing I remember doing was being angry because I was soaking, wringing wet. I turned around, and I wanted to find somebody to help me cuss out the British navy for dumping me in this 8 feet of water. Well, everybody was busily engrossed in their own duties, so I couldn't get any sympathy on that score. The next thing that I remember was I realized we were being fired on by a machine gun from the top of the cliff off to the left, several 100 yards away. The men who were with me . . . two men in my boat crew were immediately hit, one sergeant from and PFC Harris were hit by this fire from the machine gun, and I don't know how it missed me because they were right next to me. Well, anyway, this made me very angry because I figured they were shooting at me, and also, having nothing but a pistol, I felt rather helpless with this machine gun several hundred yards away. So I think it was Harris . . . when he was hit, he dropped his rifle . . . I picked up his rifle so I would have at least something that I could fight with a little greater range than the 50 yards or so that a pistol is effective at. At first, my first impulse was to go after this machine gun up here. I immediately realized that this was rather stupid . . . that our mission was to get up the top of this cliff and get on with destroying these guns that were up there. The men were all . . . the men were trained . . . as soon as they went ashore, they had their ropes and they had the order in which they were supposed to climb the ropes, and the men were all moving right in and starting to climb up the cliff. It wasn't necessary to tell this man to do this or that man to do that. Although I was the leader, everybody knew what they were supposed to do. Right at that particular stage, the only command that I really remember giving . . . I told my platoon messenger, PFC Cruz, to stay with these few men that were wounded. They had to stay at the bottom of the cliff. We got them in closer [so] that they were protected as much as possible. The next thing that I felt I better do, knowing that the landing craft containing the company commander had been sunk, together with a number of men. I thought I'd better find Col. Rudder and inform him of this event. I went down the beach maybe 25 or 50 yards and found Col. Rudder starting to climb one of the rope ladders. Well, I know he had his hands full and his mind full, and he didn't seem particularly interested in me informing him that I was assuming command of the company, and I think he told me to get the hell out of there and go climb my rope. So I went back and started up the rope. Climbing the cliff was very easy, especially after training on these cliffs that we had worked on over in England. The shelling from the warships and the bomb damage . . . a lot of it had hit the edge of the cliff and caused some dirt and large chunks of clay and shale to fall down. You could almost walk part way up the cliff . . . I'd say the first 25 feet of it really didn't entail any climbing to any extent. The cliffs were about 100 feet high. My rope . . . I went up a smooth rope and, as I said, I had no trouble at all climbing it. To my recollection of these men [Germans] on top of the cliff as we came in . . . I couldn't understand why they weren't doing more than they were doing, because, as I said, I thought we were on the defenseless on both landing on the shore and climbing up the cliff. Well, I found out later on that two things happened that practically assured [*sic*] the success of our mission, assured us getting up, and assured us all from being either killed or captured right on the shore there. First of all, the United States destroyer *Satterlee* saw what had happened. They were very close to shore, and they realized that we had no fire support. They saw the Germans on top of the cliff. I wasn't aware of this at the time. I found it out perhaps in months or almost a year later, when I read about it. But I couldn't realize what all the noise was about. I thought it was the Germans shooting at us, and this destroyer *Satterlee* seemed 400 to 500 yards off of shore and opened fire on these Germans on top of the cliff with their guns and also their antiaircraft guns. And they were the ones who provided us with fire support that enabled us to climb this cliff, and someday I would love to meet up with somebody from the destroyer *Satterlee* so I can shake his hand and thank him for this. The other thing that helped us to get up there was a rather amusing thing. Certainly the Germans have never seen anything like our rocket launchers that were firing the ropes and rope ladders up, and when these remaining nine landing craft fired six rockets each, and these went up in the air trailing smoke and fire behind them and landed on top of the cliff and partway inland, I'm sure that the Germans thought that this was some sort of a weapon, and I know it helped to make some of them hit the ground and take cover. Some of the men had tied pieces of time fuse to the end of this and lit it just before firing it, figuring the Germans will come up and see this time fuse burn, and think it was something that's going to explode at any minute, and keep them away from it. Maybe this helped. Some of the ropes were cut. Our rope was not cut . . . the rope I was climbing was not cut, and I don't think any of the ropes in our company were cut. Most of my men got up without too much trouble. As far as I know, the only men that were left at the bottom of the cliff were the two men that were wounded immediately, and one of the medics and my platoon messenger . . . that is, from my boat team. There were other casualties. I think altogether our Ranger group suffered about twenty-five casualties on the beach . . . that is, on the small beach where we landed. It was a very narrow beach . . . just about 15 or 25 feet wide at this time because the tide was coming in right fast. I'm going up the cliff now and naturally starting to realize that what we were doing, and it was kind of dangerous. However, I went over the top of the cliff and started looking for some of my men. As I said, everybody had their job and their mission, and they were moving off in small groups . . . two, three, or four in their teams to go after the three guns . . . these three casemated guns that they were to destroy. As I said, each man knew the mission of the other man, and it was set up so that there weren't any casualties. There would be other people that knew what had to be done and were capable of doing it. Also, as I got over the top of the cliff and got on this metal ground up there, my first impression was it didn't look anything at all like what I thought it was going to look like. We had any number of aerial photos and maps and sketches of what was supposed to be up there, but this tremendous bombardment from the planes and from the warships had tore up the terrain so much that I couldn't recognize anything initially up there. It was one large shell crater after the other. Well, anyway, I set out heading towards the portion of the Pointe where our guns were, where our mission took us, and we would run . . . I say "we" because I would every now and then come across other Rangers . . . run from one shell crater to the other. About this time, the Germans started shelling us from inland, and being the first time I was under artillery fire coming my way, and this was a rather terrifying experience. However, all I wanted to do was keep running and keep heading in the direction that I was supposed to be, and I felt that this was the safest place anyway because the shells were landing near the edge of the cliff, and I figured to get inland just as far as I could and as fast as I could to get away from these shell bursts. I started picking up men as we went across the terrain up there. I would run into some men of my own company and other men. You would jump into a shell hole of these craters. They were 25 feet in diameter, some of them, and there might be one or two Rangers in there. You didn't know until you jumped in the hole, and then you'd immediately, as soon as that shell had landed, you'd get out of that hole and run to the next one. And we moved right fast across this land, and, as I said, I felt safer by moving. I didn't want to stay where the shells were landing. As we got closer to the area where our three casemated guns were that were our company's objective, I started running into more and more of our men. And one time I remember we were in a small hole, and it was three or four of us there, and we saw a 40 mm antiaircraft gun. It was in an antiaircraft in placement just about 100 yards away from us, and this gun was firing direct fire with this 40 mm at Rangers who were running across the Pointe. It ranges up 100 to 200 yards. Of course, a 40 mm antiaircraft gun wasn't really designed for that, but I imagine it was pretty effective. This was the first German that I remembered seeing . . . the first live German that I saw. I had come across several dead Germans in the run across the Pointe. I don't recall seeing any dead Americans as I came across this terrain, but I did see some dead Germans. This was the first live German, and we all wanted to shoot at him, but it turned out we didn't get any opportunity. He turned this 40 mm gun in our direction, and we realized we had been seen, and everybody took out from that little hole we were in. That was the last time . . . no, while we were in this hole, one of the sergeants came over and reported that the three guns that we were to destroy were not in the casemates. They found the casemates, and the casemates were empty. Well, there went our initial mission, which was to destroy the guns. I realized that we weren't going to accomplish anything by staying in here in the middle of this no-man's land. This was, I suppose, 300 yards in from the edge of the cliff, and especially with this German antiaircraft gun in placement that knew we were there not too far away. We decided to set off . . . or I decided I would set off, and told the men what I wanted them to do. Our secondary mission, which was to move inland and to establish a roadblock on the coastal road that ran along the coast from Omaha Beach Vierville down to Grand Camp Lebain, which was down near Utah Beach. So I told the men this is what I wanted them to do, and set off for this road. Well, again, the men took off in small groups, and I did too. I waited to see if any more of the men were coming up, to tell them what I wanted them to do, and then I started across Pointe du Hoc to get out on the road myself. I remember landing in this zigzag communication trench that the Germans had dug there, and it was the deepest trench I had ever seen in my life. It was in their trench . . . the communication trenches is only about 2 feet wide, but this thing must have been at least 8 feet deep, and my first impression was "Gee, I'm safe from artillery fire in here." But being a zigzag trench, and about every 25 yards it would go off on another angle. You could only see directly ahead about 25 yards, and I was by myself at this time, and I never felt so lonesome before or, I suppose, since in all my life. Because every time I came to a corner of this communication trench where I had to make a turn to see what was in the next 25-yard section, I didn't realize and didn't know whether I was going to come face to face with a German or not. I began thinking in terms right then of maybe we were going to be captured or maybe I was going to be captured. I guess because I was by myself, this was worrying me. So this made me all the more anxious and in that much more of a hurry to get out to this coastal road to join my men, because you felt a whole lot better when there were other men around you. I went through this trench, I suppose, for 100 to 150 yards before it finally came out near the ruins of a house that was right at the entrance of the fortified position around Pointe du Hoc. Pointe du Hoc was a self-contained fort in itself. It was surrounded from the landside with minefields, with barbed-wire entanglements, and machine gun emplacements that was supposed to protect it from an attack from the land. I don't think the Germans really believed that anybody could scale the cliffs and come in from the sea. So this is where we began running into most of the German defenders was on the perimeter of this fortified area of which Pointe du Hoc was part. This is when I first saw our first American casualties. There was a German machine gun in this road leading out from the Pointe, and I came up there and I saw the first one of my men who was wounded. It was a boy named Vaughn, a T5 machine gunner, Bill Vaughn . . . a real wonderful young fellow . . . and I realized as soon as I saw him that he was dying. He had been practically stitched across with the machine gun. He wasn't in any pain because he was hit too badly. I know he knew that he was dying, and all I could do was tell him, "Bill, we'll send the medic up to look after you." There wasn't any point in me staying there with him. There wasn't anything I could do for him, and I felt the best thing for me to do was get off and get up the road where the rest of the men were. Along here, I started seeing more of our casualties. This is where the Germans started to defend more strongly. They had come out of their holes, and they were moving back and forth across the Pointe. I'm sure they were as confused as we were . . . probably a little more confused . . . and it was a series of little engagements where a group of Rangers . . . two or three Rangers would run into two or three Germans. Most of it at very close range, and usually it was whoever got the first shot off or threw the first grenade would win the little battle. I myself did not run into any Germans at this time. I did not fire a shot from this rifle I was carrying up to this point. I moved up the road and finally made contact with the two sergeants who were next in command and my fire team, and also with the 1st Sgt. Lomell who was the team commander of the other boat team from our company that had also made the beach. There was just the two boat teams . . . one commanded by myself and one commanded by 1st Sgt. Lomell. We had a little conference and talked over what we thought we ought to do, and we decided that we would go down this coastal highway several hundred yards to the right and establish a roadblock down there. Sgt. Lomell and Sgt. Hune went down this road with what men we had there . . . I suppose there were ten or twelve of them . . . and I started back to the Pointe to see if I could find any more men. As I started back, I met one of my men coming forward, who informed me that there was a sniper who had zeroed in on this road that we were moving on, and had killed I suppose half a dozen Rangers. Nearly every one was shot through the head. I started down there and saw some of these men and realized it wasn't the smartest thing in the world to be walking down this road looking for some people that I didn't even know where they were. Anyway, I turned around then and decided to go back and join these men who were out on the roadblock. We had at that time I suppose twenty men out of D Company who were with us. This was from the two boat teams. As I said, we started off with sixty-eight men and two officers. One boat sunk, which cut us down to about forty-five men, and we had about twenty men out here on the road. The other twenty-five men we found out later . . . a number of them were casualties, a few were taken prisoner, and some of them stayed back at the edge of the cliff with Col. Rudder where he established his CP back there. The other companies were doing the same thing that we were doing, which was infiltrating through to this coastal highway in small groups. As I mentioned before, no guns were in our casemates, and we got the reports from the other companies that there were no guns at all on Pointe du Hoc. The casemates were under construction and had not been completed. The Germans apparently weren't going to put the guns in until the casemates were completed. However, they had put some large logs in these emplacements, which from the aerial photos that we had seen and studied looked like the guns. So actually and up to this stage, almost this whole show had been for nothing, because our mission had been to destroy these guns to keep them from firing on the fleet, and we couldn't even find the guns. These guns that were supposed to be on Pointe du Hoc, for which all this aerial bombardment and warship bombardment and the 220 Rangers which their efforts were directed at these guns, were not on the Pointe. But at this stage, we felt rather disappointed. Not only disappointed, but I felt awfully lonesome. We realized how few men we had there. The other two companies, E and F . . . I saw the two lieutenants from each of the companies . . . it turned out that each company commander on that day was a casualty: D Company, E Company, and F Company. Each of the company commanders became casualties, and the lieutenants took over the command of each company. Lt. Armand took over the F Company, Lt. Lafery had E Company, and of course I was the surviving officer in D Company, and we got together for a few minutes at this stage to talk about what we were going to do. And we decided, insofar as we weren't going to serve any useful purpose back on the Pointe, to establish a perimeter around this road that we were supposed to cut into, try and defend ourselves, and wait for the invading force that had landed on Omaha Beach to come up. Now, the plan for D-day was that if everything went according to schedule, that we were to be relieved by a force from the 29th Division, 116th Infantry, fighting their way up from Omaha Beach at approximately 11:00 or 11:30. By then, I guess, it was about 8:00 or 8:30, so we figured we had a few hours to hold out, and that we would try to defend ourselves and wait for these fellows to come up and relieve us. We had altogether, I suppose, about sixty Rangers who were out here on the road. D Company took the right flank, E Company took the center and moved inland about 200 yards, and F Company took the left flank. I went up and joined my company up on the right flank, where they had this roadblock, and we decided to dig in on the north side of the road and to try to ambush anything that might be coming down the road from the direction of Grand Camp Lethayne. I think we saw several straggler Germans coming down the road that were brought under fire and made casualties. And then a patrol consisting of Sgt. Lemell and Sgt. Kune and one other man decided to get out and look around a little. They went inland about 100 yards from where we were along this road leading off of the hardtop coastal road, and there, lo and behold, they came on five 155 mm guns sitting alongside of the road, with ammunition stacked alongside of each of them pointed . . . actually, they were pointed towards Utah Beach, which was on the other flank and all ready to fire, but not a single German around them. This was probably one of the most fantastic things that happened in the war, as far as I'm concerned anyway. Here were these guns all ready to fire, and Lord knows the Germans needed them bad enough at this stage, and nobody around to fire them. Well, Sgt. Lomell and Sgt. Kune put thermite grenades in the brow of three of these guns to just knock them out of action, and talk some grenades into the ammunition stored there and blew up some of that. Then they came back to tell me and the rest of us what was going on, and to get some more grenades to knock the remainder of the guns out. Of course, I knew something had happened, because when that ammunition went off there was a tremendous explosion and sheet of flame from it. In the meantime, some men from E Company had come around from the other side and discovered the guns, and they knocked out the remainder of the guns. So all five of the guns were put out of action within a few minutes after they were discovered. So, in effect, we had at this stage accomplished our D-day mission, which was to knock out these 155 mm guns that were set to just fire on the transport area. Well, then we were feeling pretty good because to be able to accomplish this with practically no effort at all and no fighting at this stage, we felt that maybe things were looking up. This was, oh, I suppose, sometime in the morning . . . 9:00 or 10:00 when these guns were destroyed and put out of action. We sat out on this roadblock the remainder of the day. Different things happened. I recall that I went back or I started to go back to the Pointe to get orders from Col. Rudder to see what he wanted me to do, and on the way back, Cpl. Gordon Lunning, who was with me, and I decided that we were going to try and knock out this 40 mm gun emplacement and get the sniper that had been killing all these men as they went up and down the road. We started to stalk this particular position, which was several hundred yards away, and, as I found out, several Germans discovered us and started stalking us. Well, we fired some rounds. This was when I discovered that this rifle that I picked up on the beach wouldn't fire. The first time I laid [sic] down and had a good target at this man . . . I squeeze the trigger and nothing happens. This gun was just clogged up with dirt and mud and clay. So immediately I had to sit down and field-strip the weapon and take it apart, clean if off, and put it back together to get it working. This was when we discovered that the Germans were after us instead of us being after the Germans. So we turned around and bypassed these Germans who were starting to come up to the rear of us. There was a lot of men going back and forth. Wounded men were heading back to the Pointe. Men were coming forward with messages from the Pointe and going back there. However, most of us stayed out along this road and along this hedgerow that was several hundred yards in from the road for the remainder of D-day. I recall several times that some Germans approached and were brought under fire, and I remember one time when a large group of Germans moved down the road behind the hedgerow right opposite where we were. We were in this ditch along one side of this very narrow road, and directly across the road not 25 feet away was this hedgerow, and walking right along behind this hedgerow was fifty or sixty Germans. We decided that it wasn't a smart thing to start firing at them, because we could only see their helmets and head, and if we had fired and disclosed our position . . . we were in a ditch, and we would have been almost sitting ducks for them just when we need to. Well, anyway, we didn't fire at this stage, but we noticed that these Germans moved down around our flank and started heading inland. By then, we began to realize that the Germans weren't beaten . . . that they had an awful lot of Germans around, and there were mighty few Americans around, and we weren't in a position to do a whole lot of powerful fighting, remembering that we went in with very light equipment, very little ammunition, traveling light because we had to climb these cliffs. We had no mortars with us. We had one bazooka, some BARs, and this was the extent of our heavy weapons. The remainder was just submachine guns and rifles. This isn't the ideal equipment to beat off any kind of determined enemy attack. Later on this afternoon . . . the day, looking back, to me seems like one of the shortest days of my life. I know the name of it is the longest day, but the hours and looking back seem to go so fast. I didn't realize that time had gone this fast. About 6:00, we realized that we weren't going to be relieved by the 29th Division that day. They were having, as we found out, all kind of trouble down there themselves. So we realized that we were by ourselves out here, and for a while we weren't even sure that the Americans hadn't turned around and gone back to England and left us in there by ourselves. We knew that there was a group of Rangers back at the edge of the cliff, where Col. Rudder and the remainder of our force was. This was where they were treating the casualties. Our battalion sergeant was back there. We had some naval shore fire-control personnel there. We had some men from the 29th Division Recon who were back there with some communication men, and there were a fair number of Rangers back there who were operating from this particular perimeter. If you can visualize what this was . . . there was a perimeter around the edge of the cliff down by the beach . . . I'd say maybe 50 or 75 yards in diameter in which the casualties were, Col. Rudder and these other men that I just mentioned. And then inland almost three quarters of a mile, we had another perimeter where our sixty men from D, E, and F Companies had set up this perimeter. In between these two perimeters were the Germans, and by then they were coming out of the ground, and there was a tremendous number of them underground, as we found out. I wouldn't know the numbers, but I would say several hundred at least, and knowing the terrain and knowing these underground rooms that they had and the passages back and forth, it seemed like they were able to come aboveground, shoot, go underground, reappear maybe 50 or 75 yards away, and shoot some more. So pretty soon, people stopped going back and forth between the group that was out on the perimeter, around the hedgerows, and the group that was in the perimeter back at the edge of the cliff. We did get a few messages back and forth in the course of the day. The last directive that we received from Col. Rudder was that we were to establish a perimeter out there and spend the night out on this hedgerow perimeter. I moved the men off the road inland several hundred yards, and we tied in with the other two companies. We were around three sides of this large field. D Company was on the right flank. E Company was facing north and the center, and F Company was a continuation of E Company, and their flank was refused or bent around to the left to protect the left flank. Another platoon from the 5th Ranger Battalion, which had landed on D-day down at Omaha Beach, broke through and joined us this evening . . . I'd say about 6:00 or 7:00. Lt. Parker commanded this group. We were so happy to see him. This was the first men from Omaha that we saw, and it was the first time we realized that the invasion was there to stay, that there were other men down there, and eventually they were going to come up and join us. However, he had done almost the same thing we had done[, which] was just to move through German-held area with the Germans closing in behind him. So they joined our force and helped continue this perimeter and went down farther on the left flanks. So at this stage . . . this is about 8:00 or 9:00 at night . . . we had roughly seventy-five to a hundred Rangers . . . no, I guess it wasn't over seventy-five Rangers around this perimeter of this field. Lt. Armand and Lt. Lavery and myself had sort of got together and decided what we were going to do. Lt. Armand was the senior lieutenant, and he sort of acted as commander and told us what he would like to have us do. And then we went out and rejoined our companies and prepared to spend the night out on this perimeter. It didn't get dark in France then until I guess it was 11:00 or 11:30 at night. We had double daylight savings time that we were operating under. We pushed the time back two hours from what it normally was, and the nights were rather short then, getting dark at 11:30 and getting light about 4:30. I remember placing the men, that it was still daylight, and telling them what our mission was and what we expected to do, which was to hold this perimeter that night, and we expected to be rejoined by the other Allied troops in the morning. I had at this time eighteen or twenty Rangers from D Company. I established a CP in the corner of this hedgerow where our flank joined the flank of E Company. There was some dead Germans just down in the field just in front of us . . . 40 or 50 yards, where they had currently pitched a tent and were bivouacking there as perhaps part of the force that was manning these guns that we discovered, and I recall going down there and rooting around in this tent to see if we could find any food. We hadn't had a thing to eat since we had eaten breakfast at 4:00 in the morning. This was at 8:00 or 9:00. There is nothing really more horrible and harder to try and eat than a D-ration bar when you're really hungry and when you don't have a whole lot of water. There again we were carrying one canteen of water. Men want to hoard water when they're in combat, because you never know when you're going to get a chance to refill your canteen. At least this applied to me, and I'm sure it applied to most of the men that I knew. Well, anyway, we were hungry. We went down, looked in this tent, and I remember finding a chunk of black or dark-gray bread . . . hard, but it tasted wonderful. This was food. We ate that. We divvied it up among the few men that were right at that area there. And also I remember picking up out of this some small, white-colored cigars. I thought, well, we might find some good use for these, and I put them in my pocket, and it turned out later that this was a very good idea. We went back and we got in this perimeter this night to prepare for the night. We had put some men out in front of our lines on a listening post. Right almost as soon as it got dark . . . it must have been about 11:30 or 12:00, and everything was very quiet. We hadn't had any firing going on in our area for several hours, and we were beginning to relax and feel that the war was almost over for us anyway, and very shortly the friendly troops were going to come up, and we were going to go back to England. We had accomplished our D-day mission. All of a sudden, my first recollection is the blowing of whistles and then a lot of yelling and then a flare being fired and then a series of explosions. We found out what had happened. The Germans knew we were there. They had planned this night attack . . . a very well-planned, coordinated night attack. They had crept up within 50 to 75 yards of our position, and the whistle was the signal to start the attack. The flare was a supplementary signal. They threw grenades out in front of them and started firing, and they made this all-out attack on our position. Well, this was the most frightening moment of my . . . I guess my entire life, from being completely quiet and silent and everything to this tremendous firing outbreak going on, grenades bursting, flares, men yelling, whistles blowing, and it just seemed that there were hundreds and hundreds of Germans running towards us. We began to see them in the outline and from their firing. It wasn't real dark at night. You could make out an outline. We started returning their fire then. This first attack apparently was repulsed because they didn't break our line on this first attack. We did suffer casualties. They knocked off our listening post that we had put out in front of us. I was down in this hole right where our line joined E Company. I was in this hole with Sergeant Fate, who was the next in command of my platoon. Sgt. Lomell, who was in charge of the other platoon, was further up the hedgerow. It was sort of a loosely commanded affair. We were still thinking in terms of both teams, which meant that my men were under me and Lomell's men were under him, but at the time I was the acting company commander, and I did issue some orders to them. However, Sergeant Lomell was a real fine soldier with more military experience than I'd had, and I usually counseled with him before we decided what we were going to do. Well, anyway, my first impression was that it was going to run right over the top of us, and where I was on one flank of the line, I felt like it wasn't the right position. I thought I should get up in the center of the line where the remainder of the men were, but the flare started to fade, I said, "Look, this is what I'm going to do. We're going to get all the men together, and we're going to pull out of our line. We'll go around and make an attack in the rear of these Germans." Because we couldn't accomplish much, we couldn't fire much. Our particular flank was in a deep hedgerow. Most of the fire being returned to the Germans was from the E and F Companies, which was on this open hedgerow on the north flank. Well, anyway, I jumped up out of this hole to go with Sgt. Fate up there. I took my rifle with me, but I was carrying a cartridge belt on a pair of suspenders that supported it, and I'd taken this off just prior to this, and I left this in the hole. Well, on this belt was my canteen, a D-ration bar, my extra ammunition, and my cigarettes. So I took off, and all I had was my rifle, my pistol, my bandolier of ammunition wrapped around my neck, and the ammunition for the pistol in the belt. I didn't have water or anything to eat. I had these five cigars in my pocket. Well, anyway, I started up this hedgerow. As I went along, my men were dug into the hedgerow emplacement where the Germans had been, actually . . . foxholes . . . two to a hole, and I told them, I said, "Now, I want you to follow me, and we're going to go up here and we're going to go around and attack it in the rear." Well, one of the first holes I got to was Sgt. Lomell, and when I got up I jumped in the hole with Lomell and told him what I wanted to do. I was pretty rattled and pretty excited. He calmed me down and said, "Now, George, what do you expect to accomplish by this? First of all, you don't know how many there are. You don't know where they are. Let's talk this thing over." Well, I was perfectly willing to talk. I had calmed down a little bit at this stage. So we decided the best thing to do was hold our present position. We were well dug in. We were in deep foxholes. Apparently, the Germans didn't know exactly where we were. They were attacking an area rather than specific men. So we went back and told the men again, "Stay in your holes. Don't get out until I tell you." By then, the second German attack had hit us. This was about fifteen minutes later. The first attack, I jumped out of the hole, went up there, went back in the hole, and the Germans hit us again. The second attack overran the position held by E Company and part of F Company. These two companies decided that they couldn't hold what they had, and they decided to withdraw. They withdrew around to their left, and we did not know they were pulling out. We were over on the right, dug in this hedgerow. So the Germans made one more attack and then found out that they had captured the position. E and F had gone. They didn't know we were in this hedgerow. We were in a real thick hedgerow, very heavily overgrown with underbrush and deep holes. So the Germans had captured the positions with us in the middle of it. They didn't know it. Of course we knew it, but we weren't telling them. I was not in communication with any of my men. I was in a hole. I forget where I left Sgt. Fate . . . whether he stayed back with Sgt. Lomell or not . . . but I had gone up this line of hedgerows to try and find my men, and I got up to the edge of the position just about the time this last attack hit us. So I got in a hole up there by myself, and all of my men were in these holes. As I found out later, there was only two of the men that were discovered and captured by the Germans along this hedgerow after the attack was over. The rest of us were not discovered, even though the Germans were on both sides of the hedgerow. They were all around us. We just dug in this heavy underbrush and hid. Actually, that's what it was. All of this night, I stayed in this hole. Early the next morning, I heard a rustling in this ditch that ran through this hedgerow, and of course I was naturally scared. I figured it was the Germans coming down and digging us out, and was all set to try and defend myself when I realized they were some Americans. There were two Americans from E Company that had been left behind when E Company went back to . . . E and F Companies when they pulled out from this perimeter . . . had gone all the way back to Pointe du Hoc, back to the perimeter around the cliff. We were the only ones out there in this field. I think there was fifteen of us. These two men from E Company came in and joined us, and they got in the hole with me, and they had some water, fortunately. I don't know whether they had any food or not. I had these cigars, no matches. The matches were wet or back in my belt. I didn't have a canteen, no water. We sort of shared what little we had. They had a couple of D-ration bars and had some water. Actually, from here on in, there wasn't a whole lot exciting that happened. The Germans were in the field out in front of us, but they were in such numbers that I didn't consider it the smartest thing in the world to fire at them. We had weapons there, but there was just three of us, and there were probably a hundred Germans in this field, facing the other way, fighting the Americans who were coming up from Omaha. This was the second day that the American tanks tried to get through, and they were shelled by German artillery and forced to withdraw. So all of D plus 1 . . . we stayed in this ditch with the Germans around us. The Germans . . . we couldn't see too many. We knew they were in the hedgerow in back of us. We knew they were out in front of us, but you could only see a few of them at a time. They were good soldiers. We didn't see any Americans. During this time, we were shelled by the battleship *Texas* . . . which were shelling the Germans, actually, who were all around us. After these Germans had beaten off this tank attack coming up from Omaha, the battleship *Texas* put them under fire, and these 14-inch shells were landing in this field, some within 50 yards of where we were in these holes. This was also a terrifying experience. That shell, when it would land, would dig a hole I guess 15 to 20 feet in diameter and 4 or 5 feet deep. You could imagine what a noise it made when it went off. Unfortunately, we didn't know where the next was going to land, either, while they were firing. I can't say that I . . . I had a prayer book in my pocket . . . I'm Roman Catholic, and I did a tremendous amount of praying when I was in that ditch. I read that prayer book through from cover to cover, I suppose, a half-dozen times, and I prayed very, very sincerely for that. Actually, I suppose it might seem apropos, but since then I felt so guilty of all the things I asked for on D-day . . . asked the Lord to do for me[, which] was primarily to get me out of there alive, that I have been almost ashamed to ever ask anything since then. I think I used up all I had coming to me on D-day. Well, anyway, this brought us up to the night of D+1. The Germans had apparently pulled out that night, because we didn't see or hear any Germans around us that night. Daylight the next morning, I didn't see any Germans. I didn't hear any Germans, and I was tired of being in this ditch in this hole without anything to eat. The water was practically gone by then, and I figured we might as well get out of there and find out what was going on. So I got out of the hole and started down this hedgerow to see if any of my men were still in these holes. I realized that I hadn't talked to them or seen them . . . seen any of them since the night of D-day at roughly about 1:00 or 2:00 in the morning. They had not seen each other. Each group, and there was usually two of them in these holes down there, had no contact with the adjacent group. Now, every one of these groups felt, I'm sure, the same way I did, that we were the only Americans left out there in France or in that part of France. We figured the others had been captured or killed and we were out there by ourselves. As it turned out, there was I think fourteen of us that were still alive in the holes, with one man wounded. We found several of the men who had been killed. We found some equipment from some of our men that apparently they had taken off, and they were captured by the Germans. But all of these men were certainly glad to see me, and I was certainly glad to see them, except I almost got shot a couple of times when I come running up this hedgerow and sort of burst on them all of a sudden. I realized they hadn't seen anybody or any Americans for a long time, and anybody running up there . . . they probably figured it was the Germans. So I guess I come close to getting shot by my own men there as I came up this hedgerow. Well, anyway, we decided to say that the Germans had left our immediate area, and we were going to [go] back and find out where the Americans were. I got the men together, including the two wounded men that we had with us. Sgt. Lomell and Sgt. Frann . . . they were the two wounded men. And we got down to the road . . . coming up this road just about the time we reached it was a column of American troops, and I can remember just as plain as I'm sitting here, right up behind the lead scout was Col. Cannon, who was the commander of the 116th Infantry and since went on to become a major general or lieutenant general and commanded the troops over in Berlin . . . a very, very wonderful war record. But Col. Cannon come up this road with one hand bandaged up. He had been wounded. I know he had a weapon in the other hand. I forget what it was. We were so glad to see him. Well, Col. Cannon was all soldier, and all he wanted to know was, Where are the Germans? And all I wanted to know was, Where are the Americans at this stage? I couldn't tell him much. Naturally, I had been in this ditch for several days. He wanted to know whether the Rangers were still back at Pointe du Hoc. I said, "I didn't know that." There was firing going on over at Pointe du Hoc at this time, so this column of troops of the 116th went on up this road, and that night they fought for Grand Camp. In the meantime, our troop started back down the road. First we decided to go back to Pointe du Hoc . . . straight on back to join our troops, but they told us . . . these American troops coming through told us that the Germans were fighting back at Pointe du Hoc, so we decided to go further back this road towards Omaha to see if we could meet up with any of our men. We got back the road a half mile or a mile or so, and we found some of our men who had come up from Omaha Beach, and we had a little reunion. We got something to eat. We weren't real anxious at this stage to get back and start fighting anymore. There wasn't anybody around to tell us to go fight. We took care of our wounded. We went to an aid station there, and we got something to eat, and then we set off for Pointe du Hoc. As we came up towards Pointe du Hoc, the Germans were withdrawn. We didn't do any more fighting then, and we rejoined the remainder of our Ranger group back at Pointe du Hoc, I suppose about 12:00 on D+2. The

Lt. Kerchner receiving DSC from Lt. Col. Rudder

afternoon of this same day, D+2, the remainder of our group, which wasn't too many men at this stage. I suppose out of the 225 that we went in with, we had maybe a hundred men left. We were rejoined by the remainder of our battalion, which had landed down at Omaha Beach, and the 5th Ranger Battalion, and we set off following the 116th Infantry up the coast road towards Grand Camp. We followed the 116th. We didn't capture Grand Camp. They captured Grand Camp. And we did very little fighting there. Later the next day, heading down towards the town, some of our men captured a German battery over near Maize, with a large number of prisoners and some booty. I was not in on this particular action. We were placed in Corp Reserve, I think, at that time, and actually we stayed in Corp Reserve for several weeks. We got replacements up several weeks later, and we were given time to train these people before we ever got back and saw any more action some time after that.

Ranger Hoffman

SSGT. BILL HOFFMAN

Could you tell us what kind of career plans you had before the war started? What were you thinking about in general?

Times were tough, and I was in the CCC for three years. Then I came back and I got a job, and then came Pearl Harbor. So I went with my buddy down to the shipyard because we wanted to get onboard a gasoline tanker. But they wouldn't let us. We didn't have a seaman's card, so we just went and joined the Army.

So did you enlist or were you drafted?

I enlisted. I went to Ft. Meade, Maryland, which was a training division. Went through the basic training cycle and was supposed to ship out with the troops when they got finished. But they pulled me off orders and said they were going to keep me as an instructor on the M1 rifle. So they did that for two cycles, and then somebody came down from Regiment and said, "Who is this guy you keep pulling off orders? You can't keep him there; he doesn't have any rank." So the old man said, "I'll make him a corporal." So I didn't make PFC, I made corporal, and I continued doing that. But I used to get home on the weekends, and I got tired of hearing about all the other local guys who were overseas. So I figured I better get out of that training outfit. So luckily, in one of the morning formations, the first sergeant mentioned something about the Rangers. He said he didn't even know what it was, but if anybody's interested, come down to the orderly room after this formation and we'll talk about it. So later on I went down to the orderly room, thought maybe this is my chance to get out. I didn't like the first sergeant and he didn't like me either, so when I told him I wanted to volunteer for the Rangers, he said, "No. Get your butt out of here and get to work. Now. Get out." So I was standing outside the orderly room there and I heard somebody walk in, and it was the company commander. He asked me why I was there, and I told him what happened. He said, "I don't see any problem with this here." And he told the first sergeant to process the paperwork. So that's how I got out. Then they threw me on a big 5-ton truck and took me to Cannon Company, which was way on the other side of the post, and a bunch of guys were standing out in the field. There must have been two hundred guys standing in groups. I took my bag and kind of shuffled up to one of the groups. And then Lt. Stone and Capt. Slater came out and said, "Listen up, all you people. You guys from here over, this is D Company, 2nd Ranger Battalion." Then he introduced Lomell as his first sergeant, and Lomell came over to me and this other buck sergeant. By that time, I had made buck too. Lomell said, "You two guys go over to Cannon Company and find out when they're going to feed this bunch." So we went to the mess hall, and while we were gone, they started to interview everybody. "Were you willing to take reduction in rank to stay with this unit?" Which nobody knew anything about. "Can't promise you anything. All leaves and passes are canceled. You want to stay, fine. You don't, say so and get out." So I don't know how many guys left. Anyway, we came back and told Lomell the time to eat and all that. And that was it. After that, we were transferred to Camp Forrest for Ranger training.

So how was the Ranger training different from what you got at Ft Meade?
All the world. When I think back, it was, oh god, basic was no training at all, really. You know, you'd march, you handled the rifle. All this kind of stuff, manual arms, and all that. But this deal here with the Rangers was something else. Every place you went you had to run, and there was a whole lot of calisthenics. One of the drills was ten guys picked up a log. We had to get it up over our heads, throw it up in the air, and catch it. Then we had to put it down and do it all over again. And road marches. We had constant roadwork. [There were] 3-, 5-, 10-, 20-mile marches. Speed marches. And a lot of hand-to-hand combat. The one that sticks in my mind was, there was a sawdust pit about the size of this room, with logs on the side about this high. And they put a squad in there, or a platoon even, in the pit. Then the other platoon was supposed to get them out of there. Guys were getting broken arms and stuff from this. Really bad. But of course it took us a while to find out the secret was for two guys to get together and grab one guy and throw him out of the pit. Just physically throw him out. We also had a lot of weapons training, constant demolition training with mines, and devices to set off the explosives.

On the rifle range, have you ever heard of the concept of Maggie's drawers?
Yeah. If you shot at the target and you missed, the guy waved a red flag. Maggie's drawers.

So then after Camp Forrest, you went to Ft. Pierce, Florida?
Right. Supposed to be scouts and Ranger school, amphibious operations, stuff like that. On one training drill, we got into a rubber boat and paddled out a mile or so. Then they tipped the boat over, and we had to scramble around the water, right the thing and get back in there, and paddle back. Then another time we went swimming in the ocean, and the water was full of jellyfish. And there were a lot of sandflies everywhere, constantly. I was glad to get out of there.

I see. From there you went to Ft. Dix. Is that right?
Right. That's where we had a big formal inspection of all the gear laid out in front of the tents. After that we went up to, I think it was Camp Shanks, up in New York. And from there over to Scotland. We got on the Queen Elizabeth, and we had no escort going over. When we got to Scotland, we debarked and got on a train, and they took us all the way down to southern England, Cornwall. Bude. That's where we were billeted in private homes. They just happened to have some cliffs laying [*sic*] around the area. I don't [remember] which commando unit trained us, but they were a pretty good bunch. Mostly Scottish guys.

Do you remember the Christmas Eve party there? I guess it must have been '43 for the children of Bude?
Yeah. They had a big mob. That's the thing to do.

I guess most of you guys had extra D rations and oranges or whatever, and you would give these to the children?
Yes, but we had to give the people we were billeted with the ration cards. There were two guys to a family, so that would double rations. They made out pretty well on that. They'd welcome us in, sit by the fire, make a cup of tea. Then go upstairs, "I'll show you your bedroom." It was like being home. And then in the morning, according to what our schedule was, we would meet down in front of the theater by 6:30. But then maybe we wouldn't come back for two or three days, and the people wondered where we were. Like "What time are you going to come back for dinner?" "Can't say."

Now, would you say that the additional training you received as a Ranger really did affect your performance on the battlefield?
One hundred percent. I talk to my former CO twice a week. He's out in Albuquerque. He's ninety-one now. If it wasn't for him, I wouldn't be talking to him today. But he made me do stuff I didn't know I could do.

Now, which CO was this that you are referring to?
Jack Slater, it was. He had a little bad luck on D-day. After all this training we went through, he's in one of the assault boats, going in for the landing, and he's out in the middle of the Channel and the boat sinks. He was swamped in bad weather, but the survivors were picked up and sent back to England to get refitted. Weapons and stuff. And of

course we went on in and on up and all that. And I think we were dug in the hedgerows or somewhere, a week, ten days later, when here he comes. "Hey, Captain, where you been? The war's over." Boy, he was mad; he was mad.

So you actually told him that?

Yeah. But before that, when we heard that his boat had gone down, I got his officer's bedroll. When I opened it up, there was a nice bottle of scotch in there. All right. I talked to him today. I said, "I owe you one, Captain." He's a lieutenant colonel now. Good guy. Well, on the way up to Ft. Dix, there was so much competition between companies that fights would break out between them. So the commander said, "I'm gonna take eight men from each company and move them all around. Tone this thing down." So I went to Captain Slater on the train, and I was on my knees, "Don't move me. I don't want to leave D Company." But it worked out; I didn't have to go.

So do you think the training provided you with a good understanding of what battlefield conditions were all about?

Well, I don't know. If you've never been in combat before, you don't have a clue. People ask me, Were you afraid? No. There was nothing to be afraid of, actually. You could think this could happen, or that. But when you're there and somebody's shooting at you, then you're mad. You're mad. That's what it comes down to. But the thing to be afraid of for me was the artillery, which you can't do anything about.

Well, let's move on and talk about what your thoughts were the night before you were deployed to get on the boats to go to the invasion. What was running through your mind?

I guess it was like another maneuver. But I was up most of the night. I remember leaning on the railing of the boat, just kind of looking out at the water, and there were two or three parachutes blown up, floating by. There were three guys drowned, going the opposite way. So I thought, "What are we getting into here?" Then after that there was no time to think about anything.

So were you on LCAs or Higgins boats? Do you remember what you were thinking about at that time?

They were British. I guess they were LCAs. But there was not much time to think about anything. The lead boat was British and, I think, had those black and white stripes on, like the airplanes had on their wings. So everybody else was following him, and then the colonel decides this guy's going to the wrong place, which he was. Then all of a sudden we moved to the right, and now we're going parallel to the cliffs. Then I noticed they're shooting at us. You couldn't hear gunfire, just kuk, kuk, in the water. Then all of a sudden our three companies, D, E, and F, are headed in. D Company was supposed to go around the Pointe and come up on the other side, with no time. We're like thirty minutes late. The rest of the 2nd and the 5th were laying [*sic*] offshore waiting, and we were supposed to [send?] them out a talley-ho and then we'd all go up together. It didn't happen that way. So the rest of the 2nd and the 5th went in on Omaha, which was not too swift.

On your LCA, did you have the rocket-propelled grappling arms?

Right. There were six rockets on each boat. You had the front legs and the back legs. They had a board with holes in it, so you could adjust the angle. Lomell was gonna be the one doing the shooting. Since the cliffs were so high, you had to be so far out to get the hooks all the way up. And everything was rocketed. I was sitting right next to Lomell, and he had a little wall switch there, a toggle switch. And there was a woosh and a little smoke when he set them off. But then three rockets just hit the face of the cliff and went down. Oh darn, now what? 'Cause I had been assigned a particular rope, but I don't remember any plan Bs at all. Like, if the rope doesn't go up, do such and such. So there was a little confusion when we got off the boat, 'cause they were shooting. And you grab the rope and somebody says, "Hey, hey, that's mine." But we finally sorted it out and we went up. There were two guys who had a little rocket projector which sent up a light rope, like a clothesline. Then they would hook a heavy rope or whatever they wanted to do, to pull that up. I remember those two guys. And then we had the DUKWs with the ladders, but the Germans sunk those. They were no good. Well, they were good; it was just that it didn't work. They had a steel plate up top and a cover for two Lewis guns, and they were supposed to give us covering fire up on top while we went up the ropes, but it didn't work out that way.

So when you got off your LCA, what did you see?

Right in front of me was the cliff, and when I finally got up on top, the first thing I saw was a dead German there. No clothes on. No blood. No head. Head was gone. He was naked as a jaybird and all covered with yellow, like cordite from the explosions. The battleship *Texas* was out there firing some big ones in. So I looked at that and I thought, "That's strange. I've never seen that before." Then we moved in a little bit, and I went to this gun emplacement where I was supposed to go. I had some C-2 demolitions in my pockets, but there was no gun. That was confusing. We had seen pictures from the day before, which the British had taken, flying at cliff-top level. And the guns were there. So, OK, there's no gun. But Lomell took a patrol out and he found the guns, and that's what they got rid of them.

So when you were climbing, one of the grappling hooks had caught up there and then you pulled yourself up?

Get over, yeah. And we had studied photographs of the cliffs from the British. We thought maybe we could free-climb up at certain spots, but we couldn't tell for sure from the photos. So we just scrambled up. And they had, I think, 4-foot sections of aluminum ladders which snapped together, but that was later on. I didn't have one of those.

So at the time you were climbing, nobody was throwing grenades at you, or shooting at you?

Oh yeah, the Germans were, on top of the cliffs. They cut a couple of ropes with guys on it. And down they went.

So as you were climbing, were you looking up to see if anybody was shooting at you?

No, there was too much stuff coming down. This chalk stuff was coming down. So I was just focusing on getting to the top.

You mentioned that you looked for the guns because you had the C-2 ready to discharge it. Did all of you, whether it be noncoms or privates or whatever, know what the primary and secondary objectives were on that day?

Our unit was better briefed than a lieutenant or a captain in a regular infantry outfit. Everybody was equal. Everybody got in on the same briefing. Not like you tell the lieutenant, and the lieutenant tells the sergeant, and he tells his men. Stuff gets lost in the translation when you do it that way.

So when you got to the top, you continued to go inland. When you found out the guns weren't there, what was your secondary objective then?

We were supposed to get out to the coastal road, which wasn't too far, and secure that against any movement. That was it, but what got me was all the looking for landmarks. There was supposed to be a two-story barracks for the gun crews. That was gone. The air force just wiped it out, and the area was just shell holes. Except for the cow. There was one cow over there. All by himself.

So later that day, I guess you were on patrols, and I guess it was then when Sergeant Lomell was on a patrol and came across the 155 mm guns.

Jack Hume and Lomell both did. I wasn't with them for that.

But you were close by.

Just dug in, 'cause they were shelling the area pretty good.

And that evening there were three or four German counterattacks to try to resecure the coastal road? And you basically repelled them, you stayed your positions?

That's what we had to do, because if we hadn't done that, there was nothing at our back except the ocean. They would have run us right off the cliff. So that gave us a little incentive to try harder. We didn't get any sleep that night?

Is there anything else that you want to describe about the Normandy landings? Anything that we missed?

Just the enormity of the thing. It was so big. I got to actually look out towards the ocean and see the ships, and it was hard to believe they could put together something like that. Amazing.

So you had a great view from up on the top of the cliff then?
A good view, after we got rid of the few Germans up there. They had antiaircraft guns protecting the big guns, and they were trying to angle them down to shoot down the cliff, but they couldn't. But they had machine guns and grenades. They kept throwing those things down like crazy.

So from the time you landed on D-day until the time Brest started, which was about the middle of August, were there any notable firefights or anything important that you want to mention?
Not that I can remember. One time they said, "OK, load up in the trucks." This was going to be the attack on Brest, so we went up the peninsula there; I don't know how far. And then they stopped and the lead truck came on back. I don't know what happened there, but we didn't really go in at that time. What's that guy, that lieutenant, their platoon leader? I guess he had about four or five guys, and they went into to that Graf Spee Battery and nine thousand guys came out.

Are there specific moments of the Brest Campaign that you recall, or just a lot of firefights in that one?
We did a lot of patrolling. I used to hate that. We were mainly patrolling in the fields, at least where we were anyway.

Would you say Brest was just as difficult as the Normandy Campaign?
Oh yeah. It was tough. They were trying to elevate the guns so they could fire where we were moving in. But they couldn't do that.

OK, I guess the next major thing the Rangers were involved in was the Hürtgen Forest, from the middle of September through November. What do you recall about the Hürtgen that was different than the Normandy Campaign, for instance?
Well, the Hürtgen was a wooded area, and we were dug in because the Germans were shelling us. So we'd get those tree bursts. To me it was the land of the 6-foot trees. Man, there were beautiful forests, but they just chopped it up. So we dug holes, big three-man holes. They weren't real deep, but they were covered with logs and ponchos and dirt and stuff on top. And we stayed there for a while, patrolling from there.

Obviously the weather was much colder then, and it was raining and sleet, and so the conditions were a little worse. Would you say that the visibility was very poor in the Hürtgen?
Yeah, you couldn't see any distance. We ran into all sorts of stuff there later. And the Germans had those green uniforms on, so they were hard to see. They liked to mess around at night. That was their favorite. It was hard to get the replacement guys to stay down, and after six o'clock, anything that moves out there, shoot. One of the kids thought he saw somebody, so he said, "Halt! Who goes there?" So he stands up and there was a German with a Schmeisser, who took off right away. But there was a lot of stuff like that. And if you had to go, you had to use your helmet, because if you got out of your hole, you were dead. It was automatic. You knew that.

So the standing order for the GIs was not to get out of the hole after six o'clock? So if that's the standing order and somebody was moving, it wasn't a GI?
Right. Or, it shouldn't be a GI.

So you never set up patrols at nighttime?
Oh yeah, there were patrols that went out.

Well, then how did the other GIs know? I guess they were informed that there was a patrol going out?
The guys in foxholes got briefed that there would be a patrol passing through, and they got a separate password, just for the patrol. And when you were out on patrol, you never came back the same way. But when you came back through the line there, you better be in the right place too. Mostly it was a reconnaissance patrol, looking for any movement of trucks or people. That was about it.

Well, then I guess that would move us chronologically to Hill 400, which was the first week of December. I understand that Companies A, B, C, and E pretty much had the flanks and the security. And Companies D, your company, and F were assigned to go up the middle. Now, were you briefed about what you were trying to accomplish in advance?

Well, the patrols went out to feel around and see what was out there and where. Then they'd come back and brief the commander on that. But the object was take the hill, because the Germans had their observation post up there, and the other side was the Ruhr River. So you could see everything from where they were. We were in the town there. First they said the Germans had half of the town, but they didn't.

Was that Bergstein?

Yeah. And I remember when we were moving through the town, it was cold, wet, rainy, mud. Lots of mud. And there was one tank I remember that the turret was blown off on the side. It was dark and we were coming up, and this other column was going through us. Going back. They had been in the town and got their butt kicked. When we got in there, we used one of the houses there as a headquarters. And then in the morning, around seven o'clock, it was cold and I came down and everybody was outside. We got on the road, on both sides of it, and there was the hill. You could see it, but we had open ground between the end of the town and base of the hill. I remember walking, and then all of a sudden the artillery came in, called in by the Germans up the hill. So everybody got off to the side of the road. I moved up and behind the one house, and my platoon leader was down on his knees holding his head. I stopped and took my BAR and set it down and took his helmet off, and I didn't see anything wrong with his head. And that was it. I turned around and hollered for the medic, and that's all I remember. Then at eight o'clock that night, I woke up. I was in the same house, with a couple of tankers, 'cause they had that coverall stuff on. And I was just laying [*sic*] on a mattress. The Germans were still shelling us. I must have moved or coughed or something, and one of the guys came over and asked me if I wanted a cup of coffee. Oh, did I want a cup of coffee. So I'm saying yes, but I'm not talking. I can't talk. And so he looks at me and shrugs his shoulder and goes back. But a short time after that, someone threw a blanket on me, and that's when I saw the lieutenant sitting on the floor in the kitchen. He had a blanket on him and he was leaning up against the wall, and the whole side of the house was missing there. So pretty soon a jeep came up, and they took us down the road a couple of hundred yards. There was a half-track dumped over in the middle of the road, with all the gear thrown around. They told us to go around to the other side of the half-track and there would be a meat wagon to pick us up. So they took us back to, I think it was a forward aid station, and put me to sleep for two days. Later on I found out the medic put "Psychoneurosis, Severe" on my tag. That was the diagnosis of why I couldn't talk. So I stayed there a couple of days and they fed me, and then I went back to the outfit. I don't remember where they were, but later on up the road it happened again. This time when I woke up, I was in Paris at the First General Hospital there. I had an interview with the doctor, and he stamped the papers, "EVAC UK." And they sent me to England. But, to spice all of this up, they sent me back to a British camp, Tidworth. And the MPs who had been stationed there moved to France. So there were eight of us staff sergeants, and they told us we were going to be MPs. Because at the time, they were starting to move people back to the States, getting ready to go to Japan. So we were just guarding convoys taking men down to, I think it was Southampton, to get on a boat to go to Japan. But to top that all off, when I finally got a ride back on the *Queen Mary*, the discharge papers said, "14th Port Battalion." Like I'd never been in the Rangers. But that's where I left from, the 14th Port Battalion. What else they gonna put on there? So that ticked me off [to] no end.

When they sent you off to a forward aid station and they fed you and put you to sleep for a couple days, were you close enough to the battlefield where you could hear the guns and artillery?

No, I don't remember hearing anything. It wasn't a pyramidal tent; it was a big, long one, filled with cots and a bunch of guys snoring. It was dark in there. A guy told me to lay [*sic*] down and take these two pills. There was a canteen for the water. We called them "Blue 88s," but I don't know what they were. Then I remember somebody shaking me and telling me to get up and get something to eat. He was handing me a mess kit, and there was bright sunshine. But they didn't know what it was or how to handle it. What do they call it now, "posttraumatic stress syndrome"? In fact, in the hospital they were handing out Purple Hearts, a major and a lieutenant. When they got to me, I said, "I don't want that." They said, "You're supposed to have it." I said no. I'm thinking these other guys are really beat up. This guy's got no leg, no arm; I mean, really beat up. So they moved on to the next bunk and on out. So I don't know if what I had was a "wound." They didn't even have it classified. And I'm happy it ain't on my discharge papers.

Getting back to right before you suffered probably the concussion in the Hill 400, was that artillery barrage American, or was that German artillery barrage?

I would say German, but I don't know for sure. They had the observation post up there, so they had a good view of us.

I know that there were probably barrages from both sides, but I didn't know which one you went through. But I think that's part of the reason why the Rangers were able to get up there and hold that hill. Because the Germans were keeping their heads down due to all the artillery.

Could be. That's the thing about artillery. You don't know where it's coming from or whose it is. You can't do anything about it except maybe dig in.

I noticed that you got two Bronze Stars, is that right?

Yeah. One was for the landing, and the other one, I don't know. I must have done something. I'd have to look it up.

As a Ranger, do you think that the noncoms and commissioned officers had immediate respect from their soldiers, or do you think it took a while for them to develop that respect in the field?

It took awhile. It's like any other thing. It takes time.

So just because you were a staff sergeant, that didn't mean the private was going to respect you until he saw you leading a patrol or something.

Yeah. But the point is, you could have done away with ranks, really. Everybody did the same thing, from the company commander on down. There was nobody left behind.

What do you believe are important attributes to being a good leader in that setting?

He would have to show by example. I mean actually do. In other words, "I wouldn't ask my men to do anything I wouldn't do myself." And that should be their creed. That demands respect right there. You know, you got a real lousy job to do or whatever, and he's there. Hey, what more could you ask.

Are there any other characteristics of an effective noncommissioned officer or officer?

You gotta be sharp. You gotta know your stuff, know your subject. If you're in mortars, you gotta know the mortars inside out. If you're a rifleman or a platoon sergeant or something like that, you gotta know the tactics. And you heard stories about how an infantry outfit got really decimated, and when the battle's over and the big brass are showing up, it turns out the company commander was a corporal. That's what beat the Germans. They had too much class distinction. This guy's an officer; this guy's a peon. So when you killed a German officer, the peons didn't know what to do. They all gave up.

Do you think that Ranger training made it a more even playing field among officers, noncommissioned officers, and everybody else?

Oh yeah. Everybody could depend on everybody else. Really.

I see. Were there any other characteristics of a Ranger that made them a distinctive, elite fighting force?

The esprit de corps. Like the Marines. Semper fi. And since Omaha Beach, we had that "Rangers Lead the Way." And the other one is "Ranger Friendships Are Forever." And that's fact.

Do you think there was an attitude as well, that there may have been some characteristics within the individual that says, "I want to be the best," and just by wanting to be the best, they became the best?

Yeah, it did. You know, it was all volunteer too. I mean, each guy had his own reason for joining. And there were little things, like we got issued jump boots, instead of the buckle jobs. So right away, downtown there was this big fight with the Airborne. They questioned why we got them, because they had to complete a bunch of jumps before they could get them. Big fight.

Are there any examples of noncoms or officers that you knew of, who you would say had good leadership skills?
I thought all our noncoms were "A, number one." And they had the respect of their individual squads and platoons. They really did.

Is there one person who, for you personally, really stood out as an important leader in the 2nd Ranger Battalion? Or in your company?
Well, my old company commander. The one who went down in the boat. I had a very high regard for him. Like I say, I'm here now. I really was impressed with him. You know, I didn't know him until we first formed up, and I used to watch him. The way he talked and the way he moved, and when he called for a 10-mile road march, he was there. He had legs like a kangaroo. He could do things I could never do.

Anybody else other than Capt. Slater? Anyone else in your company or platoon?
They were all good. There were no guys who hung back or any of that stuff. They all led from the front.

What would you say would be the greatest accomplishment or the greatest legacy of the World War II group of Rangers?
Well, the initial mission, which Bradley said was almost impossible. Of course, we looked at it differently. It was a job, so we did it. Later on you say, oh wow. But I felt very lucky compared to Omaha, where the rest of those guys had to go in there. That's when they came up with that "Rangers Lead the Way."

When do you think was your greatest moment of fear in all your combat experience? Was there some particular moment that you really were scared, or that you really feared for the safety of yourself or your fellow soldiers?
There was one, and it was for myself. I forget the town we had occupied, but I think five guys were out in standing foxholes. I was back at the CP,[25] and it was time to check on them. So I go out and kind of sneak up on these guys, 'cause they would shoot you. So I was going around checking them all out. I got to talk to them a little bit because they're all kinda lonely out there. And I was on the way back to the CP again when the artillery started coming in. Oh man, hit the dirt. OK, but I didn't hit the dirt. There must have been a foundation for a house, because there was a concrete slab. And my muttons were getting in the way. I couldn't get down any further. And I could hear that voof, coming right over. Then finally it lifted and I got back, and there was a guard outside the house, and he had gotten killed. A shell hit the roof, and the shrapnel came down through his helmet. In fact, when I got back, me and my buddy found a jeep that was still runable, and the medics put him on top of the windshield in a litter. I drove him back, and my buddy was holding on to the litter. So we took him back to some abandoned German building, like a hospital. It looked like a big concrete slab. There was an entrance, and inside was full of double-decker bunks all over. Anyway, we got him back there and Doc worked on him, but he died.

So that was probably one of the moments that you had the greatest fear? Any other time? Did you have a lot of fear going up Pointe du Hoc or Brest, France, or Hill 400?
No. Well, I never got hit, and that makes a difference. You know, you get a couple of close ones and you're ticked off more than anything.

What would you say would be the saddest moment during your military experience?
Seeing some good buddies dead. You know they're not gonna get up, so that makes it hard.

Were there one or two in specific that really hurt you most? Somebody you were very close to?
They were all my buddies. You know, really. You say, oh jeez, why him? We really need him for whatever his specific job was. But after a while it's, oh yeah, it's another one. You don't care anymore.

Well, it's not that you don't care, but it's more that you're trying to survive.
Yeah, that's what it is.

If you're focusing on the sad parts, you're not gonna be an effective soldier, are you?

No I guess not. You can't dwell on that kind of stuff. That's for sure.

And that's an important survival mechanism, and they would want you to do that, right?

Yeah, you're right there.

They wouldn't want you to be thinking about it and then you get shot.

Yeah. And they told us, initially, no prisoners. OK, I was in one of these towns and the shelling started again. So I ran into a house and went down the steps to the cellar. There were five Germans there, rifles stacked. They were sitting down there and they had a candle, and they were eating out of big sardine cans. I got halfway down the stairs, and they looked at me and the guy says in German, "*Essen* [eat]." And the other one says, "*Zigerette, Zigerette*." I had five clips and five cigarettes. I threw them a pack. I went back up the stairs and left. This was in Germany.

Germany? And so the orders at the time were "No Prisoners"?

Yeah. I was supposed to shoot the five of them. I could have. They had no weapons.

But you did the right thing?

They're there, doing what they're doing, 'cause they didn't want to be there any more than I wanted to be there. At least that's the way I looked at it.

So if you would have taken them prisoner, you would have taken them upstairs, and somebody else probably would have shot them.

I don't know.

If that's what the order was.

That would have taken me out of action too. That's the trouble with prisoners; you gotta have somebody to guard them. Or if you got a wounded guy, you gotta stay with him.

Is there any particular individual that you would want to give a tribute to, or someone who you believed did an act of valor that wasn't recognized?

No. I was amazed that what I missed most about the service was the uniformity of getting things done. When I got out, everything was haphazard with no directions. Now I have no regrets.

So I understand that you carried a BAR for a while. Did you also carry a Garand for a while or a Thompson?

Yeah. Both. Anything you could lay your hands on.

What would you have personally preferred to go into battle with?

The M1 Garand. Next would be a BAR.

BAR. Because of its accuracy in short and long distances?

Yeah, it was pretty good. The weapon's good. It's the individual using it. But in the movies there's supposed to be an infantry outfit, and these guys are running around with little carbines. There were no carbines. The officers were issued carbines, and the first thing they did was throw them away and get a rifle. They also took their rank off. The Germans were great for looking for rank. And then they show some clown running around with his binoculars hanging out. Everybody didn't have binoculars [Not everybody had binoculars], and if you did, you kept it inside your jacket so the Germans didn't see it, 'cause they would think you were a leader. So everything was inside the jackets.

So I know you got an extensive training as a Ranger, but did you believe that there was a learning curve? The longer that you were in battle, the more you learned and the better you got to be as a soldier?

Oh, yeah. I would say so. They would tell us, "You could do this but you can't do that." But then we found out you could do it any way you wanted.

What are the greatest lessons you learned from your military experience? Things that really affected your life?

Organization. Organize to get things done. People ask why there's all the marching. Every place you go, you gotta be marched over. OK, let's do it your way. Everybody be over at the theater at seven o'clock. Now, you think everybody's gonna be there at seven o'clock? No. That's why they march you over there. That way, everybody's there at 7:00. Organization and discipline.

Do you think your military experience helped you see life in a different way? Learn to appreciate things more?

Well, I learned a lot about people. That overall, everybody's not nice [not everybody is nice]. Certain people have got their own little thing they have to do. It's like a learning thing, but basically it is the organization. There's a routine, so you know what you're supposed to do. Out in combat or just in garrison, there's not any difference.

What emotions do you feel when you reflect back on your military history? Would you say they're mixed feelings?

I definitely feel proud. I mean, it's not every day you can do something for your country. I ask a lot of people, What have you done for your country lately? Or your community. What have you done to improve things? But yeah, I'm proud of what I did.

When you were going through your military experience, did you realize how important this war was in the history of civilization?

No. I could see no further than the company commander at the time. This is the job; let's get her done.

You knew it was your job, you knew you had to do it, but you didn't understand how important it would be for future generations.

Well, I knew there was a war on, but maybe I wasn't old enough to know any better.

If you were to leave something for future generations and, in particular, future Rangers, what pearls of wisdom would you leave us?

I don't know. These guys are so sharp today. I can't think of anything. And when I see them, I tell them they're sharp: "We never looked like you guys do." And they do everything. They're really great. They're super. We were just the beginning. These guys know a hell of a lot more than we ever knew.

Perhaps, but if they came to you and asked you what they should strive for, what would you tell them?

Just get the job done and take care of your buddies. Which they do anyway. They follow our creed and don't leave anybody behind. And take care of everybody, and you're all family.

What would you tell a civilian to do? Is there anything you would tell us to strive for?

Sign up, and that you could do something for your country. You would think we need it now too. At this time.

So even for a civilian, do what you can to help your country.

Or just your local community. Just do something. If you're not part of the solution, you're part of the problem. You gotta do something.

1LT. CHARLES RYAN

Can you describe your experiences before World War II?

I was born in St. Louis, and within the first year of life, I lost my father from influenza. My mother's father emigrated from Ireland, while my father's family had emigrated several generations earlier from Ireland. My great-great-grandfather (Tommy Ryan) was a hunter in the early 1800s and was commissioned to accompany Lewis and Clark on their famous expedition. I grew up in St. Louis and in fact remember seeing "Butch" O'Hare when we were invited over to his home when I was a child. He was the first naval

1Lt. Charles Ryan

aviator to earn the Medal of Honor during World War II and subsequently lost his life in another mission in the Pacific theater one year later. I specifically remember that Butch on several occasions threw me into his swimming pool when I came to his house to visit. I attended CBC and played football (running back) with Babe Murphy, who was an All American. I also met Gen. Patton on a couple of occasions, met and played golf with Eddie Rickenbacker, a World War I flying ace, and developed a good working relationship with Mr. Stephen Ambrose. I also recommend reading the book *Dark and Bloody Ground*, authored by Ed Miller.

What were your interests and future employment plans prior to joining the Army?
Well, prior to joining the Army I was in school and going to college, and I had a football scholarship for Missouri University, so that was my primary interest.

Did you have a chance to complete school prior to joining the Army?
Well, I almost completed one semester, so they did give us credit for the one semester.

And then you received your draft notice?
That's a long, convoluted story. I was in the Marine Corps, the Navy Air Corps, and then I was in the Army.

How did that happen?
Well, the whole football team at Missouri U was put in what they called the B7 program, which was a Marine Corps unit. I had an eye that wouldn't pass the exam, and I tried to sneak into the Navy Air Corps with glasses, but my glasses wouldn't correct my left eye to the point where they'd accept me. So then they kicked me out of the Navy Air Corps and then they drafted me. Oh, but I had actually joined by that point.

How did you get into the Army with a bad eye?
Well, when I was taking the vision test for the Army, when it was time to check my bad eye, I covered the same eye with the opposite hand and the Doc wasn't paying attention.

Or you would have been drafted sooner?
Yes, within a month or so.

When was this?
This was in 1942.

Where were you when you heard about the attack on Pearl Harbor?
It was a Sunday morning. We were playing a touch football game, and I guess 90 percent of the guys didn't even know where Pearl Harbor was, but I had more or less followed the war since I had gone to a military school, and we were kind of involved in what was going on as far as the history and everything like that.

What were your feelings when you heard about the attack?
Oh, you know, to run down and join the service the next day.

You knew it was time to be in the Army, one way or the other?
That's right.

During your training, do you feel that the techniques that you learned and the discipline played an important role in your success on the battlefield?
To a certain extent.

Did military training provide you with a reasonable perspective of what to anticipate with regard to battlefield conditions and weather?
You're never really fully prepared for that, because when you hit the real cold weather . . . I don't know about the hot weather, but the real cold weather . . . there's no way you can prepare yourself for that.

When you were transferred to the European theater of operations?

I came over as an infantry replacement, and I arrived in Europe in January of '44.

Okay, how did you end up in the Rangers?

Well, we got a leave to London. I had a three-day pass to London, and I ran into some friends of mine who I had been in ROTC with, and they were in the Rangers, and I was telling them about all the hardships we were having at this Infantry Replacement Center, which meant doing nothing all day except lying on a bunk and trying to figure out what to do. So they said, "Why don't you volunteer for the Rangers?" So I did. Then I completely forgot about it, and then about two weeks later, my sergeant told me to grab my gear, that they were here to pick me up. And I figured, "What in the hell is going on?" 'Cause the invasion hadn't even started yet, and that's what we were mainly there for, the replacements of the infantry. So I went down and hopped in a jeep, and that's how I joined the Rangers.

And then you had some specialized training?

I didn't have too much training because they had been training for about a year and a half in England, and I joined at probably the end of March and we had a few training sessions, but that was about it.

Only a few months until D-day?

Yes.

Do you remember going to your disembarkation port in England?

Yes, I remember driving in trucks, and the English lined the road—some waving to us, others just standing, perhaps anticipating what our fate was.

What missions were the Rangers assigned on D-day?

The Rangers were assigned to two missions. The first mission was to storm Pointe to Hoc and climb the cliff and then to destroy a battery of 155 mm rifles, which had a range of 12 miles and could fire on the beachhead. So Companies D, E, and F were assigned to destroy those guns. C Company, my company, was assigned the mission to destroy the radar gun control at Pointe de le Percée, while A and B Companies were assigned to assault Dog Green Sector along with the 116th Regiment. Ultimately, A, B, and C Companies were to unite at the coastal road and attack Pointe du Hoc from an inland position if D, E, and F Companies were not successful.

Describe how you felt before the invasion.

Well, first off I was terribly seasick. Everybody was sick on the landing craft going in. We got on the craft at 12:00 midnight. Initially I was happy to get off the boat into the landing craft, but once I got in, I found out that it was twice as bad on the landing craft, and by that time, everyone was seasick on the landing craft. So it was not a happy memory. The sea was rough, and then we swirled around for several hours and finally made our run into the beach.

So did the landing craft get you close to the beach?

Well, there was a lot of confusion on D-day with regard to the landing craft. Everybody was missing their landing mark, and they were swept off course by the currents and everything like that. We were one of the few that hit our beach right on the head and landed at 6:30 in the morning, when we were supposed to land.

And what happened then, once you got off the landing craft?

Well, we got into the war, and it was like someone turning on the light switch. All of the sudden there was a war going on, and it was pretty intense.

And you were being fired at?

We landed on the western (left) flank of the Vierville Draw. There was a tremendous amount of fire. It was at low tide, and it seemed like 10 miles but it was only 200 yards of beach that we had to cross until we got to the bottom of the cliffs. And to our left flank was the 116th Regiment, and they were making the frontal attack on the Vierville Draw, which was heavily fortified. There were multiple fortified positions, which made it difficult to cross the beach, and, in fact, most of them didn't get off the beach. Within the first five minutes, they were completely wiped out, and only five men survived. B Company Rangers were coming in behind them, and they were pinned down at the beach. After we landed, we lost probably 40 to 50 percent of our men on the beach. We only had a sixty-four-man company.[26] We landed all by ourselves, and we got up to the beach wall to the cliffs,[27] and our job was to get on top of the cliffs, which we did. We immediately recognized that it would be impossible to go up the Vierville Draw. We sent a team of four climbers about 200 yards west towards Pointe du Hoc; that included Lt. Moody and Jack Stevens. They hand-climbed the cliff with their bayonets and their trench knives to the top of the cliffs. When the got to the top, they yelled down to us to come west, and threw down climbing ropes. Then the rest of the company, what was left of it, climbed the ropes; the company had reached the top of the cliff by 7:30. So technically, we were the first unit to get to the top of the cliffs on D-day.

What did you find there when you reached the top?

We were being hit with a lot of small-arms fire. And we picked up a boatload of soldiers from B Company of the 116th Regiment, and they came up the cliffs and joined us. So, at that point, we tried to consolidate our position. After scaling the cliffs, my company proceeded west to their designated position at Pointe et Raz de la Percée to knock out the radar gun control facilities that was controlling all of the artillery that was hitting our beaches. We sent a four-man patrol and realized that the radar facilities were destroyed by the preinvasion shelling from our ships and planes. The situation was chaotic, but we decided that the best action would be to take out some of the fortifications on the western slope of the Vierville Draw to eliminate these pockets that were generating intense crossfire that was decimating our troops on the beach. That's what we did; we moved east and cleaned out a bunch of machine gun nests on the west side of the Vierville Draw. However, there was a fortified house on the top that they were feeding inland troops into the area. We would clean it out, and then there would be more German troops and we would clean it out again. There was a lot of fire action all day long. And sometime around 2:00 or 3:00 or 4:00, we had secured the top of the beach. This allowed the soldiers on the beach to overrun this draw and consolidate their positions.[28] Prior to this action, the companies of the 116th Regiment (A–D Companies) and two companies of the 2nd Ranger Battalion (A and B Companies) had heavy losses on the beach. However, C Company also sustained heavy casualties on D-day; specifically, by the end of D-day, there were only fifteen wounded soldiers alive of a sixty-five-man company. We were moved out of the area after about a week and starting moving across France.

Did it ever seem like it was going to end?

The time went pretty fast; we were moving around pretty fast.

What happened the next day?

Well, that night, we were dug in and we had no idea, but we were assuming that we would get counterattacked by the enemy. We were digging in and we were getting spasmodic artillery fire all night long that day; it was a hairy night. The next day, we were joined by the A and B Companies of our battalion plus the whole 5th Ranger Battalion, which had landed to the east of us. And our primary mission was to relieve Pointe du Hoc; that is, the three companies that had landed on Pointe du Hoc that were supposed to destroy the guns on the point. That was overruled by the powers to be [powers that be]; we were directed to move inland. I had been wounded in the knee; I can't remember exactly when I got hit, but my knee just kept getting worse and it had started to bother me. So I took some prisoners down to the beach, and when I was transferring the prisoners, some doctor came up to me and told me to sit over there. I told him that I had to go back to my company, and he said, "No you don't"; I guess he thought that it was going to get infected. I could hardly walk, so they evacuated me back to England. I was in England until September, when I rejoined the unit.

You would receive replacements then?

So the replacements came in, and it would be ongoing training while you were a replacement.

How did you come across these prisoners?
These were prisoners from different units, probably between twenty and thirty prisoners. So that was my end of D-day.

What happened next; did they patch you up?
Well, I went back to England and I was there about two months, and then I joined my unit again back in France in September. And I joined my unit outside of Aachen, Germany, right on the German-French border.

What factors led to the success of the Ranger units on D-day?
We had a tough unit. We were all volunteers, and they told us how tough we were, and after a while you started to believe it. And then you find out that you aren't as tough as you thought you are. And luck played a big part of it.

As you became more accustomed to battlefield conditions, was there a learning curve with respect to survival techniques?
Oh, sure. I guess it's the animal instinct to survive that you learn certain things to do and certain things not to do, and it's something that happens over a period of time. Some guys are fast learners and some guys are not very fast, and if you don't learn quickly, you're not going to be around long. Then the battle of the Bulge started on December 16.

Where would you learn these survival techniques if not in basic training? How would you pick them up along the way?
Well, they're just certain things. There are sounds of incoming artillery. You never really hear that in basic training. Small-arms fire. A lot of times you could ignore it because you got the feel for it. Like I say, it's sort of an animal instinct. You learn when to zig and when to zag. At least, you think that you do.

So you recovered in England for several months, and you said you returned to Continental Europe in September?
Right.

Where was your unit at this time?
The Rangers are provisional companies. There are only sixty-four men in a company, and then in the battalion we had about six hundred men. We were attached to divisions. When a specific division was on the attack and if they had a particularly hard objective to take, a fortified objective, or a good defensive line, they would usually attach us to a division.

And in the autumn of '44, do you recall which division you were attached to?
Well, let's see. The 8th Division, 5th Armored, the 78th Division, the 9th Division. There were quite a few of them. Sometimes we'd only be attached for a week or a day. A couple of times we were only attached for two or three days and they'd shoot us over to another division. The 28th Division was another one. That brings us to the Hürtgen Forest.

So was there a lot of fighting there?d
Then we got into the real fighting. Well, I thought D-Day was bad, but Hürtgen Forest was a mess. And it's probably one of the few underpublicized battles that was fought in World War II, perhaps the worst battle fought in World War II. Because the United States lost more men in the Hürtgen Forest in a short period than they lost in D-day and the Battle of the Bulge. And a lot of people don't know that. They goofed up.

What happened there?
We just ran into a meat grinder. We had sent three divisions in there, and practically all of the divisions were wiped out.

So were the German soldiers dug in and well concealed?

The Hürtgen Forest was not a place to fight a war. The 82nd Airborne was also in the Hürtgen Forest, and it was like being in the foothills of the Ozark Mountains. No roads, hills; deep, hidden valleys. In depth, I think that it was probably less than 90 miles and probably 30 miles wide. And for some reason, our commanders thought that this was the way to get through to the plains of the Ruhr valley. As a result, rather than getting through it in two to four weeks, we had started in September, and by December we were still in the same position. In some respects it was worse than the Battle of the Bulge. It wasn't as cold as the Battle of the Bulge but was around 30–40 degrees, and it was constantly raining, and when you were soaked, you never warmed up. It was one of the worst battlefield experiences that I had. It was a thick forest, and you couldn't see the German soldiers until you got right up on them. We lost a lot of good men in that battle.

What was the strategy for the fighting in the fall of 1944?

You have to understand what was happening where we were. They were trying to capture the Roer River dams from September until December, and they had lost three divisions going in there, and the dams really controlled the whole northern flank or the front of the invasion, and they were afraid they'd blow the dams, flood the plain, and catch the Army out in the middle of the plain, and that would be disastrous. So we were trying to capture these dams. These dams were in a very hilly section of Germany, which was on the northern flank of the Bulge, and it was heavily defended, and there were a bunch of these hilltop fortifications or hilltop towns that were actually forts, if you want to call them that in the sense of the word. And the 28th Division got almost completely wiped out. They had to pull them off the line and regroup, and it took them a couple of months, and they were thrown down south of us in one of the holding divisions that went to the Battle of the Bulge. And they brought in the, I think, the 106th Division. They had them strung out real narrow. We were a heavy force, a heavy combat force. We had what they used to call the Varsity, which is the 1st Division, the 9th Division, and all those old good divisions, and they were making this attack and they had these hilltop towns and they were just hard to capture. We captured two or three of them two or three times and got kicked out. So the Germans swung in south of us, and we had just attacked the towns of, I think, Schmidt, Kesternich, and a few other towns, and we were in a holding position, and all of a sudden we heard the Germans were 20 miles behind us. So then we swung around south back to the west and formed a perimeter of defense holding the northern flank.

What role did religion play for some soldiers.

Well, we had many chaplains, some rabbis, some priests, some ministers. But when one of our guys, who was Jewish, said that a rabbi chaplain was having a service and asked us to go, everyone in the company went to the service. The battlefield can have a deep impact on soldiers.

Let's fast-forward then up to the Battle of the Bulge. What was your first battlefield engagement in this particular battle?

The Hürtgen Forest was on the north shoulder of the Battle of the Bulge. So we just dug in and held our position on the north shoulder, and they came in from the south and swung north to go up to Belgium. That was when all of the fighting occurred during the Battle of the Bulge.

What was the weather like in the winter of 1944, and what role did this play in the battle?

Well, I'll tell you the tremendous role. The weather up to the Bulge . . . I remember on December the seventh we made the attack on Castle Hill and Kesternich. This was a division-wide attack. But several Ranger companies took out the German positions. There were two divisions involved in it . . . two full divisions, but the Rangers achieved what other units couldn't. And the weather was getting cold and it was intermittent rain and snow. And I can't remember the exact days, but in December of 1944, all of a sudden it turned real cold and it got down to 3, 4, 5, 10 below zero. One night, it got down to 17 below zero, and it was bitter, bitter cold.

What role did that weather play during the battle?

Well, for us, it probably wasn't as bad as it was for the guys that were fighting, you know, trying to hold off the German offensive. We were in the defensive position, so we could dig in, and we did have the opportunity every once in a while to get warm, but we lost a lot of guys. I had my fingers frostbitten, and we lost a lot of guys with frozen toes and frozen fingers and stuff like that.

Did you have any special techniques for staying warm or dry?
Wear all the clothes you could.

Layers?
Layers and layers of clothes. Yeah.

Were there many injured or wounded soldiers, and how were they managed?
A lot of guys were hurt and wounded and stayed. They might go back, get patched up, and sent back because we were just short of men. We ran out of men, pure and simple.

What did you do on Christmas Eve or Christmas Day 1944?
Well, I just remember we were just sitting on a hill looking across the valley at the German lines, and that was about it. Hoping they would get some hot food up to us.

Oh, you had no special Christmas meal?
No, none that I know of.

What was your impression of the lines of communication during the battle? Do you feel that you were in touch with the commanders?
You know, when you're at a company level, the war is an entirely different thing. You don't really know what the hell is going on. Your battlefield consists of maybe 25 yards on the right to maybe 100 yards, and that's it. You don't have the big picture, the privilege of knowing what the big picture is.

Are there any individuals fallen or otherwise that you would like to pay a tribute to regarding their impact on your company?
You mean certain individuals?

Yeah, just any individual that distinguished themselves?
Oh, we had a lot of guys. Sure.

Is there any particular one you want to mention?
Oh, we had our company commander, who was a great guy. Ralph Gorenson. And our battalion commander up until the Bulge was Col. Rudder. He was a hell of a great guy. So, yeah, they were very close. We weren't like a regular Army unit. When I say a regular Army unit, I mean a regular unit. We were a pretty close, small unit, so we all knew each other pretty well.

Your colonel though; he was no longer in command?
He was taken and put in command of a regiment, and I can't recall the division, but he was put in command of this regiment, and they held a line that I learned later was called the Elsenborn Ridge, which they held for about three days and took a very hard pounding from what I understand.

It was one of the great holding actions of the battle?
Right.

What was the saddest moment during the battle or during your time in the military service?
Losing friends.

Within the Battle of the Bulge or just in your entire military experience, do you recall what was the most intense battle that you participated in or the most intense firefight?

The most intense firefight was with the capture of Castle Hill. Castle Hill or Hill 400 had a 400-meter elevation and is near the town Bergstein, just southeast of the town Hürtgen and the notorious Hürtgen Forest. The 2nd Ranger Battalion while assigned to the 8th Division, which attacked this hill on December 7, 1944. Although we were victorious in capturing this hill, the casualty rate was staggering, I believe that ninety of six hundred men in our battalion were killed.

Where was that?

This was right in the Hürtgen Forest. It was one of these hill towns that had all of their artillery spotters on top of the hill, and they could command the whole countryside and so it was heavily defended, and I think A, B, and C Company . . . D, E, and F Company lost about 70 percent of their men, and F Company lost 90 percent of their men. We took Castle Hill, and there had been two divisions that tried to take it, so we did it with less that a battalion, 125 men. Our success was in part related to the approach that was used, which involved linking our attack to an artillery barrage. Our battalion charged the hill while the barrage was still active and while the German defenders had their heads down. Some of the American GIs were killed from friendly fire during the charge. Our battalion was then assigned to the 78th Division and spearheaded the attacks on the town of Schmidt (just south of Bergstein). This town was retaken by both sides on several occasions and was also one of the most intense firefights in the war for the 2nd Ranger Battalion.

Can you describe any other memorable moments during your service?

Well, I remember specifically a few days after our battle for Hill 400 (after December 7–10, 1944); we were assigned to a regiment in the 78th Infantry Division on the outskirts of the town of Schmidt. We were in preparation for a battle to retake that town the next day. It was about 4:00 p.m., and we were all (2nd Ranger Battalion) attending a Mass for the Immaculate Conception, which we couldn't celebrate the following day due to our battle plans. It was dark, cold, and snowing during the Mass. Near the end of the service, [as] the priest said, "As you guys go into battle tomorrow," I felt a sense of peace and warmth as this intense heat and light surrounded me. As we were walking away, one of the guys next to me said, "Did you see and feel what I did back there?" "That was something else, wasn't it?" We battled for three days in Schmidt and nearly recaptured the town. However, we had to withdraw when the German forces were reinforced with some Tiger tanks. We lost nearly 30 percent of our battalion in that battle.

And when was that?

This was December the seventh.

Where were you when you heard that the Germans were massacring American prisoners?

I really don't know, but I just remember hearing about it. You're talking about the Malmedy massacre? We heard about it, you know. You heard a lot of rumors. Sometimes they were true and sometimes they weren't.

Did this change your feelings about the battle or the enemy at all?

Not really. No. Things were pretty intense with us for a long time.

You mentioned a wound you received following the invasion of D-day. Was that the only injury you sustained?

No, I got shot in the back of the neck.

When was this, and which battle?

It was in February after we broke out and went across the Cologne Plain.

Can you describe the events that pertained to your Silver Star?

I didn't receive the Silver Star until the end of the war in December of 1945, in Germany. I was playing football for the Army team in Germany when, one day, I got a call to see my CO. He told me that he had something for me, and

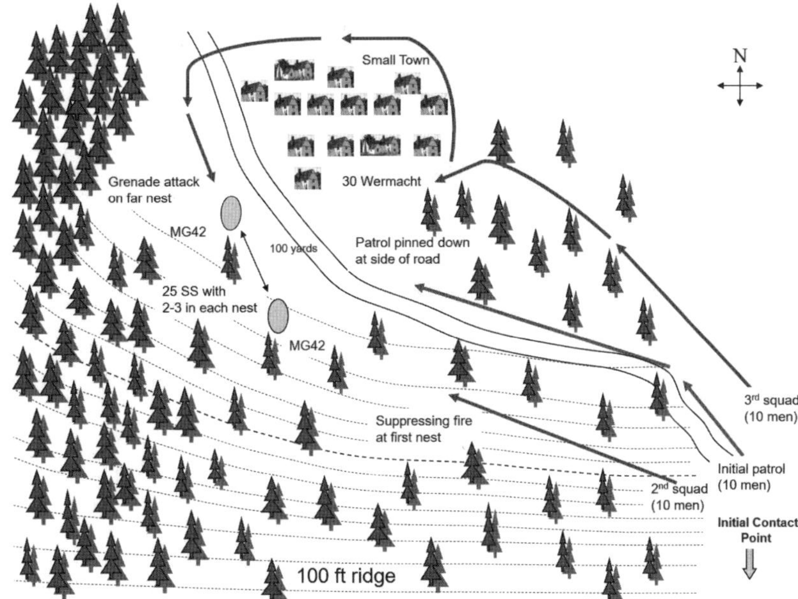

Charlie Ryan's sketch of his actions in March 1945

the citation was related to my leadership with respect to an attack of two machine gun nests in a town in Germany in the Ruhr Pocket in March of 1945. My platoon was en route to Wuppertal, approaching from the northeast. After we reached a 100-foot ridge just above a small town, we ran across a displaced person who told us that some Wehrmacht[29] German soldiers in the town below wanted to surrender. I sent a ten-man patrol to the town along the road to reconnoiter the area. Next thing I heard was a lot of small-arms fire near the road, and we found out that our first squad was attacked and pinned down by two MG42 nests near the town. Although there were about thirty Wehrmacht soldiers that surrendered in the town, we later found out that both of these nests were manned by a force of twenty-five SS across on the other side of the road. At that point, I deployed the remainder of my platoon in two ten-man squads. The first squad was directed to attack the first MG42 nest on its right flank. While they were taking on fire and diverting the attention to themselves, I led the other squad to the far side of the town. We went around the town and attacked the second nest from behind with grenades, killing the three SS soldiers. Once that nest was taken out, we continued to mop up the rest of the resisting SS and the second MG42 nest, occupied by an additional three men. Half of the SS soldiers were killed in action and the remainder surrendered.

Were there any moments of comfort or happiness during your tour of duty?

You mean during the war. Oh sure. We would be pulled back off the lines sometimes. We'd go to some little towns, you know, and have a big party and stuff like that. There were a lot of good times, and you remember the good times and you tried to forget the bad times.

How would you pass the time when you were not in a combat scenario?

Most of the time sleeping, trying to catch up on sleep. You're always tired and hungry.

How would you describe your relationship with the other soldiers in your company and with your noncoms and COs?

Oh, we were really a close-knit unit. Like I say, there were only sixty-four men in our company, and you got to know them all pretty well, and like any unit like that, you form close relationships with two or three or four guys, you know, or certain guys you bum around with; other guys you didn't.

Since you weren't with all these guys from the very first back in the States, did you feel at all like an outsider?

Oh sure, when I first went in, I was an outsider. In other words, I was a replacement, and nobody talked to you pretty much, you know. Of course, the big advantage was that none of these original guys had combat experience either, so we were all pretty much on an even keel as far as that was concerned.

But by the time that D-day occurred and you'd entered combat, you had enough time with the rest of your unit?
I got to know a few guys; there's always a few guys that will talk to you.

What impact did the war have on you?
It had a great effect; for thirty years I tried to forget about it.

What were the greatest lessons you learned from your military experience?
Well, that you can get along with anybody. Most of us have likes and dislikes as far as different people we know, but I found pretty much that you can get along with just about anybody.

If you could pass on a piece of wisdom to the next generation, something you learned from your wartime experiences, what would that be?
See, you said you weren't going to ask any hard questions. Well, I'd have to think about that. I would say that you should always try to do your best and make efforts to get along with everyone.

Where were you when you heard that Germany had surrendered?
Oh boy, I don't know. Let's see. Düsseldorf. Well, we had heard for two or three days, you know, that surrender was near. Things were pretty much collapsing everywhere, since by that time we were taking a lot of prisoners; there were very young soldiers, fourteen or fifteen years old, as well as older soldiers around forty-five or fifty, interspersed in various units to make them fight. Everybody was being very, very careful; everybody was keeping their head down.

Why?
Well, you certainly didn't want to cash in your chips if the war was ending. And I don't remember where I was specifically, but we were in some little German village, I guess, or something like that.

And how did you react?
Oh, I think somebody broke out a bottle of booze and we had a couple of drinks.

Can you describe one of the saddest moments of the war?
Yes, the day I lost my good friend George Halpin on April 17, 1945. George was a 2nd RB replacement in A Company, who I believe entered the ETO sometime at the end of the summer of 1944. Although we were not in the same company, we got to be good friends from the first time we met. We seemed to have a lot in common and got to know each other when we took liberty in Brussels in the fall. We were on patrol in the town of Laffenthall, just south of Munich. Most of the Wehrmacht were surrendering, and Dachau was freed a few days later. A German soldier who was not aware that the war had ended was hiding in a basement, fired, and hit George. I responded and eliminated the threat, and George was evacuated. A few days after VE-day, I saw one of the A Company guys and asked how George was doing. My heart sunk when he told me that he had passed away.

George Halpin

Charlie Ryan and George Halpin

How long did you remain in Europe after the Germans surrendered?
After the Germans surrendered, I stayed in Europe until January of '45.

Did you ever feel that you might be shipped to the Pacific to continue the war against Japan?
Well, that was after the war ended; we were replenished with replacements and everything like that and started training to go to Japan. And I got a chance to get into Special Services.

Which is?

Special Services . . . that's the fun and games of the Army. Taking care of entertainment and things like that. I got on one of the Army football teams. So we played football that fall.

Some of your past education and career plans?

Yeah, we had a good football team. We had a bunch of pros and all college players, and we had a good chance to travel. We went all over Europe. We went to Egypt. We went to Italy. And played in London. We played all over Europe, so it was a fun time. Gen. Eisenhower would frequently come into the locker room and cheer us on.

If you could pick just one, what do you think would be the most important contribution made by your company during the war? Perhaps in a particular battle?

Well, we were in many, many hard fights, and I guess the glamour thing was D-day. That's the one that seems to get the most publicity. First when we got out of service, nobody even thought about any of that stuff. It took everybody thirty years to forget about it.

Was it difficult to readjust to civilian life?

Not really. I was one of the lucky few that could erase it from my mind. For thirty years I didn't even think of the war. You got out and went back to school. It was just like being in the service again, without anybody telling you what to do other than the fraternity house and living it up. And probably partied too much and drank too much like everybody. I didn't talk about the war, since everybody had been in the war and had a better story. And the people that weren't in the war didn't really understand what went on in war.

Do you have any other thoughts or recollections of the Battle of the Bulge that you'd like to mention?

No, outside of being just terribly, terribly cold and hungry and miserable, I can't think of anything. I always felt that we had had it pretty tough in that winter over there, but then I read stories about those Marines at that Chosin Reservoir in Korea, where it was 30 degrees below zero, and I can imagine just how awful that could be, because we were only in maybe zero weather for maybe a week at the most. They fought there for a couple of months I think at below zero.

Do you remember the time around your twenty-first birthday in the spring of 1945?

Yes, I was then in the 78th Division and we were on the Rhine. I remember that the German planes were constantly strafing us. But, that day, I heard the sound of an aircraft that was much different, and when I looked up, I saw a German Messerschmitt Me 262 race by, and our fighters couldn't keep up with it.

Did you have many opportunities to speak with civilian populations in France, Belgium, and Germany? How were you received?

Mostly we were received very well. There were a few incidents where we were involved maybe with destruction of civilian property, and the people would be a little bit irritated with us in France and in Belgium. The Germans, they weren't irritated with us because they knew we were there to conquer them. But the French and the Belgians sometimes would get a little mad at us.

So the Germans weren't hostile? German civilians?

No, by and large the German civilians were very docile. Once they surrendered, that was it. They took directions a hell of a lot better than the French did.

Do you generally like to discuss your participation in World War II with friends and family?

No, I never discuss it.

Is there a reason for that?

Oh, I guess if you heard one war story, you heard them all.

Do you recall what thoughts you had going through all of the various campaigns?

Well, it was different at various times. At D-day, with our training and determination, we thought we were invincible, but by the end of the day, we had lost a lot of good men. As we continued to battle, one by one, we saw our buddies killed or wounded. So, at some point, after losing your buddies, one felt that it was just a matter of time and you would buy the farm. But as the war was nearing the end, you thought, well, maybe if I'm careful, I might actually survive this.

What is your general impression about your service in the military?

Well, I guess you can say that you are proud of it. A lot of times you did things that you weren't so proud of. That is the nature of war.

Do you have any other suggestions for our servicemen and women?

Yes, be on the winning side, since the losers don't fair that well.

Well, do you have anything else?

No, I really don't. I was a little surprised to receive this because I thought it had been discussed quite at length a long time ago, and I guess now with all the veterans dying off, it is the last chance to get some personal firsthand accounts.

DIARY OF CAPT. WALTER E. BLOCK
BATTALION SURGEON, 2ND RANGER BATTALION

What follows is a transcription of the unpublished personal military diary of Capt. Walter E. Block who left his established medical practice and family to become the battalion surgeon for the 2nd Ranger Battalion and ultimately an inductee within the Ranger Hall of Fame (see page 334), which offers some interesting personal insights of the Battalion's actions.

3/12/43

Saw family off in Los Angeles yesterday from Santa Barbara. They stayed at the Ambassador Hotel. I called Alice last night, long distance. They will leave Los Angeles Saturday for Chicago, and I leave tonight for Camp Forrest, Tenn.

3/13/43

Left for Camp Forrest last night. Passed through [*unreadable*] this a.m.—fond remembrances!! Heat-dust this last September!

3/14/43

Still on the train—passed through Phoenix, Tucson Arizona—El Paso this a.m. Church services aboard the train this a.m. Alice and the kids are on a train going east, but they are taking a route about 200 miles north of us, so I won't possibly be able to see them.

3/16/43

Still on the train—passed through St. Louis this a.m. Weather getting colder—

3/17/43

Arrived at Bivouac area around 7:00 a.m. today. Icy cold—about 25 miles out of Tullahoma (Camp Forrest.) Mud up to the knees, but surprisingly the next day and late this afternoon I had my first bath and shave in an icy mountain stream. It was swell!

3/18/43

Letter from Alice today. She and the children arrived in Chicago safe and sound. Thank God. There was a train wreck on Train 3 (I was on Train 4) and train personnel were killed. All my baggage was involved in the accident. I wonder if I can salvage any.

3/21/43

(Sunday) Cold—Snowing. Sleeping under pup tents. The men all shivering and running noses. However, I feel fine. I sure could go for a nice hot shower. Tried to call Alice last night in Tullahoma, but couldn't get a wire.

3/24/43

Not bad sleeping last night. Temp only 31 degrees. Yesterday was a bad one—water frozen solid. I was able to reach Alice on phone last Sunday evening. It was good to hear her voice; also the kids and my mother and father. I am going to Chicago tomorrow on a 3 day pass.

3/25/43

Pass cancelled. All personnel passes cancelled. Damn the luck—

3/28/43

In Nashville today. Plenty of hot baths and good food. Ate at a place called Kleeman's. Best piece of apple pie I ever ate. Saw 2 shows.

3/29/43

Back at camp <u>& mud</u>!

3/31/43

Sprained my ankle. Hurts like the devil. Slept poorly last night.

4/1/43

Ankle still hurting a lot. Routine duties around camp., e.g., inspection of kitchens, latrines, personnel. Got a box of candy from Alice today. She writes that she will come to Nashville to see me on the 10th, about 9 days from today.

4/5/43

In McMinneville this p.m. Good meal at Sedberry Hotel and movie. Alice is coming to Nashville this weekend. I will see her there, the Gods and general willing.

4/10/43

The Gods and "The General" were willing, and I went to Nashville today to spend the weekend with Alice—should I say a 2nd honeymoon? It was wonderful seeing her again.

4/11/43

Left Nashville and Alice today to return to camp and reached camp in a blinding rain storm.

4/12/43

Most of the outfit left today on a secret one-week mission. I am left behind "to guard the fort" with 8 men of the med. detachment.

4/14/43

Went to McMinneville to see Odell [*unreadable*] folks. Invited there for next Sunday.

4/16/43

Passed yearly physical exam for all officers today. B/P 122/72; vision 20/20-20/20; weight 142 pounds, scale 5 pounds under. My actual weight is around 147 pounds. I'm not such a bad physical specimen, I guess!

4/18/43

Squirrel hunting with Odell [*unreadable*] brother near McMinneville. No luck. Talked to Alice long distance tonight.

4/20/43

Preparation for the maneuvers.

4/21/43

Sent Alice flowers for Easter, also mother and father. Father made us a present of 100 shares of National Fuel Gas Co. stock.

4/24/43

Left maneuver area tonight. We are the blues!

4/26/43

In the Cumberland Hills. Most beautiful scenery imaginable. Dogwoods in full bloom. Made a hickory whistle for Jeffy Boy and mailed it home.

4/27/43

Cooked spaghetti out in the open overwood ashes. Best I ever ate!

4/29/43

First problem over—Blues worn (I am in the Blue Army). Sure do need a bath and clean clothes.

5/7/43

End of the second problem. Heat worse. Plenty of dust. Sissie made her 1st Communion last Sunday. I mailed her white roses.

5/11/43

Raining all day. Got the wettest I have ever been. Walking (Fording) streams—chilled through, feel fine, however. Cedar fire smoke sure burns the eyes! We are attempting to cross the Cumberland River in this problem.

5/14/43

Again it rained all of last night—I was in a pup tent, so it wasn't too bad until we were called out @4:00 a.m. The problem ended at 7:30 a.m. So "endeth" the 3rd problem—6 to go!

5/24/43

Caught in the rain again last night. This time without a pup tent up. Was I wet or was I? Soaked to the skin. Will I catch cold? I don't think so. I feel well and as strong as an ox. Well, at least an ox of 40—

5/25/43

Went up in an Army cubplane over Murfreesboro. Alice would have the w.k. conniption fit if she knew! We are on the 5th problem.

6/1/43

Start of another problem #6. I have the hotel reservation at Noel Hotel in Nashville. Wrote Alice to come this next Saturday and bring along a couple of the kids. I have a squirrel for the children, call him Sylvester. Saw a sight tonight. Thousands of fireflies silhouetted against two 2 hills (mt.?) while I was in the valley. It was a beautiful spectacle—We are with "C" Co. on this problem—Plenty of rat racing.

6/5/43

Saw Alice, Michael and Sissie in Nashville over the weekend. They all looked swell. Bought Mike a ball, Sis, broaches, and Alice a copper luster China set for our anniversary.

6/15/43

Married 14 years today. I would do it all over again as I am satisfied.

6/18/43

Alice left for Watertown with children. We (80th Ba) will leave on the 23rd and should all be together in N.Y. for next weekend.

6/21/43

No mail from Alice for 3 days.

6/25/43

On the train bound for Pine Camp—Nice trip.

6/27/43

Arrived in Pine Camp and saw my family in Watertown, N.Y. 4 hours later. They all look swell. At last we are re-united.

6/28/43

Home for the weekend with home cooking and plenty of it. We move to Carthage, N.Y., tomorrow into our own apt.

7/1/43

Iced watermelon for supper tonight with Alice and the kids. I sure have a swell family.

9/5/43

Volunteered for jungle training today. Wonder if I will be accepted. Have let the diary lapse a while. On August 22, 1943, my promotion to rank of captaincy came through. Alice, I, and Jeffy were in Chicago on a 3-day pass when it came in. Michael and Sissie were in Totem Camp, near Harrisville at the time. We moved from 413 State Street in Carthage, N.Y., on August 28 to 116 Keyes Avenue, Watertown. Not as nice a place, but it was the best to be had. Have the Studebaker with us, and I drive home every night. Pretty nice, easy life!

9/21/43

Given opportunity of joining the Rangers. Accepted it! Have to leave Friday. Alice and the children will have to drive to Chicago alone.

9/23/43

Partings are always such sad affairs! Alice went to the wheel of the car and started off at 9:45 a.m. I left for Fort Dix, N.J., at 10:00 p.m.

9/24/43

I am <u>the</u> battalion surgeon of the 2nd Ranger Battalion, a pretty rugged outfit! Arrived right into pile of work.

9/25/43

Still working—but good!

10/6/43

Left for Chicago from Philadelphia via United Airlines. Home at 9:30. Alice and Pop and Michael were waiting at the airport for me. Sissie, Jeffy, Grandma and Francine were at the house. A real reunion. I have 4½ whole days at home.

10/11/43

Left Chicago for Philadelphia via plane. Back in camp late at night. Plenty cold too.

10/20/43

Off on a 3-day problem with the Rangers to Camp Ritchie, Maryland. Sleeping out all night on the ground is ok if you have a nice warm sleeping bag. I have a sleeping bag! Will we shove off this week?

10/23/43

Back in Fort Dix. Saw plenty of historic country en route to Md. Gettysburg, etc.

11/6/43

Alice came up to see me today. Met me in Trenton. We went to Philadelphia overnight (Sat.) and then back to Trenton, N.J., on Sunday. Nice weekend, probably the last for a long time, <u>if & when</u>!

11/10/43

Left for Camp Shanks, N.Y., today near Orangeburg, N.Y. This is our P.O.E. Final "shots" for typhus here. Ouch does my arm hurt!

11/13/43

Called long distance home today. Is it for the last time that I will ever again talk to my family?

11/21/43

Michael's birthday today! I had bought him a watch and sent it to him for his birthday. I hope he likes it and will take care of it. We also embarked today, and, of all ships—The <u>QUEEN ELIZABETH</u>! The largest ship in the world.

11/22/43

I am put in charge of First Aid Post #4. There is a lot of medical work on the ship.

11/23/43

The ship sailed at exactly 3:30 today—for where? No convoy—no escort no "nuthin"!

11/24/43

Off Newfoundland—apparently—cold as the devil—smooth sea—

11/25/43

Sailing E by NE most of the day. Rough sea in afternoon. Storm at night. Lightning knocked out our radar tonight. No radar working.

11/26/43

Excitement! Ship did a complete about face—15 subs in a pack—15 miles away—running (we) like hell and zig-zagging all over the place. Spotted one plane late in p.m. (ours.)

11/26/43

Quiet all day.

11/27/43

Sailing quietly all day.

11/28/43

Arrived in Scotland (Clyde River—off Glasgow) early this a.m. Town of Green Oak on our left. Saw 5 aircraft carriers, including the "Illustrious" camped all around us. Also the battleship (British) "Renown." Stayed on boat all day.

11/29/30

On boat all day.

11/30/43

Debarked and boarded a train at 5:30 p.m. Riding all night. I developed a bad cold on the train.

12/1/43

Arrived in Bude (Cornwell County) England at noon today. Bude is a nice, quiet town near Land's End, right on the ocean. Not touched by air raids as yet. We are about 35 miles from Plymouth (air raids and Pilgrim Father).

12/8/43

Bringing the diary up to date. My foot locker where diary was kept came in today. I live at 11 Downsview Road, right across the street from the [*unreadable*] 2 blocks from the ocean. A nice home. Oh, before I forget—I have a commendation from the ship's (Elizabeth) surgeon on my "good work" aboard the ship. Quite a feather in the well-known cap! Only 1 letter from Alice since my arrival in England. Hope I get some mail soon.

12/11/43

Laid up in my room for the past 36 hours with my usual or early "bronchial" trouble as that screwy but likeable brother-in-law Maximilian would say. My landlady came in with my meal and rationed coals to keep me comfortable. The colonel (Rudder) brought me my dinner last night in my men's kit. He is a good "Joe." Hope I get better—"Rumors are beginning to fly." Sent a birthday cable to Alice and Jeffy boy. Hope they get it in time for their birthday. Today is Sunday, and I can visualize my family today—the usual Sunday from the funny—paper up. Oh, boy, if I were only home now. Hope those German bastards give up soon so I can get the hell home again—

12/17/43

I am 40 years old today! Life is supposed to begin at 40. Is my life beginning or will I go out like a "bang." Went out with my Sgt. to lay out a course for a night problem. Got into plenty of Cornish mud—hot tea in an old Cornish home—

12/24/43

Dinner at the Grenville Hotel with Freddie Wright (71 years old and a [*unreadable*] and Mrs. Schwarz child. No mail for past 4 days. Also met 2 nice lads whose dad is a POW in Japan, David & Jeremy Rees.

12/25/43

Christmas in England!

12/26/43

Had tea with the headmaster of Clifton College, Bude, Mr. Finter and his wife and son who goes to Cambridge to medical school. Had an interesting afternoon discussing Anglo-American relations and Boyle and Bernoueli's laws. Nice people. The Rees boys were in to see me. Gave them cookies and orange juice. All they could say was "Gosh."

December 31
New Year's Eve at the Grenville Hotel in Bude with
Freddie Wright's party. Nice time—Sure missed
Alice tonight!

Jan. 1st, 1944
The first day of 1944.

Jan. 4th
Left for Southampton today to inspect part of the
group who are on detached service. Southampton
sure got a "blitzing." Badly smashed up. Stayed at
the Royal Hotel. Met some British officer
commandos. Had a nice tea at the hotel and roast
veal at dinner. Imagine roast veal!

Jan. 6th
Returned to Bude this evening after riding all day.
Tired! Two letters from Alice and a cabled money
order for 129 pounds from my dad ($50). What will
I do with the money? There is no place to spend it!

Jan. 15th
Went to Plymouth today. It sure is a "blitzed up"
place. Saw the pantomime "Cinderella" in the
evening. Also saw Lady Astor and the Lord Mayer
of London at an officer dance in the latter part of
the evening.

Jan 18, 1944
Left Bude for Southampton via "peep." A cold ride.
After I arrived in Southampton, I left for London
the next a.m.

Jan. 19
In London. Saw the The King Palace and the
pantomime Cinderella again—with actress Evelyn
Laye. Very, very good.

Jan. 20
At medical aviation conference today in
Teddingham, Eng. Saw "The Lisbon Story" in the
evening at the Hippodrome.

Jan. 21
Touring London all day today and tonight was in
my first air raid. It was a lulu, too! Plenty of action.
Had another one at 5:00 a.m. on Jan 22—came
damn close. Set the house of Parliament on fire.

Jan. 22
Arrived in Folkestone at noon—close to Dover—
getting warm and hot climatically.

Jan. 29
Went to Canterbury to see the old cathedral. Left
about one hour before Jerry let loose with a big air
raid. Saw the sight from Buckburrow House where I
am staying. Very impressive. Is our "show" going to
come off? Quien sabe?

Jan. 31, 1944
"Waves" too high! No "show"—tomorrow maybe?

Feb. 1st
No!—Left Buchburrow House nr. Folkestone for
Richfield. Spent the night at Southampton in the
Hotel Royal.

Feb. 2
Arrived on the Isle of Wight this afternoon after a
dreary ferry ride. Raw, dark weather! Back to
routine work—staying at the Belgrave Hotel in
Sandown (I. of W.) Best food I ever ate in England!

Feb. 3
Beautiful Isle of Wight! It is beautiful.

Feb. 4
Climbed up a 150 foot cliff today, the last 100 feet
on a steel cable. My knees were trembling when I
reached the top. But "I dood it."

Feb. 6
Still on Isle of Wight.

Feb. 11
Went to Southampton today—plans for leaving I. of
W. made. We are going to Bude. I leave tomorrow with
the ¾-ton truck and all the medical paraphernalia.

Feb. 14
Left for Bude today instead. Arrived in time for
"chuppah" after a 7-hour ride in a ¾ weapons
carrier. Saw Dr. (Capt.) Pierzynski today at lunch
where I stopped off (315 Stat. Hospital). Also rode
through Dartmoor. What a dreary, desolate place
that is.

Feb. 17
Back to the old routine.

Feb. 28

Saw and heard the famous Menges string quartet tonight. They played Dvorak, DeBussy and Beethoven.

March 14

Still "fighting" the battle of Bude. Drove over 200 miles to Ilminster (past Taunton in Somerset) yesterday. I have a five-day leave coming up this Friday. Am going out with Lt. Majane.

March 17

Left on leave with Lt. Majane. Stopped at Exeter—saw the play "The Wind and the Rain." Also took a side day trip to Torquay and spent the night of March 18 at Cockington near Torquay—the Drum Inn. Had a wonderful time.

March 23

Back from Leave.

March 31

Preparing to leave Bude "for good" next Monday. Just finished three rugged days out "in the field." Feel okay.

April 1st

Spoke too soon. Developed a slight cough—not bad, however. Busy getting "ready" am going to use pack carrier for my aid station instead of transporting my paraphernalia by truck.

April 2nd

Left Bude for assault training center near Braunton Devon. Here I will be 4 days—Nissen Huts—not too good!

April 9th, 1944

Easter Sunday—left A.J. Center for Swanage in Dorset—beautiful place—lots of cliffs (ouch! Climbing!) and there is France only about 40 miles away, just out my window. The 2nd Easter away from home. Will I be alive this time next year? Quien sabe?—

April 11, 1944

Climbing cliffs today—muscles plenty tired.

April 12, 1944

Out on L.C.A.'s all day firing rockets (ropes) to top of cliffs.

April 14

Out to the S.S. Ben-My-Chree for LCA and rocket drill. Will be on the boat for 4 days. Out to the Red Sands of Alum Bay, Isle of Wight—very interesting work in a heavy, choppy sea.

April 16th

Climbed a 125 foot sand cliff on rope fired from rocket.

April 17

Back to base at Swanage.

April 21st

Majane (Lt.) developed a perforated peptic ulcer (my diagnosis was correct.)

April 24th

A hell of an air-raid right over our house on the top of a hill (Swanage) woof-woof went the bombs—no one hurt.

April 29

Raids every night this week except one day. Don't even get up any more—saw a beautiful demonstration of "Block-Busters" this week at Studland Bay—Eisenhower & Monty were there—pay-day tomorrow.

May 12

Busy in preparation for D-Day—met Miss Nelsen at Grosvenor Hotel Officer's Club. She was Alice's OB nurse. It is a small world after all.

May 21

Hectic days in preparation for D-Day—really went up and down some steep cliffs yesterday. I will probably go up the cliffs on D-Day with the duck ladder. Here is the theme song—

> "Be kind to your web-footed friends for a
> duck may be somebody's mother
> Be kind to your friends in the swamp
> Where it's always dismal & damp.
> Now you may think this is the end
> Well, it is——"

Sung to the tune of Sousa's Star & Stripes—
This is the last entry to be written before D-Day—If something happens to me see that my wife

Mrs. Alice Block of
2929 No. Kilbourn Ave
Chicago, Ill
gets this book—
Kiddo—I love you—

JUNE 5, 1944

This was supposed to be D-Day, but it was postponed for one day because the Channel was too rough. Sitting around on the Ben-My-Chree "just a waitin"!

JUNE 6, 1944

D-DAY—We awakened at 2:30, had breakfast at 3:00 a.m. (2 pancakes per man, small, per my orders for the last meal) and were called, "Rangers, man your stations" at 4:00 a.m. The water is rough and choppy, but it's D-Day, anyway. We leave the Mother ship exactly at 4:30 a.m. boat, 884 (LCA), Bangalore Jake (Lt. Jacob J. Hill) in front, I in back, 20 men in between. The passage is rough, men get seasick. The lad next to me vomiting in his handkerchief. We are brought into the wrong section of beach and for almost a mile have to hover close to the coast before we reach Pt. du Hoc, bad business as it gives Jerry almost 40 minutes of breathing time to get ready for us. He is ready for us, and when we reach the left flank of Pt. du Hoe he starts letting us have it. One of the 4 ducks gets it at once. Capt. Slate's craft is sunk ¼ mile out from shore. None of the craft reach the right flank of the Pointe. My craft lands at pt. X as above. We are under machine gun fire from 2 points, A and B. We crouch in a bomb crater for a few minutes, and then when the 1st riflemen reach the top, I and Bayes and South (my medics) go up to the top. T/S Karb is shot in the hand below the cliffs and never does go up to the top. Late at night Lt. Col. Trevor (Thos. Trevor care of Thames Yacht Club, Knightsbridge, London) finds me a suitable place to treat the casualties. We work all night, bandaging and dressing the wounded. We have 9 bunks into which to place the more seriously wounded. Bangalore Jake (Hill) was killed early in the a.m. He was my roommate at Swanage and was always "sending" to Sears, Roebuck & Co. for "tops" with which to blow (blow his top)—assorted sizes. Germans counter-attacking fiercely.

JUNE 7, 1944

2nd day and night at the Pointe. No relief in sight. Ammo very low. Shells rationed out. Food and water rationed. I rationed the food, water, and ammo. Col. Rudder wounded again today. He was wounded yesterday when Capt. Hargrove (a fine officer) was killed. Lt. Leagans was also killed. Lt. Baugh shot in hand and foot (seriously). Capt. Masny wounded in shoulder. Lt. McCulles wounded in head and neck. Of all the 6 officers in my billet at Swanage only Lt. Kuchner and myself are not casualties. "Rocky" Norton Lt. J.G. (Navy) was wounded by the same shell that killed Capt. Hargrove. Heinie prisoners made to act as litter bearer. Mostly young soldiers with a few Italians thrown in. Sure as hell don't look like a "master race."

JUNE 8, 1944

Third day at the Pointe as it sure looked bad. However, the Navy helped us out by blasting the coast above us and then relief came around 1:00 p.m. in the person of the 5th Rangers of the 115th Infantry—a real family reunion. Then we went on a sniper hunt, cleaning them out. Went through our first French village, St. Pierre Du Mont and then grand camps Sur La Mer got some "du pain" et "vin rouge" (for free!) from "Les inhabitants." Slept in a slit trench this night, and Jerry proceeded to give us a goose raid (but good!) He got three men of the 5th with a bomb.

JUNE 9, 1944

Still bivouacked near Osmanville.

JUNE 10, 1944

Bivouacked near a small farm about 4 miles from Colombiere. Had 2 good meals at Mme. Nicole—real eggs, cider, hot meat, potatoes and sour cream with sugar. "Café noire" Tres doucement!

JUNE 12 to JUNE 19th

Still bivouacked near the farm. Air raids every night. Gosh, the Boche are persistent.

JUNE 20th

Moved to Colombiere, but I still manage to get 1 meal a day at Mme. Nicole. Sgt. Clark and one other man go with me each day.

JUNE 22

Great excitement at the Nicole "ménage." Nine parachutists baled out near the farm just as we were eating supper. The 10th one caught on the plane. "Cette avion etait fini!" Clark and I went after the one who landed near us without arms like a bunch of damned fools! But he was an American, a Sgt. Palsidino from New York. He finished the dinner with us at Mme. Nicole's, fresh strawberries (fraises) over crème!

JUNE 23

Oh, boy, oh, boy! I am awarded a Silver Star award (orders of June 20th). Will be presented by some general tomorrow at 10:00 a.m.

JUNE 24

Yep, I was presented with the Silver Star Medal today at 10:00 a.m. by Maj. Gen. Gerow. A pretty nice-looking medal. I sent it home. Also, sent Michael a German helmet and water canteen.

JUNE 25th

Left Colombiere for Valognes VOLOGNES (Vol-an-yeah) near Cherbourg. Close to the front. Guarding prisoners, not so hot. However, it has some recompense. I am situated in a nice chalet, private, with a spring bed! I had a shave and a sponge bath, and I feel like a million.

JUNE 26th

Also slept like a million. Had to get rid of Hanlon my truck driver as he can't get along with the men. Prisoners, "thousands" of them, from young "punks" to old "gappers." Lots of Poles and Russkies in the lot, too. Raining all day. Had some fresh strawberries today from the garden. Wish we were back near Colombiere where I could run over to Mme. Nicole's and get some real food once in a while.

JULY 1ST

Still at this small town near Valognes called St. Joseph. My nice quarters are still nice. Fresh cut flowers in my room every day. Not too much hard work.

JULY 2nd

Suddenly had to move out, and we did in 2 hours' notice. We motored over to Beaumont up in the Cap De Hague port of the Cherbourg Peninsula near the little Village of Herqueville. Living out here in the woods is not as nice as it was at Valognes but still it isn't bad.

JULY 4th

The 4th of July spent out here in the open. Plenty of booby traps left by the Heinies around in the area.

JULY 12th

Still spending time on the Cap de Hague. Most all the companies are scattered out on patrols. I am conducting a private practice. Among my patients are a 2-week old baby and an 18 year old paralyzed boy. Pay is generally in eggs. Obtained a lobster from the fishing village of Osmanville. Will have a lobster dinner this coming Sunday at the village café (avec vin rouge.)

JULY 20, 1944

Still on Cap de Hague. Am living pretty comfortably. Unit was given the Presidential citation yesterday. Nice ribbon! Eating freshly caught lobsters, red and white wine, freshly slaughtered bulls, white bread, ham. Not a bad life, such as it is.

JULY 25, 1944

Just watched a procession of almost 800 Liberator 4 motored bombers returning from Germany. What a spectacle! Rumors of an impending crack-up in Germany going around—hot as a fire-cracker. Still living near Beaumont (Cap de Hague) and casualties are men fooling around with mines and demolitions. Page was blown up (literally) last Saturday night. The Colonel and I carried what was left of him on the front of a Jeep covered with flowers back to camp. What an end!

JULY 31, 1944

Still living near Beaumont. Pretty easy life! Saw a 6 year old kid tonight with what appeared to be a post-pneumonia empyema. Had him taken to the French hospital in Cherbourg. I guess I didn't lose "my hand" with children, as this youngster let me examine him without any difficult. Gave him some pineapple juice after the examination was completed. Also today tried to get an arrested Belgian out of jail for his "weeping and wailing" wife. I think it can be arranged. Three letters from Alice today. Barney is "mailed" she writes.

AUG. 6

"Nons partirons auj our d'lin!"
Leaving—"tout suite" for a new area S. of St. Lo. A midnight right ride in carivon. May be some "strafing."

AUG. 7

St. Lo is sure battered up! We are patrolling a certain area of the front—a quiet area!

AUG. 8

Advancing—on the move.

AUG. 9

In Mortain or rather this side of it as Jerry has re-captured it.

AUG. 10

Jerry is out of Mortain and we leave for another area. Every night boom-boom from the German bombers.

AUG. 12

On the move to Mayenne. Leaving Normandy another front line job!

AUG. 13

Arrived in Mayenne early in the morning with Jerry shelling the bridge to the town. Finally settled in a beautiful home, late in the morning. Everything except running water and electricity.

AUG. 19

Left Mayenne for the front lines. Base camp at Folgoet near Brest. A long ride, 20 hours, through lines of cheering populace. Rained like all fury the last 6 hours. I rode in the ambulance and stayed dry.

AUG. 21

In Folgoet church for mass today.

AUG. 23

Sent out 3 companies today on patrol. Roberts, medic in "A" Co. got it in the chest, W.I.A.

AUG. 24

I am still in front lines.

AUG. 25

Returned to base camp today. Bombardment of Brest started at 1:00 p.m. today. Boy-oh-boy, what a show!

AUG. 27

Left Le Folgoet for good and right up on the line.

SEPT. 1ST

Davis my medic got shot in the back. Evacuated him 5 minutes after he was hit with levering. Pretty dangerous n'est pas!

SEPT. 2ND to 8th

Rough work rather. We captured Lochrist Battery today. I have really worked, and I know that I have saved men's lives by rapid evacuation and prompt use of plasma (including German.) Had 2 very close calls, one from machine gun fire and art bursts.

SEPT. 9

Loafing around Lochrist.

SEPT. 10

Bivouacked near Kervaourn Chateau near St. Renan & Milizac.

SEPT. 14

Leaving Kervaourn for Le Folgoet today.

SEPT. 17

Back on the job. Took the town of La Fret (Hospital town). Plenty of (cognac and white wine.)

SEPT. 20

Back near Le Folgoet eating at Mme. Jeannie's every day with Hillis (for dinner.)

SEP. 24

Left for Landerneau, nice French town. Bought a few knick-knacks for my family.

SEPT. 28

Left Landerneau tonight at 11:00 p.m. for where? (40 plus 8 boxcars, deluxe)

SEPT. 29–30

OCT. 1–2

Spent on the train riding always due west. Reached Longuyon, France on the morning of the 3rd. Entrenched for Belgium at 8:30 a.m. and arrived at Arlon on the 3rd. A beautiful town filled with all pre-war articles. So now I am in Belgium!

SEPT. 6 [*Entries start back in September in diary*]
Still in the Arlon area. Doing some shopping and eating good food every day. The Belgians are sure hospitable folk and are much cleaner than the French. I believe their cooking is better, too.

SEPT. 8

Drove through Luxembourg today, a beautiful country. The capital city is Luxembourg and very pretty. Mostly German spoken and plenty of beer abounds.

SEPT. 10

Raining all day. I am "shacked up" in my nice, dry tent however.

SEPT. 20th

Still in Arlon area. Found a nice café where I can get thick steaks, French fried potatoes and salad—all for 60 fr.

SEPT. 30

Still loafing and resting. Working on sick call only. Bought 3 beautiful vases to send home. They were made in Longuyon, France, nearby.

OCT. 1st

Still at Arlon.

OCT. 15TH

Still at Arlon. This is a beautiful town. Quiet, sedate, gentile. Gracious living!

OCT. 21st

Left Arlon for Esch, Luxembourg near the border of Lorraine, France. A beautiful country, a beautiful town. Mostly German speaking, however. Looks as if I have to start learning German, my usual 3 word a day plan.

OCT. 24th

Bought perfume for Alice and mother for Christmas.

OCT. 26th

Hum-drum garrison life. Ho! Hum!

OCT. 28th

Had a heart check-up today at the 110th EVAC Hosp. Have had several short heart (?) pains recently. I'm a little young for a coronary in the usual sense of the world, but it's possible. Will try to get an EKG examination next time I am in the vicinity of a general hospital. I can still do 30 to 40 push-ups and about 5 one-hand push-ups, so I guess I can't be too badly off.

NOV. 2nd

Preparing to shove off tomorrow at 8:00 a.m. for "Deutschland." Esch has been a nice place. I have made many friends. Everyone has been kind to us. I will be back here again someday with my family.

NOV. 3rd

Arrived late this evening in the small town of Neudorf near Eupen, Belgium, about 4 miles from Germany. Sleeping outside in pup tents. Cold, wet, miserable!

NOV. 4TH

Went to Germany today. Saw Maj. Zorky of the old 85th Recon (5th Armored Division). Plenty of forests and sour looks from the [*unreadable*]

NOV. 8th

Moved up to the front line which is right near the town of Vossenack. "Beaucoup" fighting going on.

NOV. 10

Still in Vossenack area. Have gone out quite a few times in a litter Jeep to evacuate men. Colonel ordered me to stop as he said "You might get hit!" There is quite a kick in doing this going through a mortar barrage especially.

NOV. 15

Still in Vossenack area. No progress. Our aid station is in a concrete dug-out, which was once part of the Siegfried Line.

NOV. 19

Mail today and finally a package from home. The cherries Alice made and sent out last August 1st, as well as the apricots, arrived at last. They came in plenty fine, as all I had eaten the past two weeks have been K and C rations with an occasional sandwich brought from the rear.

NOV. 23

Thanksgiving Day but no turkey. I left the Pillbox yesterday as most of the men have been "pulled back" and relieved.

NOV. 24

We had our turkey today and everyone got a stomach cramp and diarrhea, including myself. Sure spent a miserable night. I live in an underground, log covered shelter right in the Hürtgen Forest, and there is shelling every night and most every day. Today, 2 men were hit.

Capt. Walter E. Block

NOV. 26

Geitz my medic was hit and evacuated while lugging a litter. He will lose his foot. Korb also got the cluster on his Purple Heart.

NOV. 27

I am bringing the diary up to date today, and this is the day I am writing most of the November entries. This has been without exception, I believe, the worst 3 weeks I have ever spent in the Army. Cold, rain, snow, shelling and just plain "being miserable." Sure hope the war ends soon! I was able to drive back 20 miles to Eupen and take a bath yesterday, the first one in 3 weeks. Clean clothes, warm, not hot water. Sure felt good. Took a "Gillette" blade shave this morning. "Tres beau!"

DEC. 3RD SUNDAY

Still in the Hürtgen woods just back of Vossenack and the town of Hürtgen. Plenty of artillery (enemy) shelling, both day and night. Received a Christmas package from Alice and the kids yesterday, fur lined gloves, wool scarf and wood socks. Wish I would receive mail also. Sent some money to Duffy Floral Co. to buy Alice and Jeffy flowers for their birthdays.

Last entry found. Dr. (Capt.) Block was killed at Hill 400 on December 7, 1944 when an artillery shell burst at his battalion aid station.

PART II PHOTO SECTION

Sgt. J. R. Compton and Lt. W. M. Vazsana demonstrate disarming an opponent who is armed with a knife at Camp Forrest, Tennessee, February 1943.

Left to right: Sgt. A. Colasanti, Cpl. M. Hiesenberg, and Cpl. B. Blake firing Garand, Thompson SMG, and .45 semiautomatic pistol at Camp Forrest, Tennessee, February 1943

Rangers conducting an exercise known as the "windmill" at Camp Forrest.

Two Ranger students practice "dirty fighting" techniques at Camp Forrest in January 1943.

Sgt. J. Perna practicing with his bayonet during an exercise mopping up an enemy village at Camp Forrest in January 1943

Left to right: SSgt. B. Scarboro, Cpl. S. L. Cochran, and Sgt. E. M. Draper demonstrating fighting techniques in enemy village at Camp Forrest in January 1943

This picture shows the men of the 29th Ranger Battalion training at Achnacarry in February 1943, conducting much the same training as the 1st Ranger Battalion had.

General Gerow talks with Sgt. J. O'Brien of the 29th Ranger Battalion.

Members of the 29th examine the mock graves at Achnacarry, which served as reminders not to make mistakes in combat.

Rangers training with Bangalore Torpedoes as part of beach assault training.

29th Rangers conducting a mock landing in August 1943

29th Rangers relax after a cliff-scaling exercise in August 1943.

29th Rangers setting up a 60 mm mortar during mock landings

29th Rangers conducting a mock landing in August 1943

29th Rangers practice advancing under the cover of smoke.

British lieutenant J. L. Warner provides instruction to the Rangers of the 29th Battalion in a photo dated February 1943.

29th Rangers undergo training on the BAR.

British lieutenant D. Burr provides marksmanship instruction to the 29th Battalion in February 1943.

British sergeant major T. Sawkins instructs the 29th Battalion on the use of the Thompson SMG.

The men of the 29th conduct the same log drills as their predecessors in the 1st Ranger Battalion.

2ND RANGER BN
D. Co.
Ft. Dix, NJ 1943

2nd Battalion Rangers in France, June 6, 1944

Cpl. J. Sanford and Pvt. W. Sisson report to Capt. Luthor on their mission, where they used captured German horses.

Rangers showing off captured German horses and bicycle in Normandy. *Left to right*: Pvt. L. Pye, Pvt. R. Marks, SSgt. W. Boyd, Cpl. G. Watkins, Capt. R. Prosatti, and TSgt. Goldstein.

Rangers using captured horses to run messages The mounted Ranger is TSgt. R. Woodill.

Pointe du Hoc seen a few days after the invasion

Seen here at Pointe du Hoc, the type of ladder that Rangers used to scale the cliff

Ranger in a foxhole in Normandy a few days after the invasion

Seen here in this picture taken a few days after the invasion is the beach in front of Pointe du Hoc and the type of landing craft used.

Rangers having a meal in Normandy; behind them is the aid station.

Pvt. W. Allen rests on the road outside Irsch, Germany, as 80th Division troops pass by.

Rangers in Germany in a picture dated March 3, 1945

RANGER HEADSTONES AND MEMORIALS

Ranger Banning

Ranger Biddle

Ranger McCalvin

Ranger Clendenin

Ranger Goudey

Ranger Gallo

Ranger Harding

Ranger Sowa

Ranger Ballard

COCHRAN ANDY · PFC · 300 ENGR COMBAT BN · OKLAHOMA
COHEN ROBERT · T SGT · 175 INF 29 DIV · MARYLAND
COHRON KENNETH R · CPL · 712 TANK BN · VIRGINIA
COLE EDGLE W · PVT · 262 INF 66 DIV · WEST VIRGINIA
COLLIER JAMES B · S SGT · 113 FA BN 30 DIV · NORTH CAROLINA
COLLINS HIRAM H · 1 SGT · 149 ENGR COMBAT BN · MARYLAND

COLO JOE · PVT · 262 INF 66 DIV · ILLINOIS
COLVIN GRADY E · PVT · 741 TANK BN · ALABAMA
COLWELL FRANKLIN W · S SGT · 262 INF 66 DIV · ILLINOIS
CONDON JOHN W · PVT · 501 PRCHT INF REGT · KANSAS
CONN CURTISS · PVT · 262 INF 66 DIV · KENTUCKY
CONNOLLY FRANCIS J · PFC · 2 RANGER BN · MASSACHUSETTS
CONNOR MARK B · 1 LT · 401 BOMB SQ 91 BOMB GP(H) · NEW JERSEY
CONSTANTINE TONY · TEC 4 · 262 INF 66 DIV · PENNSYLVANIA

COOK DEAN L · PFC · 262 INF 66 DIV · IOWA
COOK ROBERT W · TEC 5 · 526 ORD MAINT CO · MICHIGAN
CORE BARTON W · 1 LT · 330 INF 83 DIV · WEST VIRGINIA
CORNWELL CLINTON J · PVT · 262 INF 66 DIV · KENTUCKY
CORSON DAN W · 1 LT · 401 BOMB SQ 91 BOMB GP(H) · OHIO
COTE PHILIP G · PFC · 262 INF 66 DIV · MAINE
COTTINGHAM CLYDE JR · PVT · 23 INF 2 DIV · KENTUCKY

Ranger Connolly

Ranger Plumlee

Ranger Smith

Ranger Gardner

Ranger Gourley

Ranger Haluska

Ranger Golas

Ranger Henwood

Ranger Bowens

Ranger Hubert

Ranger Irvin

Ranger Donahue

Ranger Clifton

Ranger Oehlberg

Ranger Dolinsky

Ranger Kane

Ranger Kettering

Ranger Johnson

Ranger Machan

Ranger McWhirter

Ranger Morse

Ranger Myers

Rangers Norman Miller and Robert Miller

Ranger Page

Ranger Rafferty

Ranger Cole

Ranger Wilhelm

Ranger Raymond

Ranger Revels

Ranger Rich

Ranger Brice

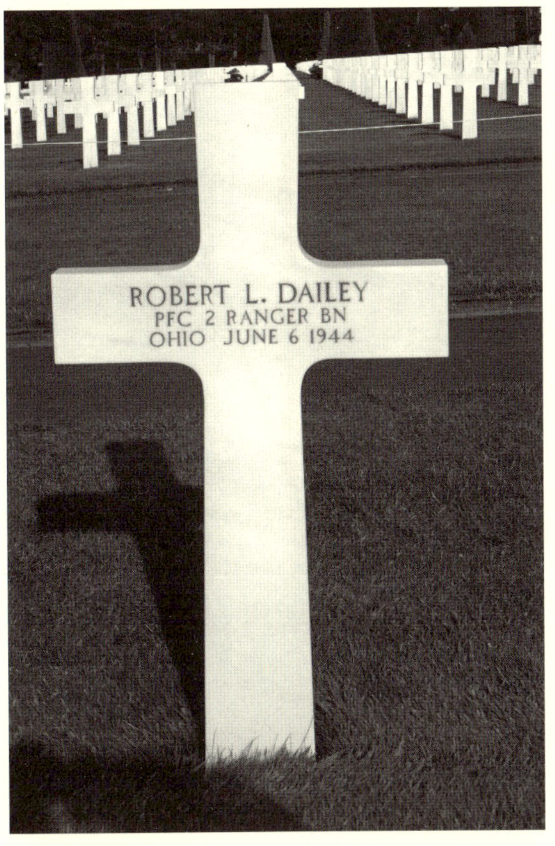

ROBERT L. DAILEY
PFC 2 RANGER BN
OHIO JUNE 6 1944

Ranger Dailey

ROBERT F. STEIN
PFC 5 RANGER BN
MASSACHUSETTS JUNE 8 1944

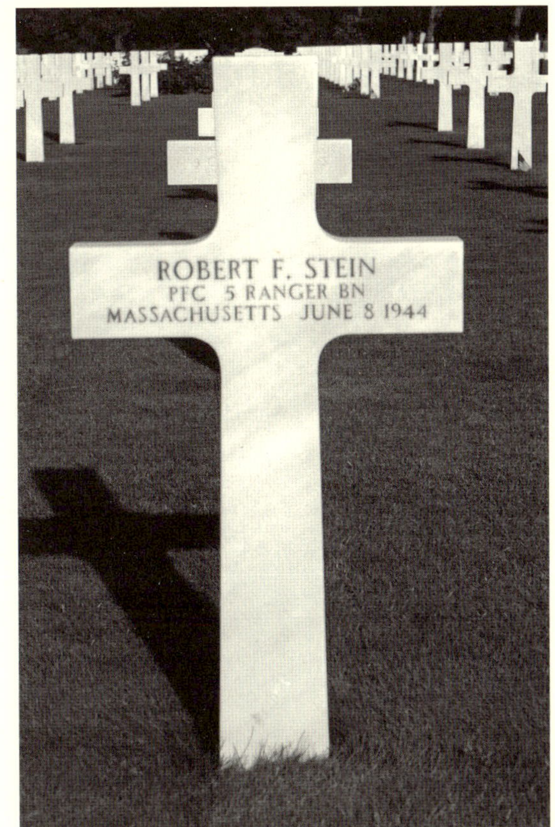

Ranger Stein

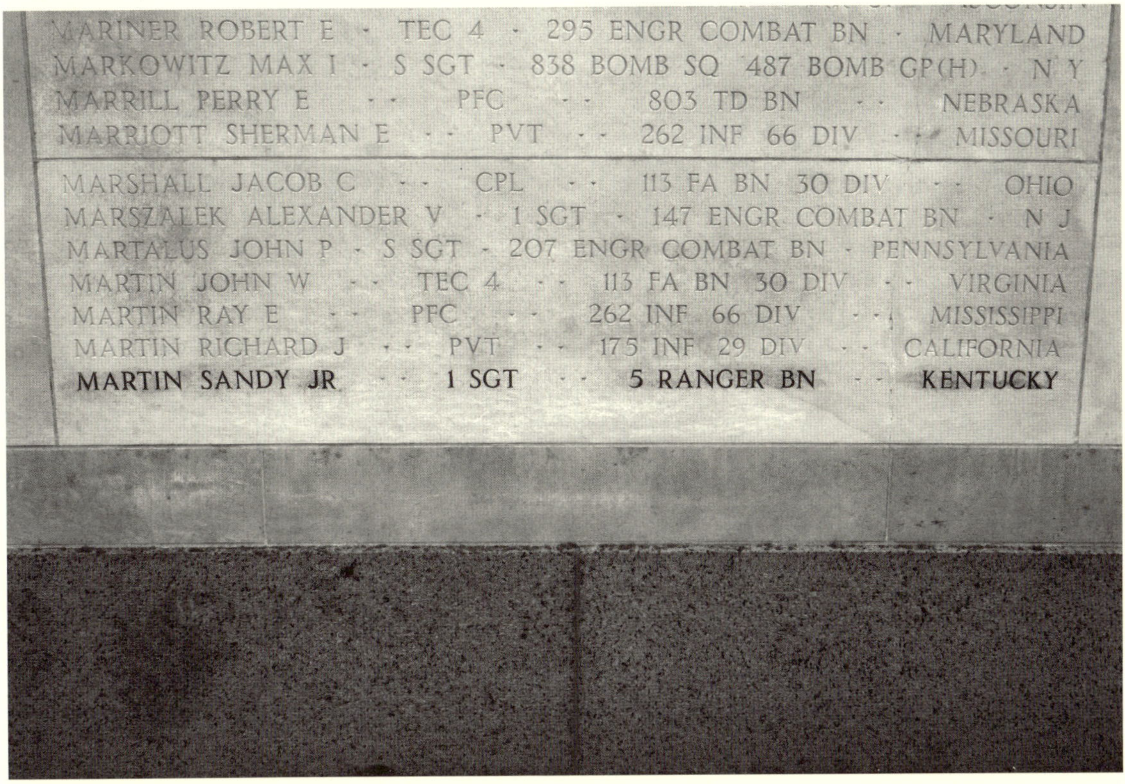
MARINER ROBERT E · TEC 4 · 295 ENGR COMBAT BN · MARYLAND
MARKOWITZ MAX I · S SGT · 838 BOMB SQ 487 BOMB GP(H) · N Y
MARRILL PERRY E · · PFC · · 803 TD BN · · NEBRASKA
MARRIOTT SHERMAN E · · PVT · · 262 INF 66 DIV · · MISSOURI
MARSHALL JACOB C · · CPL · · 113 FA BN 30 DIV · · OHIO
MARSZALEK ALEXANDER V · 1 SGT · 147 ENGR COMBAT BN · N J
MARTALUS JOHN P · S SGT · 207 ENGR COMBAT BN · PENNSYLVANIA
MARTIN JOHN W · · TEC 4 · · 113 FA BN 30 DIV · · VIRGINIA
MARTIN RAY E · · PFC · · 262 INF 66 DIV · · MISSISSIPPI
MARTIN RICHARD J · · PVT · · 175 INF 29 DIV · · CALIFORNIA
MARTIN SANDY JR · · 1 SGT · · 5 RANGER BN · · KENTUCKY

Ranger Martin

Ranger Steinen

Ranger Szerecz

Ranger Tarlano

Ranger Trainor

Ranger Vetovich

Ranger Beekler

Ranger Wassil

Ranger Reilly

Ranger Fox

ENDNOTES

1. This can cause some confusion in the study of World War II. In the German language, *Kommando* simply means "command" or headquarters, such as **Ober Kommando Wehrmacht** (OKW) or "High Command German Armed Forces," and has nothing to do with special warfare. Helpfully, the British usage of the term was Anglicized with a "c."
2. Known without affection as "Repple Depples."
3. XO is the initialism for executive officer, the second in command of the unit.
4. The Line of Departure is the designated line on a map where friendly forces move from their lines to the enemy positions.
5. Kubelwagen was a light military vehicle built by Volkswagen; roughly the equivalent of a jeep.
6. A tubular explosive device. One device could be connected to others like it for more explosive force. Being tubular, it was generally used to clear barbed-wire obstructions by being slid under the wire and then detonated.
7. See *Fatal Decision: Anzio and the Battle for Rome*, by Carlo D'Este
8. In this context, the term "commando" is German for "command" or "group" and not to be confused with the English meaning of special forces.
9. This is a Gammon grenade.
10. Nickname for German soldiers.
11. An SCR-536 handheld portable radio
12. Virginia Polytechnic Institute.
13. **Landing Craft Assault** is a landing craft used to deploy infantry.
14. An administrative billet, responsible for good order and discipline in the barracks, assigned for a specified period of time, usually twenty-four to forty-eight hours.
15. Also known as **Landing Craft Vehicle Personnel**, it derived the name "Higgins" from the manufacturer. Arguably the most common type of landing craft.
16. Branch of Criminal Investigation Command.
17. Slang term for officers who have attended OCS, which was generally about ninety days long.
18. Pronounced "duck," the acronym stands for Designed 1942, Utility, All-Wheel Drive, Dual Axles.
19. German paratroops.
20. Tracers were rounds that lit up when fired, so the shooter could see where their rounds were going. Generally, one in every five rounds were tracers. Of course, they also showed where the shooter was to the enemy, so they were often not used.
21. Quonset huts were a type of prefabricated housing for troops. Made of metal, they were better and more weather resistant than tents, but not insulated.
22. **Landing Ship Tank** is large landing craft used to deploy tanks and other armored vehicles on the beach.
23. **Landing Craft Mechanized** is a landing craft designed to carry vehicles.
24. Ammunition Supply Point.
25. Command Post.
26. Mr. Ryan was in 1st Platoon, C Company, 2nd Ranger Battalion, attached to the 1st Infantry Division, and landed adjacent to the 116th Regiment of the 29th Infantry Division at the western edge of Omaha Beach adjacent, and west of Vierville Draw on the Dog Green Sector.
27. Just west of the Vierville-sur-Mer Draw.
28. Just west of the Vierville-sur-Mer Draw.
29. Wehrmacht was the German term for all armed forces. Generally, in this sense what is meant is Heer, or regular German army, as opposed to Waffen-SS soldiers.

BIBLIOGRAPHY

Abati, Anthony. "Cisterna di Littoria: A Brave but Futile Effort," *Army History* (Fall 1991).

Altieri, James. *Darby's Rangers*, Annapolis, MD; Naval Institute Press, 2014.

Black, Robert. *Rangers in World War II*, New York: Ballantine Books, 1992.

Black, Robert. *The Battalion: The Dramatic Story of the 2nd Ranger Battalion in World War II*. Mechanicsburg, PA: Stackpole Books, 2006.

Black, Robert. *The Ranger Force: Darby's Rangers in World War II*. Mechanicsburg, PA: Stackpole Books, 2009.

Darby, William O. "US Rangers," Army and Navy Staff College Report, 1944.

Darby, William O. and Baumer, William H. *Darby's Rangers: We Led the Way*. New York: Presidio Press, 1980.

Glassman, Henry S. *Lead the Way, Rangers*. Ranger Association. 1980.

Hatfield, Thomas M. *Rudder: From Leader to Legend*. College Station, TX: Texas A&M University Press, 2011.

Heinen, Margo, and Moen, Marcia. *Heroes Cry Too: A WWII Ranger Tells His Story of Love and War*. Sidney, MT: Meadowlark Publishing, 2003.

Heinen, Margo, and Moen, Marcia. *Reflections of Courage on D-Day & the Days that Followed: A Personal Account Ranger "Ace."* Mona, MT: DeForest Press, 1999.

Knox, Robert. "A Study of Ranger Units in World War II and Korea: An Analysis of Their Successes and Failure" Master's Thesis. Chemical Corps Officer Course.

Lane, Ronald L. *Rudder's Rangers*. Longwood, FL: Ranger Associates Inc., 1979.

Mehlo, Noel F. *The Lost Ranger: A Soldier's Story*. CreateSpace Independent Publishing Platform, 2014.

O'Donnell, Patrick K. *Beyond Valor: World War II's Ranger and Airborne Veterans Reveal the Heart of Combat*. New York: Free Press, 2001.

O'Donnell, Patrick K, *Dog Company: The Boys of Pointe du Hoc*. Philadelphia, PA: De Capo Press, 2012.

Prefer, Nathan. "Rangers Led the Way at Zerf," *WWII Quarterly* (Winter 2016)

Prince, Morris. *The Road to Victory*. Sidney, MT: Meadowlark Publishing, 2009.

Ross, Robert. *US Army Rangers & Special Forces of World War II: Their War in Photographs*. Atglen, PA: Schiffer Military Books, 2002.

Sterne, Gary. *D-Day, The US Rangers, and the Untold Story of the Maisy Battery*. New York: Skyhorse Publishing, 2013.

Taylor, Thomas. *Rangers Lead the Way*. Nashville, TN: Turner Publishing Company, 1996.

Zaloga, Steven J. *Rangers Lead the Way: Point-du-Hoc, D-Day 1944*. Oxford: Osprey Publishing, 2009.

RANGER HALL OF FAMERS

1SGT. LEONARD G. LOMELL, 1994

1Sgt. Leonard G. Lomell is inducted into the Ranger Hall of Fame for his outstanding acts of heroism during the D-Day invasion of Normandy on June 6, 1944. While Serving with Company I, 2nd Ranger Battalion, 1Sgt. Lomell, though wounded, climbed the 100-foot cliffs of Pointe du Hoc, under fire from the enemy. As an acting platoon leader he led his 2nd platoon through the heaviest kind of automatic weapons fire to destroy an enemy machine gun position. He continued his courageous assault on the enemy while under devastating artillery bombardment, through two enemy lines of resistance to the rear of their position. Surrounded by the Germans, he, together with SSgt. Jack E. Kuhn, found the five big mobile coastal guns of Pointe du Hoc that were missing from the Pointe. They were hidden in an apple orchard over a mile inland from the Points. The guns were momentarily unguarded. 1Sgt. Lomell alone seized the opportunity to slip into the position and silently, with the use of thermite incendiary grenades melted together the moving parts of the traversing and elevation mechanisms and the breech blocks of the guns, thus rendering them inoperable by 0830 on D-Day. Many thousands of lives of soldiers on the landing beaches of Normandy were spared by 1Sgt. Lomell's bold, brave, and outstanding leadership in the face of such superior numbers. 1Sgt. Lomell's successful mission was in keeping with the highest traditions of the Rangers and the military service.

CAPT. WARREN E. EVANS, 1996

Capt. Warren Evans is inducted into the Ranger Hall of Fame for his extraordinary feats of courage while serving as Platoon Leader during the Djebel Berda Battle in World War II. Ranger Evans led the platoon reconnaissance over the mountain crest, identifying enemy positions and infiltration routes. This action directly resulted in hundreds of enemy POWs being captured. After conducting many hazardous night raids in rugged terrain over eight months throughout North Africa, Ranger Evans' courage and performance as first sergeant, sergeant major, and platoon leader merited his selection as company commander when the 3rd Ranger Battalion was formed. As commander of Company F, 3rd Ranger Battalion, Ranger Evans earned the Silver Star during the San Pietro Island Raid. Moving over rugged terrain, the company infiltrated and completely surprised the Germans with a ferocious attack under the cover of rain and darkness. During the infamous battle of Cisterna off the Anzio Beachhead in Italy, Ranger Evans maneuvered his company to the sound of battle and attacked into a numerically superior armed German force. Ranger Evans was taken prisoner, but his heroics would continue even after his captivity. After two failed attempts, Ranger Evans successfully escaped and returned to American lines near Liepzig, Germany. In October 1992, Capt. Evans was selected as honorary sergeant major of the 75th Ranger Regiment for extraordinary service during combat.

CAPT. WALTER E. BLOCK, 1998

Capt. Walter E. Block is inducted into the Ranger Hall of Fame for gallantry in action, courage under fire, and extraordinary medical care in the roughest of conditions. From the time he joined the 2nd Ranger Battalion in Fort Dix until his death (KIA) in the Huertgen Forest on 8 Dec 1944. Capt. Block was distinguished by his enthusiasm, courage under fire, attention to duty, and most of all, his intense concern for the health, well being and effectiveness of the 2nd Ranger Battalion. He was a physician who never hesitated to go in harm's way to care for a Ranger, a spirit his medics emulated. At Pointe du Hoc, ignoring intense fire from the enemy, he set up a temporary aid station at the base of the cliff, and directed the care of any wounded whom he could not tend to himself. After the top was gained he did not hesitate to leave the upper aid station to attend wounded in the field, frequently under heavy fire. Among those he treated was Col. Rudder who had been hit a second time while at an outpost. During the battle of Huertgen Forest the battalion suffered losses at Hill 400 equal to, or higher than, on D-Day. During this, a shell burst on the roof of the aid station killing Capt. Block while he was tending the wounded and checking on their evacuation. His gallantry in action, courage and performance in organizing medical-surgical care while under heavy fire at Pointe du Hoc was recognized in the form of a Silver Star. Later, he earned the Bronze Star and, finally, the Purple Heart.

MAJ. GEN. JOHN C. RAAEN JR., 2008

John Carpenter Raaen, Jr. was born at Fort Benning, Georgia, April 22, 1922. He was appointed to the United States Military Academy in 1939 from Arkansas. At the United States Military Academy he was appointed cadet captain and regimental supply officer and was commissioned as a second lieutenant in the Corps of Engineers upon graduation on January 19, 1943. After an initial assignment at the Engineer School he joined the 55th Armored Engineer Battalion, 10th Armored Division, located first at Fort Benning, Georgia and later in the Tennessee Maneuver Area. Here he served as a battalion staff officer and platoon leader. On September 1, 1943, he was assigned to the newly activated 5th Ranger Infantry Battalion located at Camp Forrest, Tennessee. With the battalion, he engaged in amphibious and commando training in Florida, England, and Scotland. On June 6, 1944, as headquarters company commander, he participated in the initial assault on Omaha Beach, Normandy, France. For this action he received the Silver Star and Combat Infantryman Badge. He continued in combat with the battalion through the Brittany Campaign, across France, and finally into the Saar Valley where he was injured in December 1944, and evacuated to the United States. In July 1945, he was appointed as an instructor in the Department of Ordnance at the Unites States Military Academy. In 1948, he attended the US Naval Academy Post Graduate School at Annapolis, Maryland, and following two more years' study at the Johns Hopkins University, received a master of arts degree in physics. In 1951, he was assigned as executive officer in the Ammunition Development Branch of the Office, chief of ordnance, where he remained for three years. In 1954, he attended the Command General Staff College at Fort Leavenworth. In August 1955, he became executive officer, 8th Army Ordnance Section in Korea, and in the following year assumed command of the 83rd Ordnance Battalion (Ammunition). Upon his return to the United States in January 1957, he was assigned as a project officer on the Ordnance Board at Aberdeen Proving Ground, Maryland. In mid 1959, he was reassigned as a staff officer on the Military Liaison Committee to the Atomic Energy Commission at Germantown, Maryland. In 1962, he attended the Industrial College of the Armed Forces, located at Fort Leslie J. McNair, Washington, DC. His next two years were spent in West Berlin, Germany, where he served successively as ordnance officer, assistant chief of staff, G-1, and deputy chief of staff of the Berlin Brigade. In June 1965, he was assigned as commanding officer of the United States Army Ammunition Depot at Miesau, Germany. This tour was curtailed after two months, when he returned to the United States to command the US Army Research Office, Durham, North Carolina. In January 1967, he was transferred to Aberdeen Proving Ground where he became commander of the Army Material Command's three central laboratories located there. In January 1969 he was assigned to Headquarters, United States Army Vietnam; first as chief, G4 Ammunition Division, later as chief, G4 Supply Division, and finally as deputy assistant chief of staff, G4. In December 1969, he was assigned to the Army general staff as Director of Ammunition, Office of the Deputy Chief of Staff for Logistics. He was promoted to brigadier general on July 7, 1970. He was assigned as commanding general, Headquarters Army Mobility Command on June 28, 1971. He was promoted to major general on June 3, 1972. In December 1972 he was assigned as commanding general, Headquarters Army Weapons Command, Rock Island, Illinois. Six months later, in July 1973, he organized and assumed command of the US Army Armament Command, a merger of the Weapons and Munitions Commands at Rock Island Arsenal. In September 1975, he returned to Washington, DC, as acting deputy director for the Defense Supply Agency, and in June 1976 he assumed command of the Defense Fuel Supply Center. He retired from the Army on May 1, 1979, at Cameron Station, Alexandria, Virginia.

NAMES INSCRIBED ON THE PLAQUE AT THE OBSERVATION POST, POINTE DU HOC, FRANCE

1. PFC Sammie **ADKINS**
2. PFC Volney **BEEKLER**
3. PFC Charles E. **BELLOWS** Jr.
4. S/SGT John C. **BIDDLE**
5. T/5 Charles E. **BOLLIA**
6. PFC Howard **BOWENS**
7. 1st SGT Robert M. **BRICE**
8. T/5 Charles J. **BRAMKAMP**
9. T/5 Willis C. **CAPERTON**
10. PFC Robert C. **CARTY**
11. PFC Harold E. **CLENDENIN**
12. T/5 John M. **CLIFTON**
13. PFC Raymond A. **COLE**
14. T/5 E. G. **COLVARD**
15. PFC Francis J. **CONNOLY**
16. PFC Robert L. **DAILEY**
17. PFC Joseph V. **DANIELS**
18. PFC Charles L. **DAVIS**
19. S/SGT Robert G. **DAVIS**
20. PFC John **DOLINSKY**
21. PFC James E. **DONAHUE**
22. PFC Henry S. **FARRAR**
23. T/5 Dominick F. **GALLO**
24. SGT Walter B. **GELDON**
25. PFC Wayne D. **GOAD**
26. 1st SGT Henry S. **GOLAS**
27. PFC David L. **GOUDEY**
28. PFC John S. **GOURLEY**
29. PFC Eddie W. **HARDING**
30. S/SGT Millard W. **HAYDEN**
31. SGT Kenneth A. **HENDRICKSON**
32. SGT John R. **HENWOOD**
33. 1st LT Jacob J. **HILL**
34. T/5 Percy C. **HOWER** Jr.
35. PFC Leslie M. **IRVIN**
36. S/SGT Lawrence M. **JOHNSON**
37. S/SGT James A. **KANE**
38. S/SGT Charles E. **KETTERING**
39. PFC Dennis F. **KIMBLE**
40. PVT Frank J. **KOSINA**
41. 1st LT Joseph E. **LEAGANS**
42. M/SGT Robert N. **LEMIN**
43. PFC Harold E. **LESTER**
44. T/5 Clarence J. **LONG**
45. T/5 William W. **LYNCH** Jr.
46. T/5 Charles G. **MC CALVIN**
47. PFC Andrew P. **MC CORCKLE**
48. PFC William P. **MC WHIRTER**
49. PFC James A. **MACHAN**
50. PFC George W. **MACKEY**
51. T/5 Thomas D. **MENDENHALL**
52. S/SGT Norman G. **MILLER**
53. T/5 Vayle **MILLER**
54. 1st LT William D. **MOODY**
55. PFC William D. **MYERS**
56. PFC John D. **OEHLBERG**
57. T/5 Elmer P. **OLANDER**
58. S/SGT Leon H. **OTTO**
59. PFC George **PANIAHA**
60. PFC Fred W. **PLUMLEE**
61. CAPT Joseph A. **RAFFERTY**
62. SGT Robert J. **RAYMOND**
63. PVT Rolland F. **REVELS**
64. SGT Charles E. **RICH**
65. SGT Jacob H. **RICHARDS**
66. PFC Ollie D. **RICHARDSON**
67. T/5 Raymond J. **RIENDEAU**
68. PFC John C. **SHANAHAN**
69. SGT Joseph W. **SHEDAKER**
70. PFC Earl W. **SHIREMAN**
71. T/5 Marvin A. **SIMKO**
72. S/SGT Curtis A. **SIMMONS**
73. S/SGT Frederick D. **SMITH**
74. 1st SGT Edward L. **SOWA**
75. SGT Bernard **SZEWCZUK**
76. PFC Joseph R. **TRAINOR**
77. T/5 William D. **VAUGHAN**
78. S/SGT Michael **VETOVICH**
79. PFC Robert R. **WHITEHEAD**
80. PFC George A. **WIEBURG**
81. S/SGT Benjamin H. **WIRTZ**